# New Religious Movemen

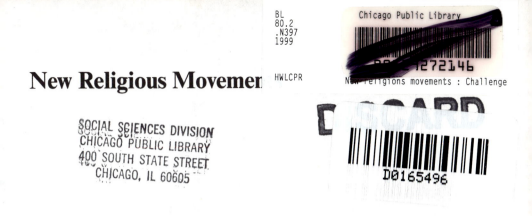

*New Religious Movements: Challenge and response* is a searching and wide-ranging collection of essays on the contemporary phenomenon of new religions. The contributors to this volume are all established specialists in the sociology, theology, law, or the history of new minority movements. The primary focus is the response of the basic institutions of society to the challenge which new religious movements represent.

The orientation of this volume is to examine the way in which new movements in general have affected modern society in areas such as economic organisation; the operation of the law; the role of the media; the relationship of so-called 'cult' membership to mental health; and the part which women have played in leading or supporting new movements. Specific instances of these relationships are illustrated by reference to many of the most prominent new religions – Hare Krishna, The Brahma Kumaris, The Unification Church, The Jesus Army, 'The Family', The Church of Scientology, and Wicca.

For students of religion or sociology, *New Religious Movements* is an invaluable source of information, an example of penetrating analysis, and a series of thought-provoking contributions to a debate which affects many areas of contemporary life in many parts of the world.

**Contributors**: Eileen Barker, James Beckford, Anthony Bradney, Colin Campbell, George Chryssides, Peter Clarke, Paul Heelas, Massimo Introvigne, Lawrence Lilliston, Gordon Melton, Elizabeth Puttick, Gary Shepherd, Colin Slee, Frank Usarski, Bryan Wilson.

**Bryan Wilson** is an Emeritus Fellow of All Souls College, Oxford. He is the author and editor of several books on sects and New Religious Movements. His recent publications include *Religion in Sociological Perspective*, *The Social Dimensions of Sectarianism*, and [with Karel Dobbelaere] *A Time to Chant: The Soka Gakkai Buddhists in Britain*. **Jamie Cresswell** is Director of the Institute of Oriental Philosophy European Centre.

# New Religious Movements
## Challenge and response

**Edited by Bryan Wilson and
Jamie Cresswell**

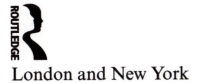
London and New York

In association with the Institute of
Oriental Philosophy European Centre

First published 1999
by Routledge
11 New Fetter Lane, London EC4P 4EE

Simultaneously published in the USA and Canada
by Routledge
29 West 35th Street, New York, NY 10001

Typeset in Times by Routledge
Printed and bound in Great Britain by
Creative Print and Design (Wales), Ebbw Vale

*British Library Cataloguing in Publication Data*
A catalogue record for this book is available from the British Library

*Library of Congress Cataloging in Publication Data*
New Religious Movements: Challenge and response
Edited by Bryan Wilson and Jamie Cresswell
Includes bibliographical references and index
1. Religions. 2. Cults. 3. Sects.
I. Wilson, Bryan. II. Cresswell, Jamie
BL80.2.N397 1999                                    98-30970
291–dc21                                            CIP

ISBN 0–415–20049–0 (hbk)
ISBN 0–415–20050–4 (pbk)

# Contents

# Contributors

**Eileen Barker** is Professor of Religion with Special Reference to the Study of Religion at the London School of Economics. She has been studying alternative religions for the past quarter of a century and has over 150 publications on the subject. These include the prize-winning *The Making of a Moonie: Brainwashing or Choice?* (Oxford, 1984) and *New Religious Movements: A Practical Introduction* (London: HMSO, 1989, 2nd edition 1999). She was elected President of the Society for the Scientific Study of Religion. In 1988, with the support of the British government and the mainstream churches, she founded INFORM (Information Network Focus on Religious Movements), a charity which provides information about alternative religions.

**James A. Beckford** is Professor of Sociology at the University of Warwick and President (1999–2003) of the International Society for the Sociology of Religion. His main publications on New Religious Movements include *Cult Controversies: The Societal Response to New Religious Movements* (London: Tavistock, 1985) and *New Religious Movements and Rapid Social Change* (London: Sage, 1986).

**Anthony Bradney** is Senior Lecturer in Law at the University of Leicester. One of his principal research interests is the relationship between religion and law in Great Britain, and he has written and lectured widely on this subject. His publications include *Religion, Rights and Laws* (1993) and (with Fiona Cownie) *The English Legal System in Context* (1996).

**Colin Campbell** is Reader in Sociology and Head of Department at the University of York. He has written widely on sociology theory, culture and cultural change, religion and the sociology of consumption, and is the author of *The Romantic Ethic and the Spirit of Modern Consumption* (Blackwell, 1987), *The Myth of Social Action* (Oxford University Press, 1996), and (with Passi Falk) *The Shopping Experience* (Sage, 1997).

**George D. Chryssides** is Senior Lecturer in Religious Studies in the University of Wolverhampton. His publications include *The Path of Buddhism* (1988); *The Advent of Sun Myung Moon* (1991) and *The Elements of Unitarianism* (1998). His forthcoming *Exploring New Religions* will be published in 1999.

**Peter B. Clarke** is Professor of History and the Sociology of Religion at King's College, University of London, and founding editor of the *Journal of Contemporary Religion*. Since the mid-1980s he has been engaged in research on African-Brazilian and Japanese new religions in Brazil.

**Jamie Cresswell** is the Director of the Institute of Oriental Philosophy European Centre. He is currently working on a PhD at the School of Oriental and African Studies, London University, on the topic of Contemporary Tibetan Buddhism and also teaches a class in Contemporary Buddhism at SOAS.

**Paul Heelas** is Professor of Religion and Modernity in the Department of Religious Studies, Lancaster University. He is the author of *The New Age Movement*, has recently edited *Religion, Modernity and Postmodernity*, and, with Linda Woodhead, is currently editing *Religion in Modern Times*.

**Massimo Introvigne**, PhD, is the managing director of the Centre for Studies in New Religions in Turin, Italy. He teaches courses and gives seminars on New Religious at the Pontifical Athenaeum Regina Apostolorum in Rome, and is the author of twenty books in Italian on New Religions and the Sociology of Religion, some of which have been translated into French and German.

**Lawrence Lilliston** is Professor of Psychology at Oakland University in Rochester, Michigan, and is also a clinical child psychologist in private practice. He has conducted field research on a variety of New Religious Movements and has published articles on the psycho-social development of children in these groups.

**J. Gordon Melton** is the Director of the Institute for the Study of American Religion in Santa Barbara, California, and the author of more than twenty-five books on religious phenomena and groups, including the *Encyclopedia of American Religions* (6th edition, 1998) and *Finding Enlightenment: Ramtha's Ancient School of Wisdom* (1998). He is currently leading the Religions Directory Project compiling the multi-volume *International Directory of the World's Religions*.

**Elizabeth Puttick**, PhD, is a sociologist of religion specialising in New Religious Movements and gender issues. She teaches courses in women and religion and world religions at the British American College, London, and is the author of *Women in New Religions* (1997)

**Gary Shepherd** is currently chair of the Department of Sociology and Anthropology at Oakland University, Rochester, Michigan. He is co-author (with his brother Gordon) of *A Kingdom Transformed: Themes in the Development of Mormonism* (1984) and also, most recently, of *Mormon Passage: A Missionary Chronicle* (1998).

**Colin Slee** is Provost of Southwark Cathedral, London.

**Frank Usarski** has lectured on *Religionswissenschaft* at the universities of Hanover, Oldenburg, Bremen, Erfurt, Chemnitz, and Leipzig. He now holds an appointment as long-term visiting professor at the Pontificia Universidade Católica, Sao Paulo, Brazil. He has recently published several papers in Germany on new religions and on traditional oriental religions.

**Bryan Wilson** is Reader Emeritus in Sociology at the University of Oxford and Emeritus Fellow of All Souls College. He is co-author (with Karel Dobbelaere) of *A Time to Chant: The Soka Gakkai Buddhists in Britain* (Oxford: Oxford University Press, 1994).

# Foreword

The Institute of Oriental Philosophy European Centre was opened at Taplow Court in 1989. It is affiliated to the IOP in Tokyo which was established in 1962 by Daisaku Ikeda, President of the Soka Gakkai International and Buddhist peace activist.

Our aim at the Institute is to create a broad base for discussion and to encourage scholarly research into various aspects of Buddhism and Oriental thought, taking an inter-disciplinary and multi-faceted approach. As well as historical, philosophical and philological research, we are particularly interested in broad themes such as the relevance of the religious traditions of Asia, particularly Buddhism, for contemporary society, the life sciences, human rights, the environment, peace studies and education. Through this work we aim to make the rich spiritual heritage of Asia a common resource for people throughout the world and to discover within these traditions a reservoir of wisdom and knowledge which is of value to today's society.

In the past we have concentrated on the creation and consolidation of a comprehensive research library containing books and journals on Buddhism, Asian religions and philosophies. We have an excellent collection of source texts and copies of the various Buddhist canons in Asian languages as well as in European languages. Two series of lectures have been held so far. 'The Wisdom of the East in Modern Society' ran for three years and included lectures on such topics as Contemporary Buddhism in Japan, Women and Buddhism, Gaia Theory and Buddhism, Astronomy and Buddhist Ideas, and Buddhism in Bath. The 'IOP Forum', our ongoing lecture series, aims to draw in specialists in the field as well as the wider public and to encourage rich and enlightening dialogue.

We aim to hold a biennial symposium on various topics related to Asian Religion and Western Thought. Our first Symposium on New Religious Movements has resulted in the publication of this present volume and I am delighted to see it appear in print as it is a valuable way to make the various findings of the Institute available to the wider community.

I hope that through our various activities and through the free and creative exchange of ideas and knowledge, we can partake, in some way, in the creation of a more peaceful and understanding world. We encourage scholars and students from all over the world to use this Institute as a forum for intellectual dialogue and exchange and to join us in these endeavours.

A number of people have assisted in this present project and I thank them all. I particularly would like to thank Dr Bryan Wilson for his hard work, valuable advice and consistent support during this process.

If you would like further information on the Institute of Oriental Philosophy, its library and activities please contact us at the address below.

Institute of Oriental Philosophy European Centre
Taplow Court
Taplow
Maidenhead
Berkshire
SL6 OER
United Kingdom
Telephone: +44-(0)1628–591244. Fax: +44-(0)1628–591244

Jamie Cresswell
Director
Institute of Oriental Philosophy European Centre

# Abbreviations

| | |
|---|---|
| ACM | anti-cult movement |
| ADFI | Association pour la Défense de la Famille et de l'Individu |
| AGPF | Aktion für geistige und psychische Freiheit |
| AFF | American Family Foundation |
| APA | American Psychological Association |
| BATF | Bureau of Arms, Tobacco and Firearms |
| BCA | Buddhist Church of America |
| BCC | British Council of Churches |
| CA | Cultists Anonymous |
| CAN | Cult Awareness Network |
| CFF | Citizens Freedom Foundation |
| COG | Children of God |
| CIC | The Cult Information Centre |
| COMA | Council on Mind Abuse |
| EMERGE | Ex-Members of Extreme Religious Groups |
| EMFJ | Ex-Mormons for Jesus |
| est | Erhard Seminars Training |
| FAIR | Family Action, Information and Resources |
| FBI | Federal Bureau of Investigation |
| FREECOG | Free the Children of God |
| FSU | Former Soviet Union |
| FWBO | Friends of the Western Buddhist Order |
| IFIF | International Foundation for Individual Freedom |
| INFORM | Information Network Focus on Religious Movements |
| IPM | Inner Peace Movement |
| ISKCON | International Society for Krishna Consciousness |
| JW | Jehovah's Witnesses |
| MMPI | Minnesota Multiphasic Personality Inventory |
| NAM | New Age Movement |
| NNRM | New New or Neo-New Religious Movement |
| NRM | New Religious Movement |
| OST | Order of the Solar Temple |
| POWER | People's Organised Workshop on Ersatz Religions |

| | |
|---|---|
| SES | School of Economic Science |
| VPA | Volunteer Parents of America |
| WCC | World Council of Churches |
| WISE | World in Scientology Enterprises |

# Introduction

*Bryan Wilson*

New Religious Movements, as sociologists have generally designated the congeries of spiritual organisations that have emerged in the last three or four decades, have now become a familiar part of the religious landscape. The phenomenon has not been confined to the western world: in parts of Africa and in East Asia, notably in Japan and Korea, religious innovations are no less in evidence. Taken altogether, a vast literature on these bodies has been produced, and the entire output – the materials produced by the movements themselves; those of their vociferous opponents; the outpourings of journalists; and the sober monographs and comparative analytical studies of academics – were it all to be brought together, would occupy a sizeable library. That there has been considerable social reaction to new religions is a matter of common observation, but the reports in the media have principally reflected parental and political concerns. Even so, with the exception of a few scholarly analyses of the media's treatment of these movements, little systematic attention has been paid to the overall way in which they and their ideologies have affected various social institutions, or to the response which has been forthcoming from these departments of state and society. The chapters in this volume seek to explore the reaction to the impact of the new religions not on individual adherents, but specifically on these major institutional spheres of contemporary society. Thus, the debate in these pages is not focused on such issues as 'brainwashing' and 'de-programming', techniques of conversion, 'love bombing' and allegedly deceitful practices of fund raising which together have constituted a prime set of issues in much of the literature, but on the societal influence and effect of the new religions.

The new movements have clearly enjoyed a measure of success in making themselves widely known, but it takes a long time for a dissenting religious body to win any degree of disinterested approval from the general public (such as, over many decades, has been gradually achieved by the Quakers and Salvation Army). Response to contemporary new religions has been polarised: on the one hand, there has been positive endorsement for a particular movement from those few whom it recruits; on the other hand, strong condemnation has been expressed from some of the parents and kinsfolk of those recruited. The negative reaction has been the primary, indeed, almost the exclusive, focus of attention by the media, which have all too often relied on the testimony of apostates to reinforce the concerns of understandably apprehensive parents.

Examining new movements from a wider perspective than that of adherents and opponents, the contributors to this volume seek to enlarge the area of enquiry by looking specifically at the relation of new religions to the major institutions of contemporary society. Thus, following two chapters on the incidence of the movements, and on their provenance and social context, Chapter 3 is devoted to the complex and at times surprising new relationships sometimes forged between new religions and modern economic organisations. Chapter 4 considers how some of the movements have had an impact on the law, and examines the legal problems which arise in relation to the movements' claims and status and to their demand to be considered equally alongside more traditional and established faiths. The media deserve attention as a major institution of the 'information society', a veritable fourth estate which increasingly dictates the agenda for public and political debate: their role in relation to NRMs is reviewed in Chapter 5.

The maintenance of public health has only in recent decades become an official matter of state policy, but health must today be regarded as very much a national institutional concern, and this aspect of life is in itself not unaffected by spiritual dispositions, as a growing body of research findings make apparent. Chapter 6 is devoted to a review of new religions and mental health in the United States where this subject has been more fully the focus of research than has been the case in Britain or in Europe generally. No overview of any process of social change would today be complete without consideration of gender differences, and Chapter 7 examines the impact of new modes of spirituality on the social role of women, who in general appear to have played a significant role in the development of New Religious Movements.

Of all social institutions exercised about the incursion of new spiritual organisations, the Churches may claim a special place: yet the agencies of long-established religion have scarcely spoken with one voice regarding NRMs. In the interests of religious freedom, on the maintenance of which all religions ultimately depend, the Churches have often been equivocal and by no means uniformly condemnatory of the new waves of spirituality. In Chapter 8, an Anglican clergyman presents a personal view of how Christians might react to these new phenomena.

Social institutions differ from one country to another, and our focus is primarily on the situation in Britain, and, more tangentially, in the United States, but to avoid British parochial insularity, a more general discussion of the world-wide emergence of new forms of spirituality is acknowledged in Chapters 9 and 10, respectively, which sample the situation overseas, specifically in the nominally monolithic Catholic contexts of Italy and Latin America. New religions in all periods appear to have stimulated opposition, sometimes including officially sponsored discrimination or persecution, but in few previous periods of western history has there been such an organised spawning of voluntary opposition groups as has been seen in response to contemporary new movements. Inevitably, attention is also paid to this most explicit response to the challenge of NRMs manifest in the self-styled anti-cult movements. Since these 'anti-cult' movements have acquired some international connections, the operations of these organisations are examined not only in the United States, where they have the longest history (Chapter 11), but also in the re-united German Republic (Chapter 12) and, in the final chapter, in Britain.

What falls outside the purview of this volume but which is a subject which calls for academic attention at the international level is the response of the state itself to manifestations of new forms of religiosity. Even among western societies, wide differences are evident, from extensive, if at times reluctant, toleration in practice in the United States and Britain, to the actual policy of hostility manifested so vigorously in France (in disregard of that country's theoretical subscription to the rights of conscience).[1] Despite the broad international trend towards greater tolerance of religious minorities, the process of enhanced freedom of conscience and human rights sometimes suffers sudden reversals. A recent case has been the hasty proposal for the revision of the post-1945 laws of religious toleration in Japan, in which the poison gas terrorism of the Aum Shinrikyō sect served as an excuse for the enunciation of new illiberal policies. A comparative world-wide study of the current policy and practice of various states towards religious diversity and the rights of minorities is much needed, but such a project would require extensive research into the social and cultural history, the religious heritage, the constitutional law, the political arrangements, as well as the traditions of toleration of different countries. The present volume is no more than a modest pointer to the desirability of some such future study. Meanwhile, we can make a small beginning by examining the way in which new religions interact with major facets of social structure.

To put into perspective the focus of current concerns, three aspects of comparative analysis may be mentioned by way of introduction. First, some brief comparisons are made between, on the one hand, contemporary New Religious Movements and, on the other, those organisations, generally referred to as 'sects', which were the New Religious Movements of earlier decades. Second, some indication is provided to illustrate the congruity and congeniality of the orientation of contemporary new religions and the ethos of the prevailing secular culture. Third, we examine the extent to which popular, media and anti-cult group stereotypes distort what social scientific investigations have established concerning new movements.

The need to examine the patterns of relationship between voluntary spiritual agencies and social institutions and constituencies is something which did not arise with any urgency in the study of earlier sectarian groups. Earlier sects were almost all variants of the dominant Christian tradition. Their basic stance *vis-à-vis* the dominant society was one of rejection, condemnation and withdrawal. Their concern was not for the redemption of the social order, but rather that of an agency offering a prospect of salvation to the individual. Those groups which harboured keen commitment to a new millennial order had no brief for the improvement of the present social system, much less for its preservation. Even those sects in which expectation of the second advent was sometimes occluded by more immediate preoccupations (as, for example, was the case with Pentecostalists in their concern with the experience of glossolalia) or groups (such as Jehovah's Witnesses) in which the second coming had been the subject of failed predictions and disappointments were, none the less, disposed to abandon responsibility for the world, save only for the prospect of still converting individuals. Their purpose was not to make over or even to ameliorate existing social institutions, since nothing was to be expected from the fallible social and political structures that had been created by sinful men. If, marginally and temporarily, the world was to become a better place, that would be an incidental consequence of the conversion of individual sinners to a holier way of life. The real prospect of betterment lay only in the total re-making of the world with the introduction of a new dispensation in the establishment of a divine kingdom, whether conceived as occurring on earth or in some heavenly realm. Even the Seventh-day Adventists, whose social reforming dispositions have led them to promote health and education, and who created, for their own following, hospitals, food factories, schools and colleges, saw this endeavour rather as a preparatory exercise for the better way of life which would follow the advent, than as a blueprint for the corrupt world to implement. In other respects, in dietary taboos and seventh-day Sabbath observance, they marked out and maintained their boundaries, insulated from the ways of the world.

By and large, it may be said that these earlier manifestations of sectarianism were concerned with personal sin, not with structural defects. Their solution for social problems, in so far as they had one for the interim dispensation in which they conceived of themselves as living, was evangelical. In contrast to a socialist commitment to the idea that improved institutions would make good men, for them the only prospect of an improved society was by the reform of individuals: if good institutions were to be created, that could only occur as men were made good (or as nearly good as Christian theology allowed). Even so, the heart of Christian sectarianism was in another place and another time-scale of salvation. These sects were not concerned to diffuse their own values into the institutional orders of existing society. They did not expect to improve the agencies of the law, or of education, much less to effect a transformation of economic practice. In general, in clear continuity with biblical injunctions, they espoused an ethic of asceticism, embraced a simple life, and surrendered both worldly ambition and responsibility for worldly well-being. Certainly, they were not content with the world as it was, but their solution to that dissatisfaction was to pin their hopes on its passing away to give place, at least for the righteous, to a better life to come.

The great majority of the new religions, diverse as they are, differ profoundly in mood and orientation from all this. Even those of them that sustain a commitment to an asceticism more typical of earlier sectarianism do not despair of this world, and do not dissociate themselves from all existing social facilities and structures, or the patterns of motivation which characterise capitalist society. Thus, the Unification Church, although it canvasses to its votaries a rather stern ascetic morality, stipulating chastity for its young members, and introducing them to a far from luxurious communal life, none the less is ready to accept modern production and business techniques in the ancillary industries, from small arms to ceramics and newspapers, which support its mission. Making a profit from street sales of candles, flowers, or the like, has been an acceptable motive both for Moonies and for the devotees of another ascetic movement, the International Society for Krishna Consciousness (ISKCON).

Clearly, other movements, specifically those whom Roy Wallis has designated as 'world-affirming',[2] go much further in endorsing the existing capitalist structure of western society and the institutions which support that structure. Indeed, 'endorsing' is perhaps too pusillanimous a term: these movements, as indicated in the chapter by Paul Heelas, are committed to making competitive market systems yet more competitive, and measure their own spiritual claims by manifestly material results. Nor is such a convergence of spiritual and material goals merely a reassertion of the old Protestant ethic: material success is, in these new religions, not an unintended consequence of conforming to the demands of religiously inspired asceticism. Indeed, asceticism has nothing to do with it. Personal comportment is not the focus of concern, except in so far as it manifests that style of positive thinking which, by one means or another, these movements seek to induce. Self-restraint, abstinence, the postponement of gratifications, and the culture of scarcity that were built into, and which may have conditioned Christian morality, are all alien to the world-affirming new religions. In these movements, spiritual power is harnessed to economic ends: religion does not dictate those ends nor prescribe moral comportment, rather, it claims to offer added impetus to everyday economic motivations.

These particular new movements are very much creatures of the times in their congeniality to the market ethos of the western world. While it cannot be easily asserted that they are demand-led, none the less it is clear that the time has passed when religious bodies could put forth a set of objective requirements for belief and behaviour and expect to command ready compliance. In a consumer-oriented society, what religion offers has to be attractive to the potential clientele. Democracy, the ethos of personal choice, education, and enhanced incomes, no doubt among other factors, have introduced, even into the realms of religious belief, the idea that, to an increasing degree, the consumer decides. Apart from the incidence of reactive rejection of contemporary values (evident among the inner communitarian core devotees of world-renouncing movements such as the International Society for Krishna

Consciousness, and some of the more fundamentalist of recently emerging Christian sects), new movements that canvass asceticism, austerity, and self-denial experience contemporary society as an unpropitious climate.

In democratic, capitalist societies, of necessity religions respond to the demands of their actual and potential votaries, and this is true not only of the newly emerging movements. Even the established Churches soften their message, or risk the loss of their constituents. Nowhere is the evidence stronger than in the United States, where the message of health, wealth, happiness, and positive life experiences has, over the last century or so, enjoyed a history of increasing acceptability and success in both minority movements and in some congregations of the mainstream denominations. Telling their audiences what they want to hear is one formula for success in some denominations. On the other hand, the staid established Churches, with their tradition of preaching against sin and of pleading as supplicants for divine mercy, as among Anglicans, English Methodists and even Catholics, appear steadily to lose ground, even though these Churches have also temporised with their charter commitments, and have come to emphasise increasingly the idea of a loving and supportive deity, and to say less about, for example, human wickedness, divine wrath, the day of judgement, and afterlife punishments. As for believers, it is clear that their strong inclination is to believe primarily, perhaps solely, in the optimistic messages which religion canvasses. Modern belief in reincarnation provides an example: although the concept has no legitimacy for Christians, opinion polls reveal that a considerable proportion of westerners espouse such a possibility. Life on earth, no longer a vale of tears, has, in a hedonistic age, been sufficiently pleasurable to persuade people that they might experience it all over again: that prospect is altogether more congenial than the orthodox Christian alternative of post-mortem punishment for a lifetime's misbehaviour.

All this is not, however, to endorse one of the prevailing theories concerning religious adherence, namely that consumers of spirituality, in making their religious commitment, make rational choices: that they calculate the usefulness of particular religious beliefs to their other life concerns; that it 'makes better sense [to] assume that people act on the basis of thoughtful, conscious assessments of the costs and benefits in making their religious decisions'.[3] Religion is, after all, primarily a matter of faith rather than of reason, in the sense that the ultimate commodity which religion purveys – salvation – is a goal, the realisation of which lies beyond empirical proof. Given such an empirically unverifiable goal, it is clearly impossible to assess rationally the best means for its attainment. Thus, religion is a non-rational enterprise, justified by something other than – perhaps something more than – rational calculation. The very term 'rational choice' among non-rational belief systems has about it something of the oxymoronic.

Even if contemporary economic concerns and the ethos of consumerism influence religion, and even if purportedly spiritual insights take on the tones of hedonism and concern for profit and success, it is in the nature of religions themselves to claim a higher legitimacy than merely such a pragmatic sanction. Some new religions may have been infected by the prevailing economic ethos, and some may employ market techniques in their own search for recruits, yet it is clear that there is no 'perfect market' of religions, no circumstance of equally diffused perfect knowledge, no equal availability of all 'products' in all contexts, and in many cases no cognisance of a competitive situation. People may inherit their religion; may remain bound to a particular denomination or tradition by social, ethnic, communal or familial loyalties; may abandon religion in spite of strong messages that it might do one good. And beyond this lies the fact that people may choose their religion on deontological moral grounds rather than on teleological assumptions.

What new religions are able to do, however, is to tailor in some measure their teachings and practices to achieve congruity between them and the changing cultural context in which they perforce operate. And in this they have a wider flexibility of response than is available to settled Church structures, caught in commitment to supposedly timelessly valid truths, and organised in structures sanctified by antiquity. Thus, it is not surprising that new movements may approximate more closely than do older ones the activities, style, and pervasive ethos of the entertainment industry: religion traditionally functioned as a form of entertainment, but as secular patterns of leisure activities have undergone transformation, older Churches have lost much of their capacity to entertain their adherents. New religions can devote resources, encourage participation, and exploit the spiritual dimensions of performance, expression, and creativity more effectively than settled Churches, whose amateurish endeavours have resulted only in the encouragement of participation in such biblically sanctioned manifestations as charismatic renewal and the less securely justified 'Toronto blessing'.[4]

The diversity of beliefs, activities, and practices of the New Religious Movements renders suspect any easy generalisations concerning them. That, in one form or another, they all offer prospects of salvation, is perhaps the highest common denominator, and salvation here covers a wide range of items, including therapeutic benefits, attitude change, material success, peace of mind, improved karma, post-mortem bliss, and perhaps much else. It is such prospects, attainable by techniques which at some point claim to transcend the empirically verifiable, that justify the designation of these organisations as religions. Their interpretations of salvific possibilities is, when compared to conventional religion, adventurous, not to say innovative. Typically, they offer their votaries fuller participation in working out, indeed acting out, their own salvation. They tend to emphasise just what the individual can do for himself, and a widely used dictum, from Soka Gakkai to Scientology and the Forums Network (*est*) is that people should learn to take responsibility for their lives.

Service for others is also a theme which with greater or lesser emphasis is to be found widely diffused among these movements, and welfare programmes of one sort or another – from drug rehabilitation courses, to campaigns against famine, refugee rehabilitation, and concern for the environment – suggest an undercurrent of altruistic potential which, if realised, would amount to the betterment of the life circumstances of a considerably more extensive public than that encompassed by these movements in themselves. Given such emphasis on the individual's need to be responsible for himself or herself and of service to others, it is perhaps not surprising that sociological investigations have concluded that typical converts to new movements are often young idealists, eager to feel that they are doing something to 'save the world'. (Saving the world is a much canvassed project expressed in one form or another, in movements as varied as the Church of Scientology, the Unification Church, Soka Gakkai International.) The recognition that adherents of new religions are often motivated by idealism stands in sharp contrast to the stereotype projected by anti-cultists and the media which asserts or implies that those joining such movements are 'brainwashed' zombies.

The issue of brainwashing is not addressed in this volume: indeed, such is the degree of concurrence established by a range of sociological investigations that the charge of brainwashing is now recognised as at best dubious. We do not seek to pursue that issue here.[5] Sociologists who have undertaken participant observation of the activities of new movements and who have become well acquainted with their members, can without hesitation reject the idea that all those who join these organisations surrender their capacity to make their own judgements. Enthusiasm there is often, and fanaticism there may be occasionally, but the type of blind allegiance that characterised the members of the Branch Davidians, the members of the Solar Temple, or the adherents of Aum Shinrikyō, is the extreme rarity, and far from being in any sense the general rule.[6]

Although social scientists display a high degree of agreement on these issues, it must be understood that they have no *parti pris* with respect to new religions. They have not come to their conclusions concerning them as a matter of dogma, or as part of a shared prospectus of liberal sentiment. They do not make *a priori* assertions of the kind which, in derogating new movements, anti-cultists have been disposed to make. The grounds on which their opinions are based are the findings of empirical enquiry. In Chapter 6, Lilliston and Shepherd demonstrate that the evidence has to be impartially examined, and the issues have to be examined separately. Thus, the motivations that prompt conversion to new movements are likely to be different from the factors that influence the continued allegiance of a second generation of adherents, and such differences must perforce be the subject of renewed scholarly enquiry. As Lilliston and Shepherd make clear, as circumstances change, so new studies will be needed. And herein lies the prime distinction between the evidence emerging from careful controlled scholarly investigation and the unsubstantiated, impressionistic, anecdotal, and self-justificatory alarmist pronouncements on new religions by anti-cult groups.

No attempt to assess the response of contemporary societies to the wave of new religions now operating can ignore the anti-cult phenomenon. Although the concern of these chapters is to review new religions in their relation to major institutions, it is entirely appropriate – indeed necessary – that the spontaneous active resistance on the part of certain interested sections of the public to one or more of the new movements should be recognised and discussed. In some respects the anti-cultists themselves betray evidence of being not entirely dissimilar in posture from they way in which they depict the movements they designate as cults. Their general attributes are single-minded fanaticism, the supreme conviction of their own righteousness, a determination to 'save' individuals from their delusions, and indeed, thereby to 'save the world'. The impetus for these movements has come in greatest measure from kinsfolk of those recruited by one or another of the new religions, and although each set of kin has usually had one or another particular movement in mind as their focus of hostility, they have made common cause to condemn a wide variety of religious bodies.

Beyond familial concerns, however, other interests have sometimes been mobilised in reaction against new religions. Some politicians have seen these issues as politically sensitive, and some have undoubtedly made political capital from taking up the cudgels. Nor have governments always maintained a neutral stance. Individual clergymen in the mainstream Churches have also sometimes pronounced on the dangers of cults. The incidence of such support for anti-cult groups has varied from one country to another, as the contributions of Melton, Usarski, and Chryssides demonstrate. In Germany, churchmen and politicians have taken a more active part than has been the case in Britain and the United States. In Germany, too, governments have become yet more embattled on the issue.

That the mainstream Churches should pronounce on other religions is altogether as expected, yet it must be said that in Britain and the United States their response has been perhaps more muted than could have been expected. In the United States, alarmed perhaps by the potential danger to their own religious freedom, Churches have sometimes intervened in court proceedings to offer a measure of guarded support for new movements. In Britain, ideas from the New Age and from the Maharishi's Transcendental Meditation have influenced some clergymen and some congregations. At a more official level, the Churches have made gestures by seeking dialogue with new religions, and by supporting the voluntary neutral agency, INFORM (the acronym for the Information Network Focus on Religious Movements), which seeks to promote research into new movements, as well as opening avenues for encounter and reconciliation between alienated parents and their converted offspring. As Provost Slee makes plain in Chapter 8, the Church tends to restate its own position, and to register, more in sorrow than in anger, their bemused response at the outcropping of so many new manifestations of self-claimed spirituality.

It is perhaps in their encounter with the law that new religious bodies come most forcefully to the attention of the public. Litigation has been abundant: libel actions; applications for charitable status; custody cases; claims for damages by apostates; allegations (usually against anti-cultists) of kidnapping and forcible 'de-programming' are among a variety of instances in which the law has been invoked either by the movements themselves or by the alienated families of converts. The more encompassing legal issues, however, relate not to specifics of this kind, but to the general question of toleration. Dissenting minorities only slowly achieved freedom of assembly, worship, and the right to proselytise. Exemption from various civil obliga- tions (from compulsory military service, from jury service, or from various health and educational provisions, for example) came even more slowly. The new movements have perhaps made fewer demands for such relaxation of civic duty than did the older Christian sects or than have recently arrived immigrant religions such as Islam and Sikhism. But they have attracted the attention of the state, largely through the activities and allegations of the anti-cult lobby.

The anti-cultists have tended to argue that just as the state takes upon itself the duty to protect citizens from, for example, drugs, drink, tobacco, and pornography, so it is incumbent on the state to do likewise relative to 'cults'. The invidious analogy leaves serious issues unresolved. Who, for instance, would determine which religious bodies were or were not to be tolerated? How would such a policy be reconciled with the declarations on religious freedom and toleration of the United Nations, the Council of Europe, and the Helsinki Accord? What would be the sanctions against persistent recusants? These wider, philosophical issues concerning how the law impinges on religious bodies, and which are explored by Bradney in Chapter 4, carry the debate into a major area of public policy. From the repressive police activities in various countries, notably the dawn raids on communities of The Family (formerly the Children of God) in Spain, Australia, Argentina, and France; and the bungling of the American author- ities in the siege of the Branch Davidian settlement at Waco,[7] it is clear that such issues are now a matter of international moment. The recent report of the French Assembly on '*sectes*' points in a similar direction. Religious toler- ation, despite the best-intended pronouncements of international agencies, is by no means a settled question, and focuses for the present very pointedly on the role and the rights of new religions.

The majority of the chapters in this volume were delivered as papers at a symposium convened by the Institute of Oriental Philosophy at Taplow Court, which is the British centre of Soka Gakkai International, of which the Institute is an ancillary organisation. Soka Gakkai itself is a lay Buddhist organisation originating in Japan in the 1930s, and is thus in itself a New Religious Movement. As facilitator of the symposium, the Institute made it clear that its interest was to promote an academic occasion for unrestrained debate among established scholars who specialised in the study of religious movements. The participants were assured of their freedom to take up whatever issues they chose, and that they would retain complete control over the content of the published papers. It became apparent that inevitably there were issues which, given the time constraints of a two-day symposium, had not featured in the presentations, and in the preparation of this volume four further papers were solicited from experts in specific fields. These are the papers by Beckford on the media; by Lilliston and Shepherd on mental health; by Puttick on women in the new movements; and – to complement the papers on anti-cult activities, by Melton on the United States, and by Usarski in Germany – the paper by Chryssides on the anti-cult movement in Britain.

## Notes

1 See Assemblée Nationale, Commission d'enquête, Report No. 2468, *Les Sectes en France*, Paris, 1996.
2 Roy Wallis, *The Elementary Forms of the New Religious Life*, London: Routledge and Kegan Paul, 1984.
3 Rodney Start and R. Finke, 'A Rational Approach to the History of American Cults and Sects', in David G. Bromley and J. K. Hadden (eds), *Religion and the Social Order*, vol. 3 (Part A) *The Handbook on Cults and Sects in America*, Greenwood, CT: JAI Press, 1993, pp. 109–25, (p. 114); for a fuller account of rational choice theory, see Rodney Stark and L. R. Iannaccone, 'Rational Choice Propositions about Religious Movements', in D. G. Bromley and J. K. Hadden (eds), op. cit., pp. 241–61.
4 For discussion of the Toronto Blessing, see the papers collected in Stephen Hunt, Malcolm Hamilton, and Tony Walter (eds), *Charismatic Christianity: Sociological Perspectives*, London: Macmillan, 1997.
5 See for example, Eileen Barker, *The Making of a Moonie: Brainwashing or Choice*, Oxford: Blackwell, 1984; Stuart A. Wright, *Leaving the Cults: The Dynamics of Defection*, Washington, DC: Society for the Scientific Study of Religion, 1987; E. Burke Rochford, *Hare Krishna in America*, New Brunswick, NJ: Rutgers University Press, 1985; David G. Bromley and J. T. Richardson (eds), *The Brainwashing/Deprogramming Controversy: Sociological, Psychological, Legal, and Historical Perspectives*, New York: Edwin Mellen Press, 1983.
6 For various accounts of the Branch Davidian movement, see Stuart A. Wright (ed.), *Armageddon in Waco*, Chicago: University of Chicago Press, 1995; on the Solar Temple, see Massimo Introvigne, 'Ordeal by Fire: The Tragedy of the Solar Temple', *Religion*, 25(3), 1995, pp. 267–83; on Aum Shinrikyō, Shimazono Susumu, 'In the Wake of Aum: The Formation and Transformation of a Universe of Belief', *Japanese Journal of Religious Studies*, 22(3–4), 1995, pp. 381–415.
7 On the mishandling of the siege of the Branch Davidian community, see Nancy T. Ammerman, 'Waco, Federal Law Enforcement, and Scholars of Religion', in Stuart A. Wright (ed.) *Armageddon*, op. cit., pp. 282–96.

# Summary of Chapter 1

New Religious Movements (NRMs) are today a world-wide phenomenon, but the current wave of such movements, which became visible in the West after the Second World War, differs from the vast majority of previous waves in that the movements arise not only within the Judaeo-Christian tradition, but also from other traditions (Hinduism, Buddhism, Islam, Shintoism, and Paganism) and from more recent philosophies or ideologies, such as psycho-analysis and science fiction. While concentrating on the situation in Europe, North America, and Australasia, Professor Barker does not ignore the growth of NRMs in Africa, Japan, Latin America, Eastern Europe, and the traditionally Christian countries of the former Soviet Union. She brings out the extraordinary variety of these movements, and indicates that while some contemporary movements manifest some of the characteristics typical of earlier new religions, the fact that many of them now have a second- or even a third-generation membership has led to some dilution of their original 'sectarian' character. She indicates that the statistical significance of new movements is not as great as their social and cultural significance, and that much of their significance lies in society's reaction to them. It is precisely this consequence for social and cultural institutions which other authors explore in subsequent chapters.

# 1  New Religious Movements

## Their incidence and significance

*Eileen Barker*

## Introduction

The subject of the incidence and significance of New Religious Movements is enormous, and the necessity to select a few points from the many that could be raised is but an invitation to anticipate at a superficial level what others will be exploring in far greater depth. I can hope to do no more than raise some of the more obvious (though sometimes forgotten) questions that relate to the challenge of the movements and to the responses to which their presence has given rise.

## Statistical significance

Despite the fact that there is a surprisingly large number of NRMs peppering the free world at the present time, and that a considerable number of persons have been affected by the movements, the real significance of new religions in modern society is not a statistical significance. Certainly, there is no indication that I have come across in the West which suggests that any one movement is showing signs of becoming a major religious tradition during the life of its first-, second- or even third-generation members. This argument is less forceful in Japan, where it has been estimated that between 10 and 20 per cent of the population are followers of one or other NRM,[1] and where a movement such as Soka Gakkai claims several million followers – but even its impressive growth seems to have reached a plateau, at least at the present time – and it should be remembered that at least 80 per cent of the population are not followers of any NRM.

## How many NRMs are there now?

The short answer is that we do not know with much accuracy what the incidence of new religions is. A somewhat longer answer starts with the simple truth that, of course, it all depends on what is meant by an NRM. Do we include each and every New Age group or do we lump them together as a single 'movement'? Do we include movements within mainstream traditions

(Opus Dei, Folkalore, the House Church movement – *each* House Church)? What about the African Independent Churches? What about the United Reform Church? Are the 'self-religions' or Human Potential groups really new *religious* movements? How new is new? What about Subud, Vedanta or possibly Jehovah's Witnesses which is the first 'sect' that comes to mind in a country such as Italy when the phrase New Religious Movement is mentioned? Might we include even the anti-cult movement – sections of it certainly exhibit several of the characteristics that 'anti-cultists' themselves attribute to 'cults'?

### Definitions of movements

There is, of course, no 'right' answer. Definitions are more or less useful, not more or less true. The definition from which I personally start – for purely pragmatic reasons – is that an NRM is new in so far as it has become visible in its present form since the Second World War, and that it is religious in so far as it offers not merely narrow theological statements about the existence and nature of supernatural beings, but that it proposes answers to at least some of the other kinds of ultimate questions that have traditionally been addressed by mainstream religions, questions such as: Is there a God? Who am I? How might I find direction, meaning and purpose in life? Is there life after death? Is there more to human beings than their physical bodies and immediate interactions with others?

### Numbers of movements

INFORM has over 2,600 different groups on its computer, the majority (but not all) of which might be called NRMs.[2] Given that there must be a good many groups about which we have not heard, it would not be unreasonable to assume that, including schisms but not branches of the same group under different names, there could be over 2,000 discrete groups in Europe. Gordon Melton, who uses a much narrower definition, which excludes the human potential groups, can provide some information on nearly 1,000 groups in America.[3] Shimazono says that scholarly estimates of the number of NRMs in Japan vary from 800 to a few thousand.[4] Several years ago, Harold Turner estimated that there were 10,000 new religions with 12 million or more adherents in among the tribal peoples of the Americas, Asia, Africa and the Pacific.[5] He would include the African Independent Churches, but untold numbers of new religions may be found in India; several hundreds exist in South America, Australia and New Zealand and in places such as the West Indies, Korea and the Philippines.

In short, while clearly dependent on the definition used, the number of NRMs according to my broad definition is likely to be in the order of four figures (two or more thousand) in the West and five figures (probably somewhere in the lower tens of thousands) world-wide.

## How many members?

Attempting to assess the incidence of the movements seems like child's play when one turns to questions concerning membership numbers. Many of the movements do not count, keep secret or distort (usually upwards) their membership figures. We know that some NRMs have only a handful of members – a score or less – while others have hundreds or thousands, with a few (but only a very few with any credibility) claiming millions.

### *Definitions of membership*

There is, moreover, a vast range of levels of membership: there are totally committed members who (like monks or nuns) devote their lives to their movement, living as a community and working full time for it; there are associate members (similar to congregational members), who may come to a centre on a weekly basis for worship or a course; and there are sympathisers (or 'nominal' members) who may be in general agreement with an NRM's beliefs and practices, but whose lives are not very widely or deeply affected by their somewhat peripheral affiliation. While for some purposes it is only committed members who are counted, at other times or in different movements, one can find included even those who have done little more than sign a piece of paper saying that they are in general sympathy with some of the movement's beliefs.

### *Double-counting*

Further confusion may arise as the result of double-counting. It is not impossible – indeed, as one moves toward the New Age end of the NRM spectrum, it is quite common – for individuals to have overlapping memberships, happily hopping from one 'self-religion' to another. It would not be impossible for committed seekers in California, Amsterdam or Highgate to spend twenty minutes in Transcendental Meditation each morning before embarking on their Tai Chi, then going on to attend a channelling session on Monday, to meet with their Co-counsellor on Tuesday, have an Alexander lesson on Wednesday, watch an Osho video on Thursday and participate in a Forum Seminar throughout the weekend. Two months later one might find them chanting 'Hare Krishna', 'Om Shanti' or, perhaps, 'Nam Myoho Renge Kyo'.

### *Turnover*

There is, furthermore, the complication of high turnover rates. Both the movements and their opponents tend to play down this characteristic of many of the better-known NRMs. On the one hand, few new religions are eager to publicise the fact that a sizeable number of their members have found the movement wanting; on the other hand, anti-cultists who are eager to defend 'the brainwashing thesis' do not wish to publicise the fact that the 'victims' not only can, but do, of their own free will, leave those very NRMs that are accused of employing irresistible and irreversible techniques of mind control.[6]

So far as our present interests are concerned, this means that it is frequently the number of people who have passed through a movement, rather than the current membership, that is counted. Being familiar with the phrase 'Once a Catholic, always a Catholic', we should not be surprised that the Church of Scientology considers all those who have ever done one of their courses to be a Scientologist, and counts them as such even if they have not been in touch with the movement for years – even, presumably, if they are among the movement's most vitriolic opponents.

And it cannot be denied that there is no way in which I, having done the course (albeit for purposes of research), cannot be an *est* graduate – or, rather, a Forum graduate. (In *that* sense – and, let me insist, in that sense only – the anti-cultists who, as a result of my participant observation, accuse me of being 'numbered' among cult members are, doubtless, correct.)

## The cultural milieu

A further point that ought to be raised so far as incidence is concerned, but which, at the same time, propels us towards the 'significance' part of my remit, is something about which Colin Campbell has written extensively: the cultic milieu.[7]

One of the features of modern society which sociologists of religion, such as Durkheim, Weber and Wilson, have frequently pointed out is that organised religion no longer has the kind of hold over social institutions that it has enjoyed in earlier periods. Religion has become increasingly a leisure pursuit that may be 'privatised', 'individualised' or even, to borrow Luckmann's term, 'invisible'. Mainstream religious organisations have suffered significant losses of membership in most of Europe and, according to some, though not all, commentators, in the United States. Anyone who has made but the most cursory of enquiries about people's religious positions in Western society will be all too familiar with the sentiment: 'You don't have to go to church to be a good Christian.'

Concomitantly, in place of a relatively homogeneous, coherent, and more or less shared culture, we have witnessed the growth of religious pluralism, interwoven with numerous social changes such as increased social and geographical mobility, universal franchise, universal education and the break-up of a traditional occupational structure, traditional values and authority structures – all of which can contribute to a dissatisfaction with, or at least a second look at, the beliefs and practices that might otherwise have been passed on by parents or others in roles of authority – thus creating a potential 'demand' (in the economic sense) for alternative ways of satisfying spiritual and religious requirements.

On the 'supply' side, although it should be remembered that most of the traditional Churches still supply more people with their religion than does any NRM, we have expanding missionary activity and escalating migration – a factor that Melton has repeatedly pointed to is the relaxing of the US immigration laws in 1965, which allowed a number of gurus to enter the United States and thus promote the growth of religions with Eastern origins. And, of course, there has been the development of a mass media (supplemented by all manner of electronic, satellite and Internet devices) swelling the variety of (broadly defined) religious resources that have become available to any one individual participating in the cultural milieu. All sorts of ideas are out there. And many of these ideas originate from, are carried by, and/or are reinforced by New Religious Movements.

This is particularly obvious with a number of New Age ideas such as person-centred spirituality and/or the potential of individual development. And, while fifty years ago none but a very small proportion of Christians would have seriously countenanced the idea of reincarnation, the European Value Surveys, the International Social Survey Programme and several other research projects tell us that anywhere between a fifth and a quarter of Europeans and North Americans now believe that we shall return to this world in another body when we have shuffled off this mortal coil. Such a belief was reported by 24 per cent of Britons – though it might be noted that several of these respondents *also* reported believing in the resurrection of the body.[8]

The point that I want to make here is that, when attempting to chart the incidence and/or significance of NRMs, we might want to be at least aware of, even if we do not include, those who are not officially members of any particular NRM. There are people who might be horrified at the thought they could be in any way connected with a 'cult', but who are, none the less, 'recipients', even carriers, of ideas and practices that are borne by, if not always born in, NRMs.

And while we are considering this category of persons loosely adding to the social significance of the movements, may I suggest that we might also recognise the existence, first, of members of the media who use and promote NRM ideas; second, of members of the mainstream religions who have picked up ideas and practices originating or transmitted by NRMs; third, of managers and other personnel in business corporations who invite and/or attend courses liberally imbued with NRM ideas and practices; and, fourth, members of the anti-cult movements who have played such a significant role in promoting the high profile that certain NRMs and their members have achieved in the past three decades or so. It is, indeed, members of the Evangelical wing of the counter-cult movement who can be credited with spreading certainly the idea, and arguably some of the practices, of ritual

Satanic abuse in North America, Western and Eastern Europe, Australia and elsewhere around the world.[9]

## Generalising about NRMs

One cannot generalise about NRMs. The only thing that they have in common is that they have been labelled as an NRM or 'cult'. The movements differ from each other so far as their origins, their beliefs, their practices, their organisation, their leadership, their finances, their life-styles and their attitudes to women, children, education, moral questions and the rest of society are concerned. Attempts to produce typologies have been limited, and even relatively useful distinctions (such as Roy Wallis's distinction between world-affirming, world-rejecting and world-accommodating religions)[10] do not really help us to anticipate with much certainty the *empirical* characteristics that might follow from the *defining* characteristics of each category. Assuredly, there is nothing to match the elegant types that Bryan Wilson elaborated for the earlier, predominantly Christian-based, sects.[11] The ever-increasing range of alternatives from all corners of the world (from relatively new philosophies such as psychoanalysis or the development of science, electronic innovations and science fiction, and the increase of UFO sightings and 'strange encounters of the third kind') have made neat, predictive models out of date almost before the ink has dried on their author's paper – or the laser has printed from their author's PC.

None the less, the anti-cult movement, much of the media and a sizeable chunk of the population continue to provide us with facile check-lists of the characteristics of NRMs as dangerous, manipulative, exploitative, and deceptive sex maniacs – or, in depictions where descriptive rather than evaluative detail is given, frequently making it difficult to distinguish 'destructive cults' from many traditional mainstream religions.

There are, however, some characteristics that make an NRM more visible and, thereby, significant *as* an NRM. One may find, for example, the first-generation enthusiasms, the unambiguous clarity and certainty in the belief systems, the urgency of the message, the commitment of life-style, perhaps a charismatic leadership, and, possibly, strong Them/Us and/or Before/After distinctions – all of which are, of course, liable to undergo significant change within a single generation.

## Who joins NRMs?

Just as there are all types of NRMs, so there are all types of people who join the movements. However, those who have joined the better-known of the current wave of NRMs in the West have been disproportionately white and from the better-educated middle classes. There are exceptions – indeed, it is worth pointing out that many of the ill-fated members of the Branch Davidians and of the People's Temple were blacks from the lower classes,[12] and that they were not as disproportionately young as those joining movements such as the Children of God, the Unification Church or ISKCON. Even the somewhat older people who have become involved with the 'self-religions' (and who may need a respectable income to pay for courses) have tended to be disproportionately in their thirties or early forties. As with other aspects of NRMs, however, we have to remember that all kinds of people of all kinds of ages, occupations, classes, ethnic groupings, educational attainments and from all kinds of religions have joined and will doubtless continue to join NRMs. And now, of course, there is a growing number of persons who have been born into an NRM. Two-thirds of the current membership of The Family are second- or even third-generation members.

## Temporal differences

The first thing that might be noted arises out of what I have already intimated: NRMs change over time. Merely the fact that time has passed means that founders have died, that young, idealist converts with few dependants or other responsibilities have grown into middle-aged parents – and a new 'born-into' generation, demanding the allocation of such resources as time and money, will have to be socialised and accommodated. Thus, like all new religions before them, the present wave of NRMs have, during the past quarter of a century, undergone changes which are all too often forgotten when the media, the anti-cult movement and, as a consequence, members of the general public talk, write or merely think about NRMs.

In a special edition of *Social Compass* that Jean-François Mayer and I recently put together to highlight changes that have occurred in NRMs over the past twenty years,[13] I argue that such changes tend to result both in the movements becoming less like each other, and, at the same time, in their becoming more like the wider society – the apparent paradox resting on the fact that modern society is a pluralist society into which the movements may merge in a number of different forms.

But it is not only the individual NRMs that change with the passage of time. Given that the structures and cultures of society are continually altering, we would expect, and do indeed find, that the 'cult scene' *as a whole* will change. The balance of public attention and the popularity of particular kinds of NRMs will vary at different times. Furthermore, these shifting scenes differ in different parts of the world.

## Spatial differences

In discussing the incidence of NRMs in Europe, Stark and Bainbridge draw a distinction between sects (schisms of mainstream traditions) and cults (innovative groups). They argue (and claim that the evidence supports the argument) that sects are likely to appear when traditional religions are strong, while cults emerge only when the traditional religions are weak.[14] Other contributors to this book provide international data, but let me, for comparative purposes, offer three very brief sketches.

### England

In England (and I am referring to England rather than to Britain or the United Kingdom), the emergence of a youth culture after the Second World War did not immediately translate into a new religious scene. Indeed, with a few exceptions such as young black males who became Rastafarians, the youth culture of the working class was and remains notable for its lack of religious manifestations – unless we were to extend our definition to include Teds, Mods, Rockers and, later, Punks and Skinheads.

Middle-class youth roughly followed the paths that their peers in North America were treading. It was not until the 1960s, towards the end of the period of militant student unrest, that a religious – or spiritual – alternative became visible to any but the few who were already involved in such an alternative. The demos faded into squats in the inner cities, into communes in sacred centres such as Glastonbury, and along the ley lines of the United Kingdom. Then the hippies started to move into more structured, but none the less religious or spiritual (rather than political) organisations – some of them of a strictly authoritarian nature. The dawning of the Age of Aquarius mingled into the Human Potential movement, which has continued to flourish – reaching into those parts of mainstream society from which other religions have been increasingly banished since the onset of a desacralization of society – or secularisation, in the Bryan Wilson meaning of the concept.[15]

Then we could observe the rise of enthusiastic religion (the charismatic, neo-pentecostal and/or restoration movements) filtering into mainstream Churches, thereby increasing the supply of one of the scarce resources – religious enthusiasm – that NRMs such as the Children of God or the Unification Church were offering in the 1960s and 1970s when many of the young people who were to join such movements were typifying the Churches as cold, hypocritical, apathetic and dominated by old ladies. It is, however, not without significance that the Holy Spirit used an NRM – the Vineyard movement – as its medium for the introduction of the 'Toronto Blessing' to certain sections of the more evangelical wing of the Church of England – a phenomenon that has become decidedly controversial in other, more conservative, sections of the Evangelical church.[16]

### Japan

As is well known, the Japanese had its modern 'Rush Hour of the Gods'[17] some time before the West had its – the former's influx of new religions occurring immediately after the Second World War, while the latter's did not really take off until the mid-1960s. There are numerous historical reasons for the differences between Japanese and Western NRMs.[18] Furthermore, since the 1970s, Japan has witnessed a new wave of movements, commonly referred to as the New New or Neo-New Religions. Aum Shinrikyō is one such NNRM, typical of the NNRMs in so far as it seems to have appealed disproportion-ately to young, well-educated people rather than to the less educated, lower-middle class and/or, especially, housewives who have been attracted to many of the earlier, post-war NRMs. The general shift, according to Shimazono, is that, while the former new religions were concerned with salva-tion and good community living in this life, the New New Religions have been less concerned about practical and *communal* problems (such as poverty, disease and family conflicts), and have placed less emphasis on altruistic ethics, concentrating more on the transformation of, and control over, the *individual*'s mind and body. In order to attain further salvation for the soul in future lives, the process of enlightenment may be pursued with the help of mystical knowledge and magical practices.

But while Shimazono typifies Aum Shinrikyō as an NNRM, he also clas-sifies it as a somewhat atypical 'isolationist' movement, and argues that the most significant development in contemporary Japan is the emergence of a magico-religious popular culture that is disseminated not through religious organisations so much as through comic books, magazines and computer games which can be read or played at any time – 'producing an instanta-neous private space'.[19]

### Eastern Europe and the traditionally Christian Former Soviet Union (FSU)

There were NRMs in Eastern Europe and the Soviet Union before 1989. Frequently they were more or less underground, and, when exposed, they sometimes suffered quite severe consequences. Several Krishna devotees were imprisoned and a couple died in Soviet jails. On the other hand, several Buddhist and New Age/Human Potential groups, while not exactly flour-ishing, were able to meet and practise quite freely in Poland, and I even managed to meet two Transcendental Meditators in the middle of the main square in Tirana before Albania's socialist regime collapsed.

But, of course, the incidence of NRMs was minute – until, that is, the Wall came down. And when it did come down the NRMs were there – several of them literally there, handing out literature with all manner of offerings. Since then, the movements have been particularly successful in Russia, and have not done badly in East Germany, Hungary and the Ukraine. There are quite a few to be found in Poland and the Czech Republic, several in Romania, Slovakia and Belorussia, and a few in Bulgaria and in the Georgian and Armenian Republics. Some intrepid members of NRMs have been found offering humanitarian aid along with salvation in the war zones of Croatia and Ngorno Karabakh.

Although there are indigenous new religions and revivals of older, folk, pagan or esoteric religions to be found in Eastern Europe and the FSU, the majority of the NRMs are from the West, many of them offering as many capitalist as spiritual wares to anyone who will listen: Unificationists offer English language classes and travel to the West, Scientologists offer management courses; but it would seem to be some of the new evangelical groups, such as the Churches of Christ planted from Boston, the Word of Life from Sweden, the Vineyard Church in the Czech Republic, or the amazingly successful Faith Church in Hungary that are really thriving.

Yet while it looked at first as though the newfound freedoms of Eastern Europe and the Former Soviet Union were presenting the new religions with a field day, whatever success they have enjoyed has generated increasing antagonism from the traditional Churches who see the movements as one of the main reasons for their lack of success in retaining what they consider to be rightfully their flock. New laws have been introduced or are in the process of being proposed to curtail the activities and, in some cases, to forbid the presence of foreign, non-established small religions. [20]

One of my doctoral students, Marat Shterin, who is comparing the NRMs in England and in Russia, is finding the difference between the reactions of the Russian Orthodox Church and the Church of England one of his most significant variables. None the less, both his and my own observations suggest that the development of the movements in Eastern Europe and the FSU differs in a number of ways from their development in the West. Perhaps this is not altogether surprising, given that they are now more experienced and, in several cases, it is a second-generation membership that is trying to establish a foothold in what are totally different surroundings. And, of course, the fact that so many of the potential converts have been brought up in an atheistic socialist state obviously has a considerable effect on what seekers are seeking.

### Cultural adaptability

The interplay between an NRM and the culture in which it originates is a familiar subject of study. A more recent interest has been investigating the way that particular movements 'travel'. In some respects, the transported NRM might appear only marginally different in whatever country it is operating. When, for example, I visit a community-based group such as the Unification Church, the Hare Krishna or The Family (all three of which I have stayed with or visited in a dozen or more different countries), I sometimes find it difficult to remember where I am, apart from being in a Moonie centre, an ISKCON Temple or a Family home – in this respect, staying with a particular NRM is rather like staying in, say, the Tokyo, Lagos or Washington Hilton – one is in a Hilton hotel – and Tokyo, Lagos or Washington just happen to be outside. One might, perhaps, notice that *some* of the other residents happen to speak a different language or have skin of a different hue – but one finds that also in the London Hilton, the Lancaster Gate Unification Centre, the Soho Krishna Temple and the Dunton Bassett Family home.

But clearly the different social contexts do, to a greater or lesser degree, affect the movements' *modus operandi* and the reception that they are given. Some manage to preserve their original beliefs and practices pretty well intact world-wide; others succeed only to the extent that they adapt – more or less – to the host culture. I have been told that there are Unificationists who are allowed to keep more than one wife in some African countries with Islamic influences.

It has already been intimated that some movements of Japanese origin are relatively successful in the West – Soka Gakkai International provides one such example – while others make less of an impression on the natives. Louis Hourmant attributes changes in the Japanese NRMs he has observed in France, such as a playing down of the magical-religious component in Reiyükai, to responses to the differences between Western and Japanese society.[21] However, Jean-François Mayer, in a Swiss context, notes that the adjustment of Mahikari has not been accompanied by a parallel diminution, although the integration of values and of the ideology promoted by Mahikari seems to be a very lengthy process for its Swiss followers.[22] Interestingly, just as the New New Religions in Japan incorporate a negation of some modern values, Mahikari members in Switzerland tend to think that their new religion brings them the sense of the sacred which they feel the conventional Churches in the West have lost.

## The significance of NRMs for individuals

### *Members*

It is obvious, but none the less worth mentioning, that the significance of an NRM – the scope and the intensity of the experience for its membership – will obviously vary from individual to individual and from movement to movement. It will also vary according to the position that individuals occupy in the movement – whether, for example, they are new converts or seasoned leaders – or, perhaps, whether they are male or female.[23] For some, joining an NRM will become and will remain the most important thing to happen in their lives – they may find direction, meaning, the hope of salvation, a sense of belonging to a like-minded community, the opportunity to develop a relationship with God, to develop their spirituality, to find their true selves or all manner of other possibilities that they felt they were denied in the 'outside world'. For others, the experience may have seemed wonderful at first but has since soured through disappointment and, perhaps, disillusionment. A few will have extremely unpleasant experiences and feel that they have been deceived, manipulated, exploited and/or robbed not only of money and material goods but also of their time and, perhaps, their innocence and, maybe, their faith in God and/or in humanity.

## Members' relations and friends

Sometimes it seems as though NRMs have an even greater significance for the relatives and friends of members than for the members themselves. While there are friends and relatives who rejoice in converts' finding a new happiness, contentment or fulfilment in an NRM, there is also a significant number of people who have had their lives profoundly and adversely affected by a friend or relative joining a new religion – and some of these people have become involved with the anti-cult movement. The metaphor of death has frequently been employed by parents who talk about feelings of bereavement; a few have even claimed that they would prefer their son or daughter to be dead rather than in 'the cult'. Husbands or wives have talked about an NRM coming between them and their partner, producing a rift that cannot be breached. One partner taking on new interests that exclude the other is not, of course, a phenomenon confined to NRMs, but it should be recognised that it can be as fraught a situation as that which arises when people discover that their partner is being unfaithful and intends to remain so.

## The significance of NRMs for the rest of society

Fifteen or so years ago, I edited a book called *New Religious Movements: A Perspective for Understanding Society*.[24] Had I the time, I would like to bring out a second volume for we have learned so much more in the intervening period about the ways in which NRMs can contribute to our understanding of society. Some of the points have already been covered and there is no space here to discuss many others. But I would like to conclude by introducing some of the ways in which sociologists of religion may be alerted to features of the wider social context in which the movements flourish or wither.

### The NRMs of the Gaps

One of the ways NRMs have been seen as being of significance is that they may occasionally function as a barometer of what at least some members of a society feel they need but is not being supplied by other means.[25] This is not so much a God of the Gaps theology as a movements of the gaps sociology. Such a perspective could – indeed has – sensitised us to perceived lacunae. There are, however, methodological problems. First, in pluralist societies, it would be foolhardy to generalise too much from particular innovations in particular NRMs. However, a rush to NRMs which are offering, say, enthusiastic rituals of worship, healing, interpretations of religious experiences might suggest a significant perceived need, rather than a chance gap or even acceptance of something because it is there rather than because it is sought. Second, while the movements might want to offer alternatives in more totalitarian societies, it would be difficult to argue that it was the positive suggestions of the NRM, rather than the repressive nature of the regime, that were responsible for the attractiveness of the 'offer' – which could, equally well, come from any dissident source – including those of a purely secular nature. But none of this is to deny that NRMs can have a significant role to play as a dissenting force in society. They can.

### Media and anti-cultists

An enormous amount of work has now been done on the ways in which the media and the anti-cult movement (ACM) have responded to the NRMs and the significance of the interaction between the various institutions. Melton explores this subject in further detail, but I would like to take two recent examples to illustrate the significance that members of a society may attach to NRMs as the result of media and anti-cult constructions of their image. In other words, what I want to highlight is the *significance of the significance* that the media and the ACM attach to the movements.

The first example illustrates how a democratic society (in this case, England) can give 'permission' to its citizens to carry out a criminal attack on a person *merely* on the grounds that s/he is the member of a 'cult'. It is the case of Kathy Wilson, a 23-year-old member of the Church of Scientology whose erstwhile friends decided that she had been brainwashed and needed rescuing. They took matters into their own hands and tried to grab her, taking a knife and a Rottweiler to assist in the kidnap. Kathy screamed. There ensued some ugly and violent exchanges as passing Scientologists came to Kathy's rescue. Despite the fact that Kathy maintained – and still maintains – that she is happy and wants to remain a Scientologist, in March 1995 a British jury unanimously acquitted the man who admitted that he had intended to 'snatch her' against her will. It was reported that his counsel had argued that:

> even though she claimed in court she did not consent to removal, it was possible her free will had been removed by the processes she had undergone in the cult and she did not have 'sufficient intelligence and understanding' to decide if she consented.[26]

What is of particular significance for our purposes is that the would-be kidnapper, who maintained that although Kathy's abduction would be 'probably against her will because she's been brainwashed and she'll be on drugs', cited as the sources of his information 'taxi drivers, a local newspaper journalist, others involved in the "rescue" of members of religious cults, as well as his own investigations'.[27] Furthermore, in a recorded interview with police, just after the incident in November 1992, he declared: 'I know I would be liable to criminal prosecution now, but no jury in the country…would see me guilty.'[28] It would seem that he was right.

My other example is from the United States, and it illustrates how the public image of an NRM can lead not to *ad hominem* but to *ad NRMinem* arguments being employed to judge something as wicked *solely* on the grounds that there is even a very slight NRM connection. It concerns the use of a slide presentation on AIDS that laid emphasis on teenage celibacy and which was promoted for use (in public and private schools, churches and doctors' offices) by such worthy citizens as a nun, a chapter leader of Concerned Women of America and a leader of Project Respect. These women then learned, at a meeting of the True Light Educational Ministry (a group 'advising people leaving cults'), that the two men who had put together the programme which they had considered so excellent happened to be Unificationists. Despite the fact that there was no evidence whatsoever that the slides had been or would be used to promote any Unification beliefs apart from that shared by the erstwhile promoters – that pre-marital sex is not a good idea – the women immediately started to advise those to whom they had previously promoted the programme that the programme should not be used.[29]

Did one of the Unificationists have a point when he suggested that it would be foolish to refuse the use of polio vaccines because one disliked their inventors' religions?

### The law

If one had to select one criterion that might indicate the extent to which a society was 'open' or 'closed', the legal position of NRMs would be a not altogether ridiculous choice. For somewhat finer tuning, the second criterion could well be the legal treatment of NRMs. I believe that this is an area where NRMs can be of particular significance in both reflecting and affecting the society in which they exist. One might look, for example, at the position of NRMs in Islamic and Soviet countries and the new legislation that has been introduced and is being contemplated in Eastern Europe and the Former Soviet Union (in Moscow, Kiev and Yerevan); one can examine the mounting number of cases that have gone to the Supreme Court in America, providing a remarkable forum for debate about the nicer points of law concerning the relative balance of freedoms between (a) individuals, (b) groups and (c) society.[30]

### Mainstream traditions in the West

There are several different issues that could be pursued so far as the signifi-cance of NRMs *vis-à-vis* traditional religions are concerned. I have already touched briefly on Stark and Bainbridge's theory about the significance of the religious situation to the growth of cults and sects, and I have briefly mentioned both the positive way in which a tradition may use the 'challenge' of the movements to incorporate changes in their own practices, and the negative reactions of the Mother Churches in Eastern Europe and the FSU. This is, of course, an area which invokes a wide range of questions about the functioning of pluralistic societies.

### NRMs as an indicator of perceived vulnerability

A further, related point of potential significance concerns not only which societies and groups within society get more or less worried about the NRMs in their midst (until recently, Finland was relatively unconcerned – and still is, compared with, say, Belgium), but also what aspects of which movements are selected for condemnation. I am not sure what the situation is now, but at one time it looked as though Britain was particularly concerned with brainwashing allegations, France with political intrigue, the United States with the break-up of the family and financial considerations, Germany with social security payments, and Japan with the effect on young people's career prospects. There are ways, as Beckford and others have suggested, in which we can learn about a society by analysing what is seen as particularly threatening.[31] Different perceptions and interpretations of the 'Satanist scare' might prove a fruitful starting point for further study in this area.[32]

### The significance of NRMs for the sociology of religion

Finally, the study of NRMs has introduced numerous methodological challenges and has taken not a few sociologists out of the ivory tower of academia into a marketplace of fierce competition in the business of social construction of reality in government circles, in the courts, the popular media and in various other venues in our pluralist society.[33]

## Concluding remarks

New Religious Movements come in a vast variety of forms. They are successful or they fail for a multitude of reasons. Facile generalisations are bound to be wrong. Some of the beliefs that are held by members of the general public are true about some of the movements some of the time but, through their studies of NRMs, social scientists have found that many of the statements in the popular media are blatantly untrue about the majority of the movements, and others refer to only a tiny proportion of their number. Much more detailed work needs to be carried out to understand the processes that occur within the movements and between them and the wider society. And, possibly more importantly, the knowledge that we have of the movements needs to be disseminated and understood more widely. Not only the NRMs, but societal reaction to them have significantly greater significance than their relatively small numbers might suggest.

## Notes

1 Susumu Shimazono, 'New Religions and the New Spirituality Movement: Two Types of Religious Movements in Advanced Industrial Societies', paper given at the Santa Barbara Center for Humanistic Studies conference, 'New Religions in a Global Perspective', Buelton, California, 16 May 1991, p. 3.
2 INFORM (Information Network Focus on Religious Movements) is a charity, based at the London School of Economics, which I founded with the support of the Home Office and mainstream Churches in 1988 in order to provide information that is as accurate and up to date as possible about new religions. It can be contacted at INFORM, Houghton St, London WC2A 2AE, England; tel. 0171–955 7654, fax 0171–955 7677, e-mail INFORM@LSE.AC.UK.
3 J. Gordon Melton, *Encyclopedia of American Religions*, 4th edn, Detroit: Gale, 1993.
4 Shimazono, op. cit.
5 Harold Turner, 'New Religious Movements in Primal Societies', in John Hinnells (ed.), *The Penguin Dictionary of Religions*, Harmondsworth: Penguin, 1984, p. 232. Second edition: *A New Dictionary of Religions*, Oxford: Blackwell, 1995, p. 350.
6 See Eileen Barker, *New Religious Movements: A Practical Introduction*, London: HMSO, 1989. Fifth impression with amendments 1995, pp. 104–5.
7 Colin Campbell, 'The Cult, the Cultic Milieu and Secularization', in Michael Hill (ed.), *Sociological Yearbook of Religion in Britain*, London: SCM Press, 1972, pp. 119–36.
8 This is not necessarily a contradiction in terms – there are a number of theologically minded people (often with Theosophical leanings) who see the two concepts as entirely complementary. It is, however, doubtful whether many of the 24 per cent have such well-worked-out beliefs.
9 See James T. Richardson, Joel Best and David Bromley, *The Satanism Scare*, New York: De Gruyter, 1991.
10 Roy Wallis, *The Elementary Forms of the New Religious Life*, London: Routledge and Kegan Paul, 1983.
11 Bryan Wilson, *Religious Sects: A Sociological Study*, London: Weidenfeld, 1970.
12 James T. Richardson, 'People's Temple and Jonestown: A Corrective Comparison and Critique', *Journal for the Scientific Study of Religion*, 19(3), 1980, pp. 239–55.
13 *Twenty Years On: Changes in New Religious Movements*, special edition of *Social Compass*, 42(2), June 1995.
14 Rodney Stark and William Sims Bainbridge, *A Theory of Religion*, New York: Peter Lang, 1987. Republished in 1996 by Rutgers University Press, New Brunswick.
15 'The Process Whereby Religious Thinking, Practice and Institutions Lose Social Significance', *Religion in Secular Society: A Sociological Comment*, Harmondsworth: Pelican, 1969, p. 14.
16 See *Religion Report*, 20 March 1995, 9(7), 1.
17 H. Neill McFarland, *The Rush Hour of the Gods: A Study of New Religious Movements in Japan*, New York: Macmillan, 1967.
18 See, for example, McFarland, op. cit. and Shimazono, op. cit. and 'New New Religions and This World: Religious Movements in Japan after the 1970s and the Beliefs about Salvation', *Social Compass*, 42(2), 1995: pp. 193–206; Susumu Shimazono, M. R. Mullins and P. Swanson (eds), *Religion and Society in Modern Japan*, Berkeley, CA: Asian Humanities Press, 1993.

19 There are quite a few signs that similar manifestations are beginning to become more prominent in the West. One of my students recently took the members of our graduate seminar on a journey through the Internet 'in search of God'. It was, as one of my other students remarked, 'something else'.

20 See Eileen Barker, 'But Who's Going to Win? National and Minority Religions in Post-Communist Society', in Irena Borowik and Grzegorz Babinski (eds), *New Religious Phenomena in Central and Eastern Europe*, Kraków: Nomos, 1997, pp. 25–62.

21 'Les Nouveaux Mouvements religieux japonais en France', *Social Compass*, 42(2), June 1995, pp. 207–20.

22 Jean-François Mayer, *Social Compass*, 42(2), June 1995, pp. 180–92.

23 See Susan Palmer, *Moon Sisters, Krishna Mothers, Rajneesh Lovers: Women's Roles in New Religions*, Syracuse, NY: Syracuse University Press, 1994.

24 Lewiston, NY: Edwin Mellen Press, 1982.

25 Warren Lewis, 'Coming-Again: How Society Functions Through its New Religions', in Eileen Barker (ed.), *NRMs: A Perspective for Understanding Society*, Toronto: Edwin Mellen Press, 1982, pp.191–215.

26 *Daily Telegraph*, 15 March 1995.

27 *Daily Telegraph*, 11 March 1995.

28 Ibid.

29 *New York Times*, 22 March 1995, pp. B1 and B6.

30 James T. Richardson, 'Minority Religions ("Cults") and the Law: Comparisons of the United States, Europe and Australia', *University of Queensland Law Journal*, 18(2), 1995, pp. 183–207.

31 James A. Beckford, *Cult Controversies: The Societal Response to the New Religious Movements*, London: Tavistock, 1985.

32 See, for example, Richardson *et al.*, op. cit.

33 Eileen Barker, 'The Scientific Study of Religion? You Must be Joking!', *Journal for the Scientific Study of Religion*, 34(3), 1995, pp. 287–310.

# Summary of Chapter 2

Without gainsaying the evident variety of NRMs with respect to both their structure and their beliefs, Professor Colin Campbell looks for certain commonalities in the thrust of cultural change which these movements represent. He notes the increased concern with environmental issues, and the enhanced importance of a much canvassed idea of 'awareness' occurring simultaneously as traditional belief in God declines, and the idea of reincarnation receives growing endorsement. His research suggests a major paradigm shift in religious orientations, from the transcendentalism of Western religion to an Eastern, immanent conception of the divine. The religious person ceases to be adequately characterised as a believer in the truth, and becomes, instead, a seeker after enlightenment. As Christianity experiences decline, Eastern religions, in both their traditional and westernised forms, thrive, while other NRMs, more explicitly recognised as psychotherapeutic systems also owe much to ideas prevalent in Eastern philosophies.

# 2　The Easternisation of the West

*Colin Campbell*

## Introduction: a changing vocabulary

Two years ago I decided that it might be possible to glean some insights into the nature and direction of cultural change by examining the evolving nature of the English language. More specifically, it occurred to me that a study of those new words which were entering the language might provide a clue to the direction in which the prevailing system of beliefs and values was evolving. Consequently, I began to scan dictionaries of New English, looking for words which had entered the language recently and which could be considered to indicate the emergence of new beliefs or attitudes, or at least, that significant changes were occurring in the meanings accorded to old ones. I made several interesting discoveries during the course of my trawl through our evolving vocabulary, but two developments in particular stood out above everything else. The one concerned that cluster of terms, such as 'green', 'ecology' and 'conservation', which could generally be subsumed under the heading of 'environmentalism'; while the other surrounded the word 'consciousness' and its synonyms (such as 'awareness'), and especially the compound term 'consciousness-raising'. These two word clusters and the meanings they embodied clearly represented new cultural developments and were, in any case, associated with new, and well-publicised, social movements. The former related to the emergence of the conservation and environmental movements. The significant word here was the use of the term 'green' to denote environmental awareness, along with the prefix 'eco-'. Both of these came into popular use in the 1970s, which was the decade when the organisations Friends of the Earth and Greenpeace were founded. The latter clearly embraced the human potential and psycho-therapy movements, as well as the more 'life-affirming' New Religious Movements and religions of the self. This was the complex world of Californian 'psychobabble', of Scientology and *est* (Erhard Seminars Training, later called Forums Network), of Encounter Groups, meditation techniques and self-help manuals designed to assist individuals 'realise their potential'.

At the same time as I was searching dictionaries of New English I was also consulting the Gallup Poll data on religious belief. This was on the assumption that any significant change in fundamental beliefs and attitudes should also be reflected here. These data are very limited in extent as well as being very crude in the measuring instruments employed, but it is none the less almost all we have to go on when attempting to assess the changing beliefs of the British people at large. I turned first to look at the evidence relating to belief in God.

Here the picture appears fairly straightforward. The percentage of the population who say that they believe in God has been steadily falling since Gallup began regular polling on this question after the Second World War. It has fallen from a figure in the low nineties to high eighties to its present figure in the mid to low sixties. Correspondingly, the percentage of the population prepared to declare that they do not believe in a God of any sort has risen from a mere 3 to 4 per cent to somewhere between 14 and 20 per cent. However, this apparently straightforward evidence for secularisation disguises the fact that this decline has been entirely at the expense of belief in the Western Judaeo-Christian conception of a personal God. For when the question concerning belief 'in a personal God' is distinguished from belief in 'some sort of spirit or life-force', then virtually all of the falling off in 'belief in God' over this period is accounted for by the fewer people who are prepared to state that they believe in a personal God. Such people now represent only about one-third of the population when, not so long ago, they constituted over half. By contrast, that proportion prepared to admit to a belief in 'some sort of spirit or life-force' has actually increased slightly in recent years.[1]

Then I turned to look at the data concerning the after-life, more especially, reincarnation. Here the situation is a rather strange one. That proportion of the population prepared to say that they believe in the standard Christian beliefs concerning heaven and hell has declined considerably (so much so that both are now minority beliefs very much on a par with belief in the Loch Ness Monster or flying saucers). However, belief in reincarnation (which is not, of course, officially part of the creed of any mainstream Christian Church), has actually been going up. About one-fifth of Britons subscribe to this belief, which is even more marked among the young. Thus, in 1978 one-quarter of 14- to 18-year-olds interviewed confessed to believing in reincarnation (as well as the impersonal rather than the personal conception of God).

The question I now had to answer was what could I make of my discoveries? Was there a connection between these four, apparently very different, findings? Could they possibly all be seen as indicating some single, fundamental change in underlying belief. Was there indeed any single thread connecting these changes? If so, what was it?

## Changing beliefs

Not one of the four concerns or beliefs which I identified could be said to be entirely new. For example, a concern with the environment has long been represented in British society by such organisations as the Countryside Commission and the National Trust, while the RSPCA and RSPB have championed the rights of animals and birds. In addition, movements which stress the importance of meditation and aim at consciousness-raising pre-date the 1960s and can be traced back to such nineteenth-century antecedents as Theosophy. Equally, evidence for belief in an impersonal God (if not for reincarnation) can be found in the Western Christian tradition. Indeed, even developments which it is often assumed were unique to the 1960s and 1970s, like concern over animal testing in the production of cosmetics (recently in the headlines because of the problems experienced by the Body Shop), actually had earlier precedents. For, back in the 1940s, there was an organisation called Beauty without Cruelty, which existed to mobilise public opinion on this issue. Equally, what is today called organic farming was largely prefigured by the Soil Association, founded in 1947. While an English organisation the Order of the Cross (founded in 1904) promoted a version of Christianity in which animal rights were central.

Yet many of these organisations (if we except, for the moment, those which embody a traditional form of countryside and animal concern, such as the National Trust, the RSPCA and the RSPB) were clearly 'fringe' or 'cultic' groups in the years immediately following the Second World War. They attracted few supporters and, on those occasions when their ideas were brought to the attention of a wider audience, the response was typically one of incredulity or ridicule. Yet today these ideas are commonplace, having entered the mainstream of cultural thought and debate. Indeed, even as I write this chapter, the headlines in the newspapers and on the television news concern the activities of animal rights activists, protesting against the export of live animals to the continent of Europe, and their subsequent rearing in veal crates. What is especially interesting about this issue is less the direct action protest adopted by this concerned minority, than the fact that there appears to be widespread popular support for their views. For here too, what was until only recently a minority view – that non-human animals should be considered to possess 'rights', and that humans have a duty to see that these are respected – now appears to have become a majority position.

It is this shift which is significant; not so much the appearance of new beliefs, but rather the widespread acceptance of ones which formerly had been confined to a minority; a shift which, it appears, really dates from the 1960s, when they were espoused by that significant and influential minority who comprised the counter-culture. However, it has taken another thirty years for significant elements of their creed to take hold among the population as a whole. The critical change here apparently took place in the 1980s, for this was the decade when environmental awareness first became fashionable as indicated by the fact that the Green Party captured a surprising 14.5 per cent of the vote in the 1989 elections for the European Parliament. But the question which needs to be considered is the extent to which these separate developments should be regarded as part of one and the same general movement, one which could well embrace other developments that have occurred over the past thirty years.

## Spiritual and mystical religion

The first thing one can say is that there is an obvious connection between the rise of the quasi-religious, therapeutic, 'consciousness-raising' movements and the two religious beliefs singled out above.[2] These clearly fit with one another, constituting elements in that form of Troeltschian 'spiritual and mystical religion' which I have had occasion to describe elsewhere.[3] Ernst Troeltsch's discussion of the distinction between church religion and sect religion has rightly become an established part of the classic canon of writings in the sociology of religion. Unfortunately the fact that this was merely a part of an essentially three-fold classification is commonly overlooked. This third element was what Troeltsch referred to as spiritual and mystical religion and, interestingly, it was this, and not church religion or sect religion, which he judged most likely to flourish in the modern world. What he had in mind was not simply the phenomenon of mysticism, which could be an ingredient in any religious tradition, but rather a religion in its own right, with its own system of beliefs. These he identified as, 'the unity of the divine ground', 'the divine seed', and the belief in spiritual evolution.[4] Prominent among these beliefs is the belief that all finite beings have their existence within God, who is the ground or the soul, the 'seed' or 'spark', of all creatures. Some form of union with God (or more properly re-union) is thus the goal of this form of religion; a goal that can only be realised through the development of the divine seed into a power capable of overcoming the world. There is, thus, a belief in a 'scale of spirituality' which marks the progression of the soul's relationship with the divine. A conception which is necessarily immanentist and denies dualism. There is no belief in a fundamental opposition of flesh and spirit or natural law and Christian miracle but merely the differences in the degree to which the finite is separated from the divine. Consequently, an ascetic temper is excluded, though there is an opposition to the selfishness and materialism of 'the world'. Indeed, it is a perspective that generally regards secular concerns as unimportant while, in placing religion above ethics, it often embraces antinomianism and Libertarianism.

This form of religion regards religious experience as a valid expression of that universal religious consciousness which is based in the ultimate divine ground; a view which leads to an acceptance of religious relativity as far as all specific forms of belief are concerned and to the doctrine of polymorphism, in which the truth of all religions is recognised. Hence, not only are the widely differing views of the central truths of Christianity tolerated, but all forms of religion are regarded as identical. Nevertheless, its own teachings, which emphasise the truths obtained through mystic and spiritual experience, are regarded as representing the 'purest' form of religion. As Troeltsch says:

> This type of mysticism becomes an independent religious philosophy, which recognises that the religious process is the same universal expression and consciousness of the metaphysical connection between absolute and finite being, and which discovers everywhere, beneath the concrete forms of religion, the same religious germ, which, however, only reaches complete and pure maturity under its fostering care.[5]

This form of religion is also syncretic. Because of its rejection of dualism and its indifference to literal truth, spiritual and mystic religion does not necessarily lead to a position of hostility in relation to secular culture. It is, of course, firmly opposed to materialism and to rationalism and to a this-worldly temper, but has an affinity with idealist and metaphysical, philosophical systems. It is also extremely individualistic – Troeltsch uses the phrase, 'radical religious individualism'[6] – with the result that it usually does not lead to the formation of organisations.

But this still leaves us with the problem of fitting the rise of environmental concern into the picture. Not that there is no evidence of a connection between environmentalism and religion, for, after a rather slow start, the world religions have begun to show some concern with ecological issues. Thus, in 1989, Pope John Paul II issued the first papal statement devoted exclusively to ecology ('Peace with God the Creator, Peace with All of Creation').[7] Then, in the following year, the World Council of Churches met to discuss 'Justice, Peace and the Integrity of Creation'; while there were religious groups actively involved in the United Nations Conference on Environment and Development in 1992 (the Rio Summit, as it was known). At the same time, some ecological organisations have turned to religion for support. In 1986, for example, the twenty-fifth anniversary meeting of the World Wildlife Federation was held in Assisi, Italy – the birthplace of the only Roman Catholic 'Ecological' Saint – while leaders of all the major world religions were invited to attend.[8] Yet such evidence as this is not really what we are looking for, as this has more to do with the reaction of established religious organisations, and does not point to links with distinctive religious beliefs.

Yet there clearly are some connections between those beliefs characteristic of mystical religion and environmentalism. Intriguingly, Greenpeace suggest (if somewhat humorously) that there may be a direct connection between reincarnation and environmentalism in one of their current advertisements, one which reads, 'When you come back as a whale, you'll be bloody glad you put Greenpeace in your will.'[9] But then the treatment of all living creatures as sentient beings, not merely capable of feeling pain, but possessed of a form of consciousness not essentially dissimilar from that possessed by humans, is a logical corollary of a belief in reincarnation (if not, technically, of a belief in the transmigration of souls). It is not so surprising, therefore, to discover that there are branches of environmentalism which resemble a spiritual, if not strictly religious, movement; ones in which 'self-development' goes hand in hand with direct action to save the planet. This deep ecology movement, as it is known, not only objects strongly against that form of 'speciesism' which puts the needs of humans above those of other forms of life, but also deliberately seeks to connect the inner world of human experience with the outer world of nature. Indeed, there is a special term, 'inner ecology', to refer to that form of meditative consciousness-raising familiar to the Troeltschian religious 'seeker'.

However, it could be objected that not all environmental issues concern sentient life and hence that this is, at best, a purely partial connection. After all, many issues which arouse concern among environmentalists, such as the fate of the ozone layer, the presence of nitrates in the water supply, or food additives, relate more to inorganic matters than to questions which relate to living creatures. But then, even here, it is a key feature of the environmental movement that in discussions of the 'elements', such as air and water (and one can include food here too), the key words 'nature' and the 'natural' are invested with powerful emotional, ethical and even spiritual resonances. Then there is also the question of that basic holism which is such a feature of environmentalism. The general notion of the interconnectedness, not just of mankind and nature, but of all life on the planet. This belief is embodied most clearly in Jim Lovecroft's Gaia hypothesis. This claim, to the effect that the planet as a whole is a self-regulating super-organism, suffused with life, clearly draws these natural elements into an environmental or ecological paradigm which is, at the least, quasi-religious.

Finally, one may note another possible connection between forms of religion and environmentalism and that is the interesting phenomenon of vegetarianism. Whatever the reasons for adopting vegetarianism, and they may, of course be either dietary or ethical, or indeed a mixture of the two, in its strict form, as Veganism, it is now officially treated as a 'religion'.[10] Given that during the Second World War a mere 100,000 people were vegetarians, while today the figure is put at between 4.2 per cent and 11 per cent of the British population,[11] this is a significant development.

## Easternisation

The thesis I would like to advance is that these developments can best be understood as constituting a process of 'Easternisation'. By this I do not simply mean the introduction and spread within the West of recognisable Eastern 'imports', whether these are products, such as spices, yoghurt and silk, practices such as yoga and acupuncture, or complete religious systems such as Hinduism or Buddhism. These developments are important and clearly should be included under this heading. Yet the introduction of 'foreign' elements such as these into an indigenous socio-cultural system may do little or nothing to change the fundamental nature of that system. They may simply be absorbed or assimilated without effecting any significant change. Indeed, these cultural imports may themselves become radically transformed as a consequence of their introduction into a new society; or, indeed, their transformation may even be required before they can be successfully accommodated. The thesis advanced here is that the traditional Western cultural paradigm no longer dominates in so-called 'Western' societies, but that it has been replaced by an 'Eastern' one. This fundamental change may have been assisted by the introduction of obviously Eastern ideas and influences into the West, but equally important have been internal indigenous developments within that system, developments which have precipitated this 'paradigm shift'. However, in order to explain more clearly just what I consider this shift to be, I shall make use of Max Weber's categorisation of the difference between East and West.

Weber's scheme for the classification and analysis of the worlds' religions was based on his extensive research on Christianity, Ancient Judaism, Hinduism, Buddhism and Chinese religion (work on Islam and further work on Early Christianity and Medieval Catholicism was under way but not completed when he died). His classificatory scheme is built on a series of dichotomies which have a logical as well as an empirical foundation. The most basic of these concerns the initial speculation concerning the nature of the divine; is it conceived of as fundamentally immanent or transcendent in nature? Weber assumed that primitive religion was fundamentally magical and animistic in character, but once society developed to a point at which there was sufficient surplus wealth to support a priesthood, then beliefs became more systematised in order to answer the problem of theodicy. This process of 'rationalisation' could take one of two directions. The one posited an immanent principle of divinity, something which is part of the world from eternity and to which man can in some sense 'adapt' himself; the other a conception of a transcendental divinity, in principle fundamentally separate from the world, controlling it from above, and in the extreme case, as having created it *ex nihilo*. These two contrasting assumptions lead to the Brahman–Atman principle in Indian religious philosophy, on the one hand, and the Semitic creator god, on the other.[12] As Weber stresses, the Eastern religious world-view rejects dualism altogether, with the world viewed as a completely connected and self-contained cosmos. Thus, that contrast between the sinful natural and the spiritual supernatural, so much a feature of Western religion, is rejected; for all the natural world is permeated with spirituality. This then is the fundamental East–West divide. To speak of 'Easternisation', therefore, is thus to talk of the abandonment of the traditional Western conception of the divine as transcendent and personal and its replacement by a view of the divine as immanent and essentially impersonal.

This Eastern model favours the Troeltschian religion of mysticism outlined earlier, with its belief in the polymorphous nature of truth, its syncretism and individualism. In addition, the Eastern concept of spiritual perfection or self-deification replaces the Western idea of salvation, the notion of a Church is replaced by a band of seekers attached to a spiritual leader or guru, while the distinction between believer and unbeliever is replaced by the idea that all beings exist on a scale of spirituality, a scale which can extend beyond this life.

This Weberian characterisation of the difference between the premises underlying East–West thought is roughly consistent with other formulations of major cultural variations. One thinks of Ruth Benedict's Apollonian–Dionysian contrast in this connection. Indeed, the significance of the classification lies in the fact that it is a contrast, with one response logically excluding the other. This point is brought out in the work of the psychologists Gilgen and Cho,[13] who devised a questionnaire to measure Eastern and Western thought in the 1970s. They identified as 'Eastern' those basic assumptions common to Buddhism, Taoism, Confucianism and Hinduism; while, by 'Western', they identified those embodied in the Judaeo-Christian religions and, to some extent, underlying Greek thought.[14] Drawing upon a wide range of sources, they identified the crucial characteristic of the former as its 'monism' in contrast to the 'dualism' of the latter. However, the full list of beliefs separating the two perspectives they summarised as:

Eastern

- man and nature are one;
- spiritual and physical are one;
- mind and body are one;
- man should recognise his basic oneness with nature, the spiritual, and the mental rather than attempt to analyse, label, categorise, manipulate, control or consume the things of the world;
- because of his oneness with all existence, man should feel 'at home' in any place and with any person;
- science and technology, at best, create an illusion of progress;
- enlightenment involves achieving a sense of oneness with the universal; it is a state where all dichotomies vanish;
- meditation, a special state of quiet contemplation, is essential for achieving enlightenment.

Western

- man has characteristics which set him apart from nature and the spiritual;
- man is divided into a body, a spirit and a mind;

- there is a personal God who is over man;
- man must control and manipulate nature to ensure his survival;
- rational thought and an analytical approach to problem solving should be emphasised;
- science and technology have given us a good life and provide our main hope for an even better future;
- action and the competitive spirit should be rewarded.

These distinctions were then embodied in a sixty-eight-item questionnaire of thirty-four pairs of statements to create an East–West scale. The scale was then tested on college students, a group of Buddhists, some transpersonal psychologists and some businessmen; a test which strongly suggested its validity.

Others have followed up this work, with results that suggest such an East–West scale is both useful and valid. Krus and Blackman[15] for example use a modified version of Gilgen and Cho's work to produce their own list of categories pertaining to East–West styles of thought.

| East | West |
| --- | --- |
| synthesis | analysis |
| totality | generalisation |
| integration | differentiation |
| deduction | induction |
| subjective | objective |
| dogmatic | intellectual |
| intuition | reason |
| anti-science | science |
| personal | impersonal |
| moralistic | legalistic |
| non-discursive | assertive |
| affiliative | power |
| ecstasis | order |
| irrational | rational |
| imaginative | critical[16] |

Further evidence to suggest that there has been a major shift from one of these pairs of contrasts to the other can be found by considering the recent history of the two major intellectual systems which comprise Western culture; that is Christianity, and secular Progressivism, especially as manifest in Socialism and Marxism. Both of these two great theoretical traditions of the West have shown clear signs of a shift towards an Eastern paradigm. The major immediate influence in both cases being, not Eastern thought as such, but German Idealistic philosophy. In the one case this was principally effected through the work of theologians, especially Tillich (in addition to the influence of Barth, Bonhoffer and Bultmann), and in the other, through social and political philosophers such as Marcuse, and the Frankfurt School more generally. Both these movements of thought had a widespread impact, the one in the form of the New Theology and the Death of God movements, the other as the New Left.

In the case of the New Theology, the critical shift was the Tillichian relocation of the divine from 'up there' to 'down here'; that is to say, from a transcendental 'out there' to an immanent 'in here' – otherwise described as 'the depth of our being'. In addition, both the New Theology and the Death of God movements constituted an assault on dogma, literalism, and organised religion, effectively mounting an attack on objective theology from the perspective of a subjective philosophy of religion. In the case of the New Left, what is significant is the rejection of the traditional social gospel of 'salvation' through political revolution or reform in favour of a belief in self-perfection through personal 'revolution' or heightened consciousness. This shift is accomplished by substituting the teachings of Freud (or, more properly Reich) for those of Marx, with the consequent redefinition of 'alienation' and 'repression' as applicable to a personal and sexual rather than a collective and politico-economic, context. This results in the perception that art, drugs and sex (together, significantly, with mystical experience) represent the avenues to personal (and hence social) reconstruction. Both revolutions can be seen to clearly involve shifts from Western to Eastern assumptions in terms of the contrasts set out above, with a general favouring of immanence over transcendence and inner, mystical, over outer, 'ascetic' responses to the world.

## Why has this happened?

If the thesis of a recent Easternisation of the West is correct, then it obviously raises important questions about exactly how and why this should have happened. Now it has already been noted that Eastern assumptions were present in the cultural profile of British life prior to their recent emergence to prominence in the 1970s and 1980s. Hence we could say that a foundation for Easternisation already existed in the form of such movements as Surrealism, Freudianism and Existentialism. This was, in large measure, the cultural inheritance drawn upon by the counter-culturalists of the 1960s, drawing in addition on new material from the East and from the culture of indigenous 'non-Western' peoples round the globe.

Yet none of this really explains why the Western paradigm lost out to the Eastern one. To appreciate this we need to recognise that the nineteenth and twentieth centuries witnessed a process in which first, the rise of science served to undermine people's faith in traditional religion, only, second, for the optimism which had been attached to science and technology to be itself undermined. It is this sequence of events which largely explains why the Eastern paradigm has come to the fore. For the Eastern paradigm is more compatible with modern thought than the traditional Western one and simply not vulnerable to an attack by science in the way that is the case with historically based religion. The extreme individualism, the anti-dualism, the relativising of truth claims, all make it comparatively invulnerable to rationalistic and scientific attack. Indeed, Eastern mystical religion tends to use the secular, humanistic attack on traditional religion to its own advantage, while also exploiting the uncertainties and disputes within science to advance mystical claims.[17]

## Problems with the thesis

The Easternisation thesis centres on the claim that there has been a fundamental sea-change in the relationship between the East and West world-views. Whereas formerly the Western view was dominant and the Eastern merely a popular, yet subordinate alternative, it is suggested here that this relationship has been reversed. Now it is those who seek to advance either a traditional religious dualism, or a scientific, rationalistic, Progressivism, who are on the defensive. For the initiative, and indeed the moral high ground, appears to have passed to those who propound monism and a vaguely spiritual or pan-psychic versions of mysticism. This change appears to be happening throughout the developed Western world (the developed East, such as Japan, is a rather different matter), most obviously perhaps in Western Europe[18] and Scandinavia, but also in North America and increasingly, one suspects, in Eastern Europe, although there are grounds for thinking that it may have progressed further in the United Kingdom than elsewhere; at least judging by the difference between British attitudes towards the question of animal rights and those prevailing on the other side of the Channel.

This is not to suggest that traditional religion has lost all power and influence. For one thing, the resurgence of Islam cannot be ignored and although this is more of a factor in the developing than in the developed world, it could still spark a reaction in the West that could favour a return to traditional forms of Christianity. Nor, given the central place accorded science in the culture of modern society, can purely secular ideologies be written off. Increasingly, however, one would expect to see them intermingled with mystic assumptions, as in the case of the Gaia hypothesis.

## Instrumental activism

One special difficulty with the Easternisation thesis concerns the problem of instrumental activism. A true shift away from a Western paradigm would require a turning towards a more resigned, if not fatalistic, attitude towards the world on the part of individuals. That is to say, a rejection of that instrumental activism which has long been so characteristic of life in the West would have to occur. But is there any sign of this? Is not Western culture still primarily world-affirming rather than world-denying in character? That the culture of the West is characterised by the pre-eminence accorded to instrumental activism has long been a taken-for-granted assumption in sociology. Talcott Parsons is probably the best-known exponent of this view. He writes:

> For contemporary American society, I assume a value system which may be called 'instrumental activism'. It involves an attitude of active mastery toward the empirical situation external to the society – both physical and psychological nature, and other societies – an attitude which favours increasing the level of adaptive flexibility primarily through increase of knowledge and economic production.[19]

Kluckhohn, Strodtbeck *et al.*, following Parsons, also stress that in contradistinction to the value-profiles of other, more traditional cultures where typically fatalist orientations prevail, modern American society is characterised by a 'doing' activity orientation, one in which 'getting things done' and 'let's *do* something about it' are stock phrases.[20] The same point is made by Cora du Bois in her reference to the importance of 'effort-optimism' in American society, and the prevalence of what she calls 'optimistic activism'[21] as exemplified by such sayings as 'If at first you don't succeed, try, try, again', or 'Let's get this show on the road'.[22]

Now, can we say that there are any signs that this orientation is no longer dominant? Perhaps not. But in one respect at least Parsons' description of this value-cluster requires modification. His claim that such an attitude favours increasing the level of adaptive flexibility through increases in 'economic production' is certainly no longer accurate. For recent years have seen a move away from productionism and the taken-for-granted assumption that continued and continuous economic growth is 'a good thing'. Increasingly, there have been calls for low or even zero-growth economic policies, calls which started with Schumacher's intriguing suggestion that Western societies should adopt 'Buddhist economics' (*Small is Beautiful*). This movement is, in turn, closely associated with calls for a move away from the employment of high technology solutions to human problems towards low technology ones. So perhaps there is after all some evidence for a move away from an emphasis upon instrumental activism.

## Conclusion

We have long been accustomed to think of the history of the modern world as involving the domination of the East by the West. At first through conquest and colonial exploitation, and then subsequently, through industrial, commercial and financial control. More recently, we have come to see the West's dominion over the East as one which is exerted increasingly through a cultural hegemony, one in which the images and ideas of the West, as purveyed by the mass media, effect a world-wide process of 'Westernisation'. If, under the influence of this presumption, any reverse influence was noted, it has generally been considered to be insignificant. Certainly there has long been a fascination in the West for 'the mysterious Orient' and for all things oriental, a fascination which has included religious ideas and attitudes. But this is usually seen as little more than a set of foot-notes to that text which is the history of the West. An enthusiasm for spices in the late Middle Ages, a passion for chinoiserie in the eighteenth century, the hippies' journey (literal and spiritual) to Kathmandu and the East in the 1960s, all these were surely incidental to the development of modern indus-trial Western civilisation as we know it. Yet today it is not at all clear that such a view is still correct.

Certainly 'Westernisation' – in the conventional sense of that word – proceeds apace in the East as well as in the Third World. That is to say, industrialisation and economic development and, now that Communism has collapsed, capitalism, are still spreading round the globe. Indeed, it would appear to be embraced eagerly by developing countries. In that respect there has been little slackening in the process of 'Westernisation'. It is in the heart-land of 'the West' itself that 'Westernisation' is facing its fiercest challenge, a challenge which is being mounted from a perspective which is, in essence, 'Eastern'. This is happening because that dominant paradigm or 'theodicy' which has served the West so effectively for 2,000 years has finally lost its grip over the majority of the population in Western Europe and North America. They no longer hold to a view of the world as divided into matter and spirit, and governed by an all-powerful, personal, creator God; one who has set his creatures above the rest of creation. This vision has been cast aside and with it all justification for mankind's dominion over nature. In its place has been set the fundamentally Eastern vision of mankind as merely part of the great interconnected web of sentient life. For just as the Great Chain of Being was the paradigm metaphor for the eighteenth century, so today there is emerging a similar overarching paradigmatic metaphor, one which represents all the earth's living creatures as interdependent, part of one natural–spiritual system. Its best expression to date has been in the Gaia theory – the Earth Mother. The Earth's living things are part of a great living being which regulates its own stability, and its strength is its overar-ching power – its paradigmatic power – to encompass all the themes identified here.

## Notes

1 By 1978 only one-third of the British population believed in a 'personal God'; but some 40 per cent believed in 'some sort of spirit, a life force'. See C. Campbell, 'The New Religious Movements, the New Spirituality and Post-Industrial Society', in Eileen Barker (ed.), *New Religious Movements: A Perspective for Understanding Society*, New York: Edwin Mellen Press, 1982, pp. 232–42.

2 The close association or affinity between the teachings of Eastern mystical reli-gions and modern therapies and psychotherapies has frequently been noted: see

Dick Anthony, Thomas Robbins, Madeline Doucas and Thomas E. Curtis, 'Patients and Pilgrims: Changing Attitudes Toward Psychotherapy of Converts to Eastern Mysticism', *American Behavioral Scientist*, 20(6), July/August 1977.

3   Campbell, op. cit.

4   Ernst Troeltsch, *The Social Teaching of the Christian Churches*, London: Allen and Unwin, 1931.

5   Ibid., p. 735.

6   Ibid., p. 377.

7   Peter Beyer, *Religion and Globalization*, London: Sage, 1994, p. 206.

8   Ibid., p. 209.

9   *Guardian*, 11 January 1995.

10   See the Home Office decision in the case of a Vegan prisoner who refused to wear prison issue leather boots: *Independent on Sunday*, 22 May 1994.

11   *Independent on Sunday*, 11 September 1994.

12   See Talcott Parsons in Max Weber, *The Sociology of Religion*, London: Methuen, 1965, p. xlvi.

13   Albert R. Gilgen and Jae Hyung Cho, 'Questionnaire to Measure Eastern and Western Thought', *Psychological Reports*, 44, 1979, pp. 835–41.

14   Ibid., p. 835.

15   David J. Krus and Harold S. Blackman, 'Contributions to Psychohistory; V. East–West Dimensions of Ideology Measured by Transtemporal Cognitive Matching', *Psychological Reports*, 47, 1980, pp. 947–55.

16   There may appear to be a contradiction between Krus and Blackman's attribution of 'personal' to the East and 'impersonal' to the West and the claim, made earlier, that the East was characterised by an 'impersonal' conception of the divine and the West by a 'personal' one. However, these pairs of attributes refer to styles of thought and not ideas themselves and it has been a characteristic of Western thought that an 'impersonal' style of thought has been employed with reference to an essentially 'personal' conception of the divine.

17   The irony here is that it is largely because of the knowledge which science has provided that we have learnt to be suspicious of modern technology. For it is science which first told us about the dangers of nuclear energy, of the threat to wildlife which insecticides represented and, more recently, of the danger to the ozone layer represented by the use of CFCs.

18   See Eileen Barker's reference to the fact that one-fifth of Europeans now say that they believe in reincarnation: Eileen Barker, 'Whatever Next? The Future of New Religious Movements', in Roberto Cipriani (ed.), *Religions Sans Frontières: Present and Future Trends of Migration, Culture, and Communication*, Rome: Ministry of Information, 1993, p. 371.

19   Talcott Parsons, *Structure and Process in Modern Societies*, New York: Free Press, 1965, p. 172.

20   Florence Rockwood Kluckhohn and Fred. L. Strodtbeck *et al.* (eds), *Variations in Value Orientations*, Evanston, IL: Row Peterson, 1961.

21   Cora Du Bois, 'The Dominant Value Profile of American Culture', *American Anthropologist*, 57, 1955, pp. 1232–9, (p. 1234).

22   Ibid.

# Summary of Chapter 3

Although the economy may be readily acknowledged as one of the major institutional divisions of modern society, the economic significance of religious commitment – apart from the debate surrounding Weber's Protestant ethic thesis – has been a relatively neglected aspect of the sociology of religion. Weber's thesis was, of course, focused precisely on this connection, but for him, and for the Puritans of whom he wrote, economic well-being was, if not exactly an unintended consequence of piety, at least not a consciously pursued dominant concern. For some of today's new religions, there is an unabashed preoccupation with the goal of teaching adherents how to achieve prosperity. It is to this sub-species of new religiosity that Dr Heelas addresses his attention, illustrating the ways in which the individual's spiritual well-being is harnessed to the realisation of his full human potential, and the implications of this association for the culture of business management in contemporary society.

# 3 Prosperity and the New Age Movement

## The efficacy of spiritual economics

*Paul Heelas*

My aim is to get all IBM's managers to experience themselves as God.
(Peter Russell, talking at Programmes Ltd)

1 My mind is centered in Infinite Intelligence that knows my good; I am one with the creative power that is materialising all my desires.
2 I now have enough time, energy, wisdom, and money to accomplish all my desires.
(Sondra Ray, *How to be Chic, Fabulous and Live Forever,* 1990, p. 81)

## Introduction

Research on the economic significance of new forms of religiosity or spirituality in the West has tended to have a relatively narrow focus. First, attention has been directed to particular New Religious Movements, such as the Unification Church and Hare Krishna, rather than to all those teachings and activities – publications, management trainings, centres, networks, groups, and individual enterprises – which clearly do not constitute 'NRMs'. And second, the majority of researchers have concentrated on how particular NRMs have set about financing themselves. Often drawing on resource mobilisation theory as their explanatory tool, this research focus directs attention away from other matters, including the ways in which spiritual teachings and practices might contribute to the efficacy of mainstream business concerns.[1]

Needless to say, it is important to study how NRMs have set about wealth acquisition. If for no other reason, this is because some have had very considerable success in this regard. It has been claimed, for example, that Scientology had assets worth $400 million as of 1986.[2] *est* and associated seminars appear to have earned even more. Activities attracted a minimum of 700,000 people during the 1971–91 period. Thinking in terms of 1991 prices – when it cost $625 to take the transformational seminar – an income of some $440 million is arrived at. Or consider Unification Church fund-raising activities in the United States. Assuming that there were 1,000 full-time fund-raisers by the close of the 1970s, David Bromley and Anson

Shupe estimate that they were then raising some $25 million a year from their street-based activities.[3]

In this context, however, I shift the focus to dwell on more general ways in which spiritual teachings and practices might – or, of course, might not – contribute to economic efficacy. I am concerned with that 'inner' realm which – it is held – contributes to the economic well-being of the individual as a spiritually empowered producer, the person not even having to work, in conventional fashion, to obtain rewards. I am also concerned with the economic well-being of those who apply spirituality within the context of mainstream business activities.[4]

## A frame of reference

To cut things down to size – and thereby having to ignore all those teachings which, like those of the Unification Church, are theistic – I concentrate on the New Age Movement, the key idea of which is that the New Age is manifested when people realise or experience their true nature. The New Age teaches a highly optimistic – as spiritual – form of humanism. The Self, itself, is to be celebrated. By nature, we are perfect. To experience the Self itself – within the person as well as within the natural order as a whole – is to experience 'God', the 'Goddess', the 'Source', the 'inner child', 'Christ consciousness', 'truth', or, simply, 'inner spirituality'.

The New Age also provides an account of imperfection. Those of us living in the everyday world do not realise what we really are – in essence – because we are functioning in terms of a false level of consciousness. We are contaminated by the artifices, the snares, of modernity. We have been socialised – indoctrinated – into believing that we can perfect ourselves only by obtaining more and more of the externals of life.

Finally, by way of introducing the New Age, a great variety of devices of spiritual disciplines are employed in order to liberate people from their mechanistic – or 'ego' – level of functioning. Many meditate; Gurdjieffians might use mathematical formulae; those belonging to the School of Economic Science sometimes turn to hard manual labour; Helen Palmer uses the enneagram; others use shamanic practices. In all cases, however, the aim is the same: 'to go within'.

Although the New Age Movement can quite readily be defined in terms of these three basic characteristics – which comprise what I call Self-spirituality – there are a number of regards in which it is marked by diversity. One, in particular, is of immediate concern.

### New worlds: from rejection to affirmation

Diversity has much to do with how the utopian life is envisaged. Since the God within has the capacity to inform virtually anything, New Agers are able to envisage very different versions of heaven on earth. And this, in turn, has much to do with how the values and products of the capitalistic main-stream are assessed.

New Age activities can be thought of as falling along a Weberian spectrum, from the world-rejecting to the world-affirming.[5] At the former end of the spectrum, the emphasis is very much on avoiding the contaminating effects of life in the mainstream. Rejecting all that is offered by capitalistic modernity, the dawning of the New Age essentially has to do with experiencing *the best of the inner world*, that is the domain of spirituality. The emphasis is very much on *detachment*. In contrast, at the latter end of the spectrum importance is attached to becoming prosperous. Inner spirituality is here utilised as a means to the end of experiencing *the best of the outer world*, rather than being intrinsically valued. Downplaying, even ignoring, the role played by detachment, the emphasis is now on *empowerment* and *prosperity*.

Between these two extremes, the majority of New Age paths teach that it is possible to experience *the best of both worlds*. Sydney Ahlstrom's term – 'harmonial religion' – can be used to characterise this intermediary position. In his words, this kind of religiosity 'encompasses those forms of piety and belief in which spiritual composure, physical health, and even economic well-being are understood to flow from a person's rapport with the cosmos'.[6] Applying the term to the New Age, it can be taken to refer to all those (totalising) paths which attach greater importance to experiences of inner spirituality and the role played by detachment than the world-affirming end of the spectrum, incorporating economic well-being while not attaching such priority to this goal as more systematic forms of world-affir-mation.

Looking at this spectrum in somewhat greater detail, the spiritually 'purist' aspect of the New Age rejects everything that has to do with this world. In the words of Dick Anthony *et al.*, 'the attainment of mundane psychological, sensory, or material conditions, such as financial success, interpersonal satisfaction, inducement of special inner sensations or moods, commitment to a certain set of beliefs' have nothing to do with the inner quest.[7] What is described as 'authentic spiritual transcendence or realisation' is all that matters. Spirituality is valued in and of itself. And from this point of view, write Anthony *et al.*, the rest of the New Age involves 'spiritual materialism'.

The *counter-cultural* aspect of the New Age is considerably less radical. As the term implies, much must still be rejected. Counter-culturalists also believe that to compete for the capitalistic externals of life is to enhance the contaminations of the ego. However, by no means all that the world has to offer is rejected. Unlike spiritual purists, counter-culturalists are intent on developing all that it is to be an authentic person. Importance is attached to what might be called 'psychological (or bodily) spirituality'. Experiences of harmony, loving oneself and others, peace and tranquillity, being healed or 'whole' are stressed; hallucinogenic drugs might be used to develop what

Anthony *et al.* describe as 'special inner sensations or moods'; inner spirituality is put to work to accord greater (expressive) value to aspects of life in this world, including personal relationships. In sum, the counter-cultural aspect can be taken to include all those activities which emphasise *Self-actualisation*. Spiritual, bodily, emotional, aesthetic, or social aspects of being human are interfused. Whether they have to do with healing, education, relationships, or being creative, the emphasis is on becoming a whole person, and in ways which are not catered for by conventional institutions. The quest for Self-actualisation, it should also be noted, is not only pursued by counter-culturalists. Some remain within the mainstream, as students for example, while seeking this goal.

The harmonial aspect of the New Age – already in some evidence in connection with the path of Self-actualisation – really comes into its own when the spiritual and the personal are combined, to varying degrees, with what the mainstream of society has to offer. It is no longer thought necessary to have to 'drop out' in order to 'tune in'. One can liberate oneself from the baneful effects of modernity while living in terms of much of what the good life – as conventionally understood – has to offer. Teachings to do with the best of both worlds – within and without – are relatively complicated. For present purposes, we can identify those to do with *mainstream-transformation* and *Self-enhancement*. Regarding the first, the basic idea is that the best of both worlds comes about when participants learn to detach themselves from – while living within – the capitalistic mainstream. This strategy, counter-cultural in that detachment and spirituality is involved, is also held to contribute to material prosperity. To 'transform' the significance of striving for money or business outcomes is supposed to release the Self, thereby enabling it to produce results – so to speak, as a by-product of being 'at cause'. Regarding the second, less importance is attached to effecting detachment and therefore to transforming the significance of mainstream results. Paths teaching Self-enhancement tend to emphasise the intrinsic value, of, say, making money. What the mainstream has to offer is now even more clearly in evidence. Fully fledged harmonial paths of this variety, in other words, offer financial, career, and status rewards, vibrant health and emotionality, all together with spirituality.

Finally, and with the emphasis now very much on world-affirmation, there are the *Self-* or *mainstream-empowerers*.[8] At the very fringe of – or beyond – the New Age, as envisaged by the purist or counter-culturalist, those concerned seek inner spirituality in order to operate more successfully in the mainstream. This is the new world of the prosperous person. 'Use the power of your mind to increase your sales', says José Silva, founder of the Silva Mind Control Method.[9] Fully convinced that it is possible to seek the God within while enjoying the benefits of what lies without, prosperity seekers thus adopt an instrumentalised form of spirituality. The theme of detachment more or less drops out of the picture. And to a greater extent than (even) the Self-enhancer, inner spirituality is accorded little intrinsic value. The shift we have been tracing – from spirituality as an end in itself to spirituality as a means to external ends – is here completed. The New Age, if that is what it can still be called, is now deeply engaged with capitalism.

The two most radical figures of the New Age – the purist and the empowerer – both suppose that capitalistic modernity is not working. But whereas the purist sees it as irredeemably flawed, the empowerer supposes that it can be made to work properly. Inner spirituality, it is clear, can serve to inform very different new worlds, each with its own distinctive nature. Running across the spectrum, there is the world to do with the intrinsics of the spiritual realm; with living as a spiritually informed person; with enjoying spiritual growth as well as the externals of life; and, finally, with obtaining and celebrating the best that the outer world has to offer. New Agers, it can safely be said, disagree about how the mainstream should be handled in order to bring about heaven on earth, their strategies ranging from comprehensive detachment to applied spirituality.

## Prosperity beyond the counter-culture

I am not going to dwell, in the present context, on the economic significance of 'right livelihood' practices of the clearly counter-cultural wing of the New Age. Thus, the kinds of activities advocated by E. F. Schumacher[10] or Charlene Spretnak and Fritjof Capra[11] are not addressed here. I turn instead to what is perhaps the most distinctive development within the New Age Movement since the 1960s, namely the elaboration and proliferation of prosperity teachings and practices.

In 1990, the University of Lancaster's Centre for the Study of Management Learning and a consultancy, Transform, ran an event called 'Joining Forces: Working with Spirituality in Organisations'. Two important centres, Findhorn (north-east Scotland) and Esalen (California), now put on similar events. This would have been unheard of when these centres were developing during the counter-cultural 1960s. A significant number of New Agers have in fact moved beyond counter-cultural antagonism to the capitalistic mainstream. Instead, they incorporate the creation of prosperity. A basic assumption – shocking for the spiritual purist or the counter-culturalist – is that there is no need for those questing within to withdraw from capitalistic institutions, specifically the world of big business. One can be active and successful in the mainstream while pursuing the goal of Self-sacralization. The mainstream, it appears, need not contaminate or otherwise reinforce ego-operations.

To the best of my knowledge, no one has provided an overview of the development of the prosperity wing of the New Age. Accordingly, I now devote some attention to the descriptive task of charting some of the things which have taken place. I also want to give an indication of the scale of activity. I then turn to the job of reflecting on the question of efficacy.

## Specialised trainings, events, businesses, and publications

The focus here is on provisions which are specifically aimed at those working in mainstream businesses. First, and almost certainly foremost, there are those trainings provided by *est* and *est*-like organisations. Werner Erhard has been central in developing ways of connecting Self-spirituality with business. Especially influenced, it would appear, by his time with Mind Dynamics at the beginning of the 1970s, Erhard went on to found *est* (the first seminar ran in October 1971). *est* itself had a prosperity aspect to it, although the application of Self-spirituality to the market-place really became focused only in 1984 when Erhard established Transformational Technologies. Erhard-based training organisations are now well established, working in Britain with such companies as Cunard Ellerman and Guinness (the latter's Breakthrough programme being derived from *est*).[12] Other specialised trainings run by *est*-like movements include those provided by Scientology, WISE – or World in Scientology Enterprises – being associated with Sterling Management Systems (for dentists and other professionals); David Singer Consultants (a leading consulting firm for chiropractors in the USA); the Concerned Business-men's Association and Uptreads (involved with marketing, organisation, and finance); Programmes Training (which I studied during the mid-1980s); Philip Hynd's Harley Young Associates (Hynd having been associated with Programmes), as well as events run by Insight (with its business division, the Insight Consulting Group, running such activities as 'Managing Accelerated Performance'); Self Transformation (which has been running 'Corporate Breakthrough' since 1986); the Living Game (corporate semi-nars); Lifespring (with its 'Leadership Program' and 'giving regular courses to corporate employees');[13] the Life Training ('People on Purpose'); and i am provide other illustrations. Then one can think of trainings organised by Silva Mind Control, an important influence at the point of which so much of all this began, namely Mind Dynamics.[14]

Second, there are those specialised trainings run by New Age Movements which do not belong to the *est* 'family'. Sannyasins – followers of Bhagwan Shree Rajneesh – have become engaged (for example, running 'Results Seminars' for companies such as IBM); Rebirthing, described by R. D. Rosen as 'unabashedly materialistic',[15] has run prosperity and money semi-nars; Maharishi Mahesh Yogi's Transcendental Meditation is to offer MBAs at its new University of Management in the Netherlands; Emissaries of Divine Light is associated with Renaissance; Nichiren Shoshu has its Business Group in London; and Subud has run outdoor management train-ings in Wales. Psychosynthesis runs events entitled, for example, 'The Two Dimensions of Corporate Growth'. And even such long-established move-ments as those (for example) deriving from Alice Bailey have entered the field (the Arcane School recently held a talk on 'The Ageless Wisdom and its Relevance to Business, Politics and Religion). It can also be observed that the Order of the Solar Temple ran trainings, an associated institution – the Academy for Research and Knowledge of Advanced Science – providing seminars and lectures for Hydro-Quebec.[16]

Third, there are those trainings (and publications) which do not appear to have such strong connections with particular New Age Movements. Almost certainly the largest single training programme to date has been that mounted by Gurdjieff-inspired Krone Associates for Pacific Bell, the telephone company setting aside $147 million for the purpose. The Pacific Institute (run by Louis Tice) is another noticeable organisation, Jeremy Main reporting that there are some 12,000 Tice-trained facilitators around the world.[17] Other organisations include those run by Tishi (follower of one of Muktananda's successors, who has recently, and somewhat controversially brought the 'Values and Vision' training to HarperCollins in Britain); Branton Kenton's Human Technology Consultants; Emerge (which has worked with Virgin Retail); I & O; Transform Ltd (partly inspired by Rudolf Steiner); the Creative Learning Consultants; Potentials Unlimited; the Results Partnership Ltd; Keith Silvester's Dialogue management training services (influenced by Psychosynthesis); Impact Factory (running the 'Money Factor'); Dave Baun's 'Charisma Training'; and Anthony Robbins' 'Unleash the Power Within' weekends. The recently opened London Personal Development Centre alone claims to provide '300 courses, workshops, seminars and lectures', 'designed to bring new creativity and vision to business'.[18] Of the many similar outfits in the United States (including, for example, Maria Arapakis' 'Careertrack'), Phoenix Communications, based in Denver, is noteworthy in that it draws on the past. Phoenix runs 'Intrepreneurship: A Non-Linear Perspective', a flyer stating that it involves 'Business Planning Based on the Model of the Medicine Wheel'.[19]

Nor should we neglect the growing literature directed at businessmen. Probably the key figure, in this regard, is the American Michael Ray. Other authors include: John Adams, Robert Campbell, Guy Damian-Knight, Roger Evans and Peter Russell, Ron Garland, Craig Hickman and Michael Silva, Gerald Jackson, Robert Pater and Roy Rowan.[20] It should be added that, typically, these authors also run events.

Another way of conveying what is going on is to draw attention to those New Age businesses, including sectors of mainstream companies, that have developed spiritual applications. One of the earliest – if not the first – New Age business is provided by the Inner Peace Movement. Founded in 1964, Gini Scott, writes of the IPM 'ideals of attaining success and abundance through spiritual growth'.[21] Programmes Ltd, Europe's largest telephone marketing agency (at least during the 1980s) provides another illustration. So does the Bank of Credit and Commerce International, the founder, Agha Hasan Abedi, hoping that it could be run in terms of Sufi mysticism. Or one might think of businesses established by Transcendental Meditation, a number of which are clustered in Skelmersdale (Lancashire). As for mainstream companies that have introduced New Age teachings and practices, one can think of IBM (Tom Jennings, Manager in Employee Development at IBM UK, being a key figure in this country); the now defunct TV-AM (where managing director Bruce Gyngell encouraged participation in Insight); another TV company in the north of England where a leading figure has attempted to encourage involvement with isa; the Clydesdale Bank; the Netherlands' third biggest bank, NMB (whose chairman, William Scherpenhuijsen-Rom, is inspired by Anthroposophy); and General Electric (where it has been reported that chairman Jack Welch has played a major role in initiating the 'transformation' of this American company,[22] and who believes that his employees need to feel rewarded 'in both the pocketbook and the soul',[23] as well as many others.[24]

Consideration must also be paid to events run by New Age centres and associated networks. Since the foundation of Findhorn in 1962, the emphasis here has tended to shift from counter-cultural Self-actualisation to a more harmonial relationship with prosperity. The 'Findhorn Foundation Guest Programmes' for Spring–Summer 1983, for example, makes no reference to the world of business whereas the 'Guest Programme' for April–December 1990 includes information pertaining to 'A Working Retreat for Consultants and Managers' and 'Intuitive Leadership'. Much of Findhorn's work in this area, it is true, remains relatively counter-cultural. But, at least for certain Findhornians, outer prosperity is by no means neglected. Thus Francis Kinsman writes that 'it is wrong for the over-enthusiastic self-explorer to denigrate the competitive outer direction of much of business',[25] elsewhere writing that business should be 'nourishing to the wallet' as well as to 'the mind, the emotions, the body and the spirit'.[26] And Lynn Carneson-McGregor, who belongs to founder Kinsman's Business Network, runs Decision Development: an organisation which aims to transform managers into 'spiritual warriors'.[27] Other centres or networks, also in Britain, have also become more prosperity-minded. The Wrekin Trust's conference, 'The Energy of Money', held in 1991, provides an illustration;[28] Emerson College, which has run 'Lifeways', provides another. Turning to the United States, Esalen, founded in the same year as Findhorn (1962), appears to have followed much the same trajectory. As Frank Rose reports, 'Laurance Rockefeller has given $25,000 to convert the Big House…into a corporate retreat';[29] and Will Schutz, once with Esalen, has organised 'The Human Element in Organisations'. Another important centre in the United States, Gurdjieffian-inspired Arica, has held Open Path Workshops, often geared to the needs of business people.[30]

Finally, another good indicator of the extent to which New Age business activities have taken root is provided by the fact that the academy has become involved. As long ago as 1984, the European Association for Humanistic Psychology, together with the Human Potential Research Project of the Department of Educational Studies of the University of

Surrey, ran a large conference on 'Transforming Crisis'. Luminaries such as Peter Russell, 'one of the first people to take human potential workshops into corporations', according to conference material, were involved. The Croydon Business School, to provide a more recent illustration, has run a two-week event, in association with the New Age Skyros Institute, on the subject of 'Innovative Management'. (IBM's Tom Jennings was one of the 'distinguished staff'.) And Ronnie Lessem, of City University Business School (London) has written a volume extolling the principles of 'metaphysical management'.[31] Thinking of my own university (the University of Lancaster), it will be recalled that the Centre for the Study of Management Learning, together with a New Age consultancy (Transform), have run a conference entitled 'Joining Forces: Working with Spirituality in Organisations'.[32] And in the United States, influential author Michael Ray is Professor of Creativity and Marketing at Stanford University. Furthermore, an increasing number of articles on New Age management and business are appearing in academic journals. The *Journal of Managerial Psychology*, for example, has run a special issue on 'Spirituality in Work Organisations' (1994, vol. 9, part 6).[33]

### Less specialised activities and publications

Generally speaking, all the items introduced above target the business person at work, in particular in the realm of management. Turning to provisions for the general public, the emphasis is less on work in the mainstream and more about 'work' on and for the Self. The promise is that the Self itself empowers the person as an autonomous 'magical' producer, the person receiving benefits even though he or she might not actually do much (if any) work in the conventional sense of the term.

The point can be illustrated by referring to all those volumes which spell out what one should do in order to become (more) prosperous. Serving as self-help manuals, they hold that affluence results once one has taken those steps which ensure that one makes contact with one's inner spirituality. Examples are provided by Louise Hay's *The Power is Within You* (1991); Sondra Ray's *How to be Chic, Fabulous and Live Forever* (1990); Anthony Robbins' *Unlimited Power* (1988); Andrew Ferguson's *Creating Abundance* (1992); Deepak Chopra's *Creating Affluence* (1993); Sanaya Roman and Duane Packer's *Creating Money* (1988); Roman's *Living with Joy: Keys to Personal Power and Spiritual Transformation* (1986) (Roman also runs workshops on money); Insight's John-Roger and Peter McWilliams' *You Can't Afford the Luxury of a Negative Thought* (1990); Rebirther Phil Laut's *Money is My Friend* (1989); Jack and Cornelia Addington's *All About Prosperity and How You Can Prosper* (1984); Marsha Sinetar's *Do What You Love, the Money will Follow* (1987); Ron Dalrymple's *The Inner Manager* (1989); Shakti Gawain's *Creative Visualisation* (1982); Stuart Wilde's *Miracles* (1988); Mark Age's *How to Do All Things: Your Use of Divine Power* (1970); Harry Lorayne's *How to Get Rich. Using the Powers of Your Mind* (1992); Al Koran's *Bring Out the Magic in Your Mind* (1993); and, from India, Swami Sivananda's *Sure Ways for Success in Life and God-Realisation* (1990) together with Luis Vas' *Dynamics of Mind Management* (1991). Very often, it should be re-emphasised, such manuals attach little or no importance to actually working to obtain wealth; what is important is getting the God within to do the work.

Another topic concerns those New Age seminars or events which are put on for the general public. A great many of these are basically to do with Self-actualisation, being primarily concerned with the experience of authentic self-hood. However, it is by no means uncommon to find mild versions of outer prosperity entering their teachings. Pagans, neo-pagans, magicians, healers and others interested in occult powers might focus on what lies within, but they are by no means always disinclined to employ 'wealth magic' – counter-cultural values notwithstanding – in order to seek what lies without.[34] The Temple of Psychick Youth, for instance, maintains that 'Once you are focused on your Self internally, the external aspects of you life will fall into place. They have to.' Given this, it is highly likely that members sometimes work on themselves to obtain external results. To give another illustration, although healing activities are primarily focused on spiritually informed well-being, guided meditations often contain references to those rewards which will 'fall into your lap' once one is 'whole'. Indeed, it is likely that hundreds of events now held weekly in Britain make some reference to prosperity or abundance. (This is not surprising, given the importance which New Agers often attach to holistic interconnectedness.)

Then there are all those activities which are of a more fully fledged harmonial nature (whether to do with self-enhancement or mainstream transformation), together with those which appear to shift even further into the external domain. The talk, at least in the promotional literature, is of 'how to unleash the innovative genius inside yourself'; how to 'reveal the underlying attitudes that limit or enhance your personal effectiveness'; how to 'clarify one's vision and values'. From large organisations like *est* and its successors ('a decisive edge in your ability to achieve'; 'a powerful practical tool') to smaller ones such as those provided by Zen Master Rama ('Get the competitive edge with Zen'), Susy Joy (with her 'Prosperity, Abundance and Manifestation' events) and Paul Jenkins' courses ('Getting What You Want'), spirituality might be promised, but in connection with much more.[35]

## Numerical significance

Since the 1960s, prosperity teachings have come to occupy an increasingly important role within the New Age Movement as a whole. Based on a survey carried out at the close of the 1970s, with 185 respondents from people engaged in 'social transformation', Marilyn Ferguson reported that the three most influential figures cited by respondents were Pierre Teilhard de Chardin (first), Jung, and then Abraham Maslow.[36] One of my research students (Stuart Rose) has recently completed a large survey (with 900 replies from readers of the New Age magazine *Kindred Spirit*. His finding that two of the three most influential figures today are Louise Hay (first) and Shakti Gawain (third) speaks for itself. (Jung has held on to second position.) Of particular significance, Rose's survey has been of 'fully fledged' New Agers. Prosperity teachings, it appears, have entered the heartland of the Movement. Key 'spiritual' figures, such as William Bloom, are now apparently contributing. (An advert for Bloom's 'Prosperity Consciousness' experiential events begins, 'Cheer up. You can be rich and have a social conscience'; he also runs 'The Money Game', promising an 'assertive attitude towards money' and talking of 'The Golden Flow of Solar Abundance'; and he has written the 'Foreword' to the launch issue of the London Personal Development Centre's *Changing Times* (1994–5).) Findhorn, with its events for managers and its 'angels in pinstripes', is no longer as counter-cultural as it was. And the prospectus of the University of Avalon, located in Glastonbury – a town which has attracted many counter-culturally orientated New Agers – advocates that 'it's time to count money onto our sacred and spiritual agendas', and runs a course on book-keeping.

In the absence of adequate ethnographic material, it is not possible to arrive at a very clear picture of the significance of prosperity (or prosperity-inclined) activities. Some organisations might present themselves as though they were oriented to the outer world. Accordingly, they use terms such as 'abundance'. In practice, however – and this requires more detailed research – such organisations might be using terms of this variety in a spiritual sense. Conversely, it could well be the case that other organisations use spiritual language in their publicity, while being, in practice, much more outward bound.[37]

Nevertheless, it would be rash to dispute the fact that the New Age is considerably more oriented to the New World of the mainstream than it was during the counter-cultural 1960s. What might be thought of as the 'Findhorn trajectory' is quite a widespread development. Leading figures have increasingly replaced the language of 'God' with the language of 'Power'; Jerry Rubin, once a Yippie, then involved with *est* and other paths within, ended life as a corporate consultant. Turning to the broader, world-wide scene, millions must have now been introduced to abundance teachings. Louise Hay currently occupies the top five places in the non-fiction listing in Brazil. New Age(y) activities are to be found in West Africa.[38] And if one is happy to apply the term 'New Age' to contemporary India or Japan, those pursuing inner-based, spiritually informed prosperity amount to very considerable numbers. (In Japan, one might think of the Institute for Research in Human Happiness, claiming to be 'the most influential religious organisation' in the nation with some 8 million members; turning to India, it is not without significance that one of the most powerful national figures – Chandraswami – provides a Tantric-inspired version of the quest for success, commercial and political.) Returning to the USA, another indication of the significance of what is going on is that an estimated $4 billion is currently being spent annually, by companies, for transformational trainings. Such trainings, it can be added, are also significant in Germany. And in Britain, my guess-estimate is that there are more than 500 training programmes. Neither should it be forgotten that the world of business is replete with humanistic trainings and assumptions. If such renderings of the search for the self are taken into account – psychological renderings of human potential having much in common with spiritual versions – the number of those who are quasi-New Age swells considerably.[39]

Publishing in 1922, Max Weber observed, 'The most elementary forms of behavior motivated by religious or magical factors are oriented to *this* world.'[40] As he goes on to make clear, he supposed that such an orientation withers with the course of history. Bryan Wilson and Karel Dobbelaere adopt much the same view: 'Advanced religions are marked by the suppression of the magical by the ethical.'[41] Enough has been said to cast some doubt on the decline of magic thesis. Modernity, it seems, can generate interest, if not direct involvement. (Evidence against the decline thesis, it can be added, is substantially enhanced if one takes into account the importance of prosperity teachings for all those Christians who believe in the power of positive thinking.)[42] The New Age might not announce its presence in the world of capitalism with quite the splendour of some of the 'enlightened entrepreneurs' of the last century – one thinks, for example, of the Congregationalist church, in Italianate style, facing the main entrance to Sir Titus Salt's mill in Saltaire – but inner spirituality is clearly being put to work: to help production, including the efficacy of the consumer to produce that which he or she personally requires.

## New Age understanding of the efficacy of prosperity practices

I will now turn to several movements and individuals to explore further how New Agers themselves see their teachings and practices coming to bear on the quest for the extrinsic. (Systematic analysis, although clearly called for, is impossible in the present context.) I first look at those which most emphasise magical productivity, namely those which attach little if any importance to actually working. I then look at those which incorporate work. Throughout, attention is drawn to the extent to which practices tend to emphasise either what lies within, or what lies without, or both.

### *Magical productivity*

Many of these practices have to do with *Self-enhancement*. Accordingly, they are of a fully fledged harmonial nature. Albeit to varying degrees, inner spirituality is taken to be of intrinsic importance. Equally, all attach considerable importance to what the mainstream has to offer.

• Case 1: Soka Gakkai International (Nichiren Shoshu Buddhism). Material outcomes are here clearly important. In the words of UK leader, Richard Causton, 'chanting Nam-myoho-renge-kyo by itself creates good fortune in the form of conspicuous benefits'.[43] At the same time, however, practices also serve to 'develop inconspicuous benefit in our lives...spiritual strengths like wisdom, hope, courage, perseverance, and humour'.[44] Serving to 'defeat the ego'[45] and to 'release...[our] Buddha potential',[46] practices serve to bring about the best of both worlds. In Wilson and Dobbelaere's summary:

> The belief of members [of Soka Gakkai International] in general was that chanting achieved all manner of benefits, and while members of longer standing tended to have grown in their appreciation of the so-called inconspicuous benefits, they were far from denying that chanting might also yield material gains of the widest variety of sorts.[47]

• Case 2: Louise Hay. Strongly influenced by New Thought, in particular by the Rev. Ernest Holmes' Church of Religious Science/Science of Mind, publications such as *The Power is Within You* advocate a somewhat more externalised version of harmonialism.[48] Prosperity, we read, involves 'time, love, success, comfort, beauty, knowledge, relationships, health, and, of course, money'.[49] Change is readily effected: 'inner changes can be so incredibly simple because the only thing we really need to change are our thoughts'.[50] 'Affirmations' – surely indicating strong commitment rather than detachment – which should be used include 'My income is constantly increasing'[51] and 'it's okay to have money and riches'.[52] The God within is at one point called 'the great chef'.[53] And in another volume Hay claims that 'Prosperity or lack of it is an outer expression of the ideas in your head', this entailing that the trick is to replace 'old limited thinking'.[54]

• Case 3: Andrew Ferguson. Influenced by experiences at Findhorn, the author of *Creating Abundance* is quite clear that 'the way to wealth creation is spiritual'.[55] Here, however, the emphasis is more on the internal aspect of harmonialism. The author is 'more concerned with personal inner growth than with monetary outer growth',[56] and the point is made that 'No amount of money can create a feeling of abundance.'[57] Importance is also attributed to detachment, obtaining £30,000 being seen as 'a beautiful example of how letting go and releasing attachment results in getting what one wanted'.[58]

It should be noted that although these three case studies have been attributed to the Self-enhancement category, all introduce – albeit, I think, marginally – features of the transformational camp. Experience of what lies within, that is to say, transforms the experience of what lies without. Causton writes of coming to 'truly appreciate the values of the conspicuous benefits that come our way';[59] Hay suggests that the enlightened person realises that 'money is truly not the answer';[60] and Ferguson notes that money 'can be properly appreciated...[once] there is something there to appreciate it'.[61]

Before looking at more clear-cut renderings of the transformational approach, we can turn to those which promise *Self-empowerment*. These involve a more forcefully instrumentalised spirituality. One goes within largely – if not entirely – to obtain that which lies without.

- Case 1: Anthony Robbins, author of volumes like *Unlimited Power*, multi-millionaire, and recently described in the press as 'Diana's guru', clearly believes in God.[62] He also attaches great efficacy to what lies within: 'The power to magically transform our lives into our greatest dreams lies waiting within us all.'[63] Furthermore, in good New Age fashion, importance is attached to moving beyond 'limiting beliefs'. However, although he occasionally writes in harmonial fashion ('the opportunity to grow emotionally, socially, spiritually, physiologically, intellectually, and financially'), the emphasis is very much on what lies in the external world. A great many strategies – given the trademark 'Optimum Performance Technologies' – are advocated, providing 'the science of how to run your brain in an optimal way to produce the results you desire'.[64] These have to do with Neuro-Linguistic Programming, adopting the right diet, and learning how to set goals, for example. We are, it seems, on the very fringes of the New Age. The 'magic' is quasi-secular; what lies within is of very little intrinsic value; and much is couched in terms of manipulating what 'genuine' New Agers would see as mere 'ego-functions'.
- Case 2: This would appear to be even further beyond the heartlands of the New Age. Written 'for victory on the corporate battlefield', *The Warrior's Edge*, as the name implies, is based on 'New Age' applications within the sphere of the military. The volume, by Colonel John Alexander, Major Richard Groller and Janet Morris, might adopt basic New Age principles – including the assumption that 'belief systems' are restrictive[65] – but the instrumentalisation of spirituality is taken to an extreme: 'There are no atheists in foxholes...When [conventional] training fails and reason is insufficient to save the day, the warrior reaches deep within, where his fundamental vision of self, God, or the universe provides the winning edge.'[66]

### Management trainings and transformational productivity

Turning now to teachings and practices which focus directly on what it is to be at work in the world of business, the inner God still has 'magical' work to do. The somewhat complicated world of 'enlightening' management trainings and 'New Age businesses' now discussed is, however, distinguished from our previous case studies by the importance attached to the *'transformation'* of the significance of the workplace.

Most generally, the idea is to transform the values, experiences and to some extent the practices of what it is to *be* at work. The New Age manager is imbued with 'new' qualities and virtues, new in the sense that they differ from those found in the unenlightened workplace. These have to do with intrinsic wisdom, authentic creativity, self-responsibility, genuine energy, love, and so on. Trainings are held to effect this shift. Furthermore, work itself is typically seen to serve as a 'learning' or 'growth environment'. The significance of work is transformed in that it is conceived as providing the opportunity to 'work' on oneself. It becomes a spiritual discipline.

The second theme is that the transformation of business depends on managers (and those whom they manage) detaching themselves from main-stream business expectations and goals. 'De-identification', as it is sometimes called, is here emphasised as being necessary to effect the shift from being 'at effect' (the ego-level of operating) to being 'at cause' (the level of operation associated with the Self itself). In turn, de-identification results in the unleashing of those magical powers which lies with the Self. Business results then ensue. And for the 'good' participant, the significance of these outcomes is transformed: from the point of view of the detached, money is no longer simply 'money'. Essentially, it has become a sign of the fact that one is in touch with one's spirituality. As for the overall outcome, transfor-mational practices – it should be apparent – are strongly harmonial. The best of both worlds can be found in the workplace. Work is valued as a means to both spiritual and 'capitalistic' ends.

Fully-fledged attempts at the transformation of business would appear to be relatively rare. Most of those involved in introducing the New Age to the workplace seem to adopt a pretty instrumentalised and world-affirming version of what inner spirituality has to offer. Attention is focused on trans-forming what it is to be a manager; business goals and ambitions would often seem to be left untransformed; little importance is attached to de-iden-tification. As an article in the *Training and Development Journal* (December 1986) puts it, 'training [is] in the use of the "higher self" for improving job performance and satisfaction' (p. 2).

However, *est* and *est*-like teachings have given rise to some comprehen-sively 'transformational' activity. Programmes Ltd, which I have discussed elsewhere, provides a good illustration.[67] Concentrating, for present purposes, on *est*, we can begin with an assertion of Erhard's: 'What I want is for the world to work...the organising principle of est is: *Whatever the world is doing, get it to do that.*'[68] The 'content' of the world, including business, is not at issue. Getting the world to work is not a matter of tinkering with external arrangements. Instead, it is a matter of coming to experience the world out of the 'context' provided by the 'de-identified' Self itself. Self-transformation transforms the values and meanings of being at work; it enables the manager to exercise 'responsibility' and 'creativity'; it enables the 'source' to obtain 'results'. Participants, it is promised, will be able 'to transform their ability to experience living so that the situations they have been trying to change or have been putting up with clear up just in the process of life itself'. Furthermore, work serves as a spiritual discipline. As Erhard puts it, 'In est, the organisation's purpose is to serve people, to create an opportunity for people to experience transformation, enlightenment, satisfaction and well-being in their lives.'[69] Among other things, setting goals and obtaining them are enlightening.[70] In short, 'the meaning of mundane work has been redeemed as a means to the sacred end of "expanding your aliveness"'.[71]

## Sanctifying capitalism

Finally, this review of New Age understanding of prosperity practices naturally leads to the question of how those concerned justify what they are doing. An obvious point, found in much of the literature, concerns radical holism. Advocates of prosperity find God in everything. Unlike counter-culturalists, who divide up in the world in (gnostic) anti-holistic fashion, the spiritual realm extends though all aspects of life, including money. As Francis Kinsman puts it, 'Holism must be appreciated in this ["competitive outer direction"] respect, too';[72] or in the words of Phil Laut, 'The material world is God's world and you are God being you. If you are experiencing pleasure and freedom in your life, then you are expressing your true spiritual nature.'[73] A closely related point concerns the belief that the world is intrinsically and permanently beneficent – a view shared, it can be observed, by those spiritual environmentalists and pagans who see nature as naturally provident. As Sanaya Roman and Duane Packer put it in *Creating Money*, 'I live in an abundant universe', continuing, 'I always have everything I need' or, as Louise Hay puts it, 'There is an inexhaustible supply in the Universe.'[74] Yet another closely related point is that our nature as spiritual beings entitles us to all that the world has to offer. In the words of Laut, 'the more spiritual you are, the more you deserve prosperity'; in Hay's to-the-point formulation, 'I deserve the best', or in Leonard Orr and Sondra Ray's formulation, 'being wealthy is a function of enlightenment', Ray elsewhere writing that 'God is unlimited. Shopping can be unlimited.'[75] Similar views, it can be noted, have been reported of the Inner Peace Movement, Scott reporting that members 'view abundance and success as a sign of evolution and growth'.[76] Bhagwan Shree Rajneesh also clearly thought that his sannyasins were entitled to celebrate the very best that the world has to offer. He frequently praised capitalism, saying in a 1982 interview that 'I don't condemn wealth, wealth is a perfect means which can enhance people in every way, and make their life rich in all ways.' He is, as he continued, 'a materialist spiritualist': a point he also justified by claiming that 'The materially poor can never become spiritual.'[77] (The reasoning here seems to be

Maslovian, the materially poor supposedly having to devote their attention to 'lower order needs' rather than to spirituality.)

Having introduced a number of the ways in which the interplay of spirituality and materiality can be justified, let me conclude with brief mention of *est*. For Erhard has provided a range of teachings which serve to legitimate work and success in the mainstream. Some graduates might pick up on the message that the world around us is our creation. (It follows from this, of course, that capitalism cannot adversely affect the future of the planet.) Other graduates might think in terms of the statement – already cited – that 'whatever the world is doing, get it to do that'. Yet others might justify wealth creation in terms of the notion that 'results' are a sign of spirituality. And then there are those graduates who suppose that the best way to bring about a transformed world is to work at the very heart of capitalism, changing the big business enterprises which dominate so much of modernity while obtaining results.

## Matters of efficacy

What are we to make of New Age understanding of the quest for prosperity? Is it possible that the practices are as wonderful as they appear? The issue of productivity is addressed by considering the role which could be played by the following:

1 magical power;
2 inner-directed wisdom;
3 transformed character;
4 work ethics;
5 handling the stresses and strains of capitalism.

### 1 Magical power: productive or counter-productive?

There is no hard evidence, from the scientific point of view, that Self-derived magic 'actually' works. It might serve, however, to encourage practitioners to focus on what they really want, thus helping to motivate them to work – in a conventional sense – in order to obtain their goals. Conversely, however, it could well be the case that those relying heavily on magical practices are less likely to make an economic impact. They are deflected from doing what is 'actually' required.

### 2 Inner-directed wisdom

I do not know of any evidence which shows that business benefits by being informed by judgements which come from the spiritual realm within. What evidence there is suggests that recourse to 'inner wisdom' is not a good way to proceed. The fate of the Bank of Credit and Commerce International provides an excellent illustration of failure. Radically de-institutionalised – to let inner spirituality run affairs – there is little doubt that its de-institutionalised nature played a major role in its demise. Surrounded by wealth, without conventional monitoring systems, managers could only too readily find their egos coming back into prominence.[78] Could it be the case that mishaps over the recent refit of the QE2 is bound up with the *est*-informed goal-setting and 'can do' outlook instilled by the trainings undergone by Cunard Ellerman?

## 3  Transformed character

It is highly likely that more skilful trainings (and perhaps the less skilful) can make a positive difference to self-understanding and experience. Trained-up managers typically regard themselves as more empowered, more responsible, more creative, more focused, more energetic, more inclined to set goals, and so on. Such changes in self-understanding and experience, I think it is fair to say, typically translate into action. A 'spiritually' informed version of the enterprising self can indeed be constructed, and one which suits the values of the enterprise culture. Certainly many companies think that trainings providing this variety of character are worth investing in.[79]

## 4  Work ethics

Research suggests that the 'Self-work ethic' (as I call it) can be highly efficacious in motivating employees. The basic idea informing the New Age work ethic is that work is valued as a spiritual discipline. By working, one works on oneself. Accordingly, one works well, with greater commitment. Evidence from Programmes Ltd strongly suggests that this ethic has played a crucial role in ensuring that a highly unlikely workforce is prepared to work exceedingly hard, at a most unlikely task (given their backgrounds and interests), making a great success of selling over the phone.[80] Under certain circumstances (involving more structured forms of transformed business than those which prevailed at the BCCI), New Age businesses can inspire and so produce the goods. Furthermore, it is also quite conceivable that New Age teachings to do with the sanctification (and therefore positive evaluation) of capitalism can serve to enhance the quality of life of employees as well as their commitment. Of particular note, those with counter-cultural interests – who might otherwise be inclined to be dissatisfied with conventional jobs – are provided with justifications for working in the mainstream. And those who have had to 'drop back' into the mainstream after a period of counter-cultural involvement can turn to those provisions, like *est*, which can handle their unease.[81] In such ways, New Age practices – aimed at 'bringing life back to work' – might thus serve to handle those problems generated by what Daniel Bell calls the 'cultural contradictions of capitalism'.[82] In other words, to the extent that 'life' is brought back to the company it can be expected that problems associated with the clash between the quest for personal authenticity or expression and the disciplined demands of the workplace, will be alleviated, if not healed.

## 5 *Stresses of capitalism*

Given the (apparent) ability of (at least some) New Age practices to make a difference to how people experience themselves, it is highly likely that numbers of people have found that New Age participation has enabled them to handle those stresses and other psychological problems generated by competitive, enterprise-culture, capitalism. The yuppie goes home from stressful work; the yuppie practises Transcendental Meditation or, perhaps more minimally, listens to New Age music; the yuppie returns, the next day, refreshed. Or again, think of the person who finds that their work activities are being adversely affected by guilt, say over a failing marriage; he or she spends several weekends taking Psychosynthesis or Relationship courses; and then feels more capable of doing a good job of work. In short, the New Age here serves to restore 'private' life to that degree of effectiveness required by the workplace.[83]

To mention an additional issue concerning the efficacy of prosperity teachings and practices, to the extent that they contribute to capitalistic modernity – including consumer culture – one has to question their role in the future of the planet. It is surely dangerous to suppose, as do certain prosperity New Agers, that the earth is infinitely 'abundant'. For beliefs of this kind deflect attention away from the quest to finding modes of production – and consumption – more suited to the longer-term 'economics' of the planet.

But whatever the case regarding matters of efficacy, and to return to how we began, one thing is for certain: prosperity teachings and practices can generate a considerable income for those supplying them.[84]

## Some broader considerations

Several additional issues deserve mention. One concerns the relationship between New Age and Christian versions of the quest for extrinsic prosperity. On first sight, there would appear to be a relatively stark contrast. Crudely, whereas the former is monistic and therefore calls upon what lies within, the latter is theistic and therefore relies on that which lies without. However (in the United States as well as elsewhere), there is a fascinating – and extremely influential – zone of interplay or fusion. Norman Vincent Peale clearly though of himself as Christian, his theistically envisaged God frequently being called into play. Reference is made to 'God's will' and to 'leaving the outcome to God'.[85] At the same time, however, we read that 'God is in you'.[86] The 'power of positive thinking' is often portrayed as being bound up with an agency which operates within the person, depending on the exercise of one's own will. Many passages could have been written by 'affirmation' New Agers such as Louise Hay.

A related consideration concerns the historical development of religious prosperity teachings in general. A great deal has, of course, been written about mind cure, positive thinking, and – to use what is probably the most useful generic term – New Thought. Typically, however, histories end with the 1960s.[87] It would be fascinating to know, for example, more about how the New Thought tradition is faring today. My impression is that it has moved even further from its theistic Christian roots, organisations like the Rev. Ernest Holmes' Church of Religious Science/Science of Mind belonging – in effect – to the New Age Movement.

Then there is the task of explaining the appeal, or development, of what is currently taking place. As formulated – in classical anthropological fashion – by Tanya Luhrmann, 'why do they [ordinary middle-class people] practise magic when, according to observers, the magic doesn't work?'[88] Clearly, this question can be tackled by way of standard anthropological theories: intellectualist (Robin Horton), symbolist (John Beattie), Durkheimian (Mary Douglas, who suggests that magic flourishes when 'group' is 'weak' and 'grid' is 'strong'), Freudian (all those who use deprivation–compensation theory) and so on.[89] There is probably some truth in all these approaches, the Durkheimian, for example, suiting our competitive, timetabled (or 'grid'-run) society. However, perhaps the most useful avenue to explore is the role played by the development of all those increasingly widespread and powerful cultural values and assumptions which lend plausibility to the idea that prosperity can be generated from within. Just to give one illustration, the (relative) boom in New Age management trainings arguably owes a considerable amount to the fact that those attracted belong to a cultural territory where they are already likely to believe in 'unlocking human potential', 'will power', 'perfectibility', 'transcending barriers', and so on: all being cultural assumptions which lend a fair degree of plausibility and attractiveness to what the New Age has to offer.[90]

Another important issue concerns the question as to whether the prosperity-inclined New Age deviates from what might be thought of as 'genuine' Self-spirituality. If the 'wisdom' of the East is anything to go by, there is certainly a case for answering in the affirmative. Detachment, we learn from the great Eastern mystical traditions, is essential. But how can those busy at work in the capitalistic mainstream become detached? Worse – from the point of view of the East, how can those who practise affirmations (for example) claim spirituality while not bothering much (if at all) with detachment? Then what are we to make of the logic, sometimes found amongst the prosperity-oriented, that detachment results in one being able to act 'from source', this naturally generating 'results' which one can then celebrate or consume. How can one perform this last act while remaining detached? Did Bhagwan enjoy his ninety-three Rolls Royces or were his drives detached? If the latter, why did he bother to use his cars? In short – and bearing in mind that academics cannot pass ultimate judgement on spiritual matters – there are certainly questions to be raised about the 'authenticity' of prosperity teachings.[91]

Finally, a note on the future. Faith Popcorn, America's 'Nostradamus of Marketing', whose company 'Brain Reserve' forecasts for sixty leading 'Fortune 500' companies, predicts that 'the next thing will be Icon Toppling. Big bad businesses...will fall over and be replaced by spiritual, entrepreneurial mainly female-led companies.'[92] I am sure that there will be plenty of similar predictions as we approach the end of the millennium. I am equally sure that they are exaggerated. However, there is no reason to suppose that – relatively speaking – spiritual economics will not continue to prosper. Since the 1960s, we have witnessed a clear pattern of growth; a clear trajectory in favour of prosperity practices. Although I have heard it said, for example, that mainstream business people will tire of expensive management trainings, and perhaps want to avoid them because they are controversial, there are no signs of a slow-down in activity. Prosperity teachings have become (relatively) well established, and at least will surely be sustained at the current level of involvement.

And even if some forms of prosperity teachings run out of momentum, one will surely continue to thrive. New Age holidays – which deserve much more detailed attention than can be provided here – have expanded rapidly during the last ten or so years. They provide a great deal. Thus if one were to go on 'The Voyage of Life' (a cruise around the eastern Mediterranean), one could go to 'Mastering Money' and 'Stress Management' workshops, or take 'Therapeutic Massage'; one would be on 'An Adventure in Self-Discovery', pleasuring the self with a holiday, and, in the process, contributing to the income of those running the voyage. This kind of thing, it is certain, is bound to continue developing, especially with the prospect afforded by the end of the decade for millennial holidays.

## Notes

1 Contrast, for example, the research focus of David Bromley and Anson Shupe, 'Financing the New Religions: A Resource Mobilisation Approach', *Journal for the Scientific Study of Religion*, 19(3), 1980, 227–39, and most of the contributions to James Richardson (ed.), *Money and Power in New Religions*, Lampeter: Edwin Mellen Press, 1988, with the additional lines of enquiry opened up by Steven Tipton, *Getting Saved from the Sixties*, London: University of California Press, 1982, and – more generally – Robert Wuthnow (ed.), *Rethinking Materialism: Perspectives on the Spiritual Dimension of Economic Behaviour*, London: William B. Eerdmans, 1995.

2 Richard Behar, 'The Prophet and Profits of Scientology', *Forbes*, 138(9), pp. 314ff. (p. 315).

3 Bromley and Shupe, op. cit., p. 236.

4 Much of what now follows draws on material presented in my *The New Age Movement: Celebrating the Self and the Sacralization of Modernity*, Oxford:

Blackwell, 1996. This volume also provides a more extensive account of the nature of the New Age Movement and other pertinent matters.

5 See Roy Wallis, *The Elementary Forms of the New Religious Life*, London: Routledge and Kegan Paul, 1984.

6 Sydney Ahlstrom, *A Religious History of the American People*, London: Yale University Press, 1972, p. 1019.

7 Dick Anthony, Bruce Ecker, and Ken Wilber, *Spiritual Choices*, New York: Paragon, 1987, p. 40.

8 Cf. Bryan Wilson, 'A Typology of Sects', in Roland Robertson (ed.), *Sociology of Religion*, Harmondsworth: Penguin, 1969, pp. 361–83 on 'manipulationist' or 'gnostic' sects.

9 José Silva, *The Silva Mind Control Method for Business Managers*, New York: Pocket Books, 1986.

10 E. F. Schumacher, *Small is Beautiful*, London: Abacus, 1974; and Schumacher, *Good Work*, London: Abacus, 1980.

11 Charlene Spretnak and Fritjof Capra, *Green Politics: The Global Promise*, New York: E. P. Dutton, 1984.

12 Ray Clancy, 'Seminars Leave Firms Divided', *The Times*, 23 July 1992.

13 Jeremy Main, 'Trying to Bend Managers' Minds', *Fortune*, 23 November 1987, pp. 77–8ff.

14 On Silva Mind Control, see José Silva, op. cit. Mind Dynamics, described by William Bartley, *Werner Erhard*, New York: Clarkson N. Potter, 1978, p. 158, as 'probably the most spectacular mind-expansion program ever staged', drew on Edgar Cayce, Theosophy, and other teachings, as well as on Silva. It was founded by an Englishman, Alexander Everett (who had previously founded an experimental school, Shiplake College, near Henley-on-Thames). His aim in Mind Dynamics was to 'get people to a higher dimension of mind, from which level their entire lives would be more effective' (cited by Bartley, p. 160). The influence of Everett on the prosperity-oriented version of the New Age is clearly seen in that Werner Erhard (*est*) and John Hanley (Lifespring), who developed their own large movements, were graduates. Everett himself later mounted new courses, including Samata. (See Jess Stearn, *The Power of Alpha Thinking: Miracles of the Mind*, New York: Signet, 1977.)

15 R. D. Rosen, *Psychobabble*, London: Wildwood House, 1978, p. 131.

16 Concerning Bhagwan's sannyasins, a leading figure at Bhagwan's community in India was recently due to come to talk to my students. He cancelled, pleading that he would be in Sweden discussing management trainings with Volvo. Concerning Nichiren Shoshu's City Business Group. Rachel Storm, 'Bourses, Boardrooms and Babylon', *International Management*, November, 1991, pp. 72–5, reports that, 'Each month members meet to chant and discuss business problems. Soeda [the founder] also advises followers in other financial centres, including Amsterdam, Luxembourg, Frankfurt, Zurich, and Milan', p. 75. (Nichiren Shoshu is now re-named Soka Gakkai International.) On the Academy for Research and Knowledge of Advanced Science, see Hugh Winsor, 'Doomsday Sect Leaves a Legacy of Destruction', *Independent*, 6 October 1994, p. 11.

17 Jeremy Main, 'Merchants of Inspiration', *Fortune*, 6 July 1987, pp. 51–4.

18 London Personal Development Centre, *Changing Times*, Sept.–Feb. 1994–5, p. 1.

19 The figure of $147 million for the Krone training is provided by Glenn Rupert, 'Employing the New Age: Training Seminars', in James Lewis and J. Gordon Melton (eds), *Perspectives on the New Age*, Albany: State University of New York Press, 1992, pp. 127–35 (p. 134). Others put the figure lower, at around $100 million. A useful account of Krone's work with Pacific Bell is provided by Kathleen Pender, 'PacBell's New Way to Think', *San Francisco Chronicle*, 23

March 1987, pp. 1, 6; see also Pender, 'PacBell Stops "Kroning"', 16 June 1987, pp. 1ff. Although Pacific Bell terminated the training before all the workforce had become involved, Krone has been more successful elsewhere. Thus, Jeremy Main, 'Merchants', op. cit., p. 53, reports that 'some Du Pont divisions have been using him for ten years'. It can be noted that there are reports of Krone activity in Britain, trainers reputedly having worked with a well-known building society, for example. As for the London Personnel Development Centre, by no means all of the courses held under its auspices are of a fully fledged New Age nature. Many appear to provide more psychological, less spiritual, renderings of human potential. But some are clearly New Age: those run by Victor Marino (with a background in Psychosynthesis), for example; or those run by Karen Kingston with her promise that 'you will learn the 10 principles of Successful Manifestation which will teach you how to connect with your Higher Self to discover what you really want, and then how to locate and remove the blocks to creating it', 'Create the Life You Really Want', *Changing Times*, London: London Personal Development Centre, 1994–5, p. 13.

20 See Michael Ray and Rochelle Myers, *Creativity in Business*, New York: Doubleday, 1986; Michael Ray and Alan Rinzler (eds), *The New Paradigm in Business*, New York: Jeremy P. Tarcher, 1993; John Adams (ed.), *Transforming Work*, Virginia: Miles River Press, 1984; Robert Campbell, *Fisherman's Guide: A Systems Approach to Creativity and Organisation*, London: Shambhala, 1985; Guy Damian-Knight, *The I Ching on Business and Decision-Making*, London: Rider, 1986; Roger Evans and Peter Russell, *The Creative Manager*, London: Unwin, 1989; Ron Garland, *Working and Managing in a New Age*, Aldershot: Wildwood House, 1990; Craig Hickman and Michael Silva, *Creating Excellence*, London: Allen and Unwin, 1985; Gerald Jackson, *The Inner Executive: Access Your Intuition for Business Success*, London: Pocket Books, 1989; Robert Pater, *How to Be a Black-Belt Manager*, London: Thorsons, 1989; Roy Rowan, *The Intuitive Manager*, Boston: Little Brown, 1986. Much of this literature, it can be noted, is informed by New Age renderings of 'New Science'.

21 Gini Scott, *Cult and Countercult*, London: Greenwood Press, 1980, p. 46.

22 Noel Tichy and Mary Anne Devenna, 'The Transformational Leader', *Training and Development Journal*, July 1986.

23 Cited by Anne Ferguson, 'Time to Tune in to New Age Ideas', *Independent on Sunday*, 14 October 1990, p. 23.

24 On NBM, see Peter Spinks, 'The Bank that Likes to Say Welkom', *Guardian*, 2 September 1987. It can also be noted that Transcendental Meditation has provided specialist literature on management trainings (see, for example, Gerald Swanson and Robert Oates, *Enlightenment Management: Building High Performance People*, Fairfield: Maharishi International University Press, 1989). Mainstream companies that have introduced New Age teachings and practices include (in alphabetical order): Barclays Bank; the Beth Israel Hospital; Boeing; British Gas; British Midland; BP; British Telecom; Campbell's Soup; Cannon; Cathay Pacific; Chemical Bank; Clydesdale Bank; Courtaulds; Daihatsu; Du Pont; Esso; the Federal Aviation Administration (USA); General Dynamics; General Motors; Guinness; IBM; Lockheed; Macro; Mars; McDonnell Douglas; NASA; Olivetti; Procter & Gamble; Scott Paper; SmithKline Beecham; Shell; the US Social Security Administration; TV-AM; the UCLA Graduate School; the United States Navy; Virgin Retail; and Whitbread. (See, for example Glenn Rupert, op. cit.)

25 Francis Kinsman, *Millennium: Towards Tomorrow's Society*, London: W. H. Allen, 1989, p. 229.

26 Kinsman, 'Business Diary', *Resurgence*, 123, June–August 1987, p. 33.

27  See Rachel Storm, 'Spiritual Warriors Attack Boardroom', *Independent on Sunday*, 13 May 1990, p. 28.
28  See Vicky Hutchings, 'Silver Tongued', *New Statesman and Society*, 20 September 1991, pp. 15–16.
29  Frank Rose, 'A New Age for Business', *Fortune*, 8 October 1990, pp. 80–6 (p. 80). See also Haidee Allerton, 'Spirituality in Work', *Training and Transformation*, June 1992, p. 1.
30  See William Henderson, *Awakening: Ways to Psycho-Spiritual Growth*, Englewood Cliffs: Prentice-Hall, 1975, p. 167.
31  Ronnie Lessem, *Global Management Principles*, London: Prentice-Hall, 1989.
32  See Richard Roberts, 'Power and Empowerment: New Age Managers and the Dialectics of Modernity/Postmodernity', *Religion Today*, 9(3), 1994, 3–13 (pp. 7–9); Paul Heelas, 'The Sacralization of the Self and New Age Capitalism', in Nicholas Abercrombie and Alan Warde (eds), *Social Change in Contemporary Britain*, Cambridge: Polity Press, pp. 139–66 (pp. 154–5).
33  Those who have written on more specialised activities, in particular management trainings, include Richard Roberts, op. cit., and Glenn Rupert, op. cit. I have provided some details (and analysis) in a number of publications, including Paul Heelas, 'Cults for Capitalism: Self-Religions, Magic and the Empowerment of Business', in Peter Gee and John Fulton (eds), *Religion and Power: Decline and Growth*, London: British Sociological Association, 1991, pp. 27–41; 'The Sacralization of the Self', op. cit.; 'God's Company: New Age Ethics and the Bank of Credit and Commerce International', *Religion Today*, 8(1), 1992, pp. 1–4; 'The New Age in Cultural Context: The Premodern, the Modern and the Postmodern', *Religion*, 23(2), 1993, 103–16; (with Leila Amaral) 'Notes on the "Nova Era": Rio de Janeiro and Environs', *Religion*, 24(2), 1994, pp. 173–80; 'The New Age: Values and Modern Times', in Lieteke van Vucht Tijssen, Jan Barting, and Frank Lechner (eds), *The Search for Fundamentals: The Process of Modernisation and the Quest for Meaning*, London: Kluwer, 1995, pp. 143–80; 'Cultural Studies and Business Cultures', in Oliver Westall and Andrew Godley (eds), *Business History and Business Culture*, Manchester: Manchester University Press, 1996. Of all the business magazines which have attended to the matter, *Training and Development* contains some of the most useful material.
34  Tanya Luhrmann, *Persuasions of the Witch's Craft*, London: Picador, 1994.
35  Marvin Harris, *America Now*, New York: Simon and Schuster, 1981; and Rachel Storm, *In Search of Heaven on Earth*, London: Bloomsbury, 1991. The latter in a chapter on 'the Prosperous Self', provides thought-provoking accounts.
36  Marilyn Ferguson, *The Aquarian Conspiracy*, London: Granada, 1982, p. 463.
37  A good example of how terms like 'abundance' lend themselves to different meanings is provided by Findhornian, Vidura Le Feuvre, 'Abundance, Progress and Blessedness on Earth', *One Earth*, Autumn, 1991, pp. 32–4. Hearing that the Findhorn community was going to hold a conference entitled 'Abundance – Accepting our Natural Heritage', she acknowledges that 'I had a little trouble with this title as it did not seem to click naturally with my usual understanding.' She then came to realise that 'abundance' was (apparently) being defined in a spiritual fashion: 'Abundance really lies in the infinite capacity of universal consciousness to create infinite possibilities of its nature' (p. 32). Accordingly, the term no longer need imply the merely materialistic.
38  On the 'New Age' in West Africa, see Rosalind Hackett, 'The Spiritual Sciences in Africa', *Religion Today*, 3(2) 1986, pp. 8–9. It is interesting to note that Soka Gakkai has branches in Lagos and Zaria (p. 9); on the New Age in Brazil, see Heelas and Amaral, op. cit., and Brenda Fucuta, 'Budismo Muda Administração de Empresas', *Jornal do Brasil*, 13 November 1994, pp. 26–7.

39 A more comprehensive assessment of the significance of prosperity teachings would have to take into account a rather different kind of New Age application from those discussed in the present context. See Heelas, *The New Age*, op. cit., Chapter 4 for further discussion. One would also have to take into account the apparently quite widespread use of astrologers, channels, and mystics in forecasting the market, making job appointments, and so on. For the situation in France, see Syliviane Sokolowski, *New Age Helping Management: The Case of Firewalking*, a paper delivered to a conference on 'Perspectives on Moralities, Knowledge and Power', European Association of Social Anthropologists, 1994. See also Adam Smith, *The I Ching Comes to Wall Street*, 1976, pp. 66–75. Nicola Legat, 'Formers: The New Navel-Gazers', *Metro*, October 1987, pp. 60–80, draws attention to a particular role performed by America's best-known channel, J. Z. Knight, namely, providing advice for those about to invest in the market (p. 72).

40 Max Weber, *The Sociology of Religion*, London: Social Science Paperbacks, 1966, p. 1.

41 Bryan Wilson and Karel Dobbelaere, *A Time to Chant: The Soka Gakkai Buddhists in Britain*, Oxford: Oxford University Press, 1994, p. 182.

42 For a comprehensive survey of magic today, see Daniel O'Keefe, *Stolen Lightning: The Social Theory of Magic*, Oxford: Martin Robertson, 1982.

43 Cited by Wilson and Dobbelaere, op. cit., p. 7.

44 Ibid., p. 23.

45 Ibid., p. 105.

46 Ibid., p. 22.

47 Ibid., p. 210. Rachel Storm, 'Bourses, Boardrooms and Babylon', op. cit., p. 75, notes that according to Hiro Soeda (a senior manager with Barclays Bank in the City of London) 'One person's *ichinen* or mind is able to affect the whole environment of the City. It can either destroy the financial centre or make it a place for prosperity and peace.'

48 Louise Hay, *The Power is Within You*, London: Eden Grove Editions, 1991.

49 Ibid., p. 146.

50 Ibid., p. 193.

51 Ibid., p. 166.

52 Ibid., p. 156.

53 Ibid., p. 38.

54 Louise Hay, *You Can Heal Your Life*, London: Eden Grove Editions, 1988, p. 118.

55 Andrew Ferguson, *Creating Abundance: How to Bring Wealth and Fulfilment into Your Life*, London: Piatkus, 1992, p. 71.

56 Ibid., p. 19.

57 Ibid, p. 71.

58 Ibid., p. 60.

59 Cited in Wilson and Dobbelaere, op. cit., p. 23.

60 Louise Hay, *The Power is Within You*, op. cit., p. 157.

61 Andrew Ferguson, op. cit., p. 150.

62 Robbins, op. cit., p. 337.

63 Ibid., p. 20.

64 Ibid., p. 39.

65 John Alexander, Richard Groller, and Janet Morris, *The Warrior's Edge: Frontline Strategies for Victory on the Corporate Battlefield*, New York: Avon Books, 1992, p. 105.

66 Ibid.

67 See Heelas, 'Cults for Capitalism', op. cit.; Heelas, 'God's Company', op. cit.; Heelas, 'The New Age: Values', op. cit.

68  Cited by Steven Tipton, 'Making the World Work: Ideas of Social Responsibility in the Human Potential Movement', in Eileen Barker (ed.), *Of Gods and Men: New Religious Movements in the West*, Macon: Mercer University Press, 1983, pp. 265–82 (p. 270).

69  Cited by Tipton, ibid., p. 276.

70  See Tipton, *Getting Saved from the Sixties*, op. cit., pp. 188–93.

71  Steven Tipton, 'The Moral Logic of Alternative Religions', *Daedalus*, Winter, 1982, pp. 185–213 (p. 203).

72  Francis Kinsman, *Millennium*, op. cit., p. 229.

73  Phil Laut, *Money is My Friend*, Cincinnati: Vivation Publishing Co., 1989, p. 14.

74  Sanaya Roman and Duane Packer, *Creating Money*, Tiburon: H. J. Kramer, 1988, p. 18; Louise Hay, *You Can Heal*, op. cit., p. 118.

75  Laut, op. cit., p. 14; Hay, *You Can Heal*, op. cit., p. 117; Leonard Orr and Sondra Ray, *Rebirthing in the New Age*, Berkeley: Celestial Arts, 1983, p. xiv; Sondra Ray, *How to be Chic, Fabulous and Live Forever*, Berkeley: Celestial Arts, 1990, p. 135.

76  Gini Scott, op. cit., p. 27.

77  Cited by Laurence Grafstein, 'Messianic Capitalism', *The New Republic*, 20 February 1984, pp. 14–16 (p. 14).

78  See Heelas, 'God's Company', op. cit.

79  More systematic evidence of the efficacy of New Age practices in transforming character cannot be further explored here. For general discussion, see Heelas, *The New Age Movement*, op. cit., Chapter 7. Peter Finkelstein, Brant Wenegrat, and Irvin Yalom, 'Large Group Awareness Training', *Annual Review of Psychology*, 1982, pp. 515–39, provide a summary of change with regard to *est* and *est*-like seminars for the general public. It is interesting to note that Douglas Rushkoff, *Cyberia: Life in the Trenches of Hyperspace*, London: HarperCollins, 1994, reports that many leading computer experts (software designers and so on) insist that they owe much of their creativity to regular immersions in 'cyberia' (that interconnected realm of being which (supposedly) fuses the pagan, the psychedelic, the spiritual and the tribal, all in the hands of the technoshaman). (And Tanya Luhrmann, op. cit., p. 114, observes that 'one or two out of every ten magicians I met had something to do with computers'.)

80  See Heelas, 'Cults for Capitalism', op. cit.; Heelas, 'The Sacralization of the Self', op. cit.; and Heelas, 'Rationalizing Religion as a Corporate Enterprise: The case of est', in James Richardson (ed.), *Money and Power in New Religions*, Lampeter: Edwin Mellen Press, 1988, pp. 223–40.

81  See Tipton, 'Making the World Work ', op. cit.

82  Daniel Bell, *The Cultural Contradictions of Capitalism*, London: Heinemann, 1976.

83  A specific example is provided by Rupert Allason, Conservative MP for Torbay and, as Nigel West, an author of thrillers. Clearly a busy man, he reports that he has 'a lot of energy' and very considerable confidence and does not feel stressed. These, and other benefits, are attributed to TM.

84  It is, of course, very difficult to assess the commercial efficacy of New Age practices. The prosperity and management literature is replete with success stories, but one cannot rule out the possibility that these are attributable to factors over and above those provided by the New Age. Some at Cunard Ellerman report that transformational trainings enabled them rapidly to save more than £1 million; others say that this was due to the company selling off rolling stock (see Storm, *In Search of Heaven*, op. cit., p. 89). According to Glenn Rupert, op. cit., p. 134, 'Upper level management [at PacBell] was very satisfied with the results of the [Krone] training. Meetings gained a better sense of direction, relations between managers improved, and productivity in company operations increased by 23 per

cent.' No doubt interpersonal relations did improve – at least among the trained – but the increase in productivity might well have been influenced by a number of variables.

85 Norman Vincent Peale, *The Power of Positive Thinking*, Englewood Cliffs: Prentice-Hall, 1952, pp. 56 and 47.
86 Ibid., p. 40.
87 See, however, David Bromley and Anson Shupe, 'Rebottling the Elixir: The Gospel of Prosperity in American Religioeconomic Corporations', in Thomas Robbins and Dick Anthony (eds), *In Gods We Trust*, London: Transaction Publishers, 1991, pp. 233–54; and Nicole Biggart, *Charismatic Capitalism*, London: University of Chicago Press, 1989.
88 Luhrmann, op. cit., p. 4.
89 See John Skorupski, *Symbol and Theory*, Cambridge: Cambridge University Press, 1976.
90 See Heelas, 'The Sacralization of the Self', op. cit., pp. 159–60; and Heelas, *The New Age Movement*, op. cit., pp. 167–8.
91 Dick Anthony, Bruce Ecker, and Ken Wilbur, op. cit., themselves involved in the New Age, attempt to pass judgement. As they argue, pp. 133–4:

> A chief aspect of the mystical glimpse-experience of ultimacy is the direct intuition that one's essence or real self is not dependent on material conditions. By thus dispelling 'ontological insecurity' – the root anxiety that one's being is vulnerable and could be lost – this experience deeply alleviates the fear and worry in life, resulting in enhanced energy, love, comfort, judgement. For the person who regards the mystical experience as true and valuable *because* it brings material and social advantage this all runs amuck. Grasping after the consequences, even subtly, contradicts the essence of the glimpse experience and tends to cancel it. A more-or-less frantic but futile attempt to keep both the state and the desired benefits typically occurs.

92 Faith Popcorn, 'A Day in the Life of', *Sunday Times* (magazine), 13 February 1994, p. 58.

# Summary of Chapter 4

In different ways and in pursuit of various ends, NRMs have found themselves confronting the law of the countries in which they operate. The law is at once a system of rules which reflect and reinforce the society in which they obtain, a form of dispute resolution and a basis in accordance with which people determine their behaviour. Yet it must also be acknowledged that the courts do not always employ the rules in a consistent way, and people – in this case, the NRMs – do not always have a full and accurate knowledge of the law. Although, traditionally, the law is said to be neutral in addressing religious issues, confrontations between the law and NRMs sometimes occur in which the operation of the law appears highly problematic. Mr Bradney explores some of these problem areas. He addresses the extent to which the position of NRMs is unique and discusses the comparisons that may be drawn with the law's treatment of other religious groups, and the sort of reforms that might be instituted.

# 4 New Religious Movements

## The legal dimension

*Anthony Bradney*

## Introduction

Before we can begin a preliminary exploration of the relationship between New Religious Movements and law in the United Kingdom it is necessary to analyse the key concepts of 'New Religious Movements' and 'law'.

As Beckford has noted, although the term New Religious Movement has been widely used in describing groups such as the Unification Church, Scientology or the Divine Light Mission:

> anyone with only a passing knowledge of even...[a] small sample of controversial groups will know that there are many more broadly comparable groups and that there are major differences between them all...[I]t becomes a problem to decide what they all have in common – if anything.[1]

As Beckford suggests, it is difficult to be certain about which groups should be included in the term New Religious Movement and how groups which are New Religious Movements are to be distinguished from other groups which are not within this category. Beckford and Levasseur have defined the term thus:

> [The phrase New Religious Movement] refers to organized attempts to mobilize human and material resources for the purpose of spreading new ideas and sensibilities of a religious nature. They are therefore intentional, collective and historically specific.[2]

For the purposes of this chapter I will accept this as a working definition of the term New Religious Movement. However, I will treat this as a soft concept, denoting a useful organising category, where it is often difficult to be sure whether individual examples of group are or are not in fact New Religious Movements. Moreover, I will seek to show that the English law's treatment of New Religious Movements is often similar to its treatment of other religious (and, indeed, non-religious groups). Adherents to New Religious Movements and the groups themselves may be treated differently, and treated less favourably, by the law, but they are not always treated differently simply because they are New Religious Movements. Rather, I will argue, they are treated differently because examples of New Religious Movements often share some of the same characteristics that cause a whole host of groups to be differently, and less favourably, treated by the law.

Defining the other key term, law, for the purpose of this chapter is a hazardous business. In the popular imagination, and in many subtle and sophisticated theories of law, law is conceived of as a thing of commands and rules. Laws are orders which tell you what to do, where disobedience is sanctioned by agents of the state.[3] If we follow this account of law, then this chapter should consider the orders that emanate from the state. In the United Kingdom, these orders are to be found either in the pronouncements of judges exercising their original jurisdiction (the common law) or in statutes and delegated legislation produced by the authority of Parliament.[4] Such a chapter would follow the traditional pattern of legal scholarship, seeking to show what legal rules apply to New Religious Movements, leavening this account with limited and largely speculative musings on the social impact of these rules. Such material will form the greater part of this chapter but to describe just this as law is, arguably, to miss important dimensions of the legal enterprise.

Even if law is a command, law is important not just for what it tells one to do. The contents of the command have a symbolic significance even if, in fact, they are not enforced.[5] For the state to say that this should or should not be done necessarily says something about the state's view of the life of the polity. If a group's behaviour is deemed unacceptable by those commands, or if a group's needs are ignored in those commands, then that says something about that group's place in society. A legal rule, on this view, is significant not only because of what it tells a New Religious Movement to do or not to do but also because of what its content says about the distance of New Religious Movements from the centre of British society.[6] However, precisely what symbolic significance these commands have depends on more than the fact that they are commands made by the state. Suppose, for example, that Parliament passes a statute but that statute is not enforced, or, once having been enforced, the statute falls into disuse. Such a statute remains a command of the state. Its legal status is unchanged by the fact that it is not used. There is still some significance in the fact that it was once passed. There is some significance in the fact that, even though it is no longer used, Parliament has not taken the time to repeal it. Yet, whatever significance is to be attached to such a statute, it is different from the significance attached to a statute that is regularly enforced. Law that is regularly enforced is more likely to influence people's behaviour. Law that is regularly enforced is more likely to reflect matters that are deemed to be of importance in the life of society. It therefore also has greater symbolic significance.

If we attach a different status to laws which are enforced then we are led on to consider what makes something law. Is the description a technical one, dividing out one species of command from another or does it in some way relate to the function that the command fulfils? Is the answer to the question, what is law, a matter of the use of language or a matter of effects in society? The dominant tradition in British legal scholarship has taken the former route. To say that something is law is simply a naming process. It says nothing about the content or effects of that thing we have said that is law.[7] Yet, we might argue that we should treat as law what actually happens in the courts. Law is what the courts decide and if they are silent or if their decisions seems to be in conflict with the words of the statue they purport to enforce, then it is that silence or those decisions which reflect what the law is.[8] Law, on this view, lies in action rather than in the books. Law is the thing that affects people's lives, not a lading list of empty rules.

The practical significance of these theoretical considerations can be seen in one area of law which has recently gained some prominence and which relates to the subject matter of this chapter, the law relating to blasphemy. Until its repeal by the Criminal Law Act 1967 the Blasphemy Act 1697 made an expression of disbelief in the Christian trinitarian view a criminal offence.[9] However, the twentieth century saw no prosecutions under this Act. The quite separate common law offence of blasphemy saw no successful prosecution between the case of *R v. Gott* in 1922 and the *Gay News* case, *Whitehouse v. Lemon*, in 1979.[10] What, then, has been the law of blasphemy in this country in the twentieth century? Should we look to both statute and the common law rule and say that that is the law or should we, like Lord Denning writing in 1949, say that '...the offence of blasphemy is a dead letter'?[11] Should we discount the *Gay News* case as an aberrant example, holding that it owes more to homophobia than to any likely resurrection of the offence?

The history of the law of blasphemy teaches us to be cautious about what we call law and not to be too simplistic in looking only to the legal rules without also paying attention to their implementation. Yet the history of blasphemy in the United Kingdom also teaches us not to ignore the importance of laws even if they are not enforced. There is some evidence, albeit limited and anecdotal, to suggest the law of blasphemy has restricted what has been published. According to Dom Moraes, George Barker's *Collected Poems* was incomplete because the publishers refused to include a poem on the grounds that it was blasphemous.[12] Equally, Muslim anger about the publication of *The Satanic Verses* was probably heightened by the fact that there was a law to prosecute blasphemies which offended Christians.[13] Neither the fact that that law protected only some Christians nor the fact that a long list of theologically blasphemous books had been published without prosecution were of any moment.[14] The existence of the law in itself gave rise to some of the anger.

Traditional legal scholarship has not just limited itself to the pronouncements of courts and to legislation passed by Parliament. It has further circumscribed itself by looking at cases considered in higher courts (generally the High Court and above) and ignoring decisions of lower courts. This has been done on the basis that such higher courts make rules which, legally, have to be followed by the lower courts. Such lower courts making unreported decisions deal with the vast majority of cases decided before the courts but, in traditional legal scholarship, have been deemed to be but shadows of the higher courts; creatures of the higher courts that are automatically obedient to them. Yet Malinowski's observation that there is a gap between what people say they should do and what they actually do, and that to have a complete picture one needs to look at both accounts, applies as much to the English courts as it did to Trobriand society. Research in the last two decades has shown that lower courts sometimes fail to follow the rules laid down in higher courts. Their decisions are usually, if not wholly at odds with the rulings of the higher courts, at least slightly at a tangent. Evidence thus far covers only a very small area of the court's activities. It is, however, consistent in pointing to the variance between what the rules suggest and what the courts do.[15] As with any other group or individual, the influence that courts have on New Religious Movements will usually be the influence of unreported lower courts and of them we can say very little more than what they do is probably somewhat different to what, legally, they should do.

One further dimension to law needs to be considered. Whatever statutes ordain and whatever courts decide, if people believe that law is something else, they will act on that belief. Their action or omission may be such as for them never to learn of their error. If, for example, a group is advised that they can only secure charitable status if their beliefs include a belief in god or gods, they may never make an official application for such status and may never find out that this advice is wrong.[16] Whether perceptions or misperceptions of the law should themselves be counted as law is a matter for dispute; that they should be taken into account when considering the effect of law is, however, quite certain.

Given the many levels of the legal enterprise, the account of the relationship between New Religious Movements and law in this chapter will necessarily be deficient. Because legal scholarship in the United Kingdom has traditionally been remiss, paying attention only to questions of doctrine, looking at rules in statutes and common law but neglecting the actual behaviour of law, the result is that our knowledge of law is frequently limited to the bare legal rules. We have statutes to consult; detailed records of the decisions of the superior courts and the guidance of academic commentaries. What happens in courts of inferior jurisdiction where most decisions are made, what perceptions people have of the law and what advice they are given about their legal rights are all things about which we know very little. Socio-legal scholarship is just beginning to reveal something about these matters.[17] Until we know more, we need to be very cautious about any generalisations that we make about the relationship between New

Religious Movements and the law.[18] For this reason, if for no other, this chapter is but a very bare beginning.

## Religious freedom under British law

Accounts of the relationship between British law and religions in the United Kingdom are few and far between. St John Robilliard's first monograph on the general relationship between religion and law in England was not followed until nearly ten years later by another book on the subject.[19] Periodical literature is similarly scarce. Part of the reason for this paucity of scholarship and research may lie in the general failure of British university law schools to produce research or scholarship which is not directed to the perceived short-term needs of the legal professions.[20] Another part of the reason may lie in the fact that there is no constitutional protection for religion in the way that there is many other legal jurisdictions. There is thus nothing on which to focus any discussion of religion and law.[21] However, the main reason why there is relatively little legal writing on the relationship between religion and law in the United Kingdom seems to be a perception that there is nothing of interest to say.

A third leader in *The Times* from 1984 continues to reflect both lay and legal opinion. 'Among those things which are held to be self-evident in British society is the principle that there should be no coercion in matters of religion.'[22] Judicial support for this view is not difficult to find. 'It is, I hope, unnecessary to say that the Court is perfectly impartial in matters of religion.'[23] 'As between different religions the law stands equal.'[24] If we follow this established view, the relationship between law and New Religious Movements is a dog that does not bark. Since the law is neutral towards religions it has no particular attitude towards New Religious Movements.[25] This approach seems to be in keeping with the United Kingdom's ideological position as a liberal democracy. While liberalism is a notoriously broad church, Rawls' statement that 'the [liberal] state is not to do anything intended to favour or promote any particular comprehensive doctrine rather than another, not to give greater assistance to those who pursue it' is likely to be accepted by most.[26] Certain general propositions about the relationship between law and religion follow from this basic starting position.

> One may say that the law–religion relationship is a natural locus of the liberal neutrality. The idea of a secular liberal state, i.e. the state which neither gets involved in matters religious nor inhibits in any way religious expression and activities has long been understood as best encapsulated by the idea of the state's neutrality towards religion.[27]

In turn, this produces the proposition that '[t]he relationship between the state and religion in modern secular nations is regulated by two principles: the separation of the state and religion, and the freedom of religion'.[28] New

Religious Movements are thus protected in the same way as Methodists or the Roman Catholic Church. The state should not interfere with them nor should it promote them.

The silence of traditional legal scholarship suggests that in Great Britain, if not perhaps in Northern Ireland, this principle of religious freedom has been accepted in the constitutional, political, and legal structure of society. Two illustrative examples might give us reason to doubt this conclusion.

First, Church and State are not separated in all of the United Kingdom. Both England and Scotland have an established Church. In the former case, establishment gives rise to a right of representation for one particular church, the Church of England, in Parliament. Archbishops of the Church of England and some Bishops sit in the House of Lords by virtue of their religious office. They have the same rights as any elected Member of Parliament.[29] They can vote on legislation. They can take part in debates. They can ask government ministers questions. New Religious Movements are outsiders to Parliament. Like all religious bodies, apart from the Church of England, there is no-one there, by right, to speak on their behalf. Many more established religious bodies may expect to find adherents of their faith amongst either the Lords or the MPs.[30] These people can speak on their behalf with more or less official authority.[31] However, this is not so with New Religious Movements. Their relatively small membership and the fact that some consciously distance themselves from the world mean that their direct representation in Parliament is unlikely.[32]

No law prevents members of New Religious Movements from becoming MPs. No law debars anyone otherwise entitled to sit in the House of Lords from sitting there because they are members of a New Religious Movement. Moreover, the presence of Archbishops and Bishops in the House of Lords may make less actual difference to the tenor of debate than one would at first suppose. Even in case of issues with an obvious religious dimension, such as the recent changes to Sunday trading laws, the Church of England, along with other mainstream churches contributing to national debates, rarely couches its arguments in religious terms.[33] Indeed, the contribution to Parliamentary debate made by the Archbishops and Bishops is very limited *per se*.[34] The point may largely be a matter of the symbolic significance which establishment gives. Nevertheless, the result is that members of New Religious Movements do not sit in Parliament while members of other religious groups do. Matters of interest to New Religious Movements are debated. Sometimes New Religious Movements themselves are debated and there is no-one there to represent those movements. We may feel that neutrality is not an obviously satisfactory way of describing this state of affairs.

A second illustrative point also shows, at a very different level, the difficulty of uncritically accepting the proposition that the law is neutral towards New Religious Movements. In 1985, Latey J refused custody of children to a

Scientologist parent commenting that 'Scientology is both immoral and socially obnoxious. Mr Kennedy [counsel in the case] did not exaggerate when he termed it "pernicious". In my judgement it is corrupt, sinister and dangerous.'[35] While Latey J stressed that the custody case was not a prosecution of Scientology, his remarks seem somewhat out of keeping with the measured tones which are normal for the judiciary in such cases.[36] One must not press this case too far. Latey J's view was the expression of an opinion by one judge in the lowest level of reported courts. Subsequently, in the Court of Appeal, Latey J's remarks were said to be 'unfortunate', though the decision itself, and his right to make the remarks, were upheld.[37] This case cannot be dismissed as an isolated example of judicial intemperance. *Hubbard v. Vosper* was an interlocutory action in a case which concerned possible copyright infringement and breach of confidence. An interlocutory action such as this is one where full argument is not heard but where a preliminary point is decided. Discussion in the case turned to the merits of Scientology. Although counsel for the plaintiff, Hubbard, the founder of Scientology, had not come to court expecting to argue this point, and so was not briefed on this matter, the court decided 'even on what we have heard so far, there is good ground for thinking that these [Scientology] courses contain such dangerous material that it is in the public interest that it should be made known'.[38]

This is not to say that there is a universal pattern in judicial pronouncements on New Religious Movements or even that the general trend is illustrated by Latey J's remarks. There are, for example, ample instances of judges making relatively positive comments about the general attitudes of Jehovah's Witnesses; thus, for example Ormrod L J's comment that 'there is nothing immoral or socially obnoxious' in the practices of Jehovah's Witnesses.[39] Even more pertinent in illustrating the proposition that the judicial attitude to New Religious Movements need not always be hostile is Ward L J's judgement in *Re ST (A Minor)*, a 1996 wardship case involving The Family, previously known as the Children of God.[40] The Family occupy a similar position to that of Scientology in the popular imagination; while Scientology is seen as being obnoxious because of perceptions about its totalitarian nature and its financial practices, hostility is directed towards The Family because of perceptions about its attitude to sexual promiscuity and sexual activity between children and adults.[41] However, the tone of Ward L J's judgment is the direct antithesis of that of Latey J. Ward L J, for example, describes The Family's evangelical activity amongst hippies in Nepal as being 'laudable', compares their concern with adherents' obedience to the rule of The Family to the demands put upon a member of a school, the army or a learned profession and describes himself as being 'filled with admiration for their total dedication to their discipleship, to their belief in the teachings of their master, Jesus Christ, and to their spreading of His Gospel'.[42]

## Freedom of belief and freedom of practice

The United States has a much more developed jurisprudence regarding religious liberty than the United Kingdom. This jurisprudence focuses on a division between freedom of religious belief and freedom of religious practice. While the former is wholly protected under the First Amendment to the American Constitution, the latter receives only limited protection.[43] This division between freedom of belief and freedom of practice can also be used to explain the British court's view of its own attitude towards New Religious Movements. The neutrality the British courts claim is a neutrality towards beliefs but not towards practices. This can be illustrated by looking at the treatment of Jehovah's Witnesses in child custody cases.

Jehovah's Witness child custody cases typically involve a divorcing couple with one Witness parent and one parent who has been a Witness and has left the movement or a parent who has never been a Witness. In an early case, *Buckley v. Buckley*, a Witness mother lost custody of her three young daughters to the non-Witness father.[44] The case was one where, usually, one would have expected the mother to win custody. Young daughters were, at the time, normally expected to go to their mothers.[45] The mother had actual custody of the children at the time of the decision, and courts tended to make custody awards in keeping with the status quo arrangement.[46] In this case the court regarded the social isolation that it saw as a consequence of membership of the Jehovah's Witnesses as being sufficient reason to award custody of the children to the non-Witness parent.[47] A series of cases have followed this general pattern. Not all cases involve Witness parents losing custody of their children where one would otherwise have expected them to win it. In some cases the courts allow Witness parents custody of their children with access arrangements which are expressly designed to prevent children being brought up in the normal Witness manner. For example, access to the other non-Witness parent might be given at dates like Christmas, Easter and the child's birthday, as these dates are not celebrated by Jehovah's Witnesses.[48] However, whatever strategy the courts choose, parents are treated differently because of social practices consequent upon membership of a particular religion. Exclusive Brethren parents have been treated in a similar manner.[49] Scottish family law treats Witness parents in the same way as English law.[50] The courts nevertheless maintain that, in acting in this manner they pay no attention to matters of religious belief. In *Wright v. Wright*, a case where a Witness father was refused access to his child because he would not give an undertaking that he would not teach the child about the Witness faith, Ormrod L J, a highly experienced family law judge in the Court of Appeal, commented:

> What it really boils down to is not a matter of the faith of the Jehovah's Witnesses being wrong or right…it is the matter of the custodial parent

holding one set of views and the non-custodial parent holding a conflicting set of views and the conflict causing damage to the child.[51]

This claim to separate matters of faith from matters of practice is not unique to the area of child custody law or to the courts. In 1979, the International Society for Krishna Consciousness set up an independent school, Chaitanya College, for the children of supporters of the movement. Because the school was intended to provide full-time education it came under the regulatory mechanism operated by the then Her Majesty's Inspectorate of Education. Adverse reports by the Inspectorate could lead to a school being closed.[52] In their report on Chaitanya College the Inspectorate made the same criticism that they had made of a number of other religious schools.

> There is no clear dividing line between the religious and academic aspects of their education. It is important, if the children are to be adequately prepared for the next stage of their education, which may not be within the Society's schools, that the curricular provision made for them should approximate more closely in pattern and purpose to the methods and expectations of the generality of schools.[53]

The Report does not, at any point, attack the religious beliefs of the school's founders. However, the Inspectorate clearly feel that an education which fits children for life within the Society, and which makes no division between the religious and the secular, does not provide full-time education within the meaning of the 1944 Education Act.[54]

New Religious Movements, like other religions, may consider it desirable to apply for registration as a religious charity. The advantages of religious charitable status can be divided into two types. First, there are the pragmatic financial and legal advantages which accrue. Charitable gifts do not have to be made to a specific human beneficiary and, contrary to the normal legal practice, may be made in perpetuity. Charities are also exempt from certain taxes.[55] There is also a more general symbolic importance in being able to register as a charity. Because the state accords charities special privileges it implicitly acknowledges some particular merit in the charities. Being accorded charitable status is, in one sense, a mark of official approval.[56] As one commentator has noted:

> [t]he leading commentaries on the law of charitable trusts in England maintain that the present state of the law is now one of virtually unqualified toleration of every religion or sect, irrespective of the truth or falsity of its doctrines.[57]

A study of the success of New Religious Movements in being accorded charitable status might be taken to suggest that this conclusion is over-hasty. This neutrality may be less real than it seems.

Academic commentators have all been agreed in thinking that Scientology should not be accorded charitable status.[58] Two difficulties are said to exist in legally registering Scientology as a charity. First, for there to be a religious charity there must normally be a notion of 'reverence to a deity'.[59] Second, if the teaching of a group is 'subversive of morality', then charitable status cannot be accorded to that group.[60] The Goodman Committee, in its report on the law of charity, went further, stating that charity law 'must exclude from charitable status what it regards as evil just as it can and does outlaw what it regards as detrimental to moral welfare'.[61] One writer has gone on to argue that a religious trust formed by a religious group which tended to break up families or which used psychological pressures on initiates would be void on public policy grounds.[62]

Those who would argue for the law's neutrality towards religion would contend that none of the above necessarily involve any movement away from the courts refusing to investigate the truth of a particular faith, or involve the courts in attempting to coerce people's beliefs. The rules, they would argue, relate to observable social practices or, in the case of the legal definition of religion for charitable purposes, rest on standard linguistic usage. There is some merit in this argument. New Religious Movements have not been entirely excluded from the ambit of charity law. It should be noted that, despite considerable external pressure, the Unification Church was able to register as a charity.[63] On the other hand, the Australian courts have rejected the English approach to the definition of religion, arguing that it is too restrictive. In *Church of the New Faith v. Pay Roll Tax Commissioners*, also a case concerning Scientology, the Australian High Court, their highest court, held that Scientology could be regarded as a religion.[64] The Australian court suggested a number of different tests for what should count as religious for charitable purposes of which the widest was '[a]ny body which claims to be religious, and offers a way of finding meaning and purpose in life'.[65]

It would be possible to examine a number of other areas of law and show how New Religious Movements have been treated but this would be merely to multiply examples. The above is sufficient to show the general pattern that is found in British law. This, then, raises the questions, is the divide between protecting religious belief and action because of that religious belief coherent and, if it is coherent, is it equitably operated in the case of New Religious Movements?

## The secular analysis of religion

The law's distinction between religious belief and religious practice is capable of logical defence. What I think is one thing; what I do is another.

Yet such a distinction can also be seen to miss the point of religion. For those who are not religious, religion can seem to be merely a cultural matter, a facet of someone's life. It can be seen as being voluntary and peripheral to personal identity. Religion is just one of many things which identifies you as a member of a group you have chosen to join. It is an addition to one's life. '[O]ne sometimes gets the feeling that religion is like stamp-collecting or playing squash, a minor hobby.'[66] However, as Dummett notes, for those who are religious, religion is obligatory and given.[67] Religion is the central focus to life. Joining a religious group is a reaction to a person's perception of the state of nature. One is a Muslim because there is Allah; a Christian because there is God. Your religion has in this sense chosen you. This is as true for members of New Religious Movements as it is for members of old-established churches.[68] The imperatives of one's religion therefore take priority over any other command including the law of the state. From belief, practice must follow. From this perspective to suggest that you are neutral to religion because you attend only to a person's actions is to deny the special status that they attach to those actions. If you judge their actions for the believer, you judge also their beliefs. Indeed, the argument can be pressed further. How would it be possible for the law to be other than neutral towards belief? Since belief is an inner matter, it is not something that the law can easily judge. The law is always more comfortable in assessing behaviour.

## Objectivity and New Religious Movements

If the conceptual distinction between religious belief and action on the basis of that belief is open to question, then the neutrality of the judicial application of this distinction to New Religious Movements is still more open to doubt. This is not to say that there is any general evidence of any conscious bias on the part of the judiciary. Rather, it is to argue that the intellectual climate within which New Religious Movements are judged in courts, and in the country at large, is one which is largely hostile to these movements. The nature of this hostility can be exemplified by looking at a religion itself antipathetic to New Religious Movements, Islam.

In recent years it has increasingly been argued that Islam is fundamentally at odds with modern Western society:

> Some people discern only the spectre of encroaching fundamentalist groups who threaten to engulf the achievements of Western-European or national cultures. They see in Islam a danger that must be banned from society, or at any rate controlled. This problematic approach stems in part from the traditional image of Islam and from anti-Islamic sentiments. The intensity of the 'moral panics', as recently witnessed in Belgium and France against the wearing of head coverings by women, particularly young girls, and the reaction to events involving Rushdie's

*Satanic Verses* and the Gulf War, show that there is no question of this being a minor issue, but of a widely held, if not always clearly formulated fear of, or aversion to Islam.[69]

Muslim commentators and others have themselves seen evidence of what they have termed a 'liberal inquisition'.

For several months [of the Rushdie affair], both Muslims and their opponents were transported into a bygone age of passion and heresy. Freedom crusades began in earnest and set out for the House of Islam. Accusations and rejoinders abounded; the obscurantism of the Muslims had to be countered with Western enlightenment. It was indeed our light and their darkness. There could hardly have been a better setting for their liberal Inquisition.[70]

What is at issue here is a clash of ideology. An Islamic ontology which is based on the revealed word of God and the priority of the community over the individual is not compatible with the sceptical, individualistic liberal framework which pervades public life in the United Kingdom. Skirmishes over isolated points like the Rushdie affair are only symptoms of a more pervasive problem of communities in conflict with each other. Rational debate about the problem is difficult because the nature and status of rationality are themselves one of the centres of disagreement. Added to this clash of ideology is simple ignorance. Islamic customs and beliefs are barely known and, where known, much misunderstood.

These arguments about the division between Islam and modern Western society may be unduly apocalyptic. At the very least, they run the risk of treating Islam as a monolith rather than as a diverse and developing religion. However, they capture the essence of the problem for New Religious Movements in the courts. New Religious Movements have much the same general relationship with Western society as does Islam: '[N]ew (religious) movements, as fundamentally religious movements, devote themselves to the timeless preoccupations of religion. Accommodating to new conditions, they may, none the less not lose sight of the basic functions of religion.'[71]

Like Islam, New Religious Movements often have a fundamentally illiberal ontology. Beckford and Lavasseur note that 'some commentators...account for the growth of NRMs as part of a reaction against the ideological disturbances of the 1960s'.[72] The result of this ideological clash can be profound in its impact.

In his measured, highly researched and generally sympathetic judgment in The Family wardship case, *Re ST (A Minor)*, Ward L J notes that:

NTs [the mother's] closing words to me were to plead with me not to denigrate the Law of Love [the central tenet of The Family's belief system]. It was an extraordinary observation from her. I would have expected her to plead with me not to remove her son.[73]

Later, in his judgment he writes '[m]y concern for NT is that she fails to put S first. The Family comes first.'[74] Ward L J's attitude, in court where the interests of the child are legally the paramount consideration, is understandable. NT's attitude, as an adherent to a religion where all that is of value is mediated through and comes directly from that religion, is equally understandable. The gap between the two is inevitable and, philosophically, unbridgeable.[75]

Finally, as with Islam, there is a general 'ignorance of the nature and characteristics of the current wave of New Religious Movements'.[76] In this atmosphere courts come to judge New Religious Movements using conceptual tools which are alien to those movements. Moreover, they come to the Movements ignorant about their nature in a legal system which is adversarial rather than inquisitorial. The problem lies in a subtle change of emphasis when courts consider more mainstream religions and when they consider those outside that mainstream. When the courts discuss Roman Catholic parents instructing their children in their faith they speak of 'religious instruction' or 'religious education'.[77] When a Jehovah's Witness parent attempts to do the same thing the courts talk about an attempt to 'indoctrinate' a child.[78] Similarly, it is difficult to believe that a court, faced with a woman wishing to enter a nunnery, would say that parents were entitled to advise their adult children not to do so 'if they think necessary, with emphasis' although this ruling was made in the case of a woman who wanted to join the Unification Church.[79] Judicial knowledge must come from the arguments of counsel and the expert evidence that is produced. Typically, in cases to date, such evidence has tended to be limited and, where it has existed, to be pathological in nature, dealing with what happens when members leave their Movement.[80] In this context it is not surprising to find that courts consistently, although not inevitably, find against New Religious Movements.

## Conclusion

Adherents to New Religious Movements share a problem in common with members of many other religions in the United Kingdom.

> Nobody [in Great Britain] can be heard to testify to their mistreatment as a believer because there is religious freedom in Great Britain. Thus their experience as a believer, as a Muslim, as a Sikh, is denied. It is not as a Hindu or a Jain that they are treated differently. It is not because they are a Jehovah's Witness or a member of the Exclusive Brethren. It is because they have an unacceptable attitude to women or the place of computers in education or whatever else it is that, for the moment,

counts as being part of the fundamental mores of Great Britain. On the one hand their beliefs result in them being less favourably treated than others with different beliefs. On the other hand they are denied the dignity of having those beliefs described as religious beliefs because they are assured that, despite their differential treatment, there is no denial of religious freedom in Great Britain.[81]

Those who write about law are inclined to see law as a solution to all social problems. This bias means that if there is a problem about religious discrimination against New Religious Movements then it follows for those who write about law that the solution should be a Religious Discrimination Act, akin to the present legislation about sex and race. It is true that the United Kingdom already has obligations under international law to protect religious freedom.[82] Domestic legislation to mirror these obligations seems natural. There are many obvious advantages to such legislation. It would both provide a focus for potential litigation, enabling the courts to deal with particular examples of discrimination, and, in doing so, it would allow the courts to build up an appropriate jurisprudence and also a greater knowledge of New Religious Movements.

There are two main problems with this solution. The first problem is pragmatic and, perhaps, capable of solution. The judges who would administer and adjudicate on any Religious Discrimination Act are the same judges who, on occasion, have been responsible for apparently discriminatory rulings in the past. Would the nature of the court process allow them to become more familiar with the New Religious Movements or would there be a perpetual state of mutual incomprehension? There is some slight reason for optimism here. In the area of child custody law, the treatment of Jehovah's Witness parents by the courts has changed over the years. While it is still arguably discriminatory, it is more accommodating to those parents. One of the reasons for this change may lie in greater judicial familiarity with the Witness movement.

The second objection to a Religious Discrimination Act is more fundamental. Neither the legislation relating to race nor that relating to sex outlaw discrimination.[83] Rather, they outlaw unjustifiable discrimination. There are still categories of permitted discrimination. This slight difference raises a host of problems. No-one would argue that religious belief is a fundamental value that, in all circumstances, overrides all other values. A devout believer who believes it is their duty to kill is not to be accommodated by any Religious Discrimination Act. The vital issue then becomes, what the boundaries of legitimate discrimination on grounds of religion are. The choice for a Religious Discrimination Act is either to set those boundaries within the wording of the statute or to leave it to the discretion of the judiciary, hoping that they will arrive at an acceptable answer through the slow accretion of case law. Given the relationship between the courts and New Religious Movements in the past, the latter answer seems unacceptable, casting the greatest burden of framing the new law on those not well equipped to deal with it. Yet to suggest that, in the current state of knowledge, Parliament is likely to arrive at any coherent or rational answer seems almost equally unlikely a proposition.

The new Human Rights Bill, incorporating the European Convention on Human Rights into UK law and thus a requirement to protect freedom of religion, brings with it many of the problems discussed above. While the European Court of Human Rights has created a jurisprudence which does not help in the protection of religious freedom, its work has not always assisted New Religious Movements.[84] In addition the Bill brings with it the problem that it is of limited application, applying, under clause 6, only to the actions of 'public authorities'. How the Bill will be applied by the courts and whether they will copy the jurisprudence of the European Court of Human Rights remain moot points.[85] Finally the Bill appears to incorporate some of the differential treatment of New Religious Movements that is found generally in English law. It seems unlikely, for example, that an adherent to a New Religious Movement will be able to take advantage of the defence under the Bill that a person 'has acted in pursuance of a manifestation of religious belief in accordance with the historic teaching and practices of a Christian or other principal religious tradition represented in Great Britain'[86] or that a New Religious Movement will be able to take advantage of the exemption under clause 6(6) that 'a person is not a public authority...if the act is done by or on behalf of a religious body exercising a jurisdiction, recognised but not created by Parliament, in matters spiritual'.

A belief in the existence of religious freedom in the United Kingdom has resulted in a failure to debate the purposes of, and the limits to, such freedom. Sudden legislation cannot cure this ill. While New Religious Movements can legitimately argue that they are ill-served by the British legal systems, sudden legislation would arguably do much harm. Nor can the position of New Religious Movements be separated from that of some other religions or, indeed, from that of other socially isolated groups.[87] Yet, to argue that New Religious Movements are not uniquely ill-served by the British legal systems is not to argue that New Religious Movements are not ill-served in an important manner. Legal systems which promote one religion and regard social practices which diverge from those common in society with suspicion have some difficulty in arguing that they are, in the philosophical sense, liberal. An important part of the solution to this problem will lie in the gradual disentanglement of state and religion:

> the state has to remain aloof from religious activities (just as it should not get involved in *anti*-religious, as contrasted to non-religious, activities and beliefs). Only by fully disentangling itself from all religion-related functions, can the law maintain its position of complete neutrality.[88]

However, an era which saw the 'Christianisation' of the state education system in England and Wales ten years ago might not be the one in which to hope for quick progress.[89]

## Notes

1  J. Beckford, *Cult Controversies*, London: Tavistock, 1985, p. 23.
2  J. Beckford and M. Levasseur, 'New Religious Movements in Western Europe', in J. Beckford (ed.), *New Religious Movements and Rapid Social Change*, London: Sage, 1986, p. 29.
3  See, most famously, J. Austin, *The Province of Jurisprudence Determined*, London: John Murray, 1963.
4  The United Kingdom is a country with several different legal systems. England and Wales together, Scotland and Northern Ireland all have separate legal systems. In some areas of law the treatment of New Religious Movements will not necessarily be the same in each legal system.
5  See T. Arnold, 'Law as Symbolism', in V. Aubert (ed.), *Sociology of Law*, Harmondsworth: Penguin, 1969.
6  Or because of what it says about the ability of New Religious Movements, either as a whole or individually, to influence the pluralistic political and social debate in British society.
7  The most influential account of this kind is to be found in H. L. A. Hart's *The Concept of Law*, Oxford: Oxford University Press, 1961.
8  K. Llewellyn *Jurisprudence: Realism in Theory and Practice*, Chicago: Chicago University Press, 1962.
9  The 1697 Act was repealed by s 13 and Schedule 4 of the Criminal Law Act 1967.
10  *R v. Gott* (1922) 16 Criminal Appeal Reports 87, *Whitehouse v. Lemon* [1979] 2 *Weekly Law Reports* 281.
11  A. Denning, *Freedom Under Law*, London: Stevens, 1949, p. 46.
12  D. Moraes, *My Son's Father* London: Secker and Warburg, 1968, p. 167. In 1976 the then Home Secretary, Merlyn Rees, said that the law of blasphemy would be used if Jorgen Thorensen made his proposed film about the life of Christ (*The Times*, 17 September 1976).
13  'The Rushdie affair has enabled us to discover that our new communities cannot appeal to legislation for protection, particularly when they cover race and blasphemy laws...because of the absence of proper recognition of their religious cultural mores.' M. Ibn Ally, 'Second Introductory Paper', in *Law, Blasphemy and the Multi-Faith Society*, London: Commission for Racial Equality, 1990, p. 22.
14  The common law offence of blasphemy protects only the beliefs of the Church of England (*R v. Chief Metropolitan Magistrate ex parte Choudhury* [1991] 1 All England Reports 306). A list of Christian blasphemous literature published in this century in the United Kingdom would include D. H. Lawrence's *The Man Who Died*, Nikos Kazantzakis' *The Last Temptation* and Michelle Roberts' *The Wild Girl*.
15  See, for example, John Ekelaar and Eric Clive with Karen Clarke and Susan Raikes, *Custody After Divorce*, Oxford: Oxford Centre for Socio-Legal Studies, 1977.
16  In a letter to the author of this chapter a representative of the Pagan Federation stated that they had received such advice from the Charity Commission when enquiring about making an application for charitable status.
17  See P. Thomas (ed.), *Socio-Legal Studies*, Aldershot: Dartmouth, 1997 and A. Bradney, 'Law as a Parasitic Discipline', *Journal of Law and Society*, 25, 1988, 75.

18 I will also ignore the possible argument that New Religious Movements are a source of social ordering that should itself be called law. The legal anthropologist, de Souza Santos, defined law as 'a body of regularised procedures and normative standards considered justiciable in a given group which contributes to the creation and prevention of disputes and to their settlement through an argumentative discourse, whether or not coupled with force' (B. de Souza Santos, 'The Law of the Oppressed: The Construction and Reproduction of Legality in Pasargada', *Law and Society Review* (12)5, 1977, at p. 10). For de Souza Santos law does not necessarily emanate from the state. Groups or communities, in the case of his study of a *favela* in Rio de Janeiro, can create legal systems in opposition to, or parasitic upon, that of the state. (See further B. de Souza Santos, *Towards a New Common Sense: Law, Science and Politics in Paradigmatic Transition*, New York: Routledge, 1995.) Wallis described the Org in Scientology as 'an elaborate and imposing bureaucratic structure' (R. Wallis, *The Road to Total Freedom*, London: Heinemann, 1976, p. 132). Courts have noted that Scientologists talk about their internal structures in legal terms such as laws and courts. (See, for example, *Hubbard v. Vosper* [1972] 2 Queen's Bench 84 at p. 99C-D) [1972] 2 Queen's Bench 84 at p. 99C-D.) Perhaps, in the light of de Souza Santos' definition, we should study Scientology's law (or the law of other New Religious Movements) in the same way that we study English law.

19 St John A. Robilliard, *Religion and Law: Religious Liberty in Modern English Law*, Manchester: Manchester University Press, 1984; A. Bradney, *Religions, Rights and Laws*, Leicester: Leicester University Press, 1993. Since then Carolyn Hamilton has published *Family, Law and Religion*, London: Sweet and Maxwell, 1995. A book by Peter Edge is currently in preparation.

20 Geoffrey Wilson, Professor of Law at the University of Warwick, once wrote '[t]he words "English legal scholarship" though high sounding have a similar function to the words "disposable paper cup". Each adjective strengthens the message that one cannot expect much in terms of long-term quality or utility from it' (G. Wilson, 'English Legal Scholarship', *Modern Law Review*, 50, 1987, at p. 819).

21 In the USA the First Amendment to the Constitution provides this focus and there is a wealth of legal writing on the subject.

22 *The Times*, 14 August 1984.

23 Per Scrutton J in *Re Carroll* [1931] 1 King's Bench 317 at p. 336.

24 Per Cross J in *Neville Estates Ltd v. Madden* [1961] 3 All England Reports 769 at p. 781.

25 Although, even on this established view, one would have to add so long as the New Religious Movement is a religion. This is an important caveat since the law does not always treat New Religious Movements as religions. (See, for example, *R v. Registrar General ex parte Segerdal* [1970] 2 Queen's Bench 697.)

26 J. Rawls, 'The Priority of the Rights and Ideas of the Good', *Philosophy and Public Affairs*, 17, 1988, at p. 262.

27 W. Sadurski, *Moral Pluralism and Legal Neutrality*, Dordrecht: Kluwer, 1990, p. 167.

28 Ibid.

29 Sir Charles Gordon (ed.), *Erskine May's Treatise on the Law, Privileges, Proceedings and Usages of Parliament*, London: Butterworths, 20th edition, 1983, pp. 4–5.

30 But not all. The Sikh case for exemption from the provision requiring those using motor-cycles to wear crash-helmets was made by Sidney Bidwell MP (*Hansard*, Standing Committee F, 23 June 1976, col. 6).

31 Thus, for example, the former Chief Rabbi, Lord Jakobovits, would comment on legislation citing at least his authority as a rabbi if not as a Chief Rabbi. (See, for

example, *Hansard,* House of Lords, vol. 496, cols 418–21 commenting on the Education Reform Bill 1988).

32  Wallis divides up New Religious Movements into three types, world-accommo-dating, world-affirming or world-rejecting (R. Wallis, *The Elementary Forms of the New Religious Life*, London: Routledge and Kegan Paul, 1984, pp. 35–6).

33  P. Regan, 'The 1986 Shops Bill', *Parliamentary Affairs*, 41, 1988, p. 218.

34  Although it can have important consequences. The then Bishop of London was, for example, partially responsible for the major reforms to religious education contained in the Education Reform Act 1988. See C. Alves, 'Just a Matter of Words? The Religious Education Debate in the House of Lords', *British Journal of Religious Education*, 13, 1991, p. 168.

35  Per Latey J in *Re B and G* [1985] Family Law Reports 134 at p. 157.

36  Ibid. at p. 135.

37  *Re B and G* [1985] Family Law Reports 493 at p. 502.

38  Per Lord Denning in *Hubbard v. Vosper* [1972] 2 Queen's Bench 84 at p. 96. Megaw LJ noted that Hubbard's counsel had not been briefed about material to defend the bona fides of Scientology in his judgment (*Hubbard v. Vosper*, op. cit., p. 100).

39  *Wright v. Wright*(1981) 2 Family Law Reports 276 at pp. 277–8. See also Sir George Baker's comment that 'no court could possibly say, or would think of beginning to say, that...children should not be brought up as Jehovah's Witnesses' (*T v. T* (1974) 4 Family Law 190 at p. 191).

40  This judgment is a High Court decision, a level of decision which is commonly reported. However, this particular decision has, to date, remained unreported and is not even available on the LEXIS database. My comments are made on the basis of a transcript of the decision supplied to me by The Family.

41  John Saliba has commented that 'there is little doubt that the Children of God/The Family has been one of the most controversial new religious groups since its appearance in the late 1960s' (J. Saliba, 'Scholarly Studies on the Children of God/The Family: A Comprehensive Survey', in J. Lewis and J. Gordon Melton (eds), *Sex, Slander and Salvation: Investigating The Family/Children of God*, Stanford, CA: Center for Academic Publication, 1994, p. 165.

42  P. 8, p. 24 and p. 30 in the court transcript.

43  'Laws are made for the government of actions, and while they cannot interfere with mere religious belief and opinions, they may with practices', *Reynolds v. United States*, quoted in L. Pfeffer, *Religious Freedom*, Skokie: National Textbook Company, 1977, p. 33.

44  *Buckley v. Buckley*(1973) 3 Family Law 106.

45  S. Cretney, *Principles of Family Law*, London: Sweet and Maxwell, 1974, p. 292.

46  *Custody after Divorce*, Oxford: Oxford Centre for Socio-Legal Studies, 1977, p. 74.

47  *Buckley v. Buckley*, op. cit. at p.107.

48  See *Re H* (1981) 2 Family Law Reports 253.

49  *Hewison v. Hewison* (1977) 7 Family Law 207.

50  *McKechnie v. McKechnie* (1990) Scottish Law Times (Sh C) 75.

51  *Wright v. Wright* (1981) 2 Family Law Reports 276 at pp. 277–8.

52  An adverse report can result in a school being removed from the register of inde-pendent schools. Continuing to operate such a school would be a criminal offence (s 70(3) Education Act 1944).

53  'Report on Chaitanya College: 24–5 May 1983', London: Department of Education and Science, 1983, p. 8.

54  Chaitanya College was sold in 1984 (K. Knott, *My Sweet Lord*, Wellingborough: Aquarian Press, 1986, p. 46).

55 A more complete examination of the legal privileges accorded to taxes is to be found in S. Bright, 'Charities and Trust for the Public Benefit – Time for a Rethink?', *Conveyancer and Property Lawyer*, 53, 1989, at pp. 29–31. See also St John Robilliard, *Religion and Law*, op. cit., pp. 68–73.

56 Although the Charity Commissioners have said registration as a charity does not indicate that the Commissioners approve of the charity's objects. (ibid., p. 66).

57 M. Blakeny, 'Sequestered Piety and Charity – A Comparative Analysis', *Journal of Legal History*, 2, 1981, at p. 211.

58 See, for example, D. Hayton (ed.), *Hayton and Marshall: Cases and Commentary on the Law of Trusts*, London: Sweet and Maxwell, 9th edn, 1991, p. 329.

59 Per Lord Denning in *R v Registrar General ex parte Segerdal* [1970] 2 Queen's Bench 697 at p. 707.

60 Per Harman LJ in *Re Pinion* [1965] Chancery 85 at p. 105.

61 *Charity Law and Voluntary Organisations (The Goodman Report)*, London: Bedford Square Press, 1976, p. 24.

62 H. Picarda, 'New Religions as Charities', *New Law Journal*, 131, 1983, 436.

63 *Report of the Charity Commissioners for England and Wales for the Year 1982* (1983, HC 370 paras 36–8 and Appendix C).

64 *Church of the New Faith v. Pay Roll Tax Commissioners*, Australian Journal Law Reports, 57, 1983, 785 at p. 808.

65 Ibid., p. 796.

66 K. Knott, *Religion and Identity, and the Study of Ethnic Minority Religions in Britain*, Leeds: University of Leeds Community Religions Project, 1986, p. 4.

67 A. Dummett, 'Race, Culture and Moral Education', *Journal of Moral Education*, 15(10), 1986, pp. 12–13.

68 See, for example, E. Barker, *The Making of a Moonie*, Oxford: Basil Blackwell, 1984, p. 124.

69 J. Rath, K. Groenendijk and R. Penninx, 'The Recognition and Institutionalisation of Islam in Belgium, Great Britain and the Netherlands', *New Community*, 18(101), 1991, p. 102.

70 S. Akhtar, *Be Careful with Muhammad!*, London: Bellew Publishing, 1989, p. 37. See also R. Webster, *A Brief History of Blasphemy*, Southwold: The Orwell Press, 1990.

71 B. Wilson, *Religion in Sociological Perspective*, Oxford: Oxford University Press, 1982, p. 133.

72 J. Beckford and M. Levasseur, 'New Religious Movements in Western Europe', in J. Beckford (ed.), *New Religious Movements and Rapid Social Change*, London: Sage, 1986, p. 34.

73 P. 39 in the original judgment.

74 P. 269 in the original judgment.

75 For a more detailed analysis of *Re ST (A Minor)* see A. Bradney 'Children of a Newer God', in S. Palmer and C. Hardman, *Children in New Religious Movements*, New Brunswick: Rutgers University Press (forthcoming).

76 E. Barker, *New Religious Movements: A Practical Introduction*, London: Her Majesty's Stationery Office, 1989, p. vii.

77 *Roughley v. Roughley* (1973) 4 Family Law 91 at p. 92, *Re M* [1967] 3 All England Reports 1071 at p. 1073.

78 *T v. T* (1974) 4 Family Law 190 at 191, *Re H* (1981) 2 Family Law Reports 253 at p. 260. *Re K* 28 March 1996 (this latter case is unreported but is available on the LEXIS database).

79 The case was the result of an application for a writ of habeus corpus by Unification Church applicants who contended that a 28-year-old woman had been kidnapped in order to get her away from the Unification Church. The court refused to make an order (*The Times*, 29 April 1982).

80  See, for example, the evidence in *Re B and G*, op. cit. *Re ST (A Minor)*, discussed above is an exception to this general rule. In addition to other witnesses 30 members of The Family and seven expert witnesses testified about the beliefs and practices of The Family. As a result of the case, perhaps surprisingly in the light of previous cases, the child who was the subject of the wardship action remained in the care and control of her mother and in The Family group in which she had been living.

81  A. Bradney, *Religions*, op. cit., p. 158.

82  Under Article 18 of the Universal Declaration of Human Rights and Article 9 of the European Convention on Human Rights.

83  S 7 Sex Discrimination Act 1975; s 5 Race Relations Act 1976.

84  See P. van Dijk and G. van Hoof, *Theory and Practice of the European Court of Human Rights*, Dervent: Kluwer, 1990, 2nd edn, pp. 397–407 and F. Jacobs and R. White, *The European Convention on Human Rights*, Oxford: Clarendon Press, 1996, 2nd edn, pp. 211–21.

85  Under clause 2 United Kingdom courts are required to 'take into account' the previous decisions of the European Court of Human Rights.

86  Clause 2(4).

87  In considering a case where a lesbian sought custody of her child Ormrod L J stated: 'It is quite obvious that their [the lesbian couple's] lives are highly abnormal. It is simple common sense to say that children ought to have a more normal life in a more normal family' (*W v. W* unreported, 4 November 1976).

88  Sadurski, op. cit., p. 196.

89  A. Stillman, 'Legislating for Choice', in M. Flude and M. Hammer (eds), *The Education Reform Act 1988*, London: Falmer Press, 1990, p. 88.

# Summary of Chapter 5

The vast majority of the general public, including those who take up strongly hostile attitudes towards NRMs, acquire such information as they have and the attitudes that they embrace from the media. Of all social institutions, the media have been most directly and vociferously concerned with new movements, and Professor James Beckford brings out the crucial role which they have played in stimulating controversy and feeding the anti-cult movement with accounts prejudicial to NRMs and often prejudicial to religion in general. Without suggesting anything in the nature of connivance, Professor Beckford indicates the ways in which journalistic interests demand controversial issues which plays into the hands of committed anti-cultists.

# 5 The mass media and New Religious Movements [1]

## James A. Beckford

## Introduction

One of the reasons why some rationalists dislike religion is that it is apparently inseparable from violent conflict.[2] The history of religious wars in Europe and Latin America in particular has often served as a justification for abandoning religion altogether. In fact, many heirs of the various Enlightenments have confidently believed that the demise of religious belief and practice would entail a lessening of social conflict. Indeed, there is an expectation that religion will cease to be a source of conflict in a largely secular society. I want to argue, on the contrary, that the very opposite has occurred in countries where reported levels of religious beliefs and belonging have been declining for many decades but where unconventional New Religious Movements have developed.

My argument is paradoxical. It suggests that some aspects of religion have become more controversial and conflictual for the very reason that general levels of religious understanding and practice are so low. Unconventional forms of religion have become especially problematic at a time when large numbers of people find even the most conventional religion alien. In these circumstances, it is the new and unusual kinds of religious groups which encounter most hostility. In their turn, these controversial groups have sometimes exacerbated matters by responding with even more hostility towards their detractors. This vicious spiral has occasionally erupted into massive conflicts and bloodshed. Jonestown in 1978 and Waco in 1993 are the most tragic examples. But I believe that there are also echoes of this process to be heard in the suspicions frequently voiced by the nominally Christian public in the UK about non-Christian minorities. Tariq Modood's characterisation of this phenomenon as 'cultural racism' is challenging but not unproblematic.[3] My concern focuses on the part played by journalists in conflicts involving so-called cults, i.e. those New Religious Movements (NRMs) which have been outstandingly controversial since their emergence in the West in the 1960s. A central theme will be that there are connections between the low-level prejudice displayed against so-called cults in everyday journalism and the spectacular conflicts which erupt from time to time around controversial NRMs.

## Controversial cults

It is not difficult to see why many of the NRMs which emerged in the USA and Western Europe in the 1960s, such as Scientology, the Unification Church[4] ('Moonies'), the International Society for Krishna Consciousness ('Hare Krishna') and the Children of God (now called 'The Family'), quickly became controversial. First, the simple fact that so many of them seemed to arrive at roughly the same time was enough to persuade some people that a new 'invasion of the body snatchers' had occurred. Second, the movements which drew on Asian philosophies and cultures tended to arouse suspicions merely for being foreign and therefore perceived as threatening. Third, the people who were targeted by the new movements were mainly young, relatively well educated, middle-class students. They were not down-and-outs or obviously deprived. This meant that their aggrieved relatives and former friends tended to have the money, connections and confidence required to make their complaints heard in centres of influence and power, at least at local levels.[5]

The list of complaints voiced against controversial NRMs grew so long that anti-cult organisations began to emerge in the early 1970s to combat what they considered to be a major menace to young people.[6] Allegations of economic exploitation, mental cruelty, the deliberate alienation of recruits from their families, deceptive recruiting practices, harmful diets and life-styles, sexual abuse and, of course, brainwashing were widespread. The high-water mark of anti-cult feeling probably occurred in the late 1970s following the death of more than 900 followers of the Revd Jim Jones at Jonestown, Guyana. This was also the period of the most rapid growth in membership of the most notorious cults.

Yet, for all the hostility and suspicion expressed towards NRMs at that time, only a tiny proportion of the population of any Western country had ever had any direct contact with any of the movements. Of course, some people came to know about them in the course of trying to 'rescue' relatives or friends from the movements' clutches. But very few people attended NRM meetings or read their literature. Nevertheless, the movements' noto-riety was confirmed many times by opinion polls which showed cult leaders to be among the most strongly disliked celebrities of their time.[7]

My own research into cult controversies was able to confirm that even people directly affected by NRMs relied for their information overwhelm-ingly on the mass media. Very few people managed or tried to contact the movements directly. Instead, they preferred to contact journalists who had published stories about the movements. Indeed, the secretiveness or defen-siveness of most controversial cults helped journalists to play a crucial role as go-betweens and arbitrators between NRMs, their members and angry outsiders. Only ex-members could rival the privileged position of a few investigative journalists; but most ex-members were understandably reluctant to talk freely about their former commitments. In these circumstances, the role of groups in the anti-cult movement (ACM) has assumed significant proportions.[8] Cult controversies cannot be properly understood unless the symbiotic relationship between these anti-cult groups and journalists is taken into account. In the cases of France and Switzerland, for example, the tendency has been for the mass media to reflect the views of the ACM or of lawyers rather than of relevant academic experts.[9] The same point has been made about Australia and the USA.[10]

## The anti-cult movement

Some anti-cult movement organisations have become influential and powerful enough to have the sympathetic ear of politicians, leading church representatives and sections of the medical and psychiatric establishments. National-level organisations have consolidated themselves, and cross-national links are slowly emerging. In short, today's ACM is much more substantial and effective than the predominantly conservative evangelical 'counter-cult' movement directed against sectarianism and marginal versions of Christianity.[11] Moreover, Jehovah's Witnesses and Christian Scientists, for example, have always been the target of critical attacks mounted by representatives of mainstream churches, and these large sectarian organisations have also had to contend with the aggressive criticism that disgruntled ex-members have showered on them. Yet, these 'established sects'[12] have rarely had to cope with the incessant barrage of highly public and politicised attacks that the ACM now routinely directs against NRMs.[13]

The fact that the ACM's dismissal of NRMs is not based on primarily theological considerations and that the aim is not usually to convert members into mainstream Christians enhances the movement's appeal to journalists. The latter find the ACM useful precisely because it attacks the very existence and *modus operandi* of NRMs without appearing to draw on doctrinal issues. It is actually common for the ACM's activists to disclaim any 'religious' intent or any animus against religion as such. They prefer the strategy of exposing alleged illegality and exploitation in NRMs. In other words, the critics' aim is to disqualify 'cults' from the category of 'religion' altogether, thereby framing cult-related problems as 'economic', 'political' or 'psychological'. The media hysteria that surrounded the rumour of the suicide of members of the Great White Brotherhood in the Ukraine in November 1993 reflected a closely related aspect of journalism, namely, ignorance or misunderstanding of NRMs' teachings. Borenstein[14] explains clearly how journalists and critics of 'cults' mistook some obscure statements made by Maria Devi Khristos, the movement's self-proclaimed Messiah, as evidence of suicidal intentions. There were also wildly inaccurate estimates of the number of her followers.

Ironically, conspiracy thinking seemed to pervade the movement *and* its critics, for:

> like the White Brotherhood, the cult's critics were more than willing to assume that 'dark forces' were secretly working toward mysterious ends. At the same time that the journalists marvelled at young people's capacity to accept the [movement's] doctrine...the majority of the reporters who covered the phenomenon proved only scarcely less prepared to suspend their belief.[15]

Nor was the misunderstanding confined to Ukrainian and Russian journalists. The same mistakes were reproduced by writers for the *New York Times*[16] and *Le Figaro*.[17]

As I argued earlier, part of the success of the ACM is due to the high degree of religious illiteracy or the simple lack of familiarity with things religious among the nominally religious sections of most advanced industrial societies. It can therefore trade on fear of the unknown at a time when so few young adults have any experience of 'normal' religion with which they can realistically compare NRMs. As a result, it is not difficult to catch the popular imagination with allegations of a sci-fi nature about the supposedly weird and dangerous goings-on inside cults. Journalists find this approach to NRMs virtually irresistible, even though, according to McDonnell,[18] 'Religion does not fit easily into the dominant world-view of most contemporary broadcasters who are often ill prepared to deal with religion, being indifferent, or occasionally, actively hostile.' At least, sensational stories about NRMs require no knowledge of religion on the part of journalists, readers or audiences. The focus on the non-religious aspects of the movements means that there is no need to tackle issues of religious belief or experience. And the parallels that are emphasised with stories of fraud and exploitation in politics, business and crime provide the audience with a recognisable script. In short, the ACM presents journalists with material which needs very little adaptation before it can be easily digested by consumers with little taste for religion – let alone religious controversies. In this sense, it is not difficult for journalists to deal with religion,[19] especially when they concentrate on expressions of religion which challenge or lie outside the scope of conventional ideas or practices. Indeed, the very controversial character of some religious phenomena is helpful to journalists because conflict can easily be made to serve as the thematic 'line' of a story. Thus, although journalists may feel uncomfortable having to report on, for example, angry protests against publication of Salman Rushdie's novel, *The Satanic Verses*, which call their own professional objectivity into question, the story-line conforms readily with the 'script' of social and cultural conflicts.

Before I analyse the ways in which the mass media's tendency to portray NRMs as controversial helps to generate and perpetuate conflict[20] I should like to insert a note of caution. I want to warn against a tendency which is marked in some academic writing about NRMs. There is a tendency to discuss NRMs in isolation and to overlook the fact that many other social phenomena, including other religious phenomena, are also reported unfairly in the mass media. For example, Meg Carter's (1995) feature article in the *Independent* on the growth of independent religious broadcasting stations in the United Kingdom claimed that journalists and programme-makers tend to be biased against religion.[21] She quoted a spokesperson for Ahmadiyya Muslim TV as claiming that, 'Only extremist ideas are newsworthy to mainstream media.' The same article also explains that this exclusive concern with extremism has made religious organisations defensive about journalists. According to Francis Goodwin, the founder of Christians in Media, 'There is a paranoia because nine-tenths of churches' contact with the media comes when they are caught on the back foot, defending themselves against something in the *News of the World*.'[22]

There is nothing particularly new about the claim that the media portrayal of virtually *all* religion tends towards the sensational, but the point needs emphasising here for two reasons. The first is that an exclusive focus on the tribulations of NRMs runs the risk of sounding like one-off special pleading or whingeing on their behalf. This only reinforces the impression that NRMs are deviant and therefore in need of special treatment. The second reason for not isolating NRMs for analytical purposes is that comparison with journalists' treatment of other phenomena can strengthen the case for demanding more professional conduct from them. Comparative studies of the media's portrayal of NRMs and of other controversial phenomena might be rewarding.

Let me give a comparative example. It is well known that journalists' reporting of crime and of court cases is uneven. Careful empirical research conducted in Scotland confirmed that a major distortion takes place: crimes involving physical violence are over-represented in Scottish newspapers by 22 per cent, and crimes involving indecency are over-represented by 13 per cent.[23] Most other types of crime are under-represented in newspaper reports. The conclusion is that journalists are selective about crime reporting and significantly biased towards the reporting of crimes of violence and indecency. We need to bear these, and similar, findings in mind when considering the unquestionably unfair reporting of NRMs' activities. Sensationalism is not the exclusive preserve of 'cult controversies'.

## The portrayal of NRMs in the mass media

### Conflict and newsworthiness

The most elementary observation about print and broadcast media's portrayal of NRMs is that the movements' activities are newsworthy only when conflicts are involved. In the quarter of a century that I have been studying NRMs in Western Europe, North America, and Japan, I have rarely found articles or programmes which did not use conflict as (a) the main occasion for the portrayal and (b) as the principal means of structuring the account. Even those accounts which aspire towards a balanced, i.e. two-sided, presentation of the issues tend nevertheless to allow the conflictual aspects to predominate. 'Cults are problematic' is the inescapable refrain of this type of journalism.[24] The audience very rarely has the opportunity to receive information about NRMs which is unrelated to conflict. The movements are only in the news when conflict is involved; and conflict concerning one movement is pounced on as an excuse for investigating all the other movements in the catch-all category of 'cults'. The aftermath of Waco was full of stories along the lines of the *Boston Globe*'s 'If you think Waco, Texas was bad, consider who could be next'.[25]

These stories about the so-called cult menace are as much about speculation as about news. They use events relating to one particular movement as a platform from which to launch 'scare' stories about the possible threat that the entire category of cults represents for other people in other places. This was an especially noticeable feature of reporting in Western European papers about the siege at Waco. In the absence, day after day, of new facts about the Branch Davidians, journalists from various countries turned to the questions of whether a comparable problem could occur in their own countries and whether the authorities there ought to be taking pre-emptive steps to avert such a possibility. Opinions were divided, but the view which prevailed was that the problem of armed cultists was a uniquely American phenomenon. Nevertheless, there was also a strong note of warning against the risk of allowing a similar conflict to develop in European countries. Vigilance was the order of the day. The virtual globalisation of mass communications thereby helps journalists to frame NRMs as primarily conflictual even in countries where the movements are virtually unknown or unproblematic.

### Conflict as the leitmotiv

Conflict is the leitmotiv which connects journalistic portrayals of NRMs. This is evident in the extensive use that journalists and programme producers make of the 'negative summary event'.[26] This is the practice of creating continuity between episodic (especially slow-moving) stories by adding a capsule summary of the negative features of the phenomenon which is in focus. This reminds the audience of the sequence of reported events into which the current story can be slotted. It also stamps a particular 'mood' on the story even if the very latest episode has not been primarily about conflict. For example, brief news reports about NRMs' attempts to buy residential property or to open new centres are often accompanied by longer 'reminders' of the movements' past conflicts and problems. What should be the most bland and innocent new items are thereby framed in a threatening fashion. And, according to Roland Campiche,[27] a Swiss television channel opened its programme on 'cults' in January 1996 by insisting that everybody was directly affected by them because 'this can happen to you too'. In a detailed analysis of French-language media construction of 'cults', following the murder–suicide of members of the Order of the Solar Temple (OST) at Cheiry and Salvan, Campiche[28] emphasised the indiscriminate way in which journalists used the term 'cult' and attributed mental instability to OST members without, however, stimulating a debate about the issues.

### Cross-references to conflict

A third aspect of the journalistic construction of cult conflicts is that stories are frequently cross-referenced to other mass media items. TV programmes, for example, use still shots of newspaper and magazine headlines as devices for emphasising shock and horror. Similarly, the still photographs of cult leaders which are sometimes used in TV programmes are shown staring out of the pages of the print media. Presumably the intention is to try to enhance the sense of realism and veracity by showing that stories about a particular NRM or leader have already appeared in the print media and must therefore be true. Since the information and images that are 'quoted' in this way between different stories and/or media tend to be overwhelmingly unflattering and critical, the effect is likely to reinforce the generally negative image of NRMs. In turn, this hardens public opinion against the movements and fuels the anti-cult campaigns. Yet, the extent to which the aftermath of the Aum Shinrikyō tragedy was reported in sensational and voyeuristic terms in Japan provoked critical responses, especially when television broadcasts repeatedly showed footage of the murder of one of the movement's top leaders at the hands of an assassin with gangster connections.[29] There were also complaints about the fact that television broadcasts frequently gave opportunities for the movement's executives to proclaim their innocence to a public audience. These appearances 'became so popular that fan clubs sprang up', according to Ishii.[30]

An allied feature of the reporting of cult-related conflicts in which the journalists have difficulty gaining access to relevant material is that they tend to substitute their own operation for the ostensibly central subject. This was especially clear in the case of Waco where access to the Branch Davidian compound was denied to journalists. The focus of many stories therefore became the media circus on the compound's perimeter. The fact that so many journalists were present seemed to guarantee the importance of the event at moments when nothing significant appeared to be happening. Writing stories about the stories being written by other journalists took the place of direct reports on the siege of the Branch Davidians. Perhaps this practice also helps journalists to cope with the competition for customers between different publications or programmes. They can keep a story running despite the lack of directly relevant material.

### Conflict feeds on stories of conflict

The next point is that, just as anti-cult activists commonly supply journalists with negative copy about NRMs, the hostile depictions of the movements in the mass media are then recycled as further evidence in the anti-cult propaganda campaigns.[31] There is in fact a mutually beneficial and reinforcing dynamic at work. It is difficult for NRM leaders or for disinterested parties to break into this cosy circle in order to challenge or correct the dominant imagery. Given the public's heavy reliance on the mass media for information about unconventional religion, the close alliance between the ACMs and journalists makes it unlikely that non-controversial, neutral or favourable material about NRMs could be published or broadcast.

The logic of suspicion which turns many investigative journalists into allies of the ACM helps to set the scene for the official agents of control. Knowing that the public has a very poor opinion of NRMs, largely as a result of stereotyping in the mass media, police officers do not take much of a risk if they take high-handed action against these unpopular movements. Journalists function as the principal gatekeepers of public opinion especially on matters with which the person-in-the-street is not normally familiar. Their overwhelmingly critical portrayal of the movements can therefore contribute indirectly towards the latter's control. Indeed, as many informed commentators on the débâcle at Waco have pointed out, the FBI, the US Department of Justice, journalists and programme-makers all tended to favour the testimony of psychological experts whose anti-cult views were well known in advance.[32] One of the many scandalous aspects of the whole affair was the studied refusal to give credence to the testimony of sociological, anthropological, historical and theological experts on controversial NRMs. Very few scholars with first-hand experience of researching these movements in their natural settings over many years would have advocated or supported the strategy and tactics adopted by the Bureau of Alcohol, Tobacco and Firearms (BATF) and the FBI. Instead, the authorities gave credence selectively to opinions rooted in individualistic abnormal psychology. This is always newsworthy, as was shown by the all-consuming fascination with the psychological condition of David Koresh. By contrast, the strictly social dynamics of exclusive, high-demand religious groups and the cultural force of apocalyptic millennialism were absent from the mass media coverage. Similar observations have been made about the lack of attention to the views of relevant academic experts in media coverage of the Solar Temple deaths and the Heaven's Gate suicides.[33]

### Conflicts, journalists and control

If the mass media portrayals of NRMs, based mainly on the one-sided evidence supplied by activists in the ACM, are sufficiently numerous and disturbing, there is a strong probability that social control agents will have to be seen to respond. Legislators and police officials in particular find themselves under pressure to say what they intend to do about the alleged wrongdoings and outrages perpetrated by cults. 'Could Jonestown happen in Britain?' or 'What are you doing to prevent another Waco happening here?' are the kind of questions put with monotonous frequency to officials in the wake of those two tragedies. Journalists seem to be relatively uninterested in the specific circumstances which led to such spectacular disasters. Instead, all the emphasis is on the *presumed and unquestioned* resemblance between the People's Temple or the Branch Davidians and 'cults' in the journalists' own countries. The authorities are forced to respond to these leading questions and are not given the opportunity to express doubts or reservations about the practice of 'lumping all cults together'.[34]

This dramatisation of the situation increases public nervousness and official defensiveness, neither of which is conducive to clear thinking and fairness. There is a danger, then, that inadvisable, panic reactions may follow. In the case of the Branch Davidians, for example:

> The ante at Waco was upped because of the intervention of television reporting. Lives were endangered because the story line was created and embedded in a pernicious dualism which legitimated the 'authorities' and discouraged unconventional perspectives and opinions. The shared mentality – the corporate mentality – was served as the cultural mainstream was reinforced, not challenged.
>
> Waco's Branch Davidians, then, were victims of a media-induced disaster, executed before the eyes of the nation on television. The polarisation that led to the catastrophe at Waco was inherent in neither the religious group itself – nor even in the FBI.[35]

Some commentators have blamed the editor of the *Waco Tribune-Herald* for running the first episode of a hard-hitting exposé of the Branch Davidians immediately prior to the BATF's assault on the compound. This allegedly broke an agreement with the BATF to withhold publication; and it probably forced the Bureau to take its ill-conceived action earlier than it had intended. On the other hand, it seems that the FBI placed considerably tighter restrictions on journalists covering the siege than is normal in similar events. In other words, the trade-off between journalists and authorities worked to the greater advantage of the latter.

Not enough attention has been given to the consequences of sensationalist depictions of religion in a secular age. To adapt the old adage, I am not trying to blame the messenger for bringing bad news but I *am* accusing the

messenger of fermenting mischief by relentlessly peddling negative stereotypes of NRMs.

### One conflict can hide another

Journalists' fascination with the tragedies of Jonestown and Waco stemmed
not only from the exotic and improbable details of the two communities'
ways of life but also from the suspicion that the cult controversies were only
the tip of the iceberg. Investigative journalists had a field day with their
inquiries into the possibility either that people in authority had bungled the
operations to prevent loss of life and/or that attempts had been made afterwards to cover up the errors made by the forces of order. In other words,
cult-related conflicts were connected with broader concerns about the use
and misuse of state power. This was especially evident in journalists'
accounts of the alleged ineffectiveness of Japanese police attempts to collect
evidence to connect the Sarin gas attacks in the Tokyo subway system to the
leaders of Aum Shinrikyō.[36]

Other examples of stories linking cults with conflicts against the state
include the bombing by police of the anarcho-ecology group, MOVE, in
Philadelphia on 13 May 1985; the killing by police in 1983 of all six followers
of Lindberg Sanders, a self-styled 'Black Jesus', in a shoot-out in Memphis;
and various armed assaults on dissident Mormons in Utah. The result is
usually a polarisation of journalistic and public opinion between, on the one
hand, the view that agents of the state acted negligently or illegally and, on
the other, the view that the same agents should have acted more decisively to
suppress the movement in question before the problem had become unman-
ageable by peaceful means. But the more general point is that it is invariably
the conflicts associated with NRMs which make them newsworthy even when
responsibility for the conflicts is attributable to the state.

An interesting twist on this theme quickly emerged in European print-
media accounts of Waco. The long and slow-moving story of the 51-day
siege provided an opportunity for journalists to investigate in depth the
issues of gun ownership and control in the USA. In fact, the amount of
attention devoted to this context of the action taken against the Branch
Davidians sometimes outweighed reports of events at Waco. The conflictual
image of cults was thereby reinforced by linking them with a separate
conflict about firearms. One conflict was 'nested' in another.

### Journalists and academic researchers

I now want to discuss some aspects of the relationship between journalistic and academic interests in NRMs. My remarks are an attempt to
place mass media portrayals of the movements in a broader context in the
hope that a clearer understanding will emerge of the differential difficulties facing journalists and academics. These two broad and heterogeneous

categories of people have different and equally legitimate reasons for wanting to know more about NRMs. But it may be naive and unhelpful to expect that they should share the same point of view or ultimately agree with one another.

The French statesman and scholar, Alexis de Tocqueville, was among the first to recognise in the mid-nineteenth century that newspapers, magazines and other printed media of communication would become more and more important to industrial societies. They would be important as replacements for 'parish pump politics' in an age of accelerating rates of social and geographical mobility. They would also act as a check on the power of politicians. They would therefore be essential to the stability and dynamism of democracy. But Tocqueville was equally far-sighted in his fears that the print-media might become an instrument of manipulation and tyranny. In fact, he had few illusions about democracy or about the temptations for democratic majorities to act and think in thoroughly oppressive and stifling ways. His only hope for the health of democracy rested on the criss-crossing, countervailing play of different interest groups and voluntary associations serviced by self-critical journalists and owners of the news media. No single group, majority or publication could be trusted to protect democracy from their separate selfish interests in controlling it.

Tocqueville's fears about the fragility of democracy have been echoed over the past 150 years by commentators from virtually every political persuasion. There is widespread agreement that free and lively media of mass communication are vital to the health of all societies. We are therefore in the debt of journalists. But, just as importantly, we must not become dependent on them. Non-journalists need to keep a critical distance from their work and to maintain a constant dialogue with them. Let me try to substantiate these general arguments by reference to the different interests that journalists and academic researchers typically have in NRMs. I shall analyse three dimensions on which the interests of journalists and researchers tend to be sharply different, whilst also insisting that each of these two categories of professional 'knowledge workers' is diverse.

### Time

For a variety of good reasons, very few journalists can afford to work on items about NRMs for longer than each 'cult controversy' lasts. This is because the owners and managers of the mass media lose their audience if the focus is not kept on 'newsworthy' stories. NRMs are only newsworthy when a problem occurs. Scandals, atrocities, spectacular failures, 'tug-of-love' stories, defections, exposés, outrageous conduct – these are the main criteria of NRMs' newsworthiness. And they tend to generate news stories and television documentaries that present the issues in terms of a polarisation between favourable and unfavourable attitudes towards 'cults'.[37] When the controversy has passed, the journalists usually have to move on to other stories. As

Wright[38] has argued, however, it is uncommon for journalists to report the concluding stages of stories which show that NRMs were not guilty of the criminal or immoral charges on which the stories were based in the first instance. He calls this 'front end/back end disproportionality'. As a result, the public rarely learns about the collapse of legal cases against NRMs or the withdrawal of accusations against them. The impression of guilt therefore lingers in public opinion. Exceptions may occur, of course, when a journalist takes time out, for example, to compile a book-length publication. But even then, the structure of journalists' books tends to reflect the same criteria of newsworthiness. And, of course, the unspectacular, non-sensational NRMs are permanently invisible in journalists' accounts.

Not only is the time that most journalists can afford to spend on 'cult' stories very limited but, equally important, there is formidable pressure on journalists and programme makers to produce their work quickly in order to be competitive in the media market. They are under pressure to provide 'instant explanations'.[39] Since they often lack the time to consult more than a few informants, it is understandable that they prefer the testimony of outspoken and willing informants who tend to take extreme positions either for or against NRMs. Journalistic stories have little place for reservations, nuances and careful comparison. But Silk (1995, 1997), Bunting (1997) and Dart (1997)[40] have explained the difficulties facing journalists who write about any kind of religion, including NRMs. In each case the explanation refers to commercial pressures and the need for journalists to be responsive to fast-moving events.

By comparison, academic researchers who are professionally concerned with NRMs tend to be just as interested in them when no controversies are apparent as when there is clear evidence of problems. This greater continuity of interest is dictated by the nature of scholars' interests and methods of research. They tend to ask questions about, for example, patterns of recruitment, retention and defection which can only be answered methodically on the basis of time-series data. Ideally, scholars also try to compare NRMs, to compare their operations in different countries, or to compare their operations in different periods of time. It is almost as if researchers considered the occasional cult controversy as a rude interruption of the routine life of NRMs – quite the opposite of most journalists. As a result, dull or boring NRMs could be just as exciting to academic researchers as the most eye-catching cult. The public may interpret academic interests in NRMs as a form of appeasement or as ivory tower indifference. Neither interpretation is fair.

## Objectivity

One person's objectivity is another person's bias. This is not a sign of cynical world-weariness on my part. It is a recognition that criteria of objectivity are variable and socially constructed. Everyone wants to be seen to be objective – but only in their own way.

How do journalists create objectivity? Their favourite strategy is to combine a dash of *vox populi* with a squirt of balance. The vox pop aspect usually consists of comments elicited from passers-by or by-standers. If these comments can be attributed to identifiable individuals, it heightens the appearance of verisimilitude and realism. Balance requires something more artful. It usually requires finding space for opposing views, in the belief that readers, listeners and viewers will mistake this adversarial structure for a representative sample of opinions. The journalist seems to have made obeisance to objectivity if a story or programme is not one-sided but two-sided. Arguments with more than two sides are usually considered too complicated for 'good' journalism. The inclusion of a non-committal contribution by an academic frequently serves as another journalistic device for constructing a kind of objectivity. It can be very uncomfortable being the filling in the sandwich!

There is no universally agreed version of objectivity among academics. And there are conflicts and tensions between academics about the objectivity of their work. But certain strategies are conventional. They include filtering out personal values and emotive language; basing findings on representative samples; comparing NRM members with matched samples of non-members; conducting research over relatively long periods of time; taking account of all available publications on a topic; and, in the sharpest contrast to journalists, participating in both mutual criticism and self-criticism. This list is far from exhaustive but it gives a clear enough indication of how academic researchers construct their versions of objectivity. It is unlikely that the items, individually or collectively, will be considered adequate grounds for objectivity in the eyes of non-academic critics.

### Practical and theoretical interests

As I indicated above, NRMs are interesting to journalists by reason of their newsworthiness as deviant, threatening, or simply weird. 'Cult' is therefore a self-contained and self-standing category which is of interest to the mass media for its own sake. Journalists need no other reason for writing about any particular NRM except that it is counted as a cult. This categorisation is sufficient to justify a story, especially if the story illustrates many of the other components which conventionally make up the 'cult' category. This puts pressure on journalists to find more and more evidence which conforms with the categorical image of cults and therefore confirms the idea that a NRM is newsworthy to the extent that it does match the category. It is no part of conventional journalistic practice to look for stories about NRMs which do *not* conform with the category of cult. Nor do journalists methodically chart the activities of NRMs which never display supposedly cultic tendencies. Journalists are in the business of, among other things, 'moral gatekeeping'. Gatekeepers do not need to concern themselves with people whose right to pass through their gates is not in moral question.

Self-critical academic researchers, on the other hand, question why and how particular moral boundaries are established and protected. The fact that some NRMs are newsworthy because they act illegally or immorally is not in itself sufficient reason to study them. It is much more likely that NRMs will be of interest to researchers because they represent part of a broader, theoretically interesting topic. NRMs may challenge, for example, prevailing sociological ideas about secularisation, the dilemmas of the liberal state, the limits of tolerance in democratic societies, the processes of religious conversion, the routinisation of charisma, and so on. In short, NRMs are interesting just as much for what they reveal about other aspects of society and culture as they are for what they reveal about themselves. And the interpretations that social scientists place on NRMs' activities are then subjected to constant criticism and testing.

## Conclusion

The mass media *can* function as one of the vital foundations of healthy democracies. But it would be a mistake to forget that they can also serve the interests of dominant groups by stifling new ideas and change. This is why portrayals of NRMs in the mass media tend to favour conservative, majoritarian distrust of novelty, dissidence, rebellion, or mere indifference. Nevertheless, journalists have on occasion played a significant role in exposing problems and scandals in NRMs and in putting pressure on errant movements to change their ways.[41] Egawa Shōko, for example, is one of the few Japanese journalists who issued warnings about the dangerous aspects of Aum Shinrikyō at a time when academic observers saw few problems with the movement.[42] It may also be true that 'While the more sensationalist sections of the media will continue to enjoy a "good" story, the more serious media have become more discerning of differences and have invited NRM representatives to present their own case.'[43] Stuart Wright[44] has also detected 'signs of improvement' in 'the general state of reporting on non-traditional religion'.

On the other hand, for the reasons that I have already discussed, the prevailing interest among journalists (or, at least, the owners and managers of the mass media) is not well adapted to the task of understanding NRMs as historically changing, but not always sensational, phenomena which reflect features of the societies and cultures in which they operate. In my opinion, the progressive growth of dispassionate, but compassionate, understanding of NRMs as social and cultural phenomena which are related in complicated ways to other phenomena is also a contribution towards a better society.

It might be tempting to conclude that journalists and academic researchers should work together in the best of all possible worlds. But the imbalance of power between them is too great for this to succeed. No, my proposal is that democratic, open societies require critical and self-critical scholarship as a counterbalance to the commercial and political forces which drive even the best journalists to limit the scope of their work on NRMs. We should not pin our hopes on the search for common ground between journalists and academic researchers. Instead, we should concentrate on improving our objective understanding of NRMs. The challenge is to counterpose information based on careful, critical scholarship to the generalisations and stereotypical images which all too often pass for 'in depth' journalism.

## Notes

1 I am grateful for permission to reprint the parts of this chapter that have appeared in the following publications: J. R. Lewis (ed.), *From the Ashes: Making Sense of Waco*, Rowman and Littlefield, 1994, pp. 143–9; *ISKCON Communications Journal*, 4, 1994, pp. 17–24; and R. Towler (ed.), *New Religions and the New Europe*, Aarhus: Aarhus University Press, 1995, pp. 99–111. I am also grateful for the criticisms offered by participants in the following meetings where earlier versions of this chapter were presented: International Conference on New Religions and the New Europe, INFORM, London, March 1993; International Conference on Religion and Conflict, Armagh City, Northern Ireland, May 1994; and the Graduate Seminar on New Religious Movements, London School of Economics, November 1995.

2 C. Candland, *The Spirit of Violence: An Interdisciplinary Bibliography of Religion and Violence*, Occasional Papers no. 6, New York: Harry Frank Guggenheim Foundation, 1992.

3 T. Modood, *Racial Equality, Colour, Culture and Justice*, London: Institute for Public Policy Research, 1994.

4 This movement is now called The Family Federation for World Peace and Unification.

5 J. A. Beckford, *Cult Controversies: Societal Responses to New Religious Movements*, London: Tavistock, 1985.

6 Anson D. Shupe, Jr and David G. Bromley, *The New Vigilantes: Deprogrammers, Anti-Cultists and the New Religions*, London and Los Angeles: Sage, 1980; Beckford, 1985, op. cit.; D.G. Bromley and A. Shupe, 'Anti-cultism in the United States: Origins, Ideology and Organizational Development', *Social Compass*, 42(2), 1995, pp. 221–36.

7 J.T. Richardson, 'Public Opinion and the Tax Evasion Trial of Reverend Moon', *Behavioural Sciences and Law*, 10(1), 1992, pp. 39–52.

8 Beckford, 1985, op. cit.; D. G. Bromley and A. Shupe, 'Organized Opposition to New Religious Movements', in D. G. Bromley and J. K. Hadden (eds), *The Handbook on Cults and Sects in America*, Greenwich, CT: JAI Press, 1993, pp. 177–98.

9 Françoise Champion and Martine Cohen, 'Les Sociologues et le problème des dites sectes', *Archives de Sciences Sociales des Religions*, (96), 1996, pp. 5–15; Roland Campiche, *Quand les sectes affolent*, Geneva: Labor et Fides, 1995; Roland Campiche, 'Le Traitement du religieux par les médias', *Etudes Théologiques et Religieuses*, 72(2), 1997, pp. 267–79.

10  J. T. Richardson, 'Journalistic bias toward new religious movements in Australia', *Journal of Contemporary Religion,* 11(3), 1996, pp. 289–302; J. T. Richardson, 'The accidental expert', *Nova Religio,* 2(1), 1998, pp. 31–43; J. T. Richardson and Barend van Driel, 'Journalists' Attitudes Toward New Religious Movements', *Review of Religious Research,* 39(2), 1997, pp. 116–36.

11  M. Introvigne, 'L'Evolution du "mouvement contre les sectes" chrétien 1978–1993', *Social Compass,* 42(2), 1995, pp. 237–47. See, as examples of mainstream Christian antipathy towards marginal movements, H. Davies, *Christian Deviations,* London: SCM Press, 1954; K. Hutten, *Seher, Grübler, Enthusiasten,* Stuttgart: Quellverlag, 1950; A. Hoekema, *The Four Major Cults,* Exeter: Paternoster Press, 1969; W. R. Martin, *The Rise of the Cults,* Grand Rapids: Zondervan, 1955.

12  J. M. Yinger, *The Scientific Study of Religion,* New York: Macmillan, 1970.

13  But see C. Wah, 'Religion as a Factor in Child Custody and Visitation Cases – Principles and Pitfalls', *American Journal of Family Law,* 6, 1992, pp. 159–66 for an indication of the kind of attacks frequently made on Jehovah's Witnesses.

14  E. Borenstein, 'Articles of Faith: The Media Response to Maria Devi Khristos', *Religion,* 25(3), 1995, pp. 249–66.

15  Ibid., p. 255.

16  *New York Times,* 13 November 1993.

17  *Le Figaro,* 14 November 1993.

18  J. McDonnell, 'Religion, Education and the Communication of Values', in C. Arthur (ed.), *Religion and the Media,* Cardiff: University of Wales Press, 1994, pp. 89–99.

19  Ibid.

20  My analysis is based partly on a systematic scrutiny of print-media items about NRMs in selected newspapers and magazines in the UK between 1975 and 1985 and partly on a thorough but more impressionistic study of the portrayal of NRMs in British, American and French newspapers and magazines since 1985.

21  M. Carter, 'Making Every Day a Sunday', *Independent,* 21 November 1995, p. 16.

22  Ibid.

23  J. Ditton and J. Duffy, 'Bias in the Newspaper Reporting of Crime News', *British Journal of Criminology,* 23(2), 1983, pp. 159–65.

24  J. A. Beckford and M. Cole, 'British and American Responses to New Religious Movements', *Bulletin of the John Rylands University Library of Manchester,* 70(3), 1988, pp. 209–24; J. A. Beckford, 'The Media and New Religious Movements', in J. R. Lewis (ed.), *From the Ashes: Making Sense of Waco,* Lanham, MD: Rowman and Littlefield, 1994, pp. 143–8; B. van Driel and J.T. Richardson, 'Print Media Coverage of New Religious Movements: A Longitudinal Study', *Journal of Communications,* 38(3), 1988a, pp. 37–61; B. van Driel and J. T. Richardson, 'The Categorization of New Religious Movements in American Print Media', *Sociological Analysis,* 49(2), 1988b, pp. 171–83; B. van Driel and J. T. Richardson, 'Journalist attitudes toward New Religious Movements', paper presented at the CIS conference, Helskinki, 1989; B. van Driel and J. van Belzen, 'The Downfall of Rajneeshpuram in the Print Media', *Journal for the Scientific Study of Religion,* 29(10), 1990, pp. 76–90.

25  Quoted by I. L. Maffett, 'Waco and the *War of the Worlds*: Media Fantasy and Modern Reality', in Lewis, op. cit., p.159.

26  K. E. Rosengren, P. Arviddsson and D. Sturesson, 'The Barsebäck "Panic": A Case of Media Deviance', in C. Winick (ed.), *Deviance and Mass Media,* Beverly Hills: Sage, 1978, pp. 131–49; Beckford, 1985, op. cit.

27  Campiche, 1997, op. cit., p. 272.

28  Campiche, 1995, op. cit.

29 Ian Reader, *A Poisonous Cocktail? Aum Shinrikyo's Path to Violence*, Copenhagen: NIAS, 1996.

30 K. Ishii, 'Aum Shinrikyo', in *Religion in Japanese Culture*, edited by N. Tamaru and D. Reid, Tokyo: Kodansha International, 1996, pp. 213–14.

31 The regular newsletter of FAIR, the main ACM in Britain, devotes a great deal of space to print and broadcast reports of problems concerning NRMs. There is no evidence that these reports are checked for accuracy or bias. It is enough that they have appeared in print.

32 Lewis, op. cit.; Stuart Wright (ed.), *Armageddon in Waco*, Chicago: University of Chicago Press, 1995.

33 Majella Franzmann, 'Mad, Bad, or Just Invisible? Studies in Religion and "Fringe" Religions', *Australian Religion Studies Review*, 10(2), 1997, pp. 5–12.

34 Eileen Barker, *New Religious Movements: A Practical Introduction*, London: HMSO, 1989.

35 C. A. Jones and G. Baker, 'Television and Metaphysics at Waco', in Lewis, op. cit., pp. 149–56.

36 Helen Hardacre, 'Aum Shinrikyo and the Japanese Media: The Pied Piper meets the Lamb of God', New York: Columbia University, East Asia Institute Report, 1995; Reader, 1996, op. cit.; M. Mullins, 'Aum Shinrikyo as an Apocalyptic Movement', in T. Robbins and S. Palmer (eds), *Millennium, Messiahs and Mayhem*, 1997, pp. 313–24.

37 Champion and Cohen, 1996, op. cit., p. 8.

38 Stuart Wright, 'Media Coverage of Unconventional Religion: Any "Good News" for Minority Faiths?', *Review of Religious Research*, 39(2), 1997, pp. 101–15.

39 Campiche, 1995, op. cit.

40 Mark Silk, *Unsecular Media: Making News of Religion in America*, Urbana, IL: University of Illinois Press; Mark Silk, 'Journalists with Attitude: A Response to Richardson and Van Driel', *Review of Religious Research*, 39(2), 1997, pp. 137–43; Madeleine Bunting, 'Reviewing the FWBO Case', INFORM seminar, London, 29 November 1997; John Dart, 'Covering Conventional and Unconventional Religion: A Reporter's View', *Review of Religious Research*, 39(2), 1997, pp. 144–52.

41 D. Mitchell, C. Mitchell and R. Ofshe, *The Light on Synanon*, New York: Seaview Books, 1980.

42 Reader, 1996, op. cit., pp. 108–10.

43 Eileen Barker, 'Plus ça change…', *Social Compass*, 42(2), 1995, pp. 165–80.

44 Wright, 1997, op. cit., p. 109.

# Summary of Chapter 6

Health is not always immediately recognised as a social institution, and yet it is clear that all modern societies devote vast resources to the maintenance of a healthy population, and the issue has been raised, particularly in connection with new religions, of whether religious affiliation as such promotes or impairs the health, especially the mental health of those who are converted. The authors examine the common assumptions made about new religions in this regard, and review the (mostly American) research which has sought to examine to what extent, if any, both traditional psycho-analytic theories, as well as popular impressions of the mental health implications of religious adherence are in any degree warranted. They review the possible effects of belonging to an NRM for children, and for adults they consider in what measure NRMs engender stress for adherents or provide means of coping with it.

# 6 New Religious Movements and mental health

*Lawrence Lilliston and Gary Shepherd*

## Introduction

A persistent notion in the public perception of New Religious Movements has been that such groups are characterised by mental illness. This notion is based on several sources of influence. Certainly the media has played a significant role, frequently featuring exposés of groups, including lurid revelations by ex-members and pictures of secret rituals and practices of the groups. Quite often – particularly on television – even relatively innocuous pictures and anecdotes are presented within a negative set, along with ominous music and arched eyebrows. The negative portrayals in the media are buttressed from time to time by real news events that seem to lend credence to the perception that New Religious Movements are inherently 'sick'. The most notable of these real-life events – the mass deaths at Jonestown – still stimulates a vivid image in the public mind. And the horrific images of Jonestown have been reinforced by recent events in Japan and Switzerland. These events are the ones that come most readily to mind when the topic of 'cults' comes up.

Reasonable people might argue that given the large numbers of New Religious Movements and the large numbers of members who have moved in and out of these groups, the tragedies everyone is aware of constitute a relatively small number of incidents. However, people do not always argue in this way: the images of New Religious Movements etched in the public mind are of emotionally deranged members, brainwashed into submission, stripped of all semblance of autonomy and self-direction, and slavishly following the whims of a sociopathic manipulative leader, perhaps even to their doom. Added to the images from the media is the public information campaign of so-called anti-cult groups who have a variety of motivations, including monetary, for stimulating and maintaining negative perceptions of New Religious Movements. This phenomenon is dealt with in greater detail in other chapters in this volume.

The popular view of the relationship between mental illness and membership in a New Religious Movement incorporates three types of possible causal paths. In one scenario, dangerous cults prey upon those who are already mentally ill or who suffer from some characterological or moral weakness. Such people are presumably easy targets for the manipulative tactics of the cult. Thus those who enter cults are thought to be already disturbed and prone to succumb to the baneful influences of destructive groups. In a second scenario, the cults deceive relatively normal, but somewhat naive, persons into attending meetings or sessions. In this scenario, recruits are initially duped into attending a meeting that appears benign, and then the cult's 'brainwashing' tactics begin. Normal people are subsequently rendered powerless and ultimately mentally ill; thus, in this view, the cult causes mental illness. A third scenario involves children who are born and reared in a cult. In this scenario, because of the pathology of the cult, those who are reared in a cult cannot be normal since they are socialised into the pathological patterns of the adult cult members.

All three of these scenarios are based upon specific ideas about the nature of New Religious Movements in interaction with theories of mental health (and illness). The popular ideas about cults are that they are completely deceptive; that they engage in powerful techniques of mind control through 'brainwashing' and programming techniques both to recruit and maintain membership; that they particularly prey upon either disturbed or naive people; and that the members are under the control of leaders who are living a luxurious life at the expense of the members. In addition to these perceptions, there is the popular view that cults are not 'authentic' religions. Most treatments of this characterisation are rather vague regarding the precise nature of an authentic religion, but the perception seems to involve the exclusion of all but rather mainstream religions from the realm of authenticity. These popular, highly negative, ideas are consistently reinforced in the media and in the literature produced by critics of New Religious Movements; they can be readily found in the popular press and in journals such as the *Cultic Studies Journal*.

These perceptions, however skewed or distorted, are seemingly supported by some attributes consistently found among New Religious Movements. Most such movements are renunciatory and involve some significant separation from past associations, including family members and friends; many groups live communally; most groups are based on new belief systems that are radically different from the mainstream and previous religious practices of members; many groups encourage or require name changes of members to reinforce their conversion to a new way of life and belief system; many groups involve a transient lifestyle; and many groups involve changes in bodily appearance, in the form of specific clothes or hairstyles, aimed at setting the members off from the larger society.[1]

Although these characteristics are not universal among New Religious Movements, when they are present, they serve to reinforce popular perceptions of mind control. Because this behaviour involves radical changes, which most people would not be willing to make, popular opinion construes it as evidence for the existence of mind control and the corollary condition of mental illness.

Mental health professionals (e.g. psychiatrists, psychologists, counsellors, and therapists) have supplemented and reinforced the negative imagery in popular perceptions. It is rather common, for instance, to see cult member-ship discussed as reflecting abnormal processes in textbooks, diagnostic manuals, and journal articles. The views of mental health professionals on religious cults rest largely on two types of argument. One is theory about the nature of abnormal mental processes, and the other is case studies of ex-members (or families of current members) of New Religious Movements who have been seen in psychotherapy. Throughout most of this century, approaches to psychotherapy and mental illness have rested on assumptions about the nature of the healthy personality. According to this view, largely grounded in psychoanalytic theory along with all its variants, normal adjust-ment is to be made within the constraints of societal norms. That is, the well-adjusted person has normative personal and sexual relationships, is a productive worker in a satisfying job, values most highly a normative family life, embraces the standard civic values and virtues, and makes some contri-bution to the maintenance of those larger societal values. Analyses of this model by Scheff [2] and others are well known in the literature on public mental health.

Thus, those who would adopt lifestyles at odds with these standards are mentally ill and not in control of their choices. According to this model, then, those who join New Religious Movements are, by definition, not making the choices normal, mentally healthy individuals made, and perforce must be mentally ill. This general model has been undergirded by psychoanalytic theory, with its elaboration of all of the complexities and nuances of psycho-sexual development, the mastery of the primary process by the ego in concert with the development of the mature superego, and the transformation and sublimation of unconscious drives and conflicts into socially acceptable and achievement-oriented behaviour. Ultimately, if all goes well, these dynamics funnel into a very narrow view of normality: family, work, and dominant cultural values as the true criteria of mental health. If all does not go well – if there are fixations or unresolved conflicts or poor ego development, for example – the individual will develop symptoms that are reflective of under-lying pathological processes. One group of symptoms that could appear would be those associated with membership in a cult. The complexity of a psycho-dynamic theory is so daunting (while at the same time being rich and fascinating) that a majority of mental health professionals have throughout most of this century accepted it, or some variant, as proven.

This perception of the validity of the accepted model of what it means to be normal, along with the theory that undergirds the model, are further buttressed by case material. Some psychotherapists see either ex-members or families of current members of New Religious Movements in psycho-therapy, and the details of their cases are consistent with the model of normality and the undergirding psycho-dynamic theory. It is important, then, to realise that the role of mental health professionals in shaping popular views of cults and their members has been extremely influential. These professionals have essentially told the public that their views of cults are correct, and have provided an intellectual rationale for that correctness.

Despite the fact that these psychological concepts have historically been widely used to explain mental health and mental illness, they have been challenged and called into question in an increasingly vigorous fashion over the past quarter of a century. A reading of textbooks in psychiatry and psychology shows that there is an increasing reluctance to embrace a narrow view of adjustment or normality. Indeed, most researchers and authors explicitly repudiate the notion that mental health can be defined in terms of overt behaviour that consistently reflects social norms. There is, rather, an increasing tendency to define adjustment in terms of personal distress rather than with reference to external standards or theoretical notions about what *should* be pathological. This tendency is being gradually reflected as well in official diagnostic manuals such as the ICD-9 and the DSM-IV,[3] and even more importantly, it is being found in the thinking of mental health professionals, who are less likely than before to interpret given behaviour – whether anxiety, for instance, or cult membership – as universally symptomatic of underlying pathology. A greater tolerance among psychotherapists for a variety of adjustive lifestyles is now present.

## Deep theories and empirical studies

There has also been a trend away from the type of theorising embodied in psychoanalytic theory. Essentially, therapists and diagnosticians have become increasingly aware that such 'deep' theories are largely comprised of unfalsifiable propositions that can never be adequately tested. And case studies, testimonials, and clinical anecdotal material – although sometimes generating interesting hypotheses – are unacceptable as scientific proof. The types of limitations and fallacies which may result if one attempts to use such examples as proof have been thoroughly documented by many writers on research design.[4] Moreover, those psychoanalytic propositions that are testable, and hence falsifiable, have not typically been supported by research. The best-known critique of an important psychodynamic concept is Loftus' work on the defence mechanism of repression.[5] Loftus traces the history of this concept and then reviews current research on memory. She concludes that this research thoroughly falsifies the Freudian concept of repression.

Hence, much of the theoretical rationale for assuming that conversion to or membership in a New Religious Movement is, *ipso facto*, symptomatic of mental illness is weak, resting as it does on a type of theory and evidence that are waning in credibility among mental health professionals.

Research on the issue of cult conversion/membership has been of two types. One is the anecdotal reports of therapists who have examined ex-members, and who have worked with their families. Best known by far of this type is the report of Margaret T. Singer in *Psychology Today*, entitled 'Coming Out of the Cults'.[6] Further anecdotal reports can be found in the most recent book by Singer, several books by Michael Langone, president of the American Family Foundation, and the *Cultic Studies Journal*, also edited by Langone.[7] These case reports are universally critical of New Religious Movements, and they all rely for their perceptions and interpretations on exactly the types of notions previously discussed. Conclusions are based upon popular ideas of mind control and involuntary membership that are combined with presumed poor social adjustment of members, either prior to or subsequent to joining the group.

These reports also rest upon the narrow view of normality previously discussed and generally upon the psycho-dynamic notions of underlying mental processes. None of these reports is systematic in nature. None of them studies groups of current members; indeed, these authors consistently and forcefully reject as invalid all research on current members. Moreover, none of these reports constitutes systematic studies of ex-members in which the population is systematically sampled and administered valid and reliable measures. All evidence is anecdotal, and although some ex-members' reports are possibly accurate, that assumption cannot be made with this type of study. These reports, offered as proof rather than as hypotheses to be tested in more systematic fashion, suffer the same fatal limitations of most such case studies, whether dealing with New Religious Movements or other groups: selective sampling, no control at all for demand characteristics, and reliability flaws inherent in all *ex post facto* research. The result of inattention to these problems is more dramatically seen by examining other, better designed systematic studies of ex-members, such as Wright's research on religious defectors.[8] Not surprisingly, systematic studies of ex-members, not limited to just those in therapy, present a different picture. For instance, perceptions of their former experiences in New Religious Movements by the great majority of subjects in Wright's study are generally quite positive. In another very important and well constructed study of ex-members, Taslimi *et al.* (1991) found that ex-members of the Shiloh Community had experienced no ill effects of past membership, had integrated well on return to the larger community, and did not differ from the general population on a symptom checklist.[9]

In contrast to the anecdotal offerings of Langone and Singer, there have also been several systematic studies of the mental health status of current cult members. Most of these studies have focused on adults, but some have focused on children. The best-known and most widely cited studies are those of Galanter.[10] Using the Minnesota Multiphasic Personality Inventory (MMPI) and conducting the first systematic psychological studies on members of a New Religious Movement – members of the Unification Church – Galanter found no evidence for a greater incidence of pathological profiles among members than among the general population. In a subsequent extensive review of direct research, such as Galanter's, as well as a review of relevant theoretical notions, Richardson concluded that there was scant evidence for poor mental health status among members of a variety of New Religious Movements.[11] It is worth noting that in this article Richardson was the first author to suggest that, in fact, for many members, the New Religious Movement experience might prove 'therapeutic' (a point that will be taken up in greater detail later in this chapter). In another volume, Saliba[12] has presented an excellent annotated bibliography of a broad range of literature on the relationship between New Religious Movement membership and mental health, and the overall picture generated by this bibliography is consistent with Richardson's conclusions that the more systematic studies find most members to be psychologically healthy.

Several more recent studies of adults who belong to New Religious Movements are supportive of the hypothesis that members are not characterised by poor mental health status. Latkin *et al.* have evaluated self-concepts among members of the now-defunct Rajneeshpuram movement,[13] surely one of the most ridiculed and vilified New Religious Movements in America's religious history. Latkin and colleagues found a high level of mental health among members, including very positive self-concepts, lower feelings of personal distress and anxiety, and greater feelings of personal autonomy and independence of thought. In another set of studies, Weiss and Mendoza employed a broad range battery of measures including clinical tests, interview data, and general personality inventories in studying members of the Hare Krishna movement.[14] Their data were quite consistent with the other studies: no evidence that the mental health status of members differed from the general population. Most recently, Sowards *et al.* studied current adult members of the Church Universal and Triumphant.[15] Using four different psychological tests, including a measure of intelligence and a psychometric diagnostic test of mental health status, these researchers found no differences from normative standards on the several mental health and symptom indicators. Interestingly, they also found higher intellectual functioning among members when compared with the general population.

In summary, then, several well-constructed, systematic studies of current members of a variety of New Religious Movements present data that converge towards a clear conclusion of absence of any unusual degree of psychopathology among these members. This conclusion contrasts greatly with the conclusion of critics who rely on anecdotal data provided by ex-members in therapy and by their families. Of course, the data from all of the systematic studies cited are group data, presented in terms of group statistics. Within those groups, there is variability, and some cases of marked psychiatric symptomatology exist. However, these cases fall far from the central tendency of all groups surveyed, thus leading to the general conclusion that good mental health is typical among adult members in all these studies.

## The effects on children

As mentioned earlier in this chapter, charges in the popular press against New Religious Movements have frequently been levelled at their treatment of children. Because of the claim that these groups are pathology-inducing, dire predictions have been made about children who have been born into these groups and reared by presumably disturbed parents. As with adult ex-members, there have appeared case examples in print and on television about children who have supposedly been abused, neglected, and psychologically manipulated by these various cult groups. According to this view, children in these groups should manifest a higher level of psychological and developmental problems than is found among children in the larger society.

Although there have been fewer studies on children in New Religious Movements than on adults, there has been some research. Lilliston studied Hare Krishna children living on a communal farm.[16] Extensive clinical diagnostic interviews were conducted along with personality, intellectual, and educational testing, and clinical behavioural checklists. Additionally, extensive naturalistic observation data were gathered over a period of several weeks. In comparison with normative standards, these children were psychologically healthy and socially well adjusted, exhibiting proportionally fewer behavioural and acting out problems than are found in the general population of children. Hare Krishna children also scored above average on tests of intelligence and educational achievement. Similar studies, employing similar methodology, were conducted with children in The Family (formerly the Children of God), and similar results were obtained: the great majority of children were found to have good mental health, superior social skills, and good intellectual functioning.[17] Finally, extensive field observation data were gathered over a three-week period on children in the Church Universal and Triumphant.[18] Although no systematic clinical work-ups or psychological testing were carried out, the behavioural observations were quite consistent with the findings obtained with Hare Krishna children and children in The Family; i.e. these children appeared well adjusted and typically free from any unusual level of overt symptomatology when compared with children in the general population.

Interestingly enough, research by Achenbach has clearly demonstrated a dramatically increased level of emotional disturbance and behavioural acting out among American children over the past fifteen years.[19] With the percentage of troubled children in excess of 20 per cent in the general population, it can be concluded that, on average, children in at least these three New Religious Movements are markedly better adjusted than other children. Thus, data from studies of children are consistent with data from studies of adults. No systematic studies of current New Religious Movement members exist that support claims that these groups are typically characterised by poor adjustment and emotional problems.

In sum, then, there is no credible evidence that New Religious Movements recruit mentally ill members, that they induce mental illness in their members, or that they raise children who are mentally ill. These studies are nevertheless limited because they are primarily oriented towards looking for the presence or absence of overt or self-reported symptomatology. While the generally low levels of symptomatology constitute a significant finding, there is much more to be explored about the interaction between mental health and membership in a New Religious Movement. One obvious point that calls for further research involves the lack of strong agreement between the findings just reviewed and data on the relationship between religion and mental health, in general.

## Mental health and religion in general

In the literature on mental health and New Religious Movements, there is scant mention of the fairly large body of work that deals with the ways in which religion may interact with mental health. Researchers in this area have tended to look at New Religious Movements as a special case that stands outside the body proper of the psychology of religion. However, this posture is justified only if New Religious Movements are seen as operating on principles that differ significantly from more mainstream religious influence. There is, of course, a vast body of social science evidence showing that similar principles are involved in the origination, maintenance, and growth or decline of religious groups, and special theories are not needed to account for contemporary New Religious Movements. This identity between many formal characteristics of all religious organisations doubtless has a corollary in terms of psychological influence. For example, the psychological processes involved in such religious phenomena as conversion, religious coping, and apostasy are probably greatly similar regardless of the religion. As mentioned previously, critics of New Religious Movements have argued that these groups do involve different processes, such as 'brainwashing', which set them apart as inauthentic religions. But this argument is refuted by both the data on the development of religious organisations and the inadequacy of the proffered psychological explanation; there is no research evidence to support the notion of 'brainwashing' as offered by critics.[20]

Research on the relationship between religion and mental health yields a picture that is quite mixed and inconclusive. Some non-empirical writers, such as Jung, Allport, and Boisen have argued that religion is positively related to mental health.[21] However, other influential writers, such as Freud and Ellis have argued for a negative relationship.[22] Empirical studies do not settle the issue. A review of over 200 studies by Batson *et al.* (1993) produces an ambiguous conclusion.[23] Some studies find a positive relationship, some find a negative relationship, and some find no relationship. The weight of evidence is slightly in favour of a negative relationship. However, these findings are inconsistent with the findings on New Religious Movement members reviewed previously which generally find members to be well-adjusted, suggesting a consistently positive relationship between religion and mental health. Although the reasons for this discrepancy are not clear and certainly must await a great deal of future research, we propose to look at the relationship between religion and mental health from the tentative perspective of a *stress–defence–coping model* of mental health and adjustment. We believe this model might lead to a possible explanation for both the mixed results found in general population studies and the more consistent results of good mental health found among New Religious Movement members.

In psychological research and theory about mental illness, the first sixty years of this century were dominated by 'grand theories' of both normal and abnormal personalities. Psychiatrists and psychologists optimistically developed theories that were assumed to encompass all human behaviour. By far the best known and most influential of these grand theories was, of course, the psychoanalytic theory of Freud and his followers. Later in the century, competitors appeared in the form of 'humanistic' approaches, the best-known example being the self-actualisation theory of Carl Rogers. These two competing types of theories differ greatly in their view of humanity. Psychoanalytic theory emphasises the essentially primitive, animal nature of people; it views us as constantly in conflict and trying to work out an accommodation between our egoistic impulses and external social constraints. In contrast, humanistic theories like that of Rogers view humans as transcending the limitations of other animals, having a basic need to be whole and to achieve their human potential. One might say that psychoanalytic theory emphasises the 'dark' side of humanity and finds that side as basic while humanistic theory emphasises the 'light' side of humanity and finds that to be basic. Theorists from these two perspectives also differ in their views on the role of religion in mental health. Psychoanalytic theorists, following Freud's analysis, have uncritically related religion to neurosis. Humanistic theorists have uncritically related religion to one's holistic and creative quest for understanding.

Many of the most important propositions of both of these theoretical approaches are essentially untestable but have a sort of fascinating, internal validity that makes them quite appealing. Both types of theories, the psychoanalytic and the humanistic, posit 'deep' processes that are not overtly visible to others, but that are assumed to exist as powerful determinants of external behaviour. Examples of these deep processes are the psychoanalytic concept of repression and the humanistic notion of striving for self-actualisation. Again, the very 'untestability' of these important propositions is part of their appeal: they simply cannot be proven wrong, and adherents are free to conjecture about what should be happening in the depths of an individual's personality according to their favourite theory. In fact, critics of New Religious Movements, particularly those connected to the anti-cult networks, do just this, arguing that followers are 'brainwashed' (a notion consistent with the psychoanalytic theory of important unconscious motivational processes) into following an inauthentic religious leader who leads them on a destructive and inauthentic path away from their self-actualisation (that might be accomplished through an authentic religious quest).

However, despite the continuing allure of such depth theories – particularly for those working in the arts and for those who seek a psychological theory as a basis for social control – more recent work in the behavioural sciences has largely rendered these kinds of depth theories anachronistic. Simply put, for the past quarter of a century, the various mental health fields have become more empirical and less oriented to grand theories. This evolution is related to several important advances, including: more and better medical research on biological factors involved in mental illness and maladjustment, such as Selye's seminal work[24] on stress and important advances in discovering the neurochemical bases of psychoses; important work on behavioural approaches, including analysis of the role of environmental factors in the etiology and maintenance of symptoms of mental illness as well as breakthroughs in the effective treatments of many problems (e.g. cognitive therapy with depression and systematic desensitisation with anxiety and phobias); and significant progress in the newly emerging multidisciplinary field of cognitive science, including a better understanding of such processes as memory, forgetting, cognitive distortions, and expectations as they relate to mental illness and health. These advances are reflected in newer textbooks and training manuals in psychiatry and psychology and in standard diagnostic sytems, such as the DSM-IV and the ICD-9-CM, which have moved from vague nosologies roughly rooted in psychoanalytic theory to more empirically based operational descriptors emphasising social functioning and environmental factors.

## Stress, defence, coping – and religion

Current approaches to the diagnosis and treatment of mental illness – and the acquisition and maintenance of mental health – tend to converge towards an empirical, functional type of approach that can be characterised as a stress–defence–coping adaptation model.[25] According to this type of model, adaptive functioning (the more commonly used term indicating mental health) and maladaptive functioning (the more commonly used term indicating mental illness) are the products of interactions between the 'stressors' one is exposed to, the effectiveness of one's defences against those 'stressors', and the coping skills one acquires as a way of warding off or dealing with future 'stressors'.[26] Each of these three interacting sets of variables – stress, defence, and coping – has behavioural components, emotional components, and cognitive components which are situated in the individual and which are frequently called 'person variables'.[27] Each set of variables is also at least partially affected by environmental factors in the form of social supports, the absence of social supports, or social threat, or they can be grounded in the person, namely, in cognitive factors such as distorted thoughts, irrational fears, and unrealistic expectations; in emotional factors, such as panic attacks, free-floating anxiety, and uncontrolled anger; or in behavioural factors such as uncontrollable dysfunctional behaviour. Defences against the stressors can be grounded in external factors, such as the social support found in good partners, good friends, and helpful social agencies who rally around the individual in crisis, or they can be grounded in the person, viz. in cognitive factors such as avoidant thinking or cognitive restructuring; in emotional factors such as an ability to relax or calm oneself or generate emotions that feel good; or in behavioural factors, such as the ability to regulate or change one's behaviour so as to achieve adaptive outcomes. Coping skills are long-term strategies that allow one to anticipate and predict potential stressors where possible, thereby enabling one to avoid the stressors. Coping skills also enable one to direct oneself towards situations where stressors are not likely to occur. Finally, if stressors cannot be avoided, which is most frequently the case, good coping skills help one prepare for anticipated stress or switch into an automatic adaptive defence mode if stress has not been anticipated.

People who have good coping skills have effective long-term planning ability and more clearly articulated value systems.[28] They also have a greater sense of self-efficacy, that is, the feeling that one can perform necessary tasks and make events turn out the way one wishes.[29] Consequently, they are better able to contextualise themselves and events, placing their lives within a broader perspective. Although people who have good coping skills are relatively effective in anticipating stressors, and thereby relatively effective in avoiding them, they do not always seek to avoid them. Because of their feelings of greater self-efficacy and their ability to contextualise, they may seek out stressors and confront them at those times when avoidance would be inconsistent with some larger purpose as defined by their value systems. As with stressors and defences, coping skills can be influenced by social supports, such as living in an environment and with people who facilitate and reinforce self-understanding and self-efficacy. Also as with stressors, such skills can have cognitive components, such as long-term planning ability and contextualising; emotional components, such as effective personal habits of control of negative emotions, the ability to relax, and self-stimulation of positive emotions; and behavioural components, including development of constructive behaviour, such as achievement or helping.

Most mental health professionals apply a model such as this to the diagnosis and treatment of psychiatric problems, even if they do not articulate the process they employ in exactly this way. Most diagnostic manuals require an elucidation of stressors, internal resources, and social factors in order to arrive at a diagnosis. And more and more, research is producing treatment packages, or regimens, aimed at one or more of these specific components. Insurance companies and government agencies increasingly require explicit use of these empirically derived treatment packages for treating particular problem components.

If we apply this stress–defence–coping model to the religion and mental health nexus, the relationship can be conceptualised as variable depending upon how religion functions within the model.[30] Thus we would postulate no general, universal role for religion in adaptation or maladaptation. Religion can be a stressor; some aspects of some religions can function as social threats by emphasising punitiveness, judgemental factors, and potential exclusion. In some cases, if religion operates as a relatively impersonal and unsympathetic system, it can create stress through lack of social supports. It seems quite likely that many people move in and out of religious groups based on their perceptions of whether or not the religion provides an adequate support system. Religion can also contribute to stress when it creates dysfunctional cognitive processes, negative emotions, or maladaptive behaviours (e.g. distorted perceptions of reality, pathological guilt, or self-destructive behaviours). Of course, religion can also serve defensive functions by either providing social support in the face of stress or by serving as the basis for cognitive, emotional, or behavioural defences against stress (e.g. more realistic perspectives on life, relief of guilt and other morbid feelings, or self-enhancing and creative behaviour).

When religion does contribute to defences against stressors, different types of religious dimensions may be adaptive for different people. For example, research has shown that different people will be drawn to different religious activities (i.e. reading scripture, praying, changing behaviour) in times of crisis depending upon the nature of the crisis and other personality variables.[31] Finally, religion may have either a negative or positive effect on long-term coping skills depending upon the theological and organisational thrust of the religion. Again, some religions may facilitate long-term coping skills, such as feelings of self-efficacy and worth by involving people in meaningful programmes and 'callings'. Other religions may militate against long-term coping skills by fostering maladaptive dependence on a leader, an organisation, or even a theological construct. These examples merely scratch the surface, but it is apparent that the question of the relationship between religion and mental health has no clear-cut single answer. Rather, it depends upon a complex relationship between the substantive characteristics /emphasis of a particular religious system and the 'person variables' of individual adherents. The complexity of this relationship has been explored fully in the important research of Pargament and colleagues on the coping functions of religion.[32]

The application of the stress–defence–coping adaptation model suggests that sometimes religion is helpful and sometimes it is hurtful. It explains why people differ in the likelihood of turning to religion in times of stress, as well as why religious education and socialisation of children have variable results. It probably also explains the variable results found in the empirical literature on the general relationship between religion and mental health.

The model may also partially explain, from a psychological perspective, the data regarding the mental health status of members of New Religious Movements.

## Stress and NRMs

Members may be initially attracted to New Religious Movements because the groups are perceived as low in stressors as compared to the outside world. In most New Religious Movements, social supports are strong and thereby serve to minimise stress. Stress is minimised not only by the presence of social supports but also in some ways by reduction of social threat. To be sure, social threat typically exists from outside the group as evidenced by the long history of persecution of such groups. However, on a day-to-day, personal interaction level, many of the kinds of social threats that are pervasive in the outside world are absent or at a low level inside the group. Examples are rudeness, random threats of violence, loss of job, drug abuse, and peer rejection. Thus, the ongoing life in many of these groups is generally protective and supportive, and this atmosphere contributes to the sense of well-being of both adults and children. Stressors may also reside in the individual in the form of cognitive distortions, negative emotions, and dysfunctional behaviour. These stressors are just as likely to be present among New Religious Movement members as in the general population. However, because of the clear prescriptive nature of regimens operating in most New Religious Movements, ongoing thought processes, emotions, and behaviour may be more consistent with group norms. Because of social supports, this consistency may be easier to maintain than it is in the more heterogeneous outside world where mixed messages of how we should think, feel, and be, abound. Thus, overall levels of stress may be lower within many New Religious Movements.

Stressors still abound, of course, in New Religious Movement environments. However, when they appear, whether in the form of some external threat or some unpleasantness within the religious group, defences may go into action more rapidly. For instance, New Religious Movements tend to provide not only long-term social support, but most also have mechanisms for intensifying social support in times of crisis, through such practices as group prayer or chanting, or group discussion. In addition to social support mechanisms, socialisation into the practices of most New Religious Movements typically involves training in personal defensive manoeuvres that reduce stress. Although most New Religious Movements would characterise these manoeuvres as theologically based religious practices and duties, from a mental health perspective they are also functional as defences. Moreover, typical defensive manoeuvres, such as meditation, chanting and prayer, thought-stopping and thought-control, focusing on positive images, expecting and stimulating positive emotions, and behavioural correction, are exactly the types of techniques that have been shown to be effective in stress reduction by mental health researchers.[33] Thus, most New Religious Movements explicitly teach techniques that empirical research has validated, although it is doubtful if members of the groups are aware of (or, in some cases, even interested in) the parallels. And of course the explanations for the effectiveness of the techniques differ greatly between mental health researchers and New Religious Group members.

Finally, New Religious Movements typically encourage long-term coping strategies as well. Social support for coping is so obviously pervasive throughout such groups that little more need be said. In addition, however, to the general social climate, individual coping skills are strongly reinforced. Long-term – indeed 'eternal' – perspectives are the norm, and every activity is infused with this awareness. Thus, the theological system contextualises the individual's life and provides an ongoing perspective of relevance and meaning from which to approach future stressors. Many New Religious Movements also emphasise self-efficacy; members come to feel themselves to be in control of their lives and destinies. The emotional climate of many New Religious Movements is relaxing and positive. Although considerable variability may exist in this regard, these are not typically tense settings. Positive emotions tend to be the norm; where this is, in fact, the case, an ongoing emotionally positive atmosphere helps inoculate against stress. Functional behaviour, including healthy personal habits, also tend to be characteristic of these groups. These healthy habits – nutritious food, abstinence from smoking and drugs, exercise, relaxation, and meaningful work – have been consistently verified as potent weapons against stress.[34]

In describing the potential stress-reducing and coping features of New Religious Movements, we are not suggesting that these groups are idyllic. There is much variability among individual members within groups, and certainly not all members provide social support and reinforce individual coping strategies, just as not all members are mentally healthy. Moreover, even within the same New Religious Movement, there is variability between settings. There are no data to indicate that members of these groups are *intrinsically* at a more developed psychological level than the general population. However, many of these groups do display those broad characteristics previously described that facilitate low stress and constitute good stress-reducing techniques. These characteristics often comprise basic structural features of the groups and their various theologies; they are not simply epiphenomena. These groups, then, typically are structured to facilitate adaptive psychological functioning. They are relatively homogeneous in comparison with the larger society, they attract members who seek these types of support systems and facilitative experiences, and those members whose needs or expectations are inconsistent with a group's structures and practices are likely to leave. Hence, it is not surprising that there is a generally high level of mental health among members of many New Religious Movements. In fact, from the perspective of mental health professionals, the data on members of New Religious Movements serve as a rough validation of the stress–defence–coping adaptation model that is increasingly employed in diagnosis and treatment.

Whether there are larger lessons for society in general remains to be seen, although the authors have suggested elsewhere that the implications of data on children may be important.[35] For example, child rearing and socialisation techniques employed in the three New Religious Movements studied by the authors – the Hare Krishnas, The Family, and the Church Universal and Triumphant – have produced children who are extremely well adjusted and adaptive in comparison with children in the larger society. Indeed, schools and parents in the larger society might benefit from adopting certain general approaches from these groups – such as tutoring, close supportive interaction with adults and older children, and establishment of a transcendent value system – to their own educational and socialisation practices. At a minimum, however, empirical psychological findings on these groups should refute critics' charges of pervasive psychopathology. Further consideration of the model discussed may provide a direction for future study.

## Notes

1 On commitment mechanisms in utopian societies, see R. M. Kanter, *Commitment and Community: Communes and Utopias in Sociological Perspective*, Cambridge: Harvard University Press, 1972.

2 T. J. Scheff (ed.), *Labeling Madness*, Englewood Cliffs, NJ: Prentice-Hall, 1978.

3 ICD-9 and DSM IV refer to the two most common diagnostic systems used world-wide. The ICD-9 (*The International Classification of Diseases – 9*) is more commonly used in Europe, and the DSM-IV (*The Diagnostic and Statistical Manual – IV*) is more commonly used in the United States. Although the two manuals differ in format, there are no substantial disagreements in terms of symptomatology or diagnostic markers for a given category. The numbers (9 and IV) also reflect the extensive revisions these manuals have undergone over the past few decades.

4 See K. E. Stanovich, *How to Think Straight about Psychology*, New York: HarperCollins ,4th edn, 1996.

5 E. Loftus, *The Myth of Repressed Memory: False Allegations of Sexual Abuse*, New York: St Martin's Press, 1994.

6 M. T. Singer, 'Coming Out of the Cults', *Psychology Today*, 12, January 1979, pp. 72–82.

7 See M. T. Singer, *Cults in Our Midst*, San Francisco: Jossey-Bass, 1995; and, for example, M. Langone, *Recovery from Cults: Help for Victims of Psychological and Spiritual Abuse*, New York: W. W. Norton, 1993.

8 S. A. Wright, *Leaving Cults: The Dynamics of Defection*, Washington, DC: Society for the Scientific Study of Religion, 1987.

9 C. R. Taslimi, R. W. Hood, and P. J. Watson, 'Assessment of Former Members of Shiloh: The Adjective Check List 17 Years Later', *Journal for the Scientific Study of Religion*, 30, 1991, pp. 306–11.

10 M. Galanter, *Cults and New Religious Movements: A Report of the Committee on Psychiatry and Religion of the American Psychiatric Association*, Washington, DC: The American Psychiatric Association, 1989.

11  J. T. Richardson, 'Psychological and Psychiatric Studies of New Religions', in L. B. Brown (ed.), *Advances in the Psychology of Religion*, New York: Pergamon Press, 1985.

12  J. A. Saliba, *Psychiatry and the Cults: An Annotated Bibliography*, New York: Garland Press, 1987.

13  See C. A. Latkin, R. Hagan, R. Littman and N. Sundberg, 'Who Lives in Utopia? A Brief Research Report on the Rajneeshee Project', *Sociological Analysis*, 48, 1987, 73–81; and C. A. Latkin, 'The Self-Concept of Rajneeshpuram Members', *Journal for the Scientific Study of Religion*, 29, 1990, pp. 91–8.

14  A. S. Weiss, 'Psychological Distress and Well-being in Hare Krishnas', *Psychological Reports*, 61 1987, 23–35; and A. S. Weiss and R. H. Mendoza, 'Effects of Acculturation into the Hare Krishna Movement on Mental Health and Personality', *Journal for the Scientific Study of Religion*, 29, 1990, pp. 173–84.

15  B. A. Sowards, M. J. Walser and R. H. Hoyle, 'Personality and Intelligence Measurement of the Church Universal and Triumphant', in J. R. Lewis and J. G. Melton (eds), *Church Universal and Triumphant in Scholarly Perspective*, Stanford, CA: Center for Academic Publications, 1994, pp. 55–66.

16  L. Lilliston, 'Personality Assessment of Krishna Consciousness Children', paper presented at the Annual Meeting of the American Psychological Association, Los Angeles, August 1985.

17  L. Lilliston, 'Children of Communal New Religious Movement Members: Psychological Functioning', paper presented at the Annual Meeting of the American Psychological Association, New York, August 1995; L. Lilliston and G. Shepherd, 'Psychological Assessment of Children in The Family', in J. R. Lewis and J. G. Melton (eds), *Sex, Slander, and Salvation: Investigating the Family/Children of God*, Stanford, CA: Center for Academic Publications, 1994, pp. 47–56; and G. Shepherd and L. Lilliston, 'Field Observations of Young People's Experience and Role in The Family', in ibid., pp. 57–70.

18  G. Shepherd and L. Lilliston, 'Children of the Church Universal and Triumphant', in J. R. Lewis and J. G. Melton (eds), *Church Universal*, op. cit., pp. 97–118.

19  T. Achenbach and C. Howell, 'Are American Children's Problems Getting Worse? A Thirteen Year Comparison', *Journal of the American Academy of Child and Adolescent Psychiatry*, 32, 1993, pp. 1145–54.

20  See D. Anthony, 'Religious Movements and Brainwashing Litigation: Evaluating Key Testimony', in T. Robbins and D. Anthony (eds), *In Gods We Trust*, New Brunswick, NJ: Transaction Press, 2nd edn, 1990.

21  C. G. Jung, *Modern Man in Search of a Soul*, New York: Harcourt, 1933; G. W. Allport, *The Individual and His Religion*, New York: Macmillan, 1950; and A. T. Boisen, *The Exploration of the Inner World*, New York: Harper, 1936.

22  S. Freud, *The Future of an Illusion*, Garden City, NY: Doubleday, 1964; A. Ellis, 'Psychotherapy and Atheistic Values: A Response to A. E. Bergin's Psychotherapy and Religious Values', *Journal of Consulting and Clinical Psychology*, 48, 1980, pp. 635–9.

23  C. D. Batson, P. Schoenrade, and W. L. Ventis, *Religion and the Individual: A Socio-Psychological Perspective*, New York: Oxford University Press, 1993.

24  H. Selye, *The Stress of Life*, New York: McGraw-Hill, revised edn, 1978.

25  D. S. Holmes, *Abnormal Psychology*, New York: HarperCollins, 2nd edn, 1994.

26  In the literature, 'coping' is sometimes used interchangeably with 'defences'. However, here the term 'coping' is employed to reflect a long-term, planning function, and the term 'defences' is used to indicate a short-term, more immediate response to stress. 'Stress' refers to the physiological and psychological response to sudden or overtaxing changes and can result in responses such as

anxiety, depression, or dysfunctional behaviour. Any individual factor that elicits the stress response is called a 'stressor'.

27 W. Mischel, *Introduction to Personality*, New York: Harcourt Brace Jovanovich, 5th edn, 1993.

28 Ibid.

29 A. Bandura, *Social Foundations of Thought and Action: A Social Cognitive Theory*, Englewood Cliffs, NJ: Prentice-Hall, 1986.

30 For a synthesis of the classical anthropological analyses of A. R. Radcliffe-Brown, *Taboo*, Cambridge, MA.: Harvard University Press, 1939; and B. Malinowski, 'Magic, Science, and Religion', in J. Needham (ed.), *Science, Religion, and Reality*, New York: Macmillan, 1925, see G. C. Homans, 'Anxiety and Ritual: The Theories of Malinowski and Radcliffe-Brown', *American Anthropologist*, April, 1941, pp. 164–72.

31 L. Lilliston and P. Brown, 'Perceived Effectiveness of Religious Solutions to Personal Problems of Women', *Journal of Clinical Psychology*, 38, 1982, 546–9; L. Lilliston and D. G. Kein, 'A Self-Discrepancy Reduction Model of Religious Coping', *Journal of Clinical Psychology*, 47, 1991, pp. 854–60.

32 K. I. Pargament and J. Hahn, 'God and the Just World: Causal and Coping Attributions to God in Health Situations', *Journal for the Scientific Study of Religion*, 25, 1986, pp. 193–207; K. I. Pargament, J. Kennell, W. Hathaway, N. Grevengoed, J. Newman, and W. Jones, 'Religion and the Problem-Solving Process: Three Styles of Coping', *Journal for the Scientific Study of Religion*, 27, 1988, pp. 90–104; K. I . Pargament, D. S. Ensing, K. Falgout, H. Olsen, B. Reilly, K. Van Haitsma, and R. Warren, 'God help Me(!): Religious Coping Efforts as Predictors of the Outcomes to Significant Negative Life Events', *American Journal of Community Psychology*, 19, 1990, pp. 793–824; K. I. Pargament, K. I. Maton and R. E. Hess, (eds), *Religion and Prevention in Mental Health: Research, Vision, and Action*, New York: Haworth Press, 1992.

33 Holmes, op. cit.

34 L. A. Pervin, *The Science of Personality*, New York: John Wiley, 1996.

35 G. Shepherd and L. Lilliston, 'Field Observation', op. cit.; L. Lilliston and G. Shepherd, 'Psychological Assessment', op. cit.

# Summary of Chapter 7

Previous chapters have considered the relationship of NRMs and the major institutions of contemporary British society as a means of refining the analysis of the challenge and the response which these movements have evoked. Social institutions do not, however, exhaust the diversity of impact which new movements have had, and one important issue arising in contemporary religion (mainstream as well as minority religion) is the way in which gender differences are accommodated. The role of women in society is undergoing profound change, but is that true of religion? It might be expected, in this climate, that new movements would themselves be vehicles for change: but are they, rather, agencies of reaction? Dr Puttick in this chapter examines the many-faceted relationship of new forms of spirituality and the often rather limited part which women have, as yet, played in their development.

# 7   Women in New Religious Movements

*Elizabeth Puttick*

## Gender roles in NRMs

The position of women in religion is paradoxical. On the one hand they are the primary 'consumers' of religion who fill the churches, keep the ritual fire burning, venerate and adorn statues of divinities. On the other hand, in most of the world's religions they are debarred from playing an active role and sometimes even from entering places of worship. Women are sometimes perceived as having an affinity with the numinous, possessing qualities of devotion, compassion, intuition and receptivity that are often associated with religiosity. Yet they may also be condemned as spiritually inferior, weak, fallen, polluted, incapable of attaining enlightenment, even literally soul-less. Accordingly, in most religions their role has been limited to the menial: arranging flowers on the altar, sweeping the temple floor, but not preaching or teaching.

Despite the enormous range of experimentation in belief and practice in NRMs, until recently there has been depressingly little evidence of significant changes in gender roles. This is mainly because most NRMs are based on world religions and tend to reflect their traditional values. Accordingly, most research on gender has found an across-the-board subordination of women, even where the ideology was non-discriminatory, especially within Christian NRMs such as the Jesus Movement and the New Christian Right. Despite some questioning of gender roles resulting in theoretical equality, in practice women are socialised into rigidly submissive roles in relation to their husbands and pastors.[1]

Asian religions have also tended to view women as spiritually inferior and deny them power and status, and Eastern-based NRMs tend to continue this tradition. In the Eastern groups she studied, Aidala found that ideologically, 'No differences were seen in the abilities of men and women to attain self perfection or "higher consciousness" which was held to be the only relevance in life.' However, translated into daily life, 'Concern for such mundane matters as the tendency of male members of the commune to avoid household chores was scorned as evidence of wrong or limited consciousness.' In other words, 'The quest for personal transcendence in such groups most often resulted in the reproduction of traditional patterns of gender relations, however refurbished with spiritual explanations.'[2]

Kim Knott, discussing the low status of women in ISKCON, suggests that it is unfair to make comparisons with the ideal of gender roles in liberated American society.[3] ISKCON is unliberated even by Indian standards; educated Indian women do not follow the policy of standing separately from men during temple functions. But the main criticism of Knott's position is that to set different standards and criteria, making a special case of religion, is to marginalise these movements even further, as well as setting dangerous precedents that can be used to maintain women's inferiority. Furthermore, it leaves open the risk of such arguments being reapplied from religious to secular life, as has happened so often historically.

The only Hindu-based NRM that directly challenges misogyny is the Brahma Kumaris movement, which Skultans describes as 'without doubt a movement where women control men. Women occupy positions of power and status, whereas men, both in their secular and religious roles are subordinate to women'.[4] In some respects it offers a complete role reversal: 'Men look after the practical aspects of living thus freeing women for higher spiritual duties.' In other words, they 'appear to be playing the role of wives'. This leads to the interesting and rare phenomenon that 'male pupil and female mentor is a typical combination'. Although Skultans does not explicitly term it a feminist movement, her study makes it clear that there is an implicit feminist ideology. This is admitted by some of the women leaders, but they prefer to emphasise their role in promoting peace and environmental concerns.

Buddhism presents the interesting paradox that despite its original freedom from doctrinal inequality, patriarchy arose and turned the religion into an overwhelmingly male-dominated institution where women were perceived as profane and polluted. This reversal was exemplified by the eight extra rules for ordained women, which are still imposed in the Theravada tradition. Buddhist misogyny has been vigorously challenged both in writing and practice, particularly in America.[5] The Friends of the Western Buddhist Order (FWBO) in Britain share in this questioning, though perhaps less radically than their American counterparts. The official line is that 'men and women enjoy equal "status" and have access to the same opportunities and facilities for serious Dharma practice', via a 'middle way between the traditional subordination of women within the sangha...and a demand for equality in a purely secular sense'.[6] Again, the practice does not always match the theory, and some members express disquiet at the under-representation of women in the higher echelons and the perceived reluctance of the movement's leader Sangharakshita to ordain women.

Research since the mid-1980s presents a more positive picture of gender roles, probably reflecting the impact of feminism throughout Western society. In some NRMs, particularly of the counter-cultural variety, women may be liberated, empowered and fulfilled. Women are more numerous in this kind of NRM, and may outnumber men by as much as 2 to 1. This is the case in the Osho movement, the Brahma Kumaris, many Wiccan, goddess-worshipping and other Pagan groups, whereas in the more traditional, authoritarian Christian sects and NRMs such as the Unification Church and ISKCON, men are in the majority.[7] This finding is important in counteracting the popular perception of women as brainwashed victims of patriarchal authority, demonstrating that they tend to choose movements offering greater scope for their abilities, while the minority who choose conservative groups may derive other benefits (see below).

## Women in power in the Osho movement

The Osho movement is the only movement, apart from the Brahma Kumaris, that has a female majority in leadership and administrative roles. Although the teachings of the leader, Osho, promoted an ideal of female discipleship that emphasised traditional feminine attributes (see below), he also advocated an equal opportunities vision of woman freed of the shackles of centuries-old conditioning, reclaiming her power:

> My own vision is that the coming age will be the age of the woman. Man has tried for five thousand years and has failed. Now a chance has to be given to the woman. Now she should be given the reins of all the powers. She should be given an opportunity to bring her feminine energies to function, to work.[8]

This ideology was reflected in the social organisation. Osho was always clearly in the position of ultimate authority, but about 80 per cent of the top jobs were held by women. His explanation for this positive discrimination was inspirational: 'I want [the commune] to be run by the heart, because to me, to be feminine is to become vulnerable, to become receptive…Yes, the ashram is run by women because I want it run by the heart.'[9] However, it can also be argued that it was logical to put women in charge of what was in effect a feminised workplace: where decision-making processes were based on intuition rather than empiricism; caring was given a higher value than efficiency; devotion and meditation were higher goals than productivity and profitability; competition was renounced in favour of co-operation.

Most of the female co-ordinators exemplified this management style, which was claimed to work well until the appointment of Sheela as Osho's deputy, who ran the American commune of Rajneeshpuram until its demise in 1985. At the time Sheela attracted great admiration and devotion from sannyasins for her energy, drive and charisma, but her ruthlessness made her increasingly tyrannical and she was largely responsible for the totalitarian regime that developed, resulting in a débâcle that brought down the whole community, including Sheela herself who served a prison sentence. It is clear that Osho bears some responsibility, at least for the choice of an unsuitable deputy if not for active collaboration, but it was an unfortunate outcome of a grand vision of female potential. However, most sannyasins felt that the experiment had been largely successful, particularly in the earlier and later phases of the movement, as a successful antidote to the technological and left-brained bias of the modern Western approach to work and the bureaucratisation of modern life.

## Discipleship: the path of feminine spirituality?

There are very few role models for women's spirituality. They may sometimes become nuns, although usually with lower status than monks and heavily constrained by extra rules, particularly in Buddhism. Religious titles betray this bias, either possessing no female equivalent or a debased meaning: priest, master, guru, pope. Only priest has the counterpart priestess, but overlaid by pagan antinomian connotations. The women's spirituality movement has revived and created a mythology of pagan priestesses, but in most religions women's priestly role is severely limited or proscribed.

One of the main paths of spiritual growth is discipleship, but in most religious traditions it has been mainly or wholly confined to men. Yet in many ways it is a highly feminine path, with its emphasis on receptivity, love and devotion to the guru and God. This is partly recognised in the Hindu bhakti tradition, which encourages the devotee to develop a feminine psychology, visualising himself as a woman and sometimes practising transvestism.[10] Some NRMs have developed this potential into a path of feminine spirituality.

ISKCON can be seen as a transitional movement in this respect, in that Prabhupada allowed women disciples but was ambivalent about their status, alternating between a mystical concept of spiritual equality with male disciples and a conservative Vedic-based belief in female inferiority. Krishna Consciousness itself is 'a feminine approach to spirituality' in that it consists of 'surrender and service to others', and ultimately to Krishna, who represents the masculine polarity.[11] Women are perceived as better socialised to practise this path, but the misogyny sometimes displayed by the movement's leader Prabhupada and his chief male disciples has resulted in lower status for women. Women also had restricted access to Prabhupada, chopping vegetables while the male devotees accompanied him on his morning walks.

Osho was clearly drawing on the bhakti tradition, taking the next logical step: if 'feminine' devotion to a male god is the primary characteristic of devotional religion, it is easier, more natural, for women to be devotees of a male god – or male master. His definitions of masculine and feminine qualities were fairly traditional, in line with Jungian psychology: emotional and intuitive attributes were seen as feminine, whereas strength, decisiveness, objectivity and the intellect itself were seen as masculine. However, the ideal that sannyasins strive towards is androgyny: a balance and integration between the qualities so misleadingly termed feminine and masculine, which is becoming increasingly commended in the New Age. Feminine qualities were also seen as central in discipleship, and women were perceived as superior in this respect: 'The disciple needs receptivity; he has to receive. Even the male disciple has to function almost in a feminine way....Hence the woman proves to be the perfect disciple.'[12]

The women's movement has been highly critical of the master–disciple relationship for its encouragement of female submissiveness to a male master. The requirement to wear a mala[13] was a particularly regressive symbol to feminists, who singled out the Osho movement for criticism on this score. Yet a number of women sannyasins had been in the women's movement prior to joining. One former leading feminist whom I interviewed answered the question of how taking on a male master connected to her feminist principles:

> It didn't strike me with much difficulty, but it did to a lot of my friends – a man's picture around my neck! But I'd been moving away for some time from feminism. I found that it was restricting me and my development spiritually. And also when I looked at the truth of my life, I found that the people who really mattered to me were my son and my lover. Feminism didn't give me a framework to explain this.

Most sannyasins found discipleship a positive and fulfilling spiritual path. The master–disciple relationship is based on deep love. Osho often used erotic imagery to convey the ecstasy of the experience: 'The disciple and teacher must become deep lovers. Only then can the higher, the beyond, be expressed.'[14] Such experiences and images are sanctified in the devotional traditions of all religions, particularly in 'marriage mysticism',[15] but is also encountered in more austere traditions such as Buddhism. One of Boucher's respondents described a 'psychic merging' with her teacher whereby she became 'so close to this person that I was really fused with him in a way that my identity was submerged. That's part of Dharma transmission, to become one with your teacher so that you can see through their eyes.'[16] However, the emphasis on 'falling in love' with the master in a kind of spiritualised version of a romantic love affair carries particular dangers for women; in the context of the intensity and intimacy of the master–disciple relationship such love may easily slide into sexuality, and thence into sexual abuse.

## Sexual abuse: the shadow side of the master–disciple relationship

Nowadays, one of the main issue for feminists regarding charismatic authority is sexual abuse, which is widespread in old and new religions within the context of general patriarchal abuse of power. It is the shadow side of the master–disciple relationship, which has darkened the reputation of a number of NRMs and the lives of their members. In the past it has often been perceived as a problem of Asian gurus encountering more permissive Western societies. However, within the last ten years, Christianity's moral hegemony has been undermined by a series of scandals regarding love affairs between evangelical preachers or priests and their parishioners, who have often been abandoned when pregnant while the priest is moved on to a new parish. One recent Christian scandal in Britain partook of all the features usually associated with charismatic leaders of NRMs. It featured Chris Brain, vicar and former leader of the 9 O'Clock Service in Sheffield. In November 1995 he admitted having had improper sexual relations with twenty of his female parishioners, as a result of which he resigned. His ministry had formerly been greatly admired by the Anglican establishment who had therefore speeded up his ordination. He had also been endorsed by the well-known American religious teacher and writer Matthew Fox, whose Creation Spirituality rituals he had adapted in his own services. Women who complained to their local bishop were dismissed as troublemakers, and 'rubbished very effectively' by Brain and his staff, although following his exposure he was condemned as a 'cult leader'.

The most wide-scale example of sexual abuse in an NRM is another Christian movement, the Children of God (COG) also known as The Family. David Berg, the leader, had multiple sexual relationships with his female followers and encouraged the membership to follow his example. The practice for which the movement is most notorious is 'flirty fishing', a recruitment technique devised by Berg and his wife for female members to bring in potential converts through prostitution. At the peak of this phase in the late 1970s, the practice spread throughout the movement's international communes, and women were working two to five nights a week. It died down because of the spread of sexually transmitted diseases, combined with the strain on family life and the increasing demands of childcare, and in 1987 the practice was stopped altogether in response to the AIDS epidemic.[17]

The abuses within the COG have been exposed, but feminist research raises further issues about the presentation and interpretation of such contentious material. One concern is the 'sexual objectification' that results from the imposition of so-called value-free, scientific methodology. Janet Jacobs particularly highlights Wallis's research on the COG as typifying 'those studies that fail to question the norms of patriarchal control that lead to the sexual exploitation of female devotees'.[18] She accuses him of dehumanising them by describing them as the group's sexual resources and not investigating or even acknowledging their responses. Jacobs herself has undertaken the most extensive research on the abuse of women by male religious leaders.[19] She describes an 'economy of love', a process of affiliation in which the female devotee hopes to be emotionally 'rescued' and loved by the guru in return for her devotion. Unfortunately, the exchange tends to break down because of the unequal power relations whereby a large number of women are competing for the love of one man and are subjected to neglect, rejection and abuse. As a result many of them leave, bitter and disillusioned by the confusion between sexual and spiritual fulfilment and the resulting exploitation.

Many gurus have been accused of sexual abuse, including Maharishi Mahesh Yogi, Muktananda, Da Avabhasa and Swami Rama. Buddhism in the West has been shaken by a number of scandals, mainly exposed through the vociferous protests of Buddhist women.[20] In particular, Chogyam Trungpa was notorious for his many sexual partners called 'consorts', as well as his alcoholism. He was exposed after his death, having chosen as his dharma heir Osel Tendzin, who died of AIDS after allegedly infecting his many partners without telling them. Sogyal Rinpoche was a protégé of Trungpa and is the best-known Tibetan lama in the West apart from the Dalai Lama. He was recently sued for $10 million by an American ex-devotee claiming sexual and physical abuse. The case was finally settled out of court, but since then there have been numerous other allegations of abuse by his female disciples.

Trungpa and Sogyal, among others, have justified sexual relationships with their students on the basis of Tantra or 'crazy wisdom', as a means of spiritual growth. Anthony and Wilber, both experienced meditators as well as academics, censure such attempts as 'a rationalisation for flamboyant acting-out and impulsivity', leading to exploitation, deep psychological wounding and spiritual disillusion.[21] Traditional Tantra at least regulates such relationships through strict ethical codes, but these are absent in most NRMs.

The women involved are not always passive victims. They may fall in love with their gurus and even actively attempt to seduce them. However, such situations are largely the result of harem-style structures where women attain power and status by being the guru's lover and are encouraged to compete for his favours. In return they are often promised special transmissions and teachings, promises which may not always be fulfilled. In addition, the qualifications for such attentions may not be spiritual. As the teacher Andrew Cohen recently commented, 'Isn't it interesting how only the youngest and prettiest women are chosen?'

Altogether, the evidence suggests that when the powerful energy of sexuality is harnessed to the drive for power and the search for enlightenment, the results are pain and disillusion for the victims, and loss of reputation for the perpetrators, which sometimes reflects on the whole tradition. Tantra may have worked in the past as a framework for such relationships and may have potential for the present under very carefully regulated conditions, but the examples of most NRMs in this tradition show that the dangers far outweigh the benefits.[22] The Dalai Lama has said that the true Tantric master is capable of drinking urine or alcohol with complete equanimity, and that the path is so difficult and demanding that there is probably nobody alive capable of walking it.

For the future it is important that sexuality in the religious context, particularly within the master–disciple relationship, is addressed, preferably by NRMs themselves. If dysfunctional family dynamics and organisational politics preclude this, abuse needs to be publicly denounced. Chris Brain was exposed after a group of his women parishioners met and agreed: 'This is not just a sex scandal, but an abuse of religious power.' Richard Baker was thrown out of San Francisco Zen Center following a mass rebellion after he was discovered to be sleeping with a trustee's wife. On a wider scale, public awareness of the extent of abuse within Buddhism emerged following the first conference on Women and Buddhism in America in 1983. The Sogyal Rinpoche case is significant partly because it established a precedent for legal action. Above all, there is a need for teachers not to exploit their position, and for women to empower themselves and take action against sexual abuse.

## Sexuality and marriage in NRMs

Historically, sects and 'cults' tend towards extremism – either asceticism or antinomianism – and contemporary NRMs continue this trend. Another option sometimes encountered – which does not stand out historically because it reflected social norms but is contentious in the modern West – is arranged or controlled marriage. The Brahma Kumaris are probably the most extreme and uncompromising example of the Eastern-based NRMs advocating celibacy, at least in Britain. The Osho movement, particularly in the 1970s, exemplifies the 'free love' ethic of the counter-culture. The 'Moonie mass marriage' provides the most dramatic example of arranged marriage.

Whatever pattern is followed, the beliefs and behaviours of religions regarding sexuality correlate with their ideas about women and femininity. Most organised religions and many NRMs are ambivalent or condemnatory about sex, leading to a polarised model of (celibate) holiness as male and (sexual) sinfulness as female. Religions that equate celibacy with purity invariably promote a dualistic, body-rejecting and misogynystic philosophy in which women are seen as Evil Temptresses whose only hope for salvation (if any exists) is to become a nun.

### *Free love and hedonism as spiritual path*

The predominant media image of the Osho movement during Osho's lifetime was of a 'sex cult' led by a 'sex guru'. However, his aim was to create a scientific yet sacramental sexuality based on a synthesis between Tantra and Reichian psychotherapy. The main lines of his teachings on sex were established in a series of lectures in Bombay in 1968, published as *From Sex to Superconsciousness*:

All our efforts to date have borne wrong results because we have not befriended sex but have declared war on it; we have used suppression and lack of understanding as ways of dealing with sex problems...And the results of repression are never fruitful, never pleasing, never healthy.[23]

In contrast to most religions, including NRMs, which are hostile or ambivalent towards sexuality, Osho taught that it is our most powerful natural energy with three levels of potential. It begins as a biological method of procreation (animal), develops into a source of pleasure and intimacy (human), and ultimately a means to self-realisation (divine). He emphasised women's potential, through their capacity for multiple orgasms, to become Tantric adepts and attain enlightenment, providing a range of techniques for the purpose.

Although the 'free love ethic' was normative in the Osho movement, sexual behaviour was as varied as elsewhere in Western society, and serial monogamy was the predominant pattern, especially among long-term sannyasins. Osho's statements on marriage are mainly critical, although he would sometimes commend its potential as 'a deep spiritual communion'. In Poona there was no encouragement for sexual partners to marry, although the 'religion' of Rajneeshism later included a marriage ceremony. Nowadays, as a response to the AIDS crisis, there is a growing emphasis on monogamy.

The main source of Pagan beliefs and practices on sexuality is the mythology of the goddess: 'Sexuality is sacred because it is a sharing of energy, in passionate surrender to the power of the Goddess, immanent in our desire. In orgasm, we share in the force that moves the stars.'[24] Much interest has focused on the Great Rite: ritual sex between the high priest and priestess in pagan rituals, but the evidence suggests that it is more often symbolic than actual. Witches do tend to worship 'sky-clad' (naked), but 'as a way of establishing closeness and dropping social masks, because power is most easily raised that way, and because the human body is itself sacred'.[25] Paganism particularly affirms the female body and provides rituals for celebrating 'women's mysteries', such as menstruation and childbirth.

The English Wiccan high priestess Vivianne Crowley perceives that the 'negative attitude to women displayed in Christianity has derived largely from negative attitudes to sex',[26] particularly following the glorification of celibacy. She describes Pagan sexual morality as simple:

there are no barriers to sexual activity with other unattached adults; but we are expected to have regard to the consequences of our actions and to ensure that we do not cause unwanted pregnancy, spread sexual disease, or mislead others as to our level of commitment to the relationship.

This means that 'For unattached adults, there are no barriers to sexual activity with other unattached adults' (although attitudes to homosexuality vary between different groups), but extra-marital sex is forbidden if it causes hurt, while rape and child–adult sex are 'anathema'.[27]

Pagans are uninterested in marriage as a legal institution, seeing it as a device to protect property and dominate women. However, a loving monogamous relationship is seen as a personal contract to be honoured. As Starhawk puts it: 'Marriage is a deep commitment, a magical, spiritual, and psychic bond. But it is only one possibility out of many for loving, sexual expression.'[28] Various Pagan groups have created colourful wedding rituals, sometimes called 'handfasting', which are often celebrated at a seasonal festival, such as the spring festival of Beltain. Alternative marriages are increasing in Britain by about 50 per cent a year, including among non-Pagans, in reaction to the outdatedness and sexism of the Judaeo-Christian rituals and the unspirituality of the civil ceremony.[29]

### The path of purity and celibacy

In contrast to sannyasin and Pagan attitudes to sexuality as gift and spiritual path, the Brahma Kumaris see it as an obstacle to enlightenment. The main method for counteracting this 'greatest vice' is to cultivate a dualistic attitude, exemplified by their mantra: 'I am a soul, my body is a garment.' The movement appears to attract people who are uninterested in sex and for whom celibacy therefore has a positive appeal. Unusually among non-monastic movements, they require celibacy for their core members, even between husbands and wives. As long as chastity is maintained, marriage and family life are allowed, even encouraged (perhaps to avoid the accusation of breaking up families). However, the married women I interviewed had been married for many years, and one admitted that this might have been a factor in easing the move into celibacy:

> Possibly our relationship had come to brother and sister anyway. He's a very modest person, and he loved it. I never told him about celibacy, I just moved out of the bedroom one day. He must have wondered, but he never said anything...I think we have a much better relationship now, it's great.

Buddhism, like Catholicism, has a developed monastic tradition. In the West, discipline tends to be looser, but Theravada and some Zen groups impose celibacy on the monks, sometimes accompanied by misogynistic attitudes. It is less usual to find women advocating celibacy in Buddhism, although the Zen teacher Kennett Roshi believes it is a precondition to attain enlightenment:

If you're married, the singleness of mind, the devotion, the oneness with that eternal can't take place, because you're dividing it off for a member of the opposite sex...If you're going to follow the eternal, *he's* the one you're gonna be fond of. He-she-it.[30]

Witnessing sexual energy without repression or indulgence is a subtle and arduous process, and may work more effectively with older, serious adepts. Most women who choose to become celibate Buddhist nuns are older and have fully experienced relationships previously. In the FWBO celibacy is practised in the long term more by older women. An 86-year-old nun at the Tibetan monastery of Samye-Ling in Scotland had been ordained in her sixties, and felt that this was a more sensible age to begin, as did a 52-year-old woman at the Theravada community of Amaravrati. A former nun in a Korean Zen monastery highlighted lack of affection as a much harder problem for women than lack of sex, and stressed the importance of clarity regarding the aim of celibacy: that it should be undertaken only as an aid to practice and not to repress the body and one's full humanity.

### *Spiritually arranged marriages*

Arranged marriages were sacralised by all the world's religions during periods when they were the cultural norm, and they still take place in some conservative sects of Western religions. Some women prefer arranged marriage with its accompanying clarity of family and gender role, despite the price of sexual restraint. There is some evidence that the women who join fundamentalist movements have suffered childhood abuse and/or broken homes, often followed by victimisation in their own relationships, which predisposes them to sacrifice freedom for stability. Some women claim that not being treated as a sex object is a benefit of such customs as covering hair and body, but the religion itself traditionally interprets them in terms of purity and pollution. In fundamentalist Christian NRMs such as the London Church of Christ, marriages are not usually formally arranged but often rely on the advice and consent of the pastor, and divorce is forbidden except for adultery. The Jesus Army is more extreme, perceiving marriage as the 'lower way', inferior to celibacy, which is promoted in *Celibate Cutting Edge*, their 'inspirational bulletin of celibacy'. In this respect the movement may be perceived as a militant version of the men's movement in which the men give up being 'feminised' and don combat gear as warriors for Jesus, also displaying misogynistic attitudes.

Eastern-based NRMs may encourage or impose arranged marriage. The 'Moonie mass marriage' is the most dramatic example, in which 2,000 or more couples may be married in one ceremony or 'Blessing', often without having even met each other beforehand. These marriages are preceded by at least six years' celibacy, followed by three years' celibacy in which the part-ners strive to become the Ideal Man and Woman (as exemplified by Mr and

Mrs Moon) before consummation is allowed. Finally, in a three-day cere-mony following a seven-day fast, the marriage is consummated in a ritual that aims to reverse the Fall precipitated by Adam and Eve's premature sexual relationship. Women may thereby attain equal or greater spiritual status than men as 'creatures of the heart' but at the price of total submis-sion to husband and guru. It is possible to refuse these marriages, but few do.

ISKCON also favours arranged marriage, though couples may come to a private understanding beforehand, and women may actively select their husband. However, they then need permission to marry from the temple president. Marital sex is permitted but only for the purpose of procreation, hedged around with restrictions. Marriage improves the social and spiritual status of women but not men, who are held to be superior to women on all levels, particularly when celibate. A woman may be perceived as 'a temptress first and a devotee second', and excluded from sharing power with the men so as not to 'sexually agitate them'.[31] However, the situation is beginning to improve now, as a result partly of the high failure rate of the marriages,[32] partly of women's greater power in the movement.

NRMs offer women a wide range of choices regarding sexuality as with other aspects of life, but it is important to recognise the consequences of some of these choices. Some women are attracted to the certainty and stability of arranged marriage and are prepared to sacrifice freedom and status, but may also suffer abuse from their husbands. Celibacy only works for a few exceptional women, and denies the affective needs. Both these solu-tions are associated with misogyny. Free love worked in the Osho movement partly because there was enough encouragement of monogamy to produce stability, whereas in the more extreme and authoritarian Children of God it caused great suffering. The more world-accepting middle way of Pagan sexuality also offers a successful model, a sacralised form of the serial monogamy predominant in Western society. Most of the support for holistic spirituality, in all religions, is from women, and it may be that body-positive immanence is inherently more female, celibate transcendence more male. The main condition for success and happiness is that women should be in control of their own sexuality and fertility.

## Motherhood and community: beyond the nuclear family

One of the main accusations against NRMs, especially from the ACM, is that they break up families.[33] Given the small numbers of people involved in NRMs and the range of beliefs and practices regarding the family, this is an exaggerated reproach. However, as on other social issues, these experimental groups provide an interesting commentary and critique on the state of family and community. As with sexual practices, the conservative NRMs attempt to revive traditional, patriarchal family structures, whereas the counter-cultural movements experiment with alternative forms, particularly the commune.

It is particularly within marriage and motherhood that feminists see woman's 'self' as most at risk of being negated. Patriarchy demands that women should sacrifice their own needs and demands to their family, valuing selflessness over self-realisation, caring for others over creation of self. Most religions sanctify motherhood as a woman's destiny and true vocation, especially the more patriarchal traditions such as Roman Catholicism, the more fundamentalist movements within all three Western religions, and NRMs like the Unification Church where Mrs Moon as a 'devoted wife and mother' is a role model for Unificationist women. Women who are themselves conservative, internalising and upholding these beliefs, may be drawn to such religions.[34] The benefits are clearly defined gender roles and stable families, but the downside is a rigid control of sexuality, work and worship by husband and elders, loss of status and opportunities for direct spiritual advancement, and a high incidence of wife and child abuse.

Conservative Christianity is now the main preserver and legitimator of traditional family values in the West, and herein lies the appeal for certain kinds of women, looking for discipline and stability in contrast to the 'decadent experiments' of secular life. The women may find it hard to give up their autonomy to a husband, particularly given 'the lack of strong sensitive men to head the godly institutions of church and family in a loving and responsible manner'. Yet this requirement is enshrined in the social organisation, as in all patriarchal society, here upheld by the Director of Counselling at Thomas Road Baptist Ministries: 'The Bible clearly states that the wife is to submit to her husband's leadership. Two-headed households are as confusing as they are clumsy.'[35] The women finally made this sacrifice, deciding 'they would rather follow than be left behind to struggle with their own individual identities'. Rose concludes: 'While they may be relatively content in their relationships with their men, their bench mark is embedded in the old system of patriarchy which continues to perpetuate the costly contradictions that trap both men and women.'[36]

The one interesting exception to this pattern of patriarchal dominance over women and children is the women's spirituality movement, where there has been a resacralisation of motherhood similar to the revival in secular society. The dangers of reverting to biological determinism through over-emphasising and romanticising female bodily existence have been incisively analysed by Ursula King as 'a form of retraditionalisation' at the expense of 'a wider human experience of self-development'.[37]

The Osho movement was the most militantly anti-family of all NRMs in the 1970s. Like R. D. Laing and other radical psychologists of the time, Osho believed the family was 'outdated', 'the most hindering phenomenon for human progress' and 'the root cause of all our neurosis'. Nevertheless, he would sometimes describe motherhood as potentially the peak of female creativity and responsibility: 'becoming the mother of a Buddha'. However, his main emphasis was firmly on self-realisation for women: 'A woman is not only capable of giving birth to children, she is also capable of giving birth to herself as a seeker of truth. But that side of woman has not been explored at all.'[38] Osho discouraged women from having children on the basis (a) that most people were incapable of positive parenting, and (b) that children were a distraction from the spiritual growth that was the main purpose of being there. The main problem for sannyasins who did have children was that the commune was set up primarily as a kind of monastery, for childless adults choosing to pursue spiritual development as the main priority. Traditionally seekers have been required to sacrifice everything, including family life, for this goal.[39] Women with children were committed to 'giving birth to themselves as seekers of truth', but also, naturally, to their children. As with sexual relationships, family life in a monastic setting can be highly problematic, setting up conflicts with the spiritual objectives. Having made the choice to be in effect a working mother, women had less time for their children and some later regretted the missed joys of motherhood. But the consensus was that even if the children had been somewhat neglected, they had still been better off in a commune than a single-parent family. Some women found motherhood and personal development compatible. One woman had found motherhood 'one of the greatest gifts that's ever happened in my life', and managed to combine it easily with meditation and communal living.

Buddhist monasteries have the same dilemma. The FWBO has experimented with various community structures and found that single-sex ones work best, reducing the psychological dependence, conflict and entanglements of family life. In America, on the other hand, there is a growing tendency for Buddhist monasteries to be non-segregated, combining single and married practitioners, sometimes including children. Mothers report a variety of experience – bitterness at the neglect of their needs; guilt at their own inadequacies; and the joys of motherhood as a path.[40]

As with other social and spiritual issues, NRMs offer women a range of options from the traditional nuclear family to childless freedom. The choices and experiences of women regarding religion have close parallels with their secular equivalents. Women who accept motherhood as their vocation and are looking for a stable, secure family life therefore tend to be drawn to conservative old and New Religious Movements. The price of these benefits, as with non-working mothers but to a greater degree, is a loss of liberty, self-determination and other possibilities for growth. Women who prefer to focus on their personal development tend to choose religions such as Buddhism, the Osho movement and Paganism. The price paid by women with children in these movements, as with career women, is the stress of combining motherhood with an often arduous regime of work and spiritual practice. However, the commune is widely endorsed as a form of social organisation offering many of the benefits of the extended family such as childcare, a stimulating environment for adults and children, the opportunity for women to be mothers without sacrificing their own development. As such, it might well be acknowledged and developed as a viable model for an increasingly single-parent society.

## Female spiritual leadership in NRMs

Stark and Bainbridge postulate that 'one of the things that attracts particularly ambitious women to cults is the opportunity to become leaders or even founders of their own religious movements'.[41] Most such women will have been frustrated, but a few have succeeded. The lack of opportunity within their own religion will sometimes drive women to convert to completely different traditions, as happened with a well-known Zen master:

> The only reason she turned away from Christianity, Roshi Kennett told me, was her incredibly deep calling to become a priest. And, as a woman, 'there was no way I could become a priest in Christianity.' It was the sexism of the Church of England that compelled her to cut loose from Christianity and finally become a monk in a foreign country, in a foreign religion, in a foreign language.[42]

The priestly role is debarred to women in many Asian religions, as in Christianity. In ISKCON conditions are improving to the point where women may now theoretically become gurus, but none have so far, intimidated by the lack of respect and role models. In the Osho movement women held most of the secular power, but Osho believed that women's spirituality lay in their capacity for discipleship rather than teaching, and that they could not become masters. This was partly because he believed women were emotionally centred, whereas men had superior minds which made it hard for them to surrender as disciples but gave them an advantage as teachers. Another reason why 'only the male mind can be a master' was: 'To be a Master means to be very aggressive. A woman cannot be aggressive. Woman, by her very nature, is receptive. A woman is a womb, so the woman can be the very best disciple possible.'[43]

The Brahma Kumaris present a similar pattern of a founder who favoured and promoted women, and has been run mainly by women since his death. In some respects the role reversal is more complete than in the Osho movement, since women are teachers as well as administrators, and there is a very clear doctrine on gender equality. They are concerned with women's issues and spiritual leadership. However, as with sannyasins, Brahma Kumaris women become core members by being fully 'surrendered', and their prominence derives from their mediumistic capacities, channelling *murlis* (sermons) from their dead founder. As a result, 'their power is veiled...through the device of possession. Women, even when they possess power, cannot be seen to wield it. Hence, the importance of spirit possession where women are the instruments or mouthpieces of a male spirit.'[44]

There are a few contemporary Indian women gurus teaching in their own right, such as Amritanandamayi, known as Ammachi or 'the hugging guru', and Mother Meera who now lives in Germany. However, these women have not founded large organisations or left bodies of teaching. This is probably largely owing to their lack of education, in contrast to the male gurus who are often highly educated – both Osho and Prabhupada were professors of philosophy. The women are bhakti gurus, but for their devotees this simplicity may be an advantage in contrast to the perceived arid intellectuality of Western religion and culture.

One of the very few women who adheres to the male style of charismatic leadership is Nirmala Devi, known as Mataji, founder of Sahaj Yoga. What is interesting is that she began as a disciple of Osho and in setting up as a guru in her own right has imitated his style, although she is publicly critical of him as he sometimes was of her. Osho claims that after they had visited Muktananda together and been unimpressed, the idea entered Nirmala's head: 'If such a fool like Muktananda can become a saint, then why can't I become a saint?'[45] Like Osho – and Gurumayi, the female successor to Muktananda – she is anti-feminist, fearing that if women behave like men they will lose their femininity. Her teaching on gender is as traditional as ISKCON's, endorsing the ideal of the Indian wife, submissive to her husband, and advocating clearly defined, traditional gender roles.

Western religion has an underground history of female leadership in sects, particularly in America where Mother Anne Lee became leader of the Shakers, Mary Baker Eddy founded Christian Science, and Ellen White founded Seventh-day Adventism. Among contemporary NRMs, the Church Universal and Triumphant was originally founded by a man, but on his death in 1973 the leadership was taken over by his wife, Elizabeth Clare Prophet, known to her followers as Guru Ma. Spiritualism has been dominated by women in America and Britain, as is channelling, its New Age derivation. The New Age itself has been created and shaped at least as much by women as men, such as Helena Blavatsky, co-founder of Theosophy, and Alice Bailey who created the Arcane School. Many of the leading figures in the turn-of-the-century occult revival were women, such as the British magician Dion Fortune. In Paganism, women are generally perceived as equal if not superior to men. Feminist witchcraft obviously has a female leadership, while most Wiccan covens have a high priest and a high priestess as equals. The best known Pagan writers are women, such as Margot Adler and Starhawk in America and Vivianne Crowley in Britain.

Most women in Christian and Eastern religion hitherto have acquired the titles Mother, Ma or Mataji. Women who positively identify with motherliness will tend towards a more feminine style of leadership. Receptivity is the most-cited quality to epitomise both femininity and spirituality, particularly in movements based on discipleship or mediumship, and the women leaders of such NRMs tend to emphasise its importance along with softness, kindness and intuition. Other qualities that women leaders have exemplified as positively feminine and beneficial for authority are practicality, intuition, tenderness, body-affirmation, caring, healing, devotion, forgiveness, holism, social engagement and social mysticism.

Probably the most flexible and relevant model of female leadership for the future is of a more androgynous kind, which steers a middle path between imitating the traditional masculine models, with the danger of taking on their flaws to an even greater degree, or adhering too closely to a feminine model, which lacks toughness in a confrontation or crisis. Osho offered women techniques and opportunities to experiment with this approach, which some adapted more successfully than others. The Brahma Kumaris also make promote this kind of integration as a leadership quality, as do many Buddhist teachers. Particularly within the meeting between East and West taking place in America, with its scope for experimentation and fruitful confrontation, many women teachers in Buddhism and other religions are leading the way towards a post-modernist, post-feminist, androgynous style of leadership.

## A new typology of spiritual needs and values

As has been demonstrated, the position and status of women vary considerably between different NRMs. The differences correlate with my new typology of religion based on Abraham Maslow's 'hierarchy of needs'.[46] The typology classifies new religions into five groups or levels according to the needs and values of their members: survival; safety; esteem; belongingness and love; self-actualisation. I then combine these five levels into two broad groupings: traditionalism (levels 1–2) and personal development (levels 3–5). I would argue that the traditionalist movements share a focus on conservative or traditional values, whereas those in levels 3–5 may be understood in terms of a spectrum of personal development from simple self-improvement to spirituality. Each level also represents clear differences in beliefs and practices regarding gender.[47]

Traditionalist movements (levels 1–2) are the most conservative, reactionary and hierarchical, comprising fundamentalist NRMs and sects within world religions. Their main appeal is to women who are confused and frightened by the complexity of the modern world. In contrast, they offer clearly defined gender roles and stable family life. They thus fulfil security needs, though often at a price of limitation and oppression. Some of these NRMs, such as ISKCON, are responding to the advances of feminism as their women members find their voices and demand greater equality. However, it is significant that these movements tend to have a male majority, sometimes 2 to 1 or higher, whereas in more liberal NRMs the ratio is typically reversed.

The appeal of NRMs focused on personal development lies in their great scope for self-expression, exploration and empowerment, sometimes beyond what is available in secular life. They attract, on the one hand, counter-cultural seekers, on the other hand women who have achieved secular/professional success and are now looking for spiritual growth. Their beliefs and practice on gender are more fluid and flexible, sometimes with a focus on androgyny, and usually including women in leadership positions. NRMs such as the Osho movement, the Brahma Kumaris, and many Buddhist and Pagan groups offer equal opportunities with no glass ceiling, and possibilities for women to combine work, marriage and motherhood with spiritual growth.

## Notes

1 Mary Harder, 'Sex Roles in the Jesus Movement', *Social Compass*, 21(3), 1974, pp. 345–53; Susan Rose, 'Women Warriors: the Negotiation of Gender in a Charismatic Community', *Sociological Analysis*, 48(3), 1987, pp. 245–58.
2 Angela Aidala, 1985, 'Social Change, Gender Roles, and New Religious Movements', *Sociological Analysis*, 46(3), 1985, 295. Similar conclusions were reached by Janet Jacobs, 'The Economy of Love in Religious Commitment', *Journal for the Scientific Study of Religion*, 23(2), 1984, pp. 155–71.
3 Kim Knott, 'Men and Women, or Devotees?', in Arvind Sharma (ed.), *Women in the World's Religions, Past and Present*, New York: Paragon House, 1987.
4 Vieda Skultans, 'The Brahma Kumaris and the Role of Women', in Elizabeth Puttick and Peter Clarke (eds), *Women as Teachers and Disciples in Traditional and New Religions*, Lewiston, NY: Edwin Mellen Press, 1993.
5 Sandy Boucher, *Turning the Wheel*, Boston: Beacon Press, 1988, and Lenore Friedman, *Meetings with Remarkable Women*, Boston: Shambhala, 1987 based their books on extensive research into the growing number of women teachers in America, who are introducing many changes through their questioning and pragmatic attitudes towards the tradition.
6 Cited in the official FWBO magazine *The Golden Drum*, November 1989–January 1990, an issue devoted to the discussion of women's issues.
7 For general research on women in NRMs see Susan Palmer, *Moon Sisters, Krishna Mothers, Rajneesh Lovers*, Syracuse, NY: Syracuse University Press, 1994; Elizabeth Puttick, *Women in New Religions* London: Macmillan, 1996; on the women's spirituality movement see Mary Bednarowski, 'The New Age and Feminist Spirituality', in J. R. Lewis and J. Gordon Melton (eds), *Perspectives on the New Age*, New York: SUNY, 1992; Nancy Finley, 'Political Activism and Feminist Spirituality', *Sociological Analysis*, 52(4), 1991, pp. 349–62; Susan Greenwood, 'Feminist Witchcraft', in Nickie Charles and Felicia Hughes-Freeland (eds), *Practising Feminism*, London: Routledge, 1995; Mary Neitz, 'In Goddess We Trust', in T. Robbins and D. Anthony (eds), *In Gods We Trust*, New Brunswick: Transaction, 1990.
8 Osho, *A New Vision of Women's Liberation,* Cologne: Rebel Press, 1987.
9 Cited by Judith Thompson and Paul Heelas, *The Way of the Heart,* Wellingborough: Aquarian, 1986, p. 93. They appear to endorse this statement, quoting a Medina sannyasin in support.
10 Katherine Young, 'Hinduism', in Arvind Sharma (ed.), *Women in World Religions*, New York: SUNY, 1987; Wendy O'Flaherty, *Women, Androgynes and Other Mythical Beasts*, Chicago: Chicago University Press, 1980.
11 Kim Knott, 'The Debate about Women in the Hare Krishna Movement', *Journal of Vaishnava Studies*, 3(4), 1995, pp. 85–109.

12 Osho, *Theologia Mystica*, Poona: Rajneesh Foundation International, 1983, p. 266.

13 A necklace of wooden beads with a locket containing Osho's photo.

14 *The Book of the Secrets*, vol. 1, Poona: Rajneesh Foundation, 1974, p. 5.

15 R.W. Hood and J.R. Hall, 'Gender Differences in the Description of Erotic and Mystical Experiences', *Review of Religious Research*, 21(2), 1980, pp. 195–207; Kees Bolle, 'Hieros Gamos', in Mircea Eliade (ed.), *Encyclopedia of Religion*, New York: Macmillan, 1987, pp. 317–21.

16 Boucher, op. cit., pp. 218–19.

17 See Gordon Melton, 'Sexuality and the Maturation of "the Family"', unpublished paper presented at the Federal University of Pernambuco, Brazil, 1994, for an extended account of sexuality in the COG.

18 'Gender and Power in New Religious Movements', *Religion*, 21, 1991, pp. 345–56.

19 Jacobs, 1984, op. cit.

20 See in Boucher, op. cit.; Friedman, op. cit.

21 Dick Anthony, Bruce Ecker and Ken Wilber (eds), *Spiritual Choices: The Problem of Recognizing Authentic Paths to Inner Transformation*, New York: Paragon House, 1987, p. 67.

22 John Stevens, *Lust for Enlightenment,* Boston: Shambhala, 1990; Miranda Shaw, *Passionate Enlightenment*, Princeton: Princeton University Press, 1994 give accounts of the Tantric tradition and the high status of women.

23 Osho, *From Sex to Superconsciousness,* Poona: Rajneesh Foundation, 1978, p. 89.

24 Starhawk, *The Spiral Dance*, San Francisco: HarperSanFrancisco, 1989, 2nd edn, p. 208.

25 Ibid., p. 97.

26 *The Phoenix from the Flame* London: Aquarian, 1994, p. 116.

27 Ibid., pp. 163–4.

28 Op. cit., p. 27.

29 This trend has attracted media attention in national newspapers and magazines, for example 'Pagans of Suburbia' in *Elle*, February 1994, and articles on alternative weddings in the *Independent*, 13 February 1995 and 24 December 1995. Even *Hello!* magazine has featured a celebrity handfasting. Graham Harvey has written a chapter on Handfastings in Druidry in Phillip Carr-Gomm (ed.), *The Druid Renaissance*, London: Thorsons, 1996.

30 Boucher, op. cit., p. 143.

31 ISKCON's official magazine *Back to Godhead,* 1991, issues 1 and 2, in which a selection of women devotees express their views.

32 One informant estimated that 50 per cent ISKCON marriages had failed.

33 Eileen Barker, *New Religious Movements: A Practical Introduction,* London: HMSO, 1989; Bryan Wilson, *The Social Dimensions of Sectarianism,* Oxford: Clarendon, 1990.

34 For example, approximately 80 per cent of white converts to Islam in Britain and America are women, who appear to be largely attracted by the high value placed on motherhood as well as the moral certainties and clearly defined gender roles.

35 Rose, op. cit., pp. 247–8.

36 Ibid., p. 257.

37 *Women and Spirituality*, London: Macmillan, 1989, p. 80.

38 Osho, 1987, op. cit. This concept is based on the Hindu doctrine that the goal of the religious life is to become *dwija*, twice-born, a rebirth into the spiritual Self.

39 Barker makes this point, citing scriptural references to Jesus's and Buddha's exhortations to their disciples (op. cit., p. 87).

40 Boucher, op. cit.

41 Rodney Stark and William Bainbridge, *The Future of Religion*, Berkeley: University of California Press, 1985, p. 414.

42 Friedman, op. cit., p. 173.
43 Osho, *The Path of Love*, Poona: Rajneesh Foundation, 1978, p. 44.
44 Skultans, op. cit., p. 52.
45 Osho, *Philosophia Perennis*, Poona: Rajneesh Foundation, 1981, p. 318.
46 Elizabeth Puttick, 'A New Typology of Religion Based on Needs and Values', *Journal of Beliefs and Values*, 18(2), 1997, pp. 133–45.
47 It should be emphasised that while levels 3–5 appear to represent 'higher' needs, no value judgement is implied. The categories are less fixed than the typology suggests; in practice most people's needs continuously fluctuate between levels, and NRMs correspondingly contain elements of all levels. See my article cited in note 46 for a fuller discussion of these issues.

# Summary of Chapter 8

Of all the social institutions which NRMs confront or affect, the Churches might be considered to be the most directly affected, and it is clear that the Churches have a virtually 'ready-made' line of response. But, as Provost Slee makes clear in this chapter, there is nothing cut and dried about clerical reaction to new movements, in confronting which the Church has a long history. Proceeding from personal experience of encounters with diverse new spiritual bodies, the Provost indicates terms in which dialogue may ensue. Whilst he notes the signal points of difference between the attitudes of mainstream Christian bodies and new movements with respect to the open-ness of their activities and their methods of seeking adherents, he does not hesitate to question the tactics and attitudes of the anti-cult movement as counter-productive in treating with contemporary NRMs.

# 8 New Religious Movements and the Churches

*Colin Slee*

## An example of the challenge

As I left Southwark Cathedral one evening recently I was accosted by a man standing in the shelter of the porch who asked if he could attend the meeting of the Friends of the Cathedral that was happening an hour or so later. I explained that it was a dinner for which people had booked and bought tickets. Whereupon he challenged me to say whether or not such attitudes could be adopted by a Christian organisation. It was then that I spotted the compulsory floppy-bound black leather Bible under his arm and my heart sank.

Then I was subjected to an inquisition. Did we think we were bringing people to a personal knowledge of the Lord Jesus? If so, how was it possible that he had seen a woman leaving the cathedral in tears an hour earlier? Did I believe we were really in touch with the Lord Jesus ourselves as evensong, which he had witnessed, was clearly nothing to do with prayer and was a travesty of the evangelist's duty to preach the word of God? – and so on. I have to confess that I eventually lost my temper and told him he was arrogant and misguided, that he had no right to interrogate me, as it happened the lady whom he had seen was French, homeless and mentally sick and that she had been greatly assisted by my staff over the past few weeks, not least in finding accommodation. I told him that he clearly had no concept of the purpose and meaning of the ancient daily Offices of the Church, of which evensong is one. That we pray at least three times every day, morning, noon and night for the people of the world, and if he would put down his Bible and open his mind to hear what was happening instead of presenting pre-cooked recipes for fundamentalism then perhaps he might begin to learn about Christianity. I did not cycle home feeling proud of myself.

I recount this story as I believe it is a small illustration of the sort of conversation and emotional reaction that so often occur between members of New Religious Movements (some Christian and others not), on the one hand, and members of what I will loosely term mainstream Churches, on the other.

For my part, there was irrational anger that everything I stood for, and my Church works for, was being subjected to an inquisition, and I felt condemned before it had every truly been examined. In spite of all my interest in NRMs and my oft repeated counsel to worried parents and relatives that they should maintain contact, keep an open mind and an ongoing discussion, I felt threatened and I felt that everything I stood for was insulted.

For his part, there was clear certainty about a straightforward faith, the Lord Jesus was the answer to everything, the church should be full to overflowing with congregations of happy people celebrating their joy in the Lord. Nobody could ever leave sad or uncured, and the hard grind of the Daily Office was irrelevant as prayer and nothing but recreation itself, pure unadulterated praise.

Ysenda Maxtone Graham illustrated my point from within the Church of England – admittedly on one of its madder fringes, last year in her book *The Church Hesitant*.[1] She told how she had visited Holy Trinity Brompton and afterwards met a local resident who said 'Have you been there recently?...*What* a change! A parade of microphones! Frightful music – guitars. I do *not* want to take my Holy Communion at a Happy Eater.'[2] It is as though people were speaking different languages. There is ample anthropological and historical evidence that different languages breed hostility because they cause fear.

## NRMs are not a new phenomenon

New Religious Movements are nothing new. Indeed, it is frequently salutary to point out to outraged Christians that Christianity itself was once a New Religious Movement.[3] Nor are new movements within Christianity a modern phenomenon, neither are syncretistic movements which gather different elements from different faith-philosophies and put them together. We have only to read the works of the early Church Fathers to see that many of them are not so much works *of faith* as works *against heresy*, to see that new movements are part of the dynamic of the Christian faith.

Arianism, the principal heresy which denied the true divinity of Christ was denounced as early as 320 AD. It led to the Emperor Constantine calling the Great Council at Nicea, the statement we now know as the Nicene Creed and the concept of *homoousios*, expressing the co-eternity and co-equality of the Father and the Son. It is well known to most followers of the music of Benjamin Britten as the Cantata 'St Nicholas' celebrates that, at Nicea, Nicholas 'pulled Arius' beard'. Gnosticism, a little earlier, in the second century, had roots in pagan religions which were integrated into Christian teaching, and eventually led to separate sects. It is fiercely denounced in the Epistle of St John and in the so-called Pastoral Epistles,[4] especially Titus and Timothy. Irenaeus, Tertullian and Hippolytus all had their work cut out defining orthodoxy against heresy.

I will not rehearse the many possible examples that arise from the

Renaissance – for instance Galileo's threat to the Church's credibility was seen in some quarters as heresy, and what is heresy, if it is not a New Religious Movement? Suffice it to say that any scholar of Church history will be able to show through the Reformation and Counter-Reformation, to the founding of Methodism, Unitarianism and the Salvation Army in the eighteenth, nineteenth and early twentieth centuries, to the emergence of New Religious Movements in the latter part of the twentieth century, that every time they are seen to pose a threat to the established system they are resisted and contradicted with considerable force. Whether or not we are witnessing an explosion of NRMs in the last few years is a study that is worth pursuing. There are complex issues to assess, not least the fact that we now live in a global village such that ideas which develop in, say, Korea or the United States, are rapidly available in all other parts of the world.

Travel, communications technology and high literacy all have their effects both as accelerators of NRMs themselves and also as possibly generating misleading data in that we now have evidence where historically little evidence of a parallel nature can be found. What we now regard as the single spread of the Christian Church throughout the Roman Empire was quite possibly seen within that empire as a proliferation of diverse new movements and cults. What we now regard as fierce polemical statements by, for instance the Reverend Tony Higton or Pastor Reinhard Bonnke, pale into insignificance beside the tracts of St Thomas More – publications which would now be seized by the obscene publications unit of Scotland Yard.

## NRMs in theological perspective

What all this does is raise the eternally difficult question of the definition of a New Religious Movement. I believe that it is possible to answer this from an ecclesiastical perspective, perhaps even a theological perspective in a manner that is different from, say, a sociological perspective.

Theologically, a New Religious Movement probably ceases to be 'New' subject to the test of the Pharisee Gamaliel in the Acts of the Apostles,[5] 'For if this idea of theirs or its execution is of human origin it will collapse; but if it is from God you will never be able to put them down, and you risk finding yourselves at war with God.'

The difficulty with Gamaliel's test is that it demands a lot of patience, a period of time and toleration on the way. The activities of NRMs raise people to a pitch of concern that does not permit a great deal of patience before the churches are asked to declare a theological perspective. For instance, the Messianic claims of the Revd Sun Yung Moon clearly place the Unification Church outside the theological perspective that would be accepted as Christian. The organisation of the Jesus Fellowship with regard to authority and orders, the shepherding and pastoring would not be recognisable as any form of priesthood in the older Christian traditions, not sufficiently rooted in the will of the people and congregation for the reformed traditions.

The second theological test of a New Religious Movement is the test from Tradition. Obviously there are debates, important debates, concerning continuity and tradition, these could engage with the period when there were two popes, or the time of the Reformation and whether the Anglican tradition is continuous with the Roman Catholic tradition or cut off by excommunication, etc. Nevertheless, in spite of all these difficulties there is an acceptance within and among the mainstream Christian Churches that they have a continuity of Tradition and teaching which has its roots in the Gospel, was received through the Aspostles and is conveyed by a process of succession in leadership and distillation in understanding. New Religious Movements frequently disregard Tradition, even see it as an impediment. The mainstream Churches regard it as a treasure and resource. I suspect that a whole lecture could usefully be delivered on this topic alone. Revelation is not in antithesis to Tradition in the mainstream Churches, it is, in part, the result of insights that occur within a dynamic of Tradition that refines and examines. Tradition also acts as an essential safety net, sifting erroneous ideas and judgements with the wisdom and experience of centuries of scholarship and Christian practice.

Institutionally I believe that the test is probably something to do with acceptance as a member of the Council of Churches Together in Britain and Ireland, or similar bodies in different nations which together form the World Council of Churches (WCC). I believe there are also clear questions with regard to the Trinitarian doctrines of mainstream Churches and their absence in some NRMs.

The WCC brought itself into being by formal resolution at a conference in Amsterdam in 1948, stating that it is 'a fellowship of Churches which accept our Lord Jesus Christ as God and Saviour'. The Council somewhat tightened up its definition in Delhi in 1961, and in 1975 in Nairobi the Council defined its functions. The emphasis on 'visible unity' in these objectives[6] places upon the WCC a role in mediation and interpretation of 'New' Movements which is both welcoming in the sense of the goal of unity and also quite severely restricting in that 'New' movements, by definition and origin, are generally in some sense both doctrinally and institutionally at odds with the Council's foundation membership otherwise they would not be *new* movements but members of an already present and recognised Church. The very nature of a new movement to some degree implies a rejection of the 'truth' as held by the historically mainstream Churches. The present debate within the Council of Churches Together in Britain and Ireland with regard to membership by the Unitarian Church is a clear example. The constitution is clearly Trinitarian, how then is it possible for the Unitarians to hold membership? Once again, a sociologist can trace the developmental pattern of foundation, definition and defence occurring in the interests of organisational integrity.

Theologically, there is a complex picture. Christian Truth is by definition open to the possibility of new revelation and yet this truth must be tested. Testing involves a certain degree of hostility, ideas must be 'tried in the fire'[7] while at the same time openness to revelation cannot be a process of all-inclusive acceptance of every new idea and movement or guru. Nevertheless the Christian understanding of our present existence and of the nature of God is entirely provisional.[8] It is therefore scriptural and theological nonsense to claim to hold an absolute or perfect faith and doctrinal creed.[9] Accordingly, the mainstream Churches cannot simply ring-fence their club as closed to anyone later than the most recent constitutional development, neither can they simply open their doors to membership by any movement that *claims* to adhere to its constitutional precepts.

New Movements pose a threat to the mainstream religions in three other ways, and these threats are not solely threats felt by the Churches. The history of 'Baha'i' in its emergence as a faith and its treatment by orthodox Islam is a clear example of threat and counterattack outside the Christian sphere. First, there is the threat posed by the implied criticism that the 'old' movements do not teach the truth about God or, at best, do so inadequately. Second, there is the threat with regard to membership. Third, there is the threat that NRMs will bring all religion into disrepute and so risk the place of historic religious tradition in culture as much as their own freedom of expression.

## Teaching truth

The conversation with which I began this chapter illustrates the knee-jerk reaction that can occur when a New Religious Movement challenges the established Churches. I suggest that this occurs more frequently on a personal level than institutionally. Nevertheless, within the mainstream Churches there are groupings which might be said to behave in a quasi-institutional manner.

The evangelical wing of the Church of England, particularly in the organised form that it takes as 'Reform' or more ecumenically as expressed through the evangelical publishing houses, has produced a steady flow of publications and denunciations of New Religious Movement teaching.[10] I would suggest that it is a handy rule of thumb that any authors and publications which use the terms 'cult' and 'sect' are by definition hostile to the generality of New Religious Movements, and that the foundation of this hostility lies not so much in disagreement about content as in a response to threat as holders of a monopoly of truth. By contrast, I suggest that any which use the term 'New Religious Movements' are consciously attempting to be neutral or academic. Nevertheless hostility can be perceived as well as actual and it can have good reason behind it as well as knee-jerk reaction.

In 1983, I was instrumental in asking the General Synod of the Church of England to address itself to the question of New Religious Movements rather than, as I perceived it, standing off in a slightly patronising and ostrich-like manner. My concern arose from a fairly constant experience of the effect of the School of Economic Science (SES) on undergraduates while I was chaplain of King's College, London, and the refusal of the then organisers even to meet me. On moving to St Albans, I found the SES not only very active in the area but also three members of my congregation involved with it and two of their spouses were expressing significant anxiety and anger concerning the effect of the SES on their family life; the third member was, in any case, single.

The question to General Synod was framed in terms which included, with the SES, the Children of God (as they were then called) and also the Unification Church. Naturally, because of the Children of God's involvement in such activities as the memorably alliterative 'flirty fishing' the motion attracted a good degree of press coverage and a banner headline in the *London Evening Standard* that day.

Synod expressed its wish that the Church should take unspecified action and passed the detailed consideration to the House of Bishops. The Bishops' discussions are of course confidential, nevertheless I am confident that they were split down the middle between those who favoured a fairly strong response to NRMs and those who were afraid, nay 'terrified' as one bishop put it to me, of actions in the courts. The bishops recognised that this was an ecumenical matter and passed it to the then British Council of Churches.

Here a new dimension appeared. The BCC recognised the problem but also recognised that freedom of expression in this country, and religious freedom in particular, are a very important part of our way of life. Any proscriptive actions encouraged by the Churches could well be misinterpreted as a response in fear to empty pews or else as a new censorship which, in the end, could emerge to affect all religious privileges. The BCC's response therefore was to encourage the formation of INFORM and also to place responsibility for NRM monitoring and relations on the desk of a permanent member of staff in an informative and enlightened manner. The response was, therefore, positive, although certainly not one which would attract media attention or approval, as it appeared cautious, academic and clearly non-confrontational.

My own development during the course of this is itself of interest. I recall Richard Harries, then Dean of King's College, London, calling it a 'crusade' against the SES. I have to say that I was not amused, and also that I believe that reluctance to be involved is consistent with expediency ethics with regard to everything from the nuclear bomb to private wealth or the National Lottery. Nevertheless there was just a smidgeon of truth in Richard's remark in so far as I had a particular axe to grind.

My own movement in attitude was from a willingness to see the SES as a 'cult' – an expression I was quite happy to see used in a book with which I collaborated[11] – to New Religious Movement; from in some sense, 'the enemy', to some sense of 'strangely misguided and potential harmful, but not always necessarily so'; from the classically imperial view of a confirmed liberal theologian to a more genuine examination of what makes people join.

I discovered several important things. The first was, and remains, that many many members of NRMs belong because they are sincere and belong because the mainstream Churches have to some degree failed them in four distinct respects.

1   Teaching
2   Information
3   Commitment
4   Acknowledgement of complexity

### Teaching

The Churches have failed to provide teaching which equips people to question NRM doctrines in a manner that exposes their inconsistency and even plain error in scriptural interpretation.[12]

### Information

They have failed them in that they are not good at selling their wares.[13] I can give examples concerning community life and contemplative prayer. I recall a conversation with Trevor Saxby of the Jesus Fellowship (previously known as the Jesus Army) in which he told me how as an Oxford student he had been a member of the well-known evangelical church, St Aldates, in Oxford. He had asked the then vicar, Michael Green, whether he and some others could explore community life together. Michael Green replied that some Christian students could get together and share a house. He then approached the curate, at that time Colin Bennett, now the Bishop of Buckingham, and received a similarly uncomprehending response. The result was that a disillusioned and sincere Trevor Saxby discovered community life at Bugbrooke – a concept which would be anathema to both clerics. When I asked Trevor Saxby if he had been referred to any of the several Anglican religious communities with houses in Oxford: the Society of St John the Evangelist, the All Saints Sisters, the Poor Clares, the Sisters of the Love of God; or even to the more evangelical communities such as those at Leigh Abbey in Devon and Scargill House in the north, he replied that none of them had ever once been mentioned.

When I had a conversation with members of the SES a frequent theme that emerged was the desire for quiet and contemplative prayer. Several members told me that they had asked their priests or ministers for help in this area and had received none. None of them had ever been referred to the Society of Retreat Conductors, the various courses and schools of meditation, to religious communities or to Spiritual Directors. It is therefore no surprise that these people went seeking elsewhere other than the mainstream churches.

I clearly recall a conversation with an undergraduate member of the SES after I had her as a member of my confirmation group for many months and, not long before her confirmation, she told me that as a result of her SES teaching she definitely believed in reincarnation. I then proceeded to go through the entire Christian teaching about the uniqueness of each person, the resurrection of Christ as an expression of atonement and forgiveness, the meaning of life eternal, and so on. It was a steep learning curve for me as well as for her as I had never ever dreamed that any confirmation candidate could seriously believe in reincarnation. Since then I have learned that many more still do!

## Commitment

The mainstream Churches might, and here I emphasise *might*, also be said to have failed people who leave them in order to join NRMs because they make insufficient demands of their members. The historic Churches have lost their grasp of commitment as a youthful ideal: organisations like the Central London Church of Christ show clearly how attractive an almost punitive regime of simple discipline can be. The mainstream Churches frequently pay the price for their more measured requirements from members. Some people join NRMs without ever attempting the mainstream Churches simply because of their reputation and a certain misguided mythology about them. One of the penalties of being historic is that they also lose the attraction of novelty.

## An acknowledgement of complexity

A theme which constantly emerges from NRM members is the seeking after 'truth'. Truth, perhaps because it has only one syllable, is conceived as being simple, easily codified and demandingly clear. This clarity may be expressed in the lifestyle of The Family, the Children of God, with its very strong emphasis on sharing all things in common, living according to the means of the giving of the local community (and DSS benefits) and communal life which extends to sexuality and child rearing as well as the simple material needs of life. Conversely, it may be expressed in the severe and quite opposite (but also fundamentalist) lifestyles of the Jesus Fellowship or the Central London Church of Christ.

The difficulty seems to me to be this. It is a feature of the search for truth in any intellectual sense that it is also a search which engages with and acknowledges complexity. The classic Anglican answer to most questions, e.g. 'What do you think about abortion?' is an 'On the one hand, on the other hand' answer. This is an answer which grapples with the complexity of the issues involved. However, it is NOT an answer which helps, satisfies or otherwise fulfils people who seek a clear, direct and uncomplicated solution. People frequently express the desire to live without the trauma of intense personal debate and the responsibility for making decisions. I suggest that the Church has somehow failed to recognise the almost contradictory claims that are being made upon it. On the one hand, the claim for simple and straightforward teaching, on the other the claim of 'truth' in a complex and highly transitional society that admits of no simple answers to difficult and demanding issues. NRMs are able to attract members precisely because they offer an apparently clear and sealed code of conduct, credal statement and solution to the woes of life. I believe it would help the Churches enormously if we could articulate this contradiction in demand and thereby give an iden-tity to the tension in which the response to NRMs is so often paralysed.

John Robinson in his little book *The Difference in Being a Christian Today* argues for a far greater maturity of faith that must emerge in a society dissolving in a state of constant change. 'For the end of the stable state means the end of *any* fixed pattern'.[14] He argues that religious language suffers from a 'language barrier' as much restricting those who are within religion as those who are not. 'This is the truth behind the "Death of God" theologians. This three-letter word "God", they are saying, has had it. Yet they insist on calling themselves theologians. They are not just atheists.'[15] Robinson's argument is one that would be recognised by most mainstream Churches, but not by all of their membership, and yet it would be completely unrecognisable to NRM members.

## Parallels

I move now to the parallels that exist between the conduct of many NRMs and the conduct of many parts of mainstream Churches. The irony seems to me to be that it is those elements within mainstream Churches who would most wish to condemn 'cults and sects' as 'antichrist' who nevertheless have the strongest parallels. There is now a reasonably large amount of literature published in evangelical circles warning students against meddling with everything from the occult to sex, and New Age to New Religion.

When I became a college chaplain, first at Girton College, Cambridge, where I had a very rude shock, and later at King's College, London, I suddenly came face to face with one of the most sophisticated and highly motivated organisations I have ever met – the Christian Union.

I found that freshers are identified before coming up for their first term, each one receives a letter of welcome from the CU, is allocated someone to visit them within hours of arrival, is invited to a prayer meeting or Bible study, frequently camouflaged as a tea party or even a drinks party, and the vulnerable – especially overseas students, the obviously frightened and homesick, and the fervent Christians, are identified. These people are then especially targeted for extra visits in their rooms, extra invitations to group meetings and extra attention when they are there. They are offered counselling, somewhere to go during the vacation, or house parties on occasional weekends in term time. They are not infrequently warned that college chaplains are not Christians. Almost none of these activities in themselves can be said to be reprehensible but the total effect is one of limitation and constraint. Students become limited to Christian-only peer groups, their free time is constrained by group activities and social mores, the university experience – stretching and stimulating – is negated by regulation and even coercion. In the worst cases I came across, people ended up having breakdowns and even in psychiatric care, in the healthier cases they chucked religion altogether, in the best cases they emerged to a mature and often humorous view of their involvement while remaining people of a discerning faith. One or two I know are now themselves college chaplains and cursing the Christian Union! It is not all bad, just as not all NRM experiences are bad, and many students find the Christian Union is a doorway to a more mature faith in due course. Professor Maurice Wiles, radical chairman of the Doctrine Commission report *Christian Believing*[16] openly declares that his Christian faith owes its existence to a Christian Union conversion experience.

You will be aware that these techniques are the 'love-bombing' techniques of NRMs. I see no difference between the students who came to me to ask for help when the Scientologists persisted in writing to them, phoning them and visiting them after they had filled in a personality test in Tottenham Court Road, and the students who came to complain that they wanted to leave the Christian Union but were in receipt of notes on their doors, being accosted at meals and visited in their room by members of the CU telling them they were on the way to Damnation.

One of the most frequent springtime activities of the Chaplain of Girton College was discussion with a steady trickle of girls who came to say they wanted to get married. A significant proportion then asked me to help them to resolve their stricken consciences because their boyfriends were unbelievers – and that term sometimes meant that they were Christians but not members of the CU. I became sick and tired of hearing 'Thou shalt not be yoked to an unbeliever'[17] and parrying with:

> If a Christian has a heathen wife, and she is willing to live with him, he must not divorce her: and a woman who has a heathen husband and willing to live with her must not divorce her husband. For the heathen husband now belongs to God through his Christian wife and the heathen wife through her Christian husband.[18]

What enraged me was that these poor girls who came in such a state had often not even had that passage, also from St Paul, mentioned to them. It was a helpful introduction to some decent New Testament study, not least because the two passages do not address exactly the same situation.

Likewise, on my visits to the Jesus Fellowship I have been told of the very careful pyramidical process by which two people who are attracted to one another within the community may approach and seek permission to meet one another, and how, if in the unlikely event that a relationship has the chance to develop with someone outside the Fellowship then that person is advised that they must leave rather than be unequally yoked.

When I was a college chaplain I even had the temerity to attend some Christian Union Bible study groups. There I discovered that only certain publishers and certain authors were acceptable as any source of reference but in any event most of the content consisted of the 'It seems to me that this passage is *really* saying...' type of comment.

When I visited the Jesus Fellowship I asked what commentaries and scholarship Noel Stanton uses in his biblical teaching. I was told, with pride, that there are probably not more than half a dozen biblical commentaries in the entire Community and that Noel's interpretation was divinely inspired so it was unnecessary to grapple with scholarship which was in any event liable to mislead.

There is an interesting area of study here also which would require much greater time and depth than are available to us now. The study of Scripture is a *sine qua non* of religious observance. The Tradition, speaking in very broad terms, of the mainstream Christian Churches has been that revelation through Scripture is by a process of examining and exploring Scripture, especially the Old and New Testaments as a fixed canon. The Tradition in the Jewish faith has been to regard Scripture as a much more flexible and dynamic text open to change as a vehicle for revelation. NRMs have adopted an approach which differs from both. I suggest that NRMs approach Christian Scripture with a predetermined perspective and set out to show how the Scriptures illuminate that perspective. The interesting contrast here would be to examine whether the same approach has not marked the development of Feminist and of Liberation Theologies, namely taking a perspective and then approaching the texts in order to see how they respond to the perspective rather than the more accustomed approach from the opposite direction in Christian Tradition.

I also enquired about the Fellowship's status with regard to the Baptist Union and the Evangelical Alliance and received vague responses in terms of the fact that previous differences were being resolved; when, however, I asked a leading Baptist what the position was I received a very different answer. It was to the effect that membership of either organisation implied an acceptance of the validity of the ministry of its members. In view of the Fellowship's steadfast refusal to accept any preacher who was not himself a member of the Fellowship, the Fellowship's part in both organisations was rendered as self-excluding.

But there are parishes who have voted to refuse women priests, there are churches who will not invite the bishop, and so on. I don't think it is possible to argue that certain doubtful practices in terms of membership of the wider church, or of discrimination within the church, are a monopoly of the NRMs and render them identifiable as in some sense extraordinary.

Such discriminatory practices are not limited to the Christian Churches only. I am not an authority on the Hare Krishna but I understand that they were regarded as highly suspect by the Asian Hindu Community in Britain for some time. This has now changed and Krishna Consciousness is becoming something of a focal point of Hindu practices in this country.

## Contrasts

Having indicated a few areas of practice where Christian Churches cannot claim to be altogether different from NRMs, I will now proceed to indicate some of the areas of contrast. The first is undoubtedly the area of transparency.

Whereas it is difficult to obtain the syllabus taught by the School of Economic Science, even clear information about their lectures[19] or copies of the Moses letters to The Family, mainstream established religious teaching is available in published catechisms, in innumerable books and is subject to critical appraisal and opinion wherever it may emerge. The correspondence in the *Independent* a few years ago between Dr Richard Dawkins, Reader in Zoology at Oxford University, and Keith Ward, the Regius Professor of Divinity, is an excellent example. The very propriety of the study of Theology, let alone a Christian faculty within the university, was challenged and defended in open correspondence.

Similarly, every church is obliged to publish its accounts – and even cathedrals (which do publish their accounts) are being enjoined by the Archbishops' Commission to adopt a uniform practice in the presentation of accounts so that simple comparability can be developed. When visiting the Fellowship I asked if it is true that their turnover two years ago exceeded £14,000,000 with a membership of only 1,000 and received no clear answer. Meanwhile the poor old Church Commissioners have been dragged through the mill in Synod, Parliament and *The Financial Times*.

Such transparency is right and it points towards truth, on the one hand, and serious concern about funds, on the other. Nevertheless the established Churches and their associated bodies are not necessarily squeaky clean. A few years ago the charity World Vision was subject to a documentary on Channel Four indicating that most of the funds raised for the Third World ended up in Germany and the United States. The programme was subject to a court action and settled out of court. World Vision has been presented to me by evangelical clergy as vindicated by this settlement whereas, because of our legal system's idiosyncracies, I suggest that the action was settled and not the truth. Channel Four may well have settled because of the costs of fighting a tendentious action with an extremely rich charity were exorbitant.

In an altogether different area there is a contrast with regard to names between the mainstream religions and NRMs. There is no doubt about

Methodist, Anglican, Roman Catholic and other churches' identity, or the identity of their sub-groups, such as aided schools. NRMs as a whole operate with a remarkable number of alternative names and identities.

The Jesus Fellowship operates a large builders' merchants called Towcester Building Supplies and staffed by members. Similarly, there is a wholefoods business 'Goodness Foods', an architects' practice and a large medical centre on one of the Northampton Housing Estates as well as the farms. I agree that it is true that not every farm owned by the Church of England has 'C of E' on a noticeboard at its gates, nevertheless there is no doubt that patients at the surgery, seeking building supplies or wholefoods are not necessarily aware of what they are supporting. Recently a friend of mine saw the Jesus Fellowship wholefoods delivery van at the kitchen entrance of Pembroke College, Oxford. I doubt if the Chaplain was aware that he was patronising an NRM when dining at High Table.

The Unification Church was at one time publishing a wide variety of literature under different auspices, the emphasis on Unity frequently leading people to believe they were in receipt of an ecumenical publication, or the emphasis on Peace or Women suggesting it was a Pacifist or Women's movement.

It was only after serious difficulties with the press that the Schools run by the SES in London published their connection – to the surprise of some otherwise unsuspecting parents.

I believe that there is a perceptible shift occurring here. The Family have recently adopted a very different approach to publicity, appointed a public relations officer and spokesman in the person of Gideon Scott and opened their doors very publicly to the press (who interestingly sometimes prefer to publish allegations without visiting to check them), to Education Inspectors, the Social Services and even Anglican clergy and sociology dons! The Unification Church has an Interfaith and Ecumenical department – whether all Christian Churches welcome the assumption behind the word ecumenical is doubtful. The Jesus Army has changed its name to Jesus Fellowship and many NRMs have found they can co-operate with INFORM as a dispassionately objective body rather than treat all interested parties from outside their own membership as necessarily hostile.

The other change has come from within academic circles and the established churches. This is, I suggest, parallel to the changes that have been occurring within interfaith dialogue generally. Hans Kung's seminal work examining Christian theological perspectives and Islam, Hindu and Buddhist faith, *Christianity and the World Religions*[20] sets out a relatively new approach with clarity.

> For it has become even clearer to me that the world religions have and must accept a concrete responsibility for world peace. This presupposes that the religion focus less on what divides them than on what they have in common. And in fact if we analyse the ethical programmes, standards,

and demands of the world religions, we discover that they do have more in common than what divides them.[21]

This approach is reflected in an increasing exchange and conversation between mainstream religious churches and the principal NRMs.

Furthermore, I would suggest that the insights derived from theological discussions between the main religions of the world will add light to the Churches' understanding of the attractions and some of the content of NRMs. For instance, the increasing concern, world-wide, with global pollution and environmental damage is especially dominant amongst young people. The approach that Buddhist and Hindu religions have to the sanctity of the created order is one which some NRMs have also adopted and expressed. Consequently there are grounds here, through theological discussions on an interfaith level, for hope that greater understanding of NRMs and of their membership may emerge. The anti-cult lobby and serious fundamentalist groups within the mainstream churches as much as within the NRMs themselves would not agree with this view.[22]

The role of women in Islam is a matter of constant controversy and the role of women in certain NRMs is clearly not hugely dissimilar.[23] I recall being told by the Jesus Fellowship that women could not preach but they were permitted to speak at meetings – 'So long as they do not spiritually bully the men.' Likewise, other fundamentalist groups, both Christian and Jewish, have a severe perspective from biblical bases on the role of women in society. There is clearly room for conversation here.

## Conclusions

The first and most important conclusion must be one of disclaimer. This chapter has attempted the dangerous and probably impossible task of drawing on a wide spectrum of examples and generalising from them, both with regard to the mainstream Churches and also the NRMs. All generalisations are by definition inaccurate and therefore my first conclusion is that all work in this sphere needs to be detailed and careful. I have only attempted to paint a broad sweep which indicates the large horizon of possibilities.

My second conclusion is that relationships between the mainstream churches and NRMs would be greatly enhanced by a large dose of humility on both sides of the divide between 'Old' and 'New' Religious Movements, and acceptance that nobody can truthfully claim to hold a monopoly on revelation.

There can be no doubt that the 'Old' religious movements have practices they condemn in other groups. It may be well if these practices were discontinued, at the very least they should be admitted where there are parallels.

Equally, NRMs must have the courage to emerge from their *Lager* mentality and be less paranoid. If they are true, then Gamaliel will be proved right, equally if they are not, then they must face the dismal prospect of reconsidering their beliefs and Gamaliel will still be right.

## Notes

1 Ysenda Maxtone Graham, *The Church Hesitant*, London: Hodder and Stoughton, 1993.
2 Ibid., p. 10.
3 Acts 11:26: 'It was in Antioch that the disciples first got the name of Christians.' Acts 17:18ff.:

> 'What can this charlatan be trying to say?'; others, 'He would appear to be a propagandist for foreign deities' – this because he was teaching about Jesus and the resurrection. So they took him before the court of Areopagus and said, 'may we know what this new doctrine is that you propound?'

4 1 Timothy 4:1: 'The spirit says expressly that in after times some will desert from the faith and give their minds to subversive doctrines inspired by devils, through the specious falsehoods of men whose own conscience is branded with the Devil's sign.' 1 John 2:18:

> My children, this is the last hour! You were told that antichrist was to come, and now many antichrists have appeared; which proves to us that this is indeed the last hour....You no less than they, are amongst the initiated; this is the gift of the Holy One, and by it you shall have knowledge. It is not because you are ignorant of the truth that I have written to you, but because you know it, and because lies, one and all, are alien to the truth.

5 Acts 5: 34–42.
6 (1) to call the churches to the goal of visible unity in one faith and in one eucharistic fellowship expressed in worship and in common life in Christ, and to advance towards that unity in order that the world may believe; and (5) to foster the renewal of the churches in unity, worship, mission and service.
7 Malachi 3:1ff.:

> Suddenly the Lord whom you seek will come into his temple; the messenger of the covenant in whom you delight is here, here already says the Lord of Hosts. Who can endure the day of his coming? Who can stand firm when he appears? He is like a refiner's fire like fuller's soap; he will take his seat rectifying and purifying; he will purify the Levites and cleanse them like gold and silver, and so they shall be fit to bring offerings to the Lord.

1 Peter 1:4ff.:

> The inheritance to which we are born is one that nothing can destroy or spoil or wither. It is kept for you in heaven, and you, because you put your faith in God, are under the protection of his power until salvation comes – the salvation which is even now in readiness and will be revealed at the end of time.
>
> This is cause for great joy, even though now you smart for a little while, if need be under trials of many kinds. Even gold passes through the assayer's fire, and more precious than gold is faith which has stood the test. These trials come so that your faith may prove itself worthy of all praise, glory, and honour when Jesus Christ is revealed.

8  Hebrews 13:14: 'For here we have no permanent home, but we are seekers after the city which is to come.'

9  1 Corinthinians 13:12: 'Now we see only puzzling reflections in a mirror, but then we shall see face to face. My knowledge now is partial; then it will be whole, like God's knowledge of me.'

10  For example, Maurice C. Burrell, *The Challenge of the Cults*, London: IVP, 1981; Caryl Mastrisciana, *Gods of the New Age*; Constance Cumbey, *The Hidden Dangers of the Rainbow*, Lafayette: Huntingdon House, 1983; Ray Livesey, *Understanding the New Age*, Chichester: New Wine Press, 1989. See also Martin Palmer's analysis of similar books in *Coming of Age*, Wellingborough: Aquarian, 1989, pp. 75ff.

11  Peter Hounam and Andrew Hogg , *The Secret Cult*, Tring: Lion Books, 1984.

12  E.g. the SES makes a lot of use of the Gospel according to St John and also the Epistles of John without ever distinguishing the different authorship or the dates and specific purposes of the Epistles as addressed to Gnosticism – which forms a part of SES teaching.

13  E.g. the emergence of TM, not least under the patronage of the Beatles, illustrates the almost total absence until that point of awareness of meditative and contemplative traditions which were centuries old in the Christian tradition.

14  John A. T. Robinson, *The Difference in Being a Christian Today*, Glasgow: Fontana, 1972, p. 61.

15  Ibid., p. 40.

16  *Christian Believing. A Report by the Doctrine Commission of the Church of England*, London: SPCK, 1976.

17  2 Corinthians 6:14 in the New English Bible 'Do not unite yourselves with unbelievers; they are no fit mates for you.'

18  1 Corinthians 7;12ff. NEB.

19  William Shaw, *Spying in Guruland*, London: Fourth Estate, 1994, p. 41:

> Afterwards, as we pour out on to the busy road outside, a couple of young women clutch each other and burst into wild laughter, running away down the street. They won't be coming again. Several are more confused, trying to work out exactly what this course in philosophy consists of. I overhear one red-haired Australian turn to his companion, and ask in puzzled tones, 'This isn't a *religious* place is it? Only it didn't make itself out to be in the advert...'

20  Hans Kung *et al.*, *Christianity and the World Religions*, London: SCM Press, 2nd edn, 1993.

21  Ibid., p. xiii.

22  'Just as certain proponents of the New Age indiscriminately roll anything vaguely religious or spiritual into one bundle and claim it for their own, so those attacking the New Age do the same. Cumbey gives an example of this in her section that purports to show that the New Age is satanic. In the opening few paragraphs she argues that satanism lies behind the New Age: 'New Agers will often admit they are worshipping Sanat Kumara, Pan, Venus, Shiva, Buddha and other pagan deities. The name Buddha literally means "Lightbearer" – the same meaning as the name Lucifer.' So Cumbey quoted by Martin Palmer in *Coming of Age*, op. cit., p. 73.

23  See especially Hans Kung, ibid., pp. 83–5.

# Summary of Chapter 9

The explicit focus of the contributions to this volume has been the institutional contexts in which NRMs have made their impact. There have, of course, been brief descriptive accounts of various movements – most of which operate internationally, some of them with a presence in virtually all advanced industrial countries – but it has not been the authors' purpose to provide a detailed analysis of the doctrines, practices and organisation of any one of them. Given this perspective, it is well to be reminded that there are other movements which arise on native soil, which do not seek to proselytise elsewhere, and which give voice to an indigenous counter-cultural spiritual tradition. Some such movements might be found in many Western cultures, but the example provided by Dr M. Introvigne is all the more telling because it arises in a country normally assumed to be monolithically Catholic. His account makes clear that new religions are by no means all deviant Christian sects, imports from the Orient or manifestations of the human potential syndrome.

# 9 Damanhur

## A magical community in Italy

*Massimo Introvigne*

Damanhur is, arguably, the largest communal group in the world today or, at least, the largest communal group in the ancient wisdom–magical tradition. Although the movement has been in existence for some twenty years, it has been the subject matter of a limited number of scholarly studies. Apart from some unpublished papers read at sociological conferences, and from an entry in my own 1990 encyclopaedical volume on 'new magical movements', *Il cappello del mago*,[1] the only studies have been authored by Italian sociologists Luigi Berzano,[2] Mario Cardano[3] and Maria Immacolata Macioti.[4] Although non-Italian social scientists have occasionally visited Damanhur, the group has been mentioned outside of Italy only in papers by Isotta Poggi, an Italian-born assistant to Dr J. Gordon Melton at the Institute for the Study of American Religion, Santa Barbara (California).[5] On the other hand – in Italy and occasionally abroad[6] – Damanhur has been featured in countless magazine articles, TV programmes and, occasionally, pieces of anti-cult literature.[7] Only in 1998 was it finally the subject of an enthusiastic book-length discussion by a British journalist, Jeff Merrifield.[8] Damanhur itself has produced through its publishing branch, Edizioni Horus, more than 150 books and booklets, mostly authored by its founder Oberto Airaudi.[9] Press and TV interest increased enormously after 1992, when the huge Underground Temple – successfully kept secret for fifteen years – was discovered (following the indications of a disgruntled ex-member) and seized by the Italian authorities for having been built in breach of a number of zoning requirements. Damanhur later won the subsequent court case. This chapter will shortly place Damanhur within the alternative spirituality tradition of its Italian region, Piedmont (Piemonte). It will detail its origins, history and worldview. It will explore the meaning of the Underground Temple and raise some sociological questions on the structure and future of the community, and on its relationship with the New Age in Italy.

## Alternative spirituality in Piedmont

Damanhur is situated in Piedmont, less than 30 miles north of the city of Turin. Before 1861 – when the Kingdom of Italy was established – Italy was divided into a number of small states. Piedmont and the island of Sardinia, together with some districts presently part of France, constituted the Kingdom of Sardinia, ruled by the House of Savoy. Although early Savoy rulers were rather conservative – and, in the eighteenth and early nineteenth century, hostile to the Enlightenment – things changed in the 1840s. For a number of reasons, Turin – a university city – became the home of the most progressive and liberal intellectual renewal in Italy; the renewal in turn produced leading politicians and the Kings themselves. Under the leadership of Prime Minister Count Camillo di Cavour (1810–61), the Kingdom of Sardinia eventually became the Kingdom of Italy under what Cavour called the 'artichoke policy'. Little by little, through war, international alliances and negotiated settlements, the Kingdom of Sardinia added – one after the other – all the small Italian states to the crown of the Savoy family. By 1861, the Kingdom of Sardinia encompassed all of Italy excluding Rome and the surrounding area, still ruled by the Pope. Rome was eventually invaded and made the capital of the Kingdom of Italy (established with this name in 1861) in 1870. The unification of Italy under the liberal House of Savoy was seen as a threat to the continuous existence of an independent state ruled by the Pope in Central Italy. The Count of Cavour and other leading politicians in Piedmont had a frankly anti-clerical orientation. Savoy politics were actively opposed by the Vatican and by the Catholic Church, including in Piedmont itself. This, in turn, only increased the anti-clerical measures of the Count of Cavour and his associates, and many leading Catholic clergymen in Piedmont suffered imprisonment and exile. Within the frame of this policy, Piedmontese governments were extremely tolerant – for the standards of their time – towards alternative spirituality, seen as another way to harass the largely predominant Catholic Church. American New Religious Movements such as Mormonism and, later, Seventh-day Adventism were allowed into Piedmont (while they were prevented from entering any other Italian state). Although statutes against magic and witchcraft remained on the books, Turin became a surprisingly tolerant city as far as the activities of occult and magical groups were concerned. As a result, not unexpectedly, occult leaders, spiritualist mediums and practitioners of magnetism and mesmerism, fleeing the more hostile conditions prevailing in other Italian states (and, occasionally, France, Austria and Belgium), settled in Turin. The capital of Piedmont became, between 1850–80, one of Europe's main centres for occultism and spiritualism. In 1890 – twenty years after the Italian army had conquered Rome – the political function of alternative spirituality in Turin had exhausted itself, and the prosecution of a number of spiritualist mediums and mesmerists in a celebrated trial marked the end of this occult spring.

The reason why Turin became the home of many occult and spiritualist groups, thus, has nothing to do with the alleged esoteric interests of the Savoy family (largely a legend). It should rather be explained within the political situation and the hostility between the governments of Piedmont and the Catholic Church during the process that eventually led to the unification of Italy. One of the results of the Savoy politics of tolerating a number of occult and spiritualist groups in Turin was the production of a propaganda literature, particularly in Rome and Naples, accusing the government of Piedmont of protecting 'satanists'. The label of 'City of the Devil' for Turin was largely generated by this propaganda, and has remained with the city ever since, although in the twentieth century the number of occult and spiritualist groups in Turin has not been exceptional if compared with other large Italian and European towns.[10] On the other hand, it is not untrue to say that Turin's occult spring of 1850–90 has left a certain legacy. The Theosophical Society and the splinter United Lodge of Theosophists have been particularly active in Piedmont's capital. A succession of local independent groups in the Theosophical or 'ancient wisdom' tradition has also been founded in Turin throughout the twentieth century. Finally, it should be mentioned that the existence in Turin from the times of Napoleon of what is now the largest Egyptian Museum in the world is not unconnected to the birth of a number of occult groups inspired by Egyptian rituals and religion.[11]

## The origins and history of Damanhur

Oberto Airaudi was born in Balangero, in the Lanzo valleys, north of Turin, in 1950. A precocious young man, he published at the age of 15 a book of poetry, and at the age of 17 *Cronaca del Mio Suicidio* ('A Chronicle of My Suicide'), a rather morbid book where he announced in a literary form his 'possible' suicide.[12] At the same time, Airaudi was fascinated by Turin's occult milieu. He visited a number of healers and 'pranotherapists' (healers claiming to use the force of 'prana' by raising their hands and, occasionally, by physical manipulations) and learned the secrets of their profession, quite popular in Italy in the 1970s. Soon, Airaudi became a successful 'pranotherapist' himself, with offices in a number of different small towns of Piedmont. He was also interested in spiritualism – and later co-authored a spiritualist manual[13] – and became familiar with Turin's Theosophical subculture. In 1974 he had enough friends and clients to establish its own organisation, the Horus Centre, along with a School of Pranotherapy.

Almost immediately after the establishment of the Horus Centre, Airaudi mentioned to the members that they should eventually organise to live communally. In 1975 steps were taken to buy a property in the valley called Valchiusella, between the villages of Baldissero Canavese and Vidracco. The valley is situated between Ivrea (one of Italy's 'technocities' and the home of the computer company Olivetti) and Castellamonte (a famous town in Italy for the manufacture of china). In 1976 a settlement was established under the name of an ancient Egyptian city, Damanhur, with two dozen pioneers. Damanhur was officially inaugurated as a community in 1979. In 1981 the previous by-laws were modified into a 'Constitution', a move emphasising that the community regarded itself as 'separate people' and even 'an independent state'. The Constitution was revised in 1984, 1986 and 1987, until – in 1989 – it was re-issued as the *Constitution of the Nation of Damanhur*. In fact, anti-cultists and some local authorities had actively opposed the definition of Damanhur as a 'state', and the 1989 text opted finally for the word 'Nation'. At any rate, Damanhur has a 'government' of its own and a currency, the credit (*'credito'*), whose value is, however, regulated on the Italian lira and whose function is largely symbolic. From its very beginning, the 'citizens' of Damanhur in part work in the community and in part have outside work but return to the community after their working day is finished. Although exceptions existed, a large majority of the original pioneers were young adults who had finished high school. A few had college degrees, and a small group included skilled workers with no high school training. Couples were admitted and children were raised in small units composed of a number of families. Very soon Damanhur had its own day-care centre, pre-school and elementary school (an intermediate school, for children age 11–14, was set up in 1994). After a few conflicts local authorities have accepted the autonomy of these schools. Yearly examinations by school authorities of the nearby municipalities have confirmed that the educational standards of Damanhur schools are high, and the results scored by children are higher there than average.

The growth of Damanhur has been continuous. There were 200 'citizens' in 1985 and 450 in 1998. Since according to the Constitution a community could not exceed 220 members, Damanhur is now a 'federation' of a number of different communities, all located within a radius of 20 miles in the Valchiusella valley. There are at present an 'autonomous region', Damyl; two communities, Etulte and Tentyris; and two 'federal regions', Rama and Valdajmil. In fact, there is a continuum of homes in the valley, each inhabited by ten to fifteen people, including children. Some services are centralised in Damyl, including the schools. Damyl also houses the 'open temple', an impressive open structure with statues of Greek and Egyptian divinities, and a larger open area with symbols of different religious traditions where a market is held every Sunday, when the community opens its gates to welcome tourists and visitors.

The products of the community are sold also through normal commercial channels (including international duty free shops as far away as in Saudi Arabia and Abu Dhabi). Damanhur is reputed for its health food products, china and jewellery. Paintings by community artists (including the founder, Oberto Airaudi) are also sold to the general public. More surprisingly, Damanhur has a high percentage of computers (one for every six 'citizens') and one of the community's resources is the sale of software. Although self-sufficiency is a stated goal, even today a percentage of 'citizens' have jobs outside. In addition to the 450 'citizens' (all residents in the community homes), Damanhur is composed of some 300 'associated members'. The latter live in their own homes, the vast majority in the province of Turin, but contribute economically to the community and visit at the weekend and when special celebrations are held. At least another 1,000 people are regularly in touch with Damanhur and attend the courses of the Free University of Damanhur, in Turin and elsewhere, but do not contribute or tithe regularly and are not regarded as 'members'. The Constitution suggests that 'citizens' deed all their properties to the community, but in fact areas of private property have always been kept and the economic arrangements of Damanhur have passed through various phases.[14]

The organisation of the family in Damanhur has attracted considerable hostile interest. Couples may join the community and continue as such, although they should live communally with other families in one of the valley homes. On the other hand, many 'citizens' have joined Damanhur unmarried and have entered into one of the community marriages, stipulated as a contract which provides for a 'provisional' marriage for one, two and three years. When the contract expires, the marriage could be renewed or dissolved. The sensationalist press has always equated the Damanhur system of marriage to free love. Damanhur's 'citizens' counter that a significant percentage of the marriages are regularly renewed. They claim that against the hypocrisy of the larger society – where marriages are theoretically 'forever' but in many cases end in divorce – the possibility of checking periodically whether a real marriage still exists results in better couples. It may, they say, in fact contribute to the stability of the families. Children, at any rate, spend a significant portion of their time in the community schools and other communal activities. As usual, conflicts – and lurid, but often inaccurate reports on the family arrangements of Damanhur – have arisen in child custody cases when only one of the parents has left the community. Disgruntled ex-members have also informed the press of Damanhur's practice of 'programming' the birth of each new child according both to the economical possibilities of each unit and to astrologically defined times. In many tabloid articles this has simply been reported as the couples of Damanhur 'having sex only when Airaudi gives his permission', actually a caricature of Damanhur's 'programmed births' project.

## Damanhur's world-view

According to sociologist Luigi Berzano, Oberto Airaudi's world-view shows elements of four different religious traditions: Egyptian, Celtic (including Christian Celtic), occult–theosophical and New Age. Although when asked, any 'citizen' of Damanhur would insist that the community's world-view is absolutely new and original, in fact the influence of a larger theosophical and occult tradition is, at times, evident. Many ideas popular in the New

Age have been incorporated in the community's literature. However –
contrary to other New Age Meccas in Europe – Damanhur is not vegetarian. In fact its restaurant (open to the public) excels in the preparation of
meat specialities. (The list of wines is also rich, in the tradition of Piedmont
but unlike in many New Age vegetarian restaurants.) Vegetarian meals are
available, but Airaudi himself is not vegetarian and does not abstain from
wine (although all 'citizens', according to the Constitution, should abstain
from tobacco and drugs, and the provision is strictly enforced). Although no
world-view may be entirely new, it should also be recognised that Airaudi
has integrated elements of different origin in a rather original synthesis.

Damanhur does not accept being called polytheistic. 'Only one God
exists', but it is impossible to contact him directly. God remains largely
unknown and we can access him only through *the* gods, the 'Intermediate
Deities'.[15] Only nine 'Primeval Deities' are self-generated; all the others have
been created by humans but, not unlike the Jungian archetypes, now have an
existence of their own. Not to be confused with the 'Intermediate Deities' –
or the gods – are 'entities', which include angels, nature spirits and demons.
While today the entities are 'subtler' than humans, the first human was a
'Primeval Deity' who – according to a Gnostic myth with a long history in
the hermetic and esoteric tradition – was the victim of a fall and lapsed into
the present union with the body. Many Deities and entities voluntarily
followed the humans into their exile and may now help us when we try to
return to our original 'subtler' state (according to a scheme whose theosophical origin is apparent). Our return to the original condition may be made
easier by different sciences, including modern physical science but also
magic, alchemy and 'selfic', the science studying the particular properties of
spiral-like forms (called 'self' in Damanhur). Through these techniques the
'citizens' of Damanhur also learn to recognise the 'synchronic lines' which
constitute the Earth's nerves (the Earth – as in many occult and New Age
traditions – is considered as a living being). The very site of Damanhur was
selected because of the 'synchronic lines' converging in the valley, and
knowing the 'lines' is essential in order to communicate with distant places
and even to programme our future reincarnations.

Damanhur's cosmology includes the early generation of three 'Mother
worlds' – the world of human beings, the world of plants, and the world of
nature spirits – that are not capable of communicating between themselves
but generate 'Echo worlds' through which the 'Mother worlds' become able
to communicate. Each race has an 'astral tank' (a concept similar to the
'akashic memory' of the Theosophical tradition). Human beings may get in
touch, through particular techniques, with the human 'race mind' (the
'astral tank' of the human race), but they may find very useful information
also in the 'race minds' of animals. To this effect, each human being may
enter into a special magical relation with an animal by assuming its name. In
fact all the 'citizens' of Damanhur are identified not by their family names
but by the name of an animal. The founder used to be called Hawk – an

allusion to Horus – although today he is referred to simply as Oberto. Among citizens one finds names such as Elephant, Kangaroo, and so on. Today – as a later development – each 'citizen' is now identified by two names, normally the first of an animal and the second of a plant. Animal names also serve the obvious sociological purpose of marking the community's 'otherness', a purpose also served by the 'citizen's' customs of greeting each other (but not outsiders) with the words 'With you' ('*Con te*') rather than with the more usual 'Good morning' or 'Good evening'. Parapsychological experiments and other classical techniques of the occult–esoteric milieu are still occasionally used in Damanhur, but much more important are the visual arts as a tool for self-transformation and the use of a distinctive esoteric language (that 'citizens' regard as an ancient secret language rediscovered by Damanhur) – written both in Latin characters and in ideograms – and of musical themes and dance movements corresponding to this language. Oberto Airaudi has devised rituals – including ritual dresses – in order to facilitate the reintegration of humans into their original exalted condition, and at the same time the reintegration of Mother Earth threatened by an ecological disaster. Although observers may note that Egyptian symbols are somewhat predominant, Airaudi insists that the Egyptian religion is no more important than other traditions in building Damanhur's new synthesis. Egypt, he mentioned in a recent interview with the undersigned, has also been used in the Temple as a convenient *external* symbolism in order to hide more esoterical truths that Damanhur was not prepared to share with the outside world.

## The Underground Temple

Only in 1992 – due to unpredictable external circumstances – it became clear to outside observers that the main 'work' for the 'citizens' of Damanhur was not the building of a self-sufficient community, nor the performance of certain rituals and dances in the Open Temple. The most important work was the building of the Underground Temple. To the completion of this building is magically linked, in Damanhur's inner world-view, the salvation of the whole Planet Earth. Scholars – having ignored the very existence of the Underground Temple for many years – may now overestimate its central role in Damanhur. The spiritual and magical experience connected with the arts remains central in the community, but a significant part of the artistic enterprise appears to be centred on the Underground Temple.

Damanhur has been a remarkably stable community, with the number of defections actually lower than in non-communal New Religious Movements. Accordingly, lawsuits by former members – although not unknown – have not been a significant problem, and have normally been settled. In 1985, however, Filippo Maria Cerutti – a former member of the 'government' of Damanhur – left the community and sued Airaudi, asking for compensation for his former services and financial contributions (although Cerutti, a rich man, had never donated all his fortune to the community). In this case the evaluations by Cerutti and by Damanhur of what would have been a fair settlement were so far apart that an amicable solution proved impossible, and the case went to court. Cerutti – who had been part of Damanhur's inner circle – threatened to expose the existence of the Underground Temple. When, in 1992, it became clear that no settlement was possible, Cerutti contacted a District Attorney, Bruno Tinti, telling him the amazing story of a huge temple located under a small mountain, with miles of galleries and rooms. Although initially sceptical, the judge ordered a raid. Following Cerutti's indications, the tax police were able to uncover a large number of secret passages and technologically advanced devices hidden one after the other in the very heart of a small mountain, leading, one after the other, to hidden rooms of almost incredible magnificence.

Building temples, of course, is not a criminal offence in Italy, but Airaudi and Damanhur's 'government' were accused of the breach of zoning regulations and statutes requiring building permission. In 1993 the City of Vidracco, having jurisdiction on the Underground Temple, ordered its destruction. Due to the opposition of a considerable part of the public opinion – including social scientists and the artistic community – the order was never enforced. An inspection by state engineers ascertained that the underground works had not damaged the mountain (but rather consolidated it). On the other hand, authorities in charge of the preservation of the cultural patrimony of Piedmont decided that the Temple was a significant work of art and should be preserved. The court case was finally decided in 1996, and was largely favourable to Damanhur. Not only is the Temple safe from legal threats, but the community may now continue its work to expand it.

The Italian authorities in charge of the preservation of the works of art seem to have correctly assessed the artistic value of the Underground Temple when they declared it a protected 'collective artistic work'. For the outside visitor it is a breathtaking experience, offering – room after room – amazing and unexpected discoveries. The artworks (mainly stained-glass windows, frescoes and mosaics) are reminiscent of Byzantine, Egyptian and Greek models but also of Liberty's, the department store, and Art Deco, all these styles merged into a unique Damanhur perspective. One of the main rooms is the Water Room, dedicated to the Mother and the female principle, with a spectacular dolphin mosaic. The Earth Room has eight huge columns and a bull mosaic, dedicated to the male principle. The Glass Room, with the largest underground dome in the world, made of 60,000 small glass pieces, is the site of Damanhur's most important rituals. In addition to the three main rooms, there are apparently never-ending corridors, with stained-glass windows, Egyptian-style frescoes, many secret passages (often unsuspected and astonishing) and smaller rooms for parapsychological and magical experiments. Particularly significant is the Room of the Spheres, where big glass spheres are each connected to the always present 'self' (i.e. a metal spiral). Through these spheres the 'citizens' of Damanhur may get in touch with the continents and direct their magical energy where it is mostly needed. All in all, it is impossible to describe the Underground Temple, called the Temple of Man ('Tempio dell'Uomo', without using gender-inclusive language, although women are prominent in the leadership of Damanhur). There are literally miles of corridors, and thousands of statues, windows and paintings. In fact, each member of the community makes with his or her own hands a statue symbolically representing his or her connection with the animal whose name each 'citizen' has selected.

Entering the Underground Temple – an experience for the time being reserved to a small number of non-'citizens', including state and local officers, social scientists and some journalists – is, as sociologist Maria Immacolata Macioti has written, 'entering into a fairy tale.'[16] Although rituals are performed in the Temple, one understands that the most important ritual has been – for the last sixteen years – the construction of the Temple itself. The need for secrecy has precluded the use of noisy modern technological devices. Probably the secret was doomed from the beginning: it was very unlikely that it could be kept forever, even if the number of 'apostates' who defect from Damanhur is small. However, the very fact that the secret of so huge a project has effectively been kept for a decade and a half by some 500 people, with no hint reaching the anti-cultists or the press, is the real 'miracle' of Damanhur. On the other hand, the experience of Damanhur should be re-evaluated taking into account the Temple. Like the early Mormons in Nauvoo, the 'citizens' of Damanhur regard among their most sacred duties building the Temple, and all the other experiences – including the economic structure of the community – have among their aims allowing them time enough for their building enterprise. For this reason, Airaudi considers it extremely important that Damanhur should now be allowed to continue the construction. In his vision, the construction should continue to be the most important spiritual activity of the 'citizens' for some decades.

## The future of Damanhur

It is not impossible that the unwanted disclosure of the Underground Temple in 1992 will start a new phase for Damanhur. It has already compelled the community to engage in a closer dialogue with local and national authorities and with the public at large. Cerutti's 'revelations' have in fact made Damanhur a more important target for anti-cultists than it used to be. In 1992 the Roman Catholic Bishop of Ivrea, in whose Diocesan territory Damanhur is located, Mons. Luigi Bettazzi, released a document on the community. Bettazzi confirmed that no one could at the same time become a 'citizen' of Damanhur and remain a Roman Catholic in good standing. Even some Damanhur leaders regarded this statement as reasonable. Bettazzi, however, also accused Damanhur of 'immoral practices' and 'brainwashing', without further details and apparently following the anti-cult literature on the subject.[17] Ironically, Bettazzi is a controversial Bishop in Italy for his extremely liberal political views.

The birth of Damanhur could be described according to the well-known Stark–Bainbridge typology of audience cults, client cults and cult movements.[18] Damanhur's experience shows that a leader and his or her followers could pass subsequently through the three stages. Damanhur started as an audience cult including the readers of Airaudi's popular books. When Airaudi started a professional career as a 'pranotherapist' and healer, his regular clients moved from the audience cult to the client cult stage. Finally, Airaudi was capable of organising his clients into a movement, which eventually became communal.

The communal form of Damanhur, on the other hand, is not really typical of the Italian New Age. The New Age is – particularly in Italy – a network of independent and loosely structured groups.[19] Damanhur is anything but loosely structured. It claims to be a 'nation' with a 'government', a 'constitution' and a well-established hierarchy. It was developed before New Age became a household name in Italy, although it subsequently incorporated some (but not all) of New Age's most popular ideas. It will probably survive what J. Gordon Melton has called 'the demise of the New Age'.[20] Structured and hierarchically organised movements such as Damanhur were not really part of the New Age network, although they found many of their followers within the New Age milieu. In this respect it would be interesting to compare Damanhur to another community in Piedmont, the Green Village ('Villaggio Verde') of Cavallirio (Novara).[21] Although Damanhur and the Green Village have in common a theosophical reference, the Green Village is an 'open' community where only a dozen of people live but members of many different groups of the Theosophical and New Age milieu gather, particularly on Sunday, to perform a variety of different activities. Damanhur, on the other hand, is not an 'open' community. Although it welcomes visitors of different persuasions, in order to be a 'citizen', one has to share the rather precise world-view of Oberto Airaudi (although he insists that his world-view is evolving, and would not use the word 'religion').

Even the notion of 'movement', or 'New Religious Movement', fails to capture what Damanhur exactly is. Damanhur is, in fact, a community, and Oberto Airaudi insists that he has decided that it should *not* become a 'movement'. Discussing the matter with Airaudi, it becomes clear that what he does not like in the idea of 'movement' is the geographical dispersion of the members in a large territory. He claims that all attempts to organise settlements too far from the original location of Damanhur have not been successful. Damanhur could still grow in the future, but Airaudi would prefer that all the settlements – part of what the Constitution calls a 'federation' – remain in the Valchiusella valley, or at least in the province of Turin. It is true that Damanhur places great emphasis on computing, and that computer links could be easily established at longer distances. On the other hand, it is crucial for Airaudi that all the 'citizens' could meet regularly, share the life of one and the same community (and – as we now know – attend the Underground Temple rituals and participate in its never-ending construction). This has made Damanhur a selective community (all new 'citizens' have to pass through a probationary period before joining) with little interest in proselytism. The number of people who discover Damanhur through the lectures of Oberto Airaudi, the books and the possibility of visiting on Sunday as tourists results already in more applications to join than the community is prepared to accept. Groups of people who have visited Damanhur coming from as far away as Los Angeles have been counselled to 'do their own thing' and keep some sort of loose association without joining as 'citizens' or 'associates'. In other words, building the community is more important for Oberto Airaudi and his friends than taking a message to the outside world (although this second aspect has not been completely neglected, thanks to the publishing house, the magazines and the lectures). Building the Underground Temple and performing the rituals are more important than attracting new converts. This is probably also due to an esoteric and not yet fully disclosed apocalyptic vision of the fate of Planet Earth.

Oberto Airaudi will not turn 50 before the year 2000 and the group – despite being itself more than twenty years old – is still in an early and charismatic phase. Incidents such as the one involving the forced disclosure of the Underground Temple may accelerate the Weberian processes of routinisation of the charisma and lead to new directions. It would become increasingly difficult for the community – particularly if it continues to be successful – to avoid or prevent its own institutionalisation as a movement.

## Notes

1 See my *Il cappello del mago: I nuovi movimenti magici dallo spiritismo al satanismo*, Milan: SugarCo, 1990, pp. 87–90.
2 Luigi Berzano, 'Religione e autoperfezionamento', in Maria Immacolata Macioti (ed.), *Maghi e magie nell'Italia di oggi*, Florence: Angelo Pontecorboli Editore, 1991, pp. 141–86; republished in an updated version as 'Damanhur: un monastero per famiglie nell'età dell'acquario', in L. Berzano, *Religiosità del nuovo areopago: credenze e forme religiose nell'epoca postsecolare*, Milan: Franco Angeli, 1994, pp. 143–70; L. Berzano, *Damanhur: popolo e comunità*, Leumann (Turin): Elle Di Ci, 1998.
3 Mario Cardano, *Lo specchio, la rosa e il loto: uno studio sulla sacralizzazione della natura*, Rome: SEAM, 1997.
4 Maria Immacolata Macioti, 'Il tempio sotterraneo di Damanhur', *Ars Regia*, IV, 19, July–August 1994, pp. 4–9.
5 See e.g. Isotta Poggi, 'Alternative Spirituality in Italy', in James R. Lewis and J. Gordon Melton (eds), *Perspectives on the New Age*, Albany, NY: State University New York Press, 1992, pp. 271–86.
6 See for example the lengthy article by Javier Sierra, 'El secreto de Damanhur', *Mas allá de la ciencia* 50, April 1993, pp. 38–51.

7   See, for examples of an anti-cult treatment of Damanhur, Pier Angelo Gramaglia, *La reincarnazione*, Casale Monferrato (Alessandria): Piemme, 1989, pp. 384–92; Cecilia Gatto Trocchi, *Viaggio nella magia*, Rome and Bari: Laterza, 1993, pp. 59–72. For a criticism of the anti-cult book by Gatto Trocchi (an anthropologist) see my 'A proposito di viaggi nella magia', *La Critica Sociologica* 106 (Summer 1993): pp. 127–34. In 1998 anti-cult comments on Damanhur found their way, together with more balanced comments coming from scholarly literature, in the Italian police's report *Sette religiose e nuovi movimenti magici in Italia* (Rome: Ministero dell'Interno, 1998: pp. 87–9). The report is, in general, more moderate than similar French, Belgian or German documents. It also mentions a pending investigation on Damanhur generated in 1993 by claims of disgruntled ex-members in an Italian TV talk show and still unresolved.

8   Jeff Merrifield, *Damanhur: The Real Dream*, London: Thorsons, 1998.

9   For a comprehensive bibliography of Damanhur's own writings see Berzano, 'Damanhur: un monastero per famiglie nell'età dell'acquario', op. cit., pp. 166–70.

10  See, on this point, my 'La città delle meraviglie: spiritualità alternative, nuove religioni e magia a Torino', *Ars Regia*, III, 12, May–June 1993, pp. 24–35; and *Indagine sul satanismo: satanisti e anti-satanisti dal Seicento ai nostri giorni*, Milan: Mondadori, 1994.

11  See, on this point, Alessandro Bongioanni and Riccardo Grazzi, *Torino, l'Egitto e l'Oriente fra storia e leggenda*, Turin: L'Angolo Manzoni Editrice, 1994. What is known to the Mormons as the Book of Abraham in the *Pearl of Great Price* was 'translated' by the Mormon prophet Joseph Smith by interpreting papyri originally excavated in Egypt by the archaeologist Antonio Lebolo. The latter, a native of Castellamonte (near Turin, and in fact not far from present-day Damanhur), was an associate of Turin's Egyptian Museum.

12  Oberto Airaudi, *Cronaca del Mio Suicidio*, Turin: CEI, 1968.

13  Oberto Airaudi and U. Montefameglio, *Lo Spiritismo*, Turin: MEB, 1979.

14  See Berzano, 'Damanhur: un monastero per famiglie nell'età dell'acquario', op. cit., pp. 146, 150.

15  See 'Gabbiano' (Mauro Gagliardi) (ed.), *La Via Horusiana – il libro: princìpi e concetti fondamentali della scuola di pensoero di Damanhur*, 2nd edn, Turin: Horus, 1988, pp.104–10. Further information has been supplied in personal interviews by 'citizens' and leaders of Damanhur, including Oberto Airaudi.

16  Macioti, 'Il tempio sotterraneo di Damanhur', op. cit., p. 5.

17  Mons. Luigi Bettazzi, 'Parliamo di Damanhur', *Il risveglio popolare*, 22 October 1992, p. 3.

18  See Rodney Stark and William Sims Bainbridge, *The Future of Religion: Secularization, Revival, and Cult Formation*, Berkeley, CA: University of California Press, 1985, pp. 26–30. More recently, Bainbridge has recommended not using the word 'cults' when mentioning his 1985 typology because of the derogatory meaning it has assumed in the meantime.

19  See my *Storia del New Age 1962–1992*, Piacenza: Cristianità, 1994.

20  See J. Gordon Melton, 'The Future of the New Age', unpublished paper presented at the RENNORD 1994 conference, Greve, Denmark, August 1994.

21  See Isotta Poggi, 'An Experimental Theosophical Community in Italy: The Green Village', *Theosophical History*, IV, 4–5, October 1992–January 1993, pp. 149–54.

# Summary of Chapter 10

Augmenting the transcultural focus of the subject, Professor Clarke takes as his specific framework for analysis one particular cultural context, but within that context examines a congeries of imported new religions originally carried by alien immigrants – the Japanese in Brazil. His chapter sharpens the perception of new movements as a world-wide phenomenon. These religions have diverse life-histories, as they are disseminated from their country of origin, adapt to new cultural conditions and eventually influence increasing proportions of the indigenous population. Their initial success depends on their immigrant base, but in adapting to their new circumstances, those immigrants also infuse into an old culture new patterns of spirituality, different normative assumptions and new value systems.

# 10 Japanese New Religious Movements in Brazil

## From ethnic to 'universal' religions

*Peter B. Clarke*

## Introduction

Although their presence in Brazil dates back to the 1920s it was not until the 1960s that Japanese New Religious Movements, of which there are now at least thirty-two, began to make an impact beyond the boundaries of the Japanese immigrant communities. Today several of these movements claim a membership – a very difficult term to define precisely – of over 100,000 with two, Seicho no-Ie (House of Growth) and Sekai Kyuseikyo (Church of World Messianity) claiming more than 2 million followers, the vast majority of whom are Brazilians of non-Japanese origin. This chapter offers some insights into the reasons why and the ways in which these movements sought to move beyond their ethnic base in the Japanese community and insert themselves into the wider Brazilian society.

Japanese new religions are known as *shinko shukyo* (newly arising religion) and *shin shukyo* (new religion), terms which came into use among journalists and scholars in the 1950s, and since the 1960s the latter term has been the more widely used of the two. There is also a third label in use and that is the controversial term 'new, new-religions' (*shin shinshukyo*) which is intended to indicate a more recent stage in the development of the 'new' religions and is applied in particular to those movements such as Mahikari (True Light), Shinnyoen and Agonshu (Agama Sutra Sect) that rapidly increased their membership in the 1970s and 1980s while others such as the Soka Gakkai (Value Creation Society) were considered to have peaked.

Establishing a chronological framework of Japanese 'new' and 'new, new' religions is not without its difficulties. Four positions have been adopted regarding periodisation, the first of which looks to the beginning of the nineteenth century as the starting point. Those who take this position point to the rise and popular appeal at the time of new religions based on mountain worship such as Fuji-Ko. The second proposed starting date is the middle years of the nineteenth century when Kurozumikyo (the Teachings of Kurozumi), Tenrikyo (the Teaching of Heavenly Truth) and Konkokyo (the Teaching of the Golden Light) began to attract followers. The principal reason for this choice of starting point is that all three movements were to have a great influence on later Japanese New Religious Movements.

For similar reasons others look to the beginning of the twentieth century as the most appropriate starting point stressing the importance of the influence of Omotokyo (the Great Origin) and Reiyukai (Society of Friends of the Spirit) on 'new' religions in Japan. The fourth position on the starting date suggests the beginning of the post-World War II era when, with the introduction of the principles of religious freedom and the separation of 'Church' and State, many new movements began to flourish.

There are problems with all four starting points and these have been examined elsewhere.[1] It could be argued that the 'new' movements of the beginning of the nineteenth century that were to influence later ones were too few to constitute a solid basis for a trend in this direction. The third position which places the starting date at the beginning of the twentieth century overlooks the important influence of those earlier movements mentioned when discussing position two. Against the fourth position it can be said that it pays insufficient attention to the continuity between pre- and post-World War II 'new' movements such as Soka Gakkai. This leaves position two as the one favoured by many students of Japanese 'new' religions.[2]

Problems do not end with dating; the question of what to include in the category of 'new' religion is also difficult. 'New' religions draw heavily on the established religions for their teachings and there are no clear and precise ground rules for distinguishing between a renewal movement within an established religion and a 'new' religion as such. Many observers adopt the position that if the movement in question has a new founder and a new name, then it is new, although it might serve the same functions as the older movement from which it has emerged.

## The salient features of Japanese NRMs

The majority of 'new' and 'new, new' Japanese religions fit the category of manipulationist movements as described by Bryan Wilson.[3] That is, their main concern is with the provision of a modern, relevant faith in a society whose traditional belief systems are not easily accommodated to the new conditions created by the rapid process of urbanisation and industrialisation which Japan has experienced over the past 150 years and particularly since World War II. Moreover, as a result of the war Japan has had to re-evaluate how it sees itself and how it presents itself to the wider world, the 'new' and 'new, new' religions often presenting it as peacemaker and protector of the environment.

Other shared features of the 'new' and the 'new, new' religions include the emphasis they place on spiritual healing, on miracles and on the importance of ensuring that the ancestors are at rest. Most, moreover, are built on the personality of a charismatic founder usually regarded as an *ikigami*, that is one possessed by a deity. The differences between these religions can often be attributed to the differences in the personality of the founder or leader in question.

With few notable exceptions, these religious movements tend to be highly syncretistic, holding to a mixture of beliefs and practices derived from a number of Japanese traditional religious sources and in some cases also from outside Japan, for example, from Christianity, Hinduism and the New Thought movement of the late nineteenth century and from Western occult sources. Almost all have a strong faith in the continuing presence and power of the spirits of the dead to cause harm if left unpacified and almost all are convinced of their power to purify and heal. This attention to the spirits of the dead and to the ancestors is expressive of the view that life and death are not polar opposites and at the same time it can be interpreted as an affirmation of the primacy of life over death. It also has to be understood in the context of the link between shamanism and ancestor worship that is to be found in many 'new' and 'new, new' Japanese religions.

Almost all of the 'new' and the 'new, new' movements are millenarian, stressing that the end is near and that a new earthly paradise of peace, harmony, happiness and plenty is at hand for those who follow their precepts and that catastrophe and doom await those who do not. Nostradamus is a popular figure whose prophecies of imminent disaster are used by a number of movements to create among followers a spirit of dedication and enthusiasm and to strike fear into the indifferent and the waverer.

While the 'new' and 'new, new' religions pursue, albeit with varying degrees of endeavour and emphasis, the most elemental goals of Japanese religion – the attainment of personal well-being, the purification of the souls of the departed and the veneration of the ancestors – they also modify the methods of recruitment and to some degree the content of this religion. The modern architectural style of their places of worship is another mark of the distinctiveness of the 'new' and the 'new, new' religions as is the emphasis placed on and the energy put into recruitment.

The message itself, though derived from old sources, often contains 'new' emphases and elements including the stress on pacifism, environmental care and protection, and world transformation. These 'new' and 'new, new' movements also make great use of the mass media and modern technology to communicate their message and enlarge their following. In their pursuit and use of the benefits of modernity for this and other purposes, tradition is not neglected. Although rarely valued purely for its own sake, tradition is drawn upon as a spiritual, psychological and emotional resource to cope with the stresses and strains of modernity.

The Japanese 'new' and 'new, new' religions are contemporary expressions of Japanese religiosity that in certain respects constitute a critique of the older, more established traditions. Furthermore, they are often less hierarchical and less dominated by a priestly class, thereby assigning much more importance to the lay members. Indeed, as a leading spokesperson for Seicho-no-Ie pointed out, they could quite correctly be interpreted as the vanguards of the development of non-establishment, essentially lay spirituality and religion in Japan.

Their protest goes beyond attacking what they perceive to be the doctrinal inadequacies and defects of the older religious movements that espoused the political and military aims of the state. Others have been anti-establishment including Tenrikyo with its cry of 'reform of the world' (*ya naoshi*) and Omotokyo with its 'reconstruction of the world' (*yo no tatekai*). This opposition has sometimes met with repression from governments while appealing to many ordinary Japanese citizens.

Another dimension of 'newness' is the provision of techniques by means of which members can secure the benefits to be derived from the sacred teachings and practices which the founders of the movements have uncovered. Toda Josei of Soka Gakkai reportedly referred to the movement's mandala as 'a machine that turns out happiness'.[4]

The teachings are often presented as entirely new in the sense that they are put forward as the first ever correct interpretation of a particular sacred text or tradition. For example, the founder of Myoho Renge Shu, Tamei Nicherei, formerly a member of Soka Gakkai, maintains that the latter's claim that its founder Nichiren Daishonin (1222–82) was the reincarnation of the Boddhisattava Jogyo (i.e. the representative of the Buddha's virtue of true self) is based on an incorrect reading of history which, properly understood for the first time only now, points to himself as the Jogyo.

Thus, 'new' or 'new, new' movements sometimes see themselves as presenting what can amount to a radical, alternative version of a long-held belief or set of beliefs. Agonshu is another example of this. Although it had been in existence for some time previously, in 1978 its founder Seiyu Kiriyama Kancho claimed he had discovered new, hidden truths by reading early Buddhist texts known as the *Agama sutras*, texts which had previously been given little attention in Japan. Able to discover the hidden, inner meaning of these texts Kiriyama uncovered a direct and rapid road to Buddhahood (*jobutsu-ho*) for the living, and, just as importantly, for the spirits of the dead. For there is a need to ensure that the latter attain Buddhahood or *jobutsu* if the living are to be at peace and to secure well-being and prosperity.[5]

The new religions also tend to be more international and universalistic in their vision and outreach than the older, more established religions, regarding it as their mission to bring peace and fulfilment to the whole world. This in part explains their missionary endeavour in many countries outside Japan, beginning in Brazil with Omotokyo (religion of the Great Origin) in the late 1920s.

The term 'new, new' does not suggest a radical discontinuity between those movements to which it is applied and the 'new religions'. It is not even chronologically meaningful in every case. The term 'new, new' has been applied, for example, to Agonshu, the roots of which can be traced back to the early 1950s. However, Agonshu began to flourish only in the late 1970s and throughout the 1980s, while movements such as Soka Gakkai and Seicho no-Ie were considered to have peaked by that time. It is chiefly this factor, and their greater emphasis on traditional spiritual explanations of life accompanied by a strong belief in miracles, the greater degree of importance attached by them to ancestors and to tradition in general and their strikingly lively, thrusting, dynamic approach to the dissemination of their message – making for a close resemblance to the Christian televangelist Churches of North America – that have earned them the label 'new, new' religions (*shin shinshukyo*).

## The response to modernity

Both the 'new' and the 'new, new' religions have demonstrated more concern than the established religions for the effects on the individual and society of modernity and contemporary change and offer many Japanese beliefs and practices that enable them to respond to the rapid economic, political and cultural changes that their country has witnessed during the past 150 years and particularly since the end of World War II. At the highest level of generality this is principally why they appeal. Movements also provide a community structure to those in urban areas who lack close links with family or friends.

The modern garb in which they present Japanese core values such as the importance of the pacification of the ancestors and the spirits of the dead, notions of spiritual causality of illness, the emphasis on this-worldly success and happiness, also attracts many. Those in the West who join these movements often stress the relevance of their beliefs and practices to daily life and find compelling their notions of spiritual causality and the control over their life that this explanation of illness offers. Their already mentioned concern with peace and environmental issues likewise attracts by giving members and would-be members the sense that, far from being powerless and incapacitated by modernity, they can actually control and harness it in ways compatible with personal happiness and the good life here on earth.

The appeal of the 'new' and the 'new, new' religious movements is variable. Very broadly speaking, in the Japanese context many of these movements display the characteristics of revitalisation movements: they rework and reshape traditional beliefs, rituals and symbols in such a way as to make them relevant to the social, cultural and spiritual needs and aspirations of the present.[6] Outside Japan their appeal is necessarily different. For the most part, with a few notable exceptions, the 'new' and 'new, new' Japanese religions that have established themselves in countries in the West are confined in terms of membership to Japanese living abroad and their spouses or relatives who are often European or American. This is the case, for example, in Canada[7] and in the United States where only Zen and Macrobiotics have found mass appeal outside the Japanese-American community.[8]

## The Brazilian context and the Japanese heritage

Official Japanese immigration to Brazil dates back to the arrival of 781 immigrants on the steamer *Kasato Maru* on 18 June 1908 at the port of Santos in the state of São Paulo, having left Kobe three weeks earlier on 28 April.[9] Some of the first settlers, now in their nineties, are still alive. Most were employed as agricultural labourers on the coffee, cotton and banana plantations.

For many of the pre-World War II Japanese settlers in Brazil Japanese remains their only language while many second (*nisei*) and third (*sansei*) generation Brazilians of Japanese descent are bilingual, speaking both Japanese and Portuguese and know virtually nothing about the history, culture, religious beliefs and practices of their parents and grandparents. They were often thoroughly 'catholicised' and until relatively recently that meant the rejection of all that was 'non-Catholic'. Often one finds that the younger generation of Brazilians of Japanese descent have never visited the temple frequented by their parents and the *butsudan* (Buddhist shrine) or *Kamidana* (Shinto household altar) are usually in the parents' bedroom and it is only the latter who pray and place offerings there.

Many of the Japanese settlers, especially the second (*nisei*) and third (*sansei*), generations have joined Christian denominations as in California.[10] Japanese-Brazilians have their own Assemblies of God church in São Paulo, and a considerable number of the second and third generations are Catholics[11] while in California the Methodist Church appears to have the largest number of Japanese-American worshippers.[12] In Brazil there has also been a movement of Japanese to Umbanda and on a lesser scale to Spiritism. Japanese temples in turn attract many from Umbanda, Spiritualism and Catholicism. These temples are known locally as *igrejas* or churches. Much of the terminology used in speaking about Japanese religion in Brazil is Catholic while in the United States it is Protestant. In Brazil naming rites are referred to as *baptism* and the main temple ceremony is called the *mass,* while the one who presides over the rituals is the *padre* or priest and the head monk is the *bispo* or bishop. In California Jodo Shinshu or True Pure Land Buddhism which, in cities such as San José draws 99 per cent of its members from the Japanese-American community, uses the word church instead of temple, is known as the Buddhist Church of America (BCA) and uses the title reverend instead of monk. It also introduced a nativity service for the Buddha that parallels Christmas and celebrates the day of his enlightenment as *Jodo-e* on 8 December, the popular Christian feastday of the Immaculate Conception. In California Buddhist wedding and funeral ceremonies have also been influenced by Christianity and practices such as grace before meals have been introduced into Buddhist homes.[13]

In Brazil the Buddhist temples are sought out principally for the healing that they offer. In the temple precincts there are numerous shrines to Jizo, the bald

Buddhist figure who protects travellers, children and the souls of the dead. The Japanese *santos* (saints) do not always perform exactly the same role as in Japan or conform precisely to the image people have of them there. In Brazil both role and image have been somewhat modified by the differing demands and requirements of life there. The same process of domestication is also marked in Afro-Brazilian religion also known as Candomble or Umbanda where the image and understanding of the role and function of certain of the gods of African origin have been changed almost beyond recognition.

Assimilation in terms of religious language and 'saintly' roles and functions notwithstanding, the Japanese Buddhist traditions in Brazil have retained much of their Japanese heritage in terms of beliefs, rituals, outlook and architectural style, among other things.

There is often more than one Japanese Buddhist tradition in the same locality. The largely Japanese town of Suzano, situated some 50 km to the east of São Paulo with a population of 180,000, is home to numerous Japanese old, 'new' and 'new, new' Japanese religions. Among the 'new' religions are Soka Gakkai with a membership of around 1,000 families, and Risshokoseikai, Omotokyo, Tenrikyo, Seichono-Ie, Buts-Ryu-Shu (Followers of Buddha), all of which have far fewer members. The most active and largest of the 'new, new' movements in Suzano is Mahikari, and Kofuku-no Kagaku (Science of Human Happiness), although still very small, has recently been increasing the number of its adepts in the town.

Suzano has a Japanese Buddhist temple belonging to the Honpa Honganji temple of the Amida or Pure Land Buddhist tradition, which is affiliated to the Mother temple in Kyoto, the *Jodo Shinshu Honganji-ha* – often referred to as Nishi (western)-Honganji. The *Shinshu Otaniha* or Higashi (eastern) Honganji-ha tradition of Pure Land Buddhism is also present in Suzano but does not appear to be as strong as the Nishi Honganji. There are also two Shingo temples.

The tradition of Pure Land Buddhism has a Chinese prototype and owes its origins in Japan to Honen (1133–1212) who divided Buddhism into two types: one in which people attempt to gain enlightenment through disciplined self-effort and one in which people seek to be born in the Pure Land, the spiritual state of oneness with ultimate reality, through reliance on the mercy of Amida Buddha. Honen himself followed the second type, giving as his reasons his belief that the saving power of Amida Buddha was absolute and his conviction that people were so deeply enmeshed in sin as to be incapable of achieving enlightenment through their own efforts. Honen was convinced that in this final period of history (*mappo*) in which Buddhism had degenerated into little more than an empty shell, the only way to salvation was through reliance on the merciful compassion of Amida Buddha. All forms of ritual and meditation were left to one side in favour of the *nembutsu* practice, that is, the chanting of the invocation *Namu-Amida-Butsu*, meaning devotion to the Amida Buddha.

One of Honen's best known disciples Shinran (1173–1262) founder of

Jodo Shinshu (True Pure Land Buddhism) basing himself on the Larger Sutra of Immeasurable Life went further than his master in rejecting the possibility that individuals could save themselves by their own efforts. Instead, he insisted that the compassion and saving power of Amida were absolute. More precisely, Shinran's doctrine of predestination asserted that the compassion and saving power of Amida had already in fact been effective in that all had already in principle been saved by these means although many perhaps were unaware of this. Shinran also brought Buddhism closer to ordinary life by teaching that while secular, worldly values and aspirations do not constitute an authentic basis for living, nevertheless people should not break off their ties with the world. He rejected the idea of a religious elite and attempted to abolish the distinction between religious virtuosi and lay people, claiming that it was not necessary to lead a monastic, celibate life in order to be a devout Buddhist and live up to its highest ideals. Rather, it was perfectly possible to live in the world, marry and bring up a family and achieve the same goals as a monk. His teachings had a wide appeal and his movement is one of the largest Buddhist movements in present-day Japan.

One of Suzano's two Shingon temples, the Igreja Buddhista Nambei Yugazam Jyomiyoji, is possibly the largest Japanese Buddhist temple in Latin America. Shingon (True Words) Buddhism is the oldest tantric Buddhist sect in Japan founded in 815 by Kukai, posthumously known as Kobo Daishi (774–835), who brought the teachings from China. More precisely, the temple is a branch of the Shingon movement known as Shingon Shugendo, reportedly founded by En-no-ozunu (posthumously honoured as Jinpen Daibotsatsu), the seventh-century shamanistic mountain ascetic. The sect features the climbing of sacred mountains, mountain worship and magical rituals and the temple in Suzano is appropriately situated in elevated woodlands outside the town.

The Shingon movement bases its teachings on the *Dainichi* and *kongocho* sutras and one of its main practices for the attainment of Buddhahood is the chanting of the secret words of the Mahavairochana Buddha. It claims that its esoteric teachings were transmitted from the Mahavairochana Buddha to Vajrasattva and on down through Nagarjuna, Nagabodhi, to Vajrabodhi and Amoghavajra, who brought the teachings from India to China in the eighth century. It was in Ch'ang-an in China that the Japanese priest Kobo Daishi studied these teachings from 804–6 under the master Hui-Kuo before returning to Japan and founding a temple on Mount Koya in 816 and another at To-ji in 823. The sect divided on Kobo Daishi's death into the Ono and Hirosawa schools and today there are numerous branches of Shingon. Both the Pure Land (Jodo Shinshu) and the True Word (Shingon) traditions of Buddhism were brought to Brazil in the first instance by immigrants from Japan.

A great deal of the activity in the Buddhist temples in Brazil revolves round the statue of Jizo, the above-mentioned saint, who, according to one of its four monks, is '*mais para as mulheres, para as pessoas que querem bebê* (more for women, for people who want children)'.

The present enthusiasm for temple building and involvement in religion was not a feature of Japanese immigrant culture in Brazil prior to World War II. Perhaps the extent to which the immigrants failed to practise any form of religion until the 1950s has been exaggerated. However, among the reasons why religion was not central to their lives until the 1950s was the widespread belief that they would one day return to Japan, a notion found in so many first-generation immigrant communities, including Asians in Britain.[14] Moreover, a principal element of Japanese religion, the cult of the ancestors, was not something which they felt it was necessary to perform in Brazil, for this cult was performed for them in their absence by their kinsfolk in Japan. The myth of the return ran deep in the culture of the Japanese settlers, the death of one of the members in Brazil being referred to as the 'death of a visitor: a morte do visitante', or 'death in a foreign land: a morte alheia'.[15] The lack of organised religion among the Japanese immigrants prior to World War II was partly compensated for by the Japanese school. The immigrant school became, once a month, a virtual shrine for the recitation of the Imperial Rescript on Education of 1890. As in Japan, the Rescript was solemnly and religiously venerated as if it were a deity, and the principal of the school assumed the role of a monk wearing white gloves as he recited the relevant excerpts on filial piety and loyalty in front of the portrait of the Emperor, the symbol of power and authority and the focal point of reverence and respect. There was a groundswell of Shinto and nationalistic sentiment in Brazil during and after the end of World War II.[16] Those immigrants in particular who belong to the *kachi-gumi* or victory group that refused to accept that Japan had been defeated formed the *Yasukuni ko* (Yasukuni association) to assist with the maintenance of the Yasukuni Jinja where all the Japanese war dead are enshrined as *kami* (gods), and constructed a miniature of this shrine at Marilia in the south-west of the state of São Paulo.

On the other hand, by the 1950s ever increasing numbers of Japanese immigrants had decided to settle permanently in Brazil and many more were soon to achieve middle-class status. Large numbers were moving into the towns while those who remained in the rural areas became producers, land owners and distributors of farm and other products. Not only were *Butsudan* (Buddhist altars) popular, but more households installed *kamidana* (Shinto altars) and more shrines were constructed.

The most developed Shinto shrine and movement in Brazil today is Hokkoku Dai Jingu (Great Shinto Shrine of Brazil) or Iwato Jinja (in Japanese mythology this is the name of the place where the sun Goddess Amaterasu concealed herself in distress at her brother's perverse behaviour only to be coaxed out of it by other deities). Hokkoku Dai Jingu was established as Kaminoya Yaoyorozu Kyo (the Dwelling of the Myriad Deities) in 1966 at Aruja to the north-east of São Paulo by the nonagenarian Suzuko Morishita, the daughter of a Shinto ascetic (*gyoja*). Today people look upon her as a *sensei* (teacher) or one who receives messages from the gods (*miko*). In 1968 the movement acquired the status of the Brazilian branch of the Ise Jingu, the spiritual centre of Japanese Shinto and shrine of the imperial ancestors. There are a number of smaller, auxiliary shrines at the Aruja sanctuary complex including one that has all the typical features found at a shrine of a protector deity of the land and people, an *uji-gami*. Syncretism is in evidence in some of the smaller shrines which house together Buddhist images such as Jizo and Catholic images of Jesus and Nossa Senhora da Aparecida (Our Lady of Aparecida, patroness of Brazil). In a recent interview with this writer, Suzuko Morishita explained this syncretism by saying that there were no racial divisions in the life beyond, only in this life, and that since her message has its source in the realm of the gods it was meant for all peoples. This may explain why the movement she founded has a substantial number of non-Japanese-Brazilians among its estimated 10,000 members.[17]

The first of the new religions to evangelise in Brazil in the 1920s were largely Shinto-derived, Tenrikyo (the Religion of Heavenly Truth) founded in 1937 and Omotokyo (Religion of the Great Origin) started in 1892. Among the other predominantly Shinto movements in Brazil are: Kurozumikyo founded in 1814 by the Shinto priest Kurozumi Munetada (1780–1850) and Konkokyo founded in 1859 by Kawate Bunjiro (1814–83).

New religions that are not strictly speaking Shinto often manifest Shinto features. This holds, for example, for Seicho-no-Ie (House of Growth), Sekai Kyuseikyo (Church of World Messianity) and Perfect Liberty Kyodan. Seicho-no-Ie (House of Growth) which became known in Brazil soon after it was founded in Kobe in 1932, through the writings of its founder Masaharu Taniguchi, contains both Buddhist and Shinto elements in its beliefs and practices and even some Christian and New Thought ideas. Its highly elaborate Shinto shrine houses the tutelary deity Ookumi-mushi-no-kami, the protector god of happy marriages and economic prosperity, who is the principal deity of the Great Shrine of Izumo in Shimane Prefecture in southeastern Japan. In Brazil this deity has acquired several other roles including that of ruling god of other countries (*Gaukoku-tsukasa-no-kami*) who protects the Japanese and their descendants living in other lands, and is also the protector of agriculturalists living in frontier zones (*kaitaku-no-kami*).

Following the Shinto model, several of the new religions emphasise that their object of worship serves as the protector of the land of Brazil and continue to utilise the Shinto–Buddhist–Folk practices of Shugendo, in particular *kaji-kito*, incantations and prayers, with a view to exorcising evil influences and guaranteeing economic prosperity.

## The process of Brazilianisation

As previously pointed out, the 1950s saw the Japanese community place increasingly less emphasis on returning home to Japan and much more on settling permanently in Brazil. That meant creating the *ie* or household there which in turn entailed the development of a more formal set of religious rituals and traditions, and in particular of ancestor worship. Indeed, by the late 1950s, the older generation of Japanese Brazilians had begun to refer to themselves as 'the ancestors', indicating that they would require the appropriate burial rites and ceremonies in Brazil. And in a number of cases, ashes of dead relatives were imported from Japan itself to become the foundations of the ancestral shrine.

Some new movements consciously strove to retain their Japanese character in full throughout the 1950s and into the 1960s and a few continue today in this vein. Those that have resisted enculturation are generally numerically small while those that adapted increased their numbers exponentially for a period of twenty years, growing beyond all recognition, but now seem to have reached their peak and to be on a downward spiral.

Tenrikyo (Heavenly Wisdom) is one example of a movement that has not sought to adapt. It arrived in Brazil in 1929 shortly after Omotokyo (the Great Origin). Like several other Japanese new religions, Tenrikyo was founded by a woman, Miki Nakayama, the daughter of a farmer, who received her first revelations in 1837. She taught that the Heavenly Kingdom was drawing near, bringing to an end a world of sickness and poverty.[18] Her appeal was in the main to the farming communities that had lost their property and status during the period of the Meiji land reforms in the second half of the nineteenth century. Tenrikyo has around 150,000 teachers and an estimated membership of 1.5 million who worship God the Parent, the creator and sustainer of life. Miki Nakayama is both the shrine of God the Parent, and the mediatrix between this God and humanity.

This movement, the cosmology of which places Japan at the centre of the universe and depicts the Japanese as the original and supreme race, is prototypical of many of the 'new' Japanese religions, combining as it does elements of Shintoism and Buddhism while emphasising the laws of karma and reincarnation.

Japanese new religions, whatever their doctrinal and ritual basis, are more numerous and strongest in the south of Brazil, particularly in São Paulo although several of these have expanded north to the states of Bahia and Pernambuco in recent times. Sometimes compared to multinational companies or businesses,[19] some spread their message mainly through their publications and count regular subscribers as members or associate members. As we have seen, Seicho no-Ie (House of Growth) is widely regarded as the largest of the Japanese new religions in Brazil, followed by Sekai Kyuseikyo (Church of World Messianity), Soka Gakkai (Value Creation Society), and Perfect Liberty Kyodan (the Religion of Perfect Liberty). Some of the new religions are very recent, have few facilities and are still preoccupied with laying their foundations. Among the newer and much smaller movements is Kofuku-no Kagaku (Institute for Research in Human Happiness), reportedly one of the largest and fastest-growing movements in Japan. This movement entered Brazil in 1992 and by March 1996 had recruited over 2,000 members most of them from the City of São Paulo or from Greater São Paulo and the remainder from other states including Matto Grosso do Sul and Parana.

As increasing numbers of *nisei* and *sansei* turned to Catholicism in the 1950s, in part to enter more fully into Brazilian society, it became evident that if the new religions were to expand they would be obliged to concentrate their efforts on attracting other members than Japanese-Brazilians. This in turn entailed, as in North America, the shedding of much of their Japanese heritage and adapting their language and ritual to the needs and requirements of the wider Brazilian society. Movements that followed this path met with remarkable success in a very short space of time. For example, Seicho no-Ie membership was estimated at 15,000 in 1968, 99 per cent of whom were of Japanese descent. By 1988 the membership had risen to *c.* 2,400,000, 85 per cent of whom were not of Japanese descent.[20] In the mid-1960s this movement began the process of indigenisation with the establishment of a department of doctrine using Portuguese as the language of instruction and communication. In 1967 its review was translated into Portuguese as *Acendedor* and sent to Brazilians of non-Japanese origin for the first time. Also in 1967 reading circles for Brazilians at large were formed for the first time.

Seicho no-Ie also took the decision to advertise itself as a philosophy rather than a religion thus allaying fears which some Catholics and other Christians might have had about joining a non-Christian religion and this has undoubtedly assisted its growth in Brazil. Furthermore, where it once emphasised that its doctrines and ethics would make its members 'good Japanese' it began to stress, in line with the pursuit of Brazilianisation by many of the *isseis*, that its teachings and practices would assist members to become 'good Brazilians'. Although Perfect Liberty Kyodan and Sekai Kyuseikyo did not expand so spectacularly, they nevertheless made impressive headway among the wider Brazilian population by a similar process of adaptation of their teachings, practices and ethos. Perfect Liberty Kyodan, which has some 400 churches and an estimated 500,000 adepts in Japan,[21] has been active in Brazil since 1957 and has turned Aruja City on the outskirts of São Paulo into its sanctuary for Latin America, carrying over to that part of the world the concept of Holy or Sacred Place found in Japan. Members from Argentina, Bolivia, Peru, Paraguay and the other Spanish-speaking countries of Latin and Central America gather there, emphasising its spiritual significance. Spiritual healing once attracted large numbers to this movement but for the past decade or more the practical ethical guidance which it offers for daily life in a modern environment appears to have an equal if not even greater appeal.[22] Perfect Liberty and other Japanese new religions did perform and still do perform a similar role in Japan, enabling people from the rural areas and smaller towns to find a means of coping with the demands made on them in an increasingly fragmented, rapidly changing urban environment. While there has been considerable adaptation, and although there is much variation from movement to movement, it should be noted that authority and control rest ultimately with Japan in the case of virtually all the Japanese new and 'new, new' religions in Brazil.

## Conclusion

In the absence of reliable statistics and with the mostly vague and open-ended notion of membership it is extremely difficult to estimate the size of the Japanese new and 'new, new' religions in Brazil. This notwithstanding, those associated with these religions probably have to be counted in millions rather than thousands. These movements, although from another culture, owe their success in Brazil to a considerable degree to the fact that they were able to build on an already existing substratum of beliefs similar in certain respects to the ones they taught. Latin and Central America and Caribbean societies generally have for long had contact with some of the key beliefs and practices preached by the Japanese new religions including the idea of reincarnation, the spiritual roots of sickness and healing and the cult of the dead through their indigenous traditions.

Looking beyond the specifically religious sphere, the Japanese new movements do not as yet exert anything approaching the degree of influence on the art, architecture, music, diet, dress, language and literature, the economy or the health system or the social structure as, for example, the African–Amerindian–Catholic or the Spiritist movements. Moreover, unlike these other religions, they are much more class-based and class-oriented. They have hardly touched the life of the poorer sections of society. None the less, the trade in *butsudans* (Buddhist household altars) and *kamidanas* (Shinto household altars) in São Paulo, and the building of impressive Buddhist temples and Shinto shrines there and throughout the state, are signs that the beliefs and practices of Japan are no longer simply an exotic appendage to the religious and cultural life of Latin America's largest and most economically and industrially advanced region.

## Notes

1 P. B. Clarke 'Japanese "Old', "New" and "New, New" Religions in Brazil', in P. B. Clarke and J. Somers (eds), *Japanese New Religions in the West*, Folkestone, Kent: Curzon Press/Japan Library, 1994, pp. 150–61.
2 N. Inoue (ed.), *New Religions: Contemporary Papers in Japanese Religions*, (2), Tokyo: Kokugakuin University Institute for Japanese Culture and Classics, 1991.
3 B. R. Wilson, *Religious Sects*, London: Weidenfeld and Nicolson, 1971.
4 H. N. McFarland, *The Rush Hour of the Gods: A Study of New Religious Movements in Japan*, New York: Macmillan, 1967.
5 I. Reader, *Religion in Contemporary Japan*, Basingstoke and London: Macmillan, 1991.
6 A. Wallace, 'Revitalisation Movements', in *American Anthropologist*, 58(2), 1956, pp. 264–81.

7  M. Mullins, 'The Transplantation of Religion in Comparative Sociological Perspective', in *Japanese Religions*, 16(2), July, 1990, pp. 43–62.
8  J. Gordon Melton and C. Jones, 'New Japanese Religions in the United States', in Clarke and Somers , op. cit., pp. 33–54.
9  H. Saito, *O Japonês no Brasil*, São Paulo: Editora Sociologia e Política, 1961. For a detailed account of the daily life of early Japanese immigrants in the state of São Paulo, see T. Handa, *Memórias de um immigrante Japonês no Brasil*, São Paulo: T. A. Queiroz, 1961.
10  B. M. Hayashi, *For the Sake of Our Japanese Brethren*, Stanford, CA: Stanford University Press, 1995.
11  *Uma Epopéia Moderna: 80 Anos da Imigração Japonesa no Brasil*, São Paulo: Editora Hucitec, 1992.
12  Hayashi, op. cit., p. 4.
13  K. Yanagawa (ed.), *Japanese Religions in California*, Tokyo: University of Tokyo, Dept. of Religious Studies, 1993, p. 35.
14  M. Anwar, *The Myth of Return*, London: Heinemann, 1979.
15  T. Maeyama, 'O Antepassado, o Imperador e o Imigrante: Religião e Identificação de Grupo dos Japoneses no Brasil Rural (1908–50)', in *Estudos Brasileiros: Integração e Assimilação dos Japoneses no Brasil*, São Paulo: Centro dos Estudos Nipo-Brasileiros, 1971, p. 430.
16  Ibid.
17  P. B. Clarke, interview material from field work, São Paulo, May 1995.
18  R. S. Ellwood Jnr, *Tenri-kyo: A Pilgrimage Faith* Tenri, Nara: Oyasato Research Institute, Tenri University, 1982.
19  H. Nakamaki, 'The Indigenization and Multinationalization of Japanese Religion: Perfect Liberty Kyodan in Brazil', in *Japanese Journal of Religious Studies*, 18, 1991, pp. 213–41.
20  *Uma Epopéia*, op. cit., pp. 544ff.
21  P. B. Clarke, interview material from field work at Perfect Liberty Kyodan headquarters at Tondabayashi, April 1996.
22  Y. Fujikura, *Alguns Aspectos de Inculturação no Trabalho Missionário da PL no Brasil* (Mestrado: Ciencias da Religião, São Paulo: Pontificia Universidade Catolica (PUC), 1992.

# Summary of Chapter 11

Quite apart from the challenge which NRMs presented within the context of major social institutions were the more explicit patterns of response which they evoked initially from those concerned to defend (as they saw it) the integrity of the family and to protect young people. First in the United States, and then widely in other Western cultures, voluntary agencies arose, so-called 'anti-cult' movements, sometimes specifically claiming to be family defence organisations. Dr Melton traces the career of these organisations in America, their development from groups of amateur activists into quasi-professional vigilante organisations, until in more recent years the ardour of this response to new religions appears to have considerably waned.

# Summary of Chapter 5

# 11 Anti-cultists in the United States

## An historical perspective

*J. Gordon Melton*

## Introduction

The approaching end of the twentieth century has seen the decline of what became an important reactionary social movement in the West in the last quarter of the twentieth century. The anti-cult movement was a response to the global religious diversification in the decades since World War II, but owed its origin to the noticeable rise of new Asian and occult religions in the United States in the early 1970s. The post-war spread of what became known as new religions followed two very different patterns in Europe and North America.

A gradual penetration of the European nations by 'new' religions (i.e. Asian religions) began soon after the dust settled from, not so much World War II, as the Chinese revolution and the declaration of Indian independence. Migrants brought their religions into the nations of Europe through the colonial systems, especially into England, France, and Holland, and by the government-sponsored migration of needed labourers into Germany and Switzerland. At the same time, Western vagabonds began their now legendary treks into Asia in search of spiritual wisdom only to return to their homeland as initial converts to unfamiliar (to the rest of us) faiths. The change was gradual and problems with migrants tended to focus on ethnic and racial issues rather than religion. Much of the new religious life was and still is confined to the migrant ghettos, but increasingly religious teachers visited and then settled in Europe. They increased the religious diversity already created by the home-grown religious dissidents who had emerged as founders of new alternative religious communities through the nineteenth and twentieth centuries. Beginning with the formation of the Swedenborgian church, numerous new religions (alternatives to traditional Christianity) emerged in Europe. Most notable were the post-Mesmerist magical (Rosicrucian, Neo-templar, and Martinist) orders that appeared in France, Spiritualism which diffused across the continent from Great Britain and Paris, and Theosophy. Through the twentieth century, almost every country from Bulgaria (Great White Brotherhood) to Denmark (Martinus Institute), to Great Britain (New Age Movement, Wicca) contributed to the emerging pluralism as Gnosticism revived in the climate of post-Enlightenment religious freedom.

In America the pattern of diversification was quite different due to the passing of a series of laws in the first decades of this century which prevented migration from Asia. The culminating Asian Exclusion Act of 1924 was in force until the fall of 1965 when it was rescinded as a result of Presidents Kennedy and Johnson calling upon the member nations of the Southeast Asian Treaty Organisation to support the war effort in Vietnam. The price of co-operation was the removal of insulting and discriminatory immigration policies against member countries by the United States. One result was the sudden influx of hundreds of thousands of Asians into the United States and the opening of the country to the endeavours of Asian religious missionaries (usually arriving under such titles as swami, bhagwan, yogi, guru, pir, sensei, or master).

The sudden availability of Asian teachers coincided with a unique situation in American life, the coming of age of the post-war baby boom generation. That very large generation had been a problem for more than a decade as it put pressure on the public school system which had to find space and teachers to accommodate them, and now confronted the business community with the need for jobs, jobs which were simply unavailable. One response was the development of a new subculture, the street-people culture. The street people emerged in urban centres across the United States but was especially pronounced along the Pacific Coast where both the climate and a socially tolerant society provided them with the greatest degree of freedom. One aspect of the new subculture of special importance to its religious development was the swelling of the subculture each summer by college kids (especially those rich enough not to have to work all summer) who idealised the lifestyle of the street people and joined them for their annual vacation period.

Thus in America, as new religious leaders began to pour into the country at the end of the 1960s, they joined those indigenous leaders already actively working this self-selected 'lost' generation living on the streets. Swami Prabhupada (Hare Krishna) began in Greenwich Village, Yogi Bhajan (Sikh Dharma) in Los Angeles, and the Unification Church in Eugene, Oregon, and Washington, DC. They were joined by several groups founded in the United States, most prominently the Church of Scientology and the groups of the Jesus People movement, as well as the imports from Europe (Wicca, Friends of Meher Baba). Earlier Alan Watts, who became the great populariser of Zen, had migrated from England. Each of these groups adapted itself to the generation on the streets, and their love of psychedelic drugs, and took a high percentage of their early recruits from among them.

The penetration of the street-people culture by new religions might have largely gone unnoticed were it not for the large number of summer hippies who swelled their ranks. Many of the recruits to the new religions came from these vacationers who found membership in a new religion to be a welcome alternative to their return to college life and the prospect of a career which had been wished upon them by their middle- and upper-middle-class parents. While the majority of parents were quite tolerant of their son's or daughter's new religion, some were quite upset, not so much with their flirting with a new faith but their dropping out of school, their turning over their income/inheritance to a strange foreign group, and/or their assuming a position in the religion as their life's career. To put it bluntly, how does a secular parent tell acquaintances that his/her offspring has become a missionary working the streets for a low status religion rather than a doctor, lawyer, or executive?

The actual number of young adults who dropped into the new religions was low, but just enough had dropped earlier career plans that by the early 1970s a few upset parents began to voice their anger publicly and quickly found that they were not alone. The first networks of what was to become a national movement began to emerge. The alarm over what was occurring was also sounded by the Jewish community. In 1972, several evangelical Christian organisations announced plans for what was to be known as 'Key '73', a massive door-to-door campaign designed to present every household in America with the evangelical gospel. Among those who quickly signed on in support were the many Jewish evangelism groups who saw an opportunity to canvas the Jewish community in which they had been quietly working since the 1920s. The leadership in the Jewish communities across the country reacted quickly and denounced the effort. In the process of negotiating their concerns with the leaders of the Key '73 campaign, they became aware of a host of other missionary groups both Christian (Unification Church, Children of God, the Way International) and Eastern (primarily Zen and Hindu guru-led) groups which were accepting Jewish converts. The formation of the Jews for Jesus in the San Francisco Bay Area was especially disturbing. The Jewish communal organisations across the country have been prominent supporters of the anti-cult organisations for the last quarter of a century.[1]

## From FREECOG to CFF[2]

The first of the new religions to attract major controversy was a Christian evangelical group, one of the early Jesus People groups, which had emerged around a former holiness minister, David Berg, in southern California. As early as the 1970s informal groups of parents began investigating the group, which had begun among the street people enjoying the sand and surf at Huntington Beach. The loosely organised beach ministry had changed dramatically in 1969 when members heeded a prophecy by Berg on impending doom for California. After eight months of wandering across America, Berg emerged as Moses David and his followers as the Children of God.[3]

Parents concerned about their offsprings' involvement in the group formalised their anger and concern in 1972 by forming the Parents Committee to Free Our Sons and Daughters from the Children of God, later shortened to Free the Children of God (or FREECOG), the first of the anti-cult groups. They tried direct appeals to their family members, and in their failure to persuade them to return to their former life, tried more coercive measures and sought the intervention of law enforcement agencies. These efforts culminated in the actions of the Attorney General of the state of New York who in 1974 issued a report on the Children of God, accusing them of a laundry list of crimes, but took no action as most of the alleged crime occurred outside of his jurisdiction and most of the members, following Berg's vision of leading a world-wide missionary organisation had left the United States.

The efforts of FREECOG, including their taking out ads in newspapers in southern California, brought media coverage as well as inquiries from parents whose young adult offspring had affiliated with other new groups. Thus it was that in late 1973 the leadership of FREECOG transformed their organisation into the more broadly based Volunteer Parents of America. VPA soon folded due to organisational inadequacies and was superseded by the Citizens Freedom Foundation, arguably the most successful of the 1970s anti-cult groups. Originally CFF was confined to California, but similar organisations under a variety of names sprang up around the country. They included the Citizens Organised for Public Awareness of Cults (Greensboro, North Carolina), Personal Freedom Foundation (Baltimore, Maryland), and Love Our Children, Inc. (Omaha, Nebraska). These organisations were generally based around the zeal of one or two people, constantly limited financially, and experienced a rapid turnover as members (i.e. parents) resolved their personal situation in some manner and dropped out.

During the mid-1970s, several attempts were made to construct a national umbrella organisation which could co-ordinate the efforts of the many local groups and make some national impact. In 1976 the Ad Hoc Committee Engaged in Freeing Minds was able to entice Senator Robert Dole (of Kansas) to hold hearings at which parents and others could present their complaints. However, both the committee and a second national organisation, the International Foundation for Individual Freedom, proved ineffective and soon passed from the scene.

The anti-cult movement of the 1970s never satisfactorily resolved its essential problem. Members actually opposed the new religions for two specific reasons. One group had religious qualms with the new religions and did not want their offspring to associate with any group other than the one in which they were raised. The larger percentage, however, were angered that their young adult offspring had rejected parental guidance and had given up on higher education and a 'normal' career for membership and work within a cult. But neither concern fell into the realm of government concerns. Adults, even young ones, had a perfect right to change careers and religious affiliation, and government and law enforcement officials were largely unresponsive to parental demands for intervention. Thus that very real concern had to be recast and the parental concern groups had to change into anti-cult groups, and the leadership began a search for both an alternative programme (given the inactivity of the courts and police), and an articulate ideology which shifted attention from the unacceptable choices of the youthful convert and to the organisations which they had joined.

The process of demonising the new religions began very early. During the days of FREECOG, members had encountered the polemic literature which had been circulating for a generation in evangelical circles. That literature had branded the different non-Christian and heretical groups as 'cults', a term quickly adopted to designate the targeted new religions. Prior to the mid-1970s, almost all material on cults had been written by Protestant Christians, and the acceptance of the term by the anti-cult groups created a rather complex pattern of interaction. The term 'cult' was already familiar to many people and evangelicals were already concerned about the new 'cults' which had emerged in the decade after 1965. Some of the Christian counter-cult groups had both a stable organisation and a national distribution system for their literature. At the same time, the more prominent Christian writers on cults, such as Walter Martin, clearly understood those who branded conversionist groups like the new religions as manipulative and deceitful could easily turn on Evangelical Christian groups and attack them on the same ground. Only a few Evangelicals joined sociologist Ron Enroth in aligning themselves with the new anti-cultists.

The existence of the Christian counter-cult literature also continually presented problems for anti-cultists since they could not build a programme around their true concern (disapproval of their children's choices), and had to generate a polemic against 'cults' in general. Christian literature also broadly attacked 'cults', but centred the attack upon some older more successful groups and included some large influential groups such as the Mormons and Unitarians, and even Roman Catholics. Each time the anti-cult movement gained some audience with legislators, seeking to persuade them to act against cults, their efforts were undermined by the Christian literature. Circulated around a state assembly, outspoken legislators tended quickly and tactfully to withdraw support from any legislation that would suggest disapproval of the religious affiliation of their fellow legislators.

## Programme and ideology

Even before finding a perspective which would justify the attack upon the new religions, anti-cultists hit upon a programme. Actually, it appears that the first de-programmings took place even prior to the founding of FREECOG. Reportedly, the process was developed by Theodore 'Ted' Patrick, at the time an employee of the state of California, who had become concerned about his son's and a nephew's encounter with the Children of God. He met some COG people and allowed them to evangelise him. He would later call their conversionist activity 'brainwashing', by which he meant that the group manipulated people to the extent that they were turned into robots and mental slaves. The anti-COG groups adopted the 'mind control' terminology and in its first newsletter, the Citizens Freedom Foundation defined de-programming as:

> the process of releasing victims from the control of individuals and organisations who exploit other individuals through the use of mind control techniques. Once released, the victims, rid of the fear that held them in bondage, are encouraged to again think for themselves and to take their rightful place in society, free from further threats to their peace and security.[4]

Not covered by the formal definition, de-programming, as touted by CFF and practised by Patrick, involved the detaining of the subject (sometimes kidnapping them off the street) and forcing them to participate in an intense harangue denigrating COG (or some other group) and its leader. The victim of the de-programming was suddenly cut off from any support supplied by other members of the groups and confronted with the emotional outpouring of parents and other family members begging them to renounce the group and straighten up their lives. The number of de-programmings increased steadily through the decade. Patrick quit his job with the state and became a full-time professional de-programmer in late 1971. His book describing his work appeared in 1976.[5]

While de-programmings were by no means successful in all cases (and exact numbers are difficult to determine), enough were successful that some of those who went through the process joined the ranks of the de-programmers and/or became prominent advocates of the anti-cult perspective. As the coercive nature of the process became better known, it became the subject of a variety of court actions. On several occasions Patrick was tried and convicted, though he usually received only a token sentence.

Drawing upon the ideas undergirding the practice of de-programming, a mechanistic perspective of religious conversion in general (which had hung on in many psychological circles) and popular hysteria over Chinese thought-control practices used against American prisoners during the Korean War, the leaders of the anti-cult movement by 1975 were freely using the term 'brainwashing' to describe the process of becoming and remaining involved in a new religion. Potential members were described as psychologically vulnerable individuals who combined an intense youthful idealism with an inability to adjust to their social situation, especially in college.

According to the developing polemic, it was this naive young individual who was attacked by the cult. The first step was, through deceit, to trick the person to attend a group event. There, without revealing their true goals, the group leaders began a subtle process of manipulation which began with the staged smiles, openness, and happiness expressed by members of the group.

Before the potential recruit had time to think about what was occurring, he would be enticed (coerced) into membership and then held in that membership by the repeated application of subtle psychological techniques. The recruit gradually lost his/her ability to think or to choose another way. The understanding of this process was in fact developed from a superficial presentation of the recruitment process of one group, the Unification Church of Rev. Sun Myung Moon, who often recruited street people by first inviting them to dinner and only after the potential recruit gained a favourable impression of the group did a discussion of group belief and practice begin. However, on the whole, new religions had a more standard approach that began with an introduction to the group. There was, in fact, no way to hide what was occurring when one first visited a Hindu temple whose members adopted Indian dress.

Early anti-cultists found substantiation for the use of 'brainwashing' as a descriptive term from psychologist Robert Jay Lifton whose *Thought Reform and the Psychology of Totalism*[6] described the processes of thought control used in the Korean prison camps and compared them with the various practices operative in different social groups including revivalistic religious groups.

Not only was de-programming seen as necessary to 'freeing' a person psychologically trapped in a group, but some form of continued post-de-programming counselling was also recommended. Jean Merritt, a psychiatric social worker, and one of the first psychological professionals attracted to anti-cultism, saw the treatment of ex-cult members to be a difficult but significant part of their return to normalcy. In an open letter written in 1975, she noted:

> Ex-members are so weak once they have been presented with the realities of how they have been psychologically, financially and sometimes sexually abused, that they have need of constant attention. Ironically, this causes the parents and professionals to act similarly to the cults in their close surveillance. Once there is some restoration of ego functioning, the weaning process takes place again and hopefully the person is on the way to recovery. Some that are not so fortunate have to be hospitalised because they are so dependent, suicidal, or because they have suffered complete breaks with reality. The recovery process takes almost a year, for the person to be back to where they first began in the cult.[7]

This added perspective on the problems of people who have been de-programmed led to the formation of several rehabilitation centres, the most famous being the Freedom of Thought Foundation in Tucson, Arizona, and they continue to be an important part of the de-programming efforts.

Once the various local anti-cult groups began to associate with each other on a national level, they also began to appeal to the government to handle the 'cult' problem. They found a sympathetic ear in the person of Kansas Senator Robert Dole, but the hearing provided parents of members of the new religions with very little beyond a media event. Dole did write letters to both the Internal Revenue Service concerning the tax status of the Unification Church and to the Justice Department attempting to set up a meeting between the Attorney General and two scholars identified with anti-cult movement, but neither letter led to any action.

The dead-end in Washington was followed by a series of actions at the state level. Over the next few years, a number of bills were introduced into state legislatures calling for various repressive measures against the new religions. Some bills focused upon accusations of criminal activity, but most attempted to make involvement in new religions a concern of mental health professionals. For example, the legislation in Vermont, introduced in 1976, looked at such diverse alleged activities of groups as fraudulent fund-raising activities, tax evasion, and the possible mental subjugation of citizens. A bill introduced in Texas in 1977 called for an investigation of reported mind control activity by cults. All of these bills failed to pass; and as the decade drew to a close, it appeared that the anti-cult movement was dying a slow death. Then everything changed on 18 November 1978.

## Jonestown and the revival of anti-cultism

On 18 November 1978, Congressman Leo J. Ryan, those who had accompanied him to Guyana to visit the communal settlement of the People's Temple, and some 900 followers of the Temple, including its leader Jim Jones, died in combined acts of murder and suicide. In spite of the many books that have appeared, including several by survivors, what occurred at Jonestown is still far from clear. Some facts such as how many died by murder and how many by suicide may never be known. However, many of the facts await only the release of the mass of documents assembled by the House of Representatives committee set up to investigate the event, especially the death of Congressman Ryan. To date, those documents, including papers relative to a number of independent investigations by various national, state, and local government agencies remain locked up, immune to release under Freedom of Information requests, apparently for reasons of national security. Interestingly enough, Patricia Ryan, the daughter of Leo Ryan, and an anti-cult activist since the early 1980s, broke with the anti-cult perspective on Jonestown and charged in a suit filed against the Central Intelligence Agency that the United States government was responsible for her father's death.

Whatever questions remain concerning the events at Jonestown, there is a clear picture of the role that Jonestown played in the revival of the anti-cult movement. As the story of the disaster at Jonestown began to unravel in the media, the group suddenly became a 'cult'. It became the subject of a US Senate hearing and then a Congressional investigation, and over the next two years, anti-cultists worked to turn it into the symbol of everything that was bad about the new religions. Thus 1979 became a bumper year for books on the issue of cults. The efforts to attack new religions through state legislatures were renewed and, finally, a more or less stable national anti-cult organisation emerged.

Senator Robert Dole took the lead in responding to Jonestown. Even before the Congress had prepared for hearings on Ryan's death, Dole organised a set of hearings based upon the suggestion that Jonestown was a harbinger of tragedies about to break forth from the youth-oriented new religions such as the Unification Church. The hearing, originally set up to provide a platform for anti-cult spokespersons, turned into a sideshow as spokespersons for the new religions demanded equal time and as civil libertarians and a new group of scholars who had studied new religions through the 1970s rose to counter the accusations of anti-cultists with the data of their research. Dole's zeal and public support for the anti-cultists were considerably softened by the entrance into the hearings of a senator from Utah, who happened to be a Mormon.

The actual hearings on Ryan's death were not as spectacular as they could have been as much of the work was done behind closed doors and the real findings of the committee were never revealed. In the end, a five-volume report was released but it was somewhat lost in the flood of journalistic productions. Not only were a dozen or more books on Jonestown released, but a host of books on new religions as cults appeared. Many of these books were accounts of former members' life and break with a group, all concluding that the proper reaction would be support of anti-cult activities.[8]

In the wake of Jonestown, anti-cult bills appeared in Massachusetts, Illinois, Minnesota, Connecticut, Pennsylvania, Texas, Maryland, Oregon, and most importantly New York. These bills varied widely in their sophistication and support. Most were defeated at the hearing stage as civil libertarians, representatives of mainline churches, and experts on new religions mobilised against the legislation. The one exception was New York where the Unification Church, the best known and most disliked of the several new religions, had its headquarters and seminary. The Unification Church had been an issue in the state as it pursued a state charter for the seminary at Barrytown; and in 1977, one state assemblyman had sponsored one of the more frivolous anti-cult bills which would have made it a felony for anyone to found or promote a 'pseudo-religion', whatever that was. The 1980 New York legislation, generally known as the Lasher Bill after its author Assemblyman Howard Lasher, would have amended the mental health codes to allow parents widespread powers of conservatorship for purposes of de-programming their offspring, specifically adult offspring, who joined one of the new religions. The bill passed the assembly twice but was vetoed by the governor on both occasions. By the time of the second veto, it had become obvious that such legislation was not going anywhere nationally and further efforts, which were taking a significant amount of anti-cult resources, were abandoned.

Possibly for the long run, the most important result of the Jonestown tragedy was the revitalisation and reorganisation of the anti-cult movement. Taking the lead in that reorganisation was the old Citizens Freedom Foundation (soon to become known as the Cult Awareness Network, CAN) and the relatively new American Family Foundation. In November 1979, a date appropriately chosen to coincide with the first anniversary of Jonestown, sixty-five people from thirty-one anti-cult groups met in Chicago to reorganise the ineffective International Foundation for Individual Freedom. IFIF had been too decentralised to accomplish its self-assigned task, but now there was an agreement to seize the initiative provided by Jonestown. After some debate a decision was made to reorganise around the Citizens Freedom Foundation, the strongest of the regional groups. CFF became the Citizens Freedom Foundation–Information Services, and the 1979 meeting was designated as the first of what became annual national meetings. Different tasks were assumed by regional affiliated groups in Minneapolis, Pittsburgh, and southern California.

The new organisation still did not provide the strength many felt was needed by the movement, and in 1983 a five-year plan was placed before CFF's leadership. It suggested that CFF needed to build a more stable organisation which could gain legitimacy in the public eye as the most knowledgeable source of information on cults. Four specific goals were set: gain financial stability, develop professional management, create an efficient communications system, and publish a quality newsletter. As a first step in implementing this programme, in 1984, CFF changed its name to Cult Awareness Network of the Citizens Freedom Foundation and soon became known simply as the Cult Awareness Network. A central headquarters was established in Chicago, and an executive director hired (since 1987, Cynthia Kisser). The national office was organised to respond to inquiries from the media, academia, and individuals. An aggressive public relations programme was initiated to place the Cult Awareness Network before the public.

Simultaneously with the reorganisation of CFF, the American Family Foundation (AFF) was founded under the leadership of John Clark. Clark, a psychiatrist in practice in Weston, Massachusetts, and an adjunct professor at Harvard, had been the leading public spokesperson for the anti-cult movement through the 1970s, but had been largely silenced after receiving a formal reprimand from the Massachusetts Psychiatric Association. In contrast to the very activist approach of CFF/CAN, AFF was conceived as an organisation of professionals who would focus upon research and education. It provided a place where academics, psychological professionals, and social scientists could relate to the movement and launched a programme of public education and issued a set of publications centred upon *The Advisor*, its newsletter, and the *Cult Studies Journal*, modelled upon standard academic journals. A number of the publications were authored by Clark as chairman of the executive committee and psychologist Michael Langone, AFF's director of research.

The emergence of AFF and the reorganisation signalled an important transition in the anti-cult movement. The many anti-cult groups which had formed around the country in the 1970s had been created and led largely by parents concerned with the membership of their sons and daughters in the more controversial of the new religions: the Unification Church, Scientology, Hare Krishna, the Children of God, The Way International, the Divine Light Mission, and several evangelical Christian groups. These groups were never large, the largest being The Way International which peaked at about 12,000 members. Only a small minority of parents were ever concerned about these groups and by the early 1980s, only a few had been able to sustain any zeal, either because their problem had been resolved or they had decided to live with the unhappy situation.

However, in the meantime, in their effort to gain the support of the courts and government agencies to their cause, the parents discovered that they needed the assistance of a variety of experts who became their spokespersons. The most important of these were psychological professionals, some of whom were quick to identify with the plight of parents who were disturbed at the 'loss' of their offspring to the religious life. The professionals became expert witnesses in court cases and addressed the legislative hearings attempting to investigate the cults.

Already in the mid-1970s some professionals who had become identified with the cause of the parent groups formed Return to Personal Choice under the leadership of psychiatric social worker Jean Merritt. The organisation, headquartered in Lincoln, Massachusetts, welcomed psychological professionals, lawyers, and clergy into membership. The relatively small Return to Personal Choice was superseded by the American Family Foundation and its more expansive programme, and Merritt moved to Washington, DC, as the head of AFF's Government Affairs Program, which has shown some substantial effect in influencing government officials with the anti-cult perspective. Meanwhile, through the early 1980s, in large part as CFF implemented the goals of its five-year plan, the professionals also assumed control of the organisation. Since the renaming of the CFF in 1984, the majority of the board members and speakers at the annual conference have been professionals (a natural change given the attempts of the organisation to gain legitimacy). CAN and AFF developed contemporaneously and tried to project an image as quite separate organisations. Over the decade, however, the organisations developed interlocking boards and several joint programmes which had made it ever more difficult to distinguish them.[9]

The transition to professional control was also somewhat dictated by the intense controversy over de-programming which hit CFF in the early 1980s. De-programming had been an important, if erratic, element in the anti-cult programme through the 1970s. The various anti-cult organisations kept in touch with de-programmers and served as contact points for parents who wished to avail themselves of their help. By the mid-1970s, a number of professional de-programmers were operating in both North America and Europe. Some of these were former cult members and others simply entrepreneurs. Immediately after Jonestown the number of de-programmings (and concurrently the number of de-programmers) rose dramatically. The Unification Church, the Hare Krishna, and The Way International were the primary targets, though other groups labelled as cults also came under attack.

The spread of de-programming created a strong reaction. Besides its traditional critics, a number of people who had been successfully de-programmed began to denounce the handling they had received from the de-programmers. Christian counter-cult spokespersons led by Walter Martin separated themselves publicly from the use of what he considered 'unChristian tactics' in the attempt to win people from membership in the new religions. Also, the new centralised CFF began to realise that it stood legally vulnerable for the activities of its members around the country, including de-programmers. Thus in 1981 it took steps to separate itself from the actual practice of de-programming and the possible excesses of its practitioners. In a public statement, CFF withdrew support, as an organisation, from kidnapping or holding a person against his/her will and advocated what is usually termed 'exit counselling', a form of anti-cult counselling into which the member enters voluntarily. That formal separation, of course, changed very little in fact. The policy statement in no way prevented individual board members or executives such as Cynthia Kisser from openly praising de-programming and de-programmers.

Also, in spite of that formal distancing, through its activist members around the country, CFF/CAN continued to refer people to de-programmers. It regularly invited professional de-programmers to speak at its meetings and to be present at its annual conferences where contacts could be made. The conferences also serve as a forum for ex-members to testify to the successful transition they have made as a result of de-programming. (In the mid-1990s it was also revealed that contrary to its stated public policy, CAN had paid de-programmer Galen Kelly a monthly stipend for many months during the early 1990s.)

Through the 1980s the Cult Awareness Network had developed as a true 'network' in the contemporary use of that term. The national board and office in Chicago 'networked' with a number of independent experts and activists and with the loosely affiliated local groups and activists around the country. In turn, its local leaders also 'networked' with a number of de-programmers, only a few of whom were formal members of the Network. Thus while the organisation 'officially' distanced itself from de-programming, in fact it fully advocated and supported the practice by its choice of speakers for its meetings, by providing a context in which de-programmers and potential clients met, and by directing people to de-programmers through its network. De-programmers, especially those who lacked a public profile, relied upon referrals through the CAN network for a steady supply of paying clients.

## International anti-cultism

Almost simultaneously with the emergence of anti-cult organisations in the United States, organised anti-cult sentiment appeared in Europe. This sentiment was occasioned by the movement of the Children of God into Europe in the early 1970s, the highly publicised tour of Rev. Moon to Europe in 1972, and the European expansion of the Church of Scientology. As early as 1973 de-programmers from America went to Europe to seize Americans who had moved there as members of the different groups and stayed on to de-programme various European converts.

By the mid-1970s individual anti-cult groups, largely drawing on the American literature, organisational model, and language, began to form. Among the earliest was Family Action, Information and Rescue (FAIR) in England, the Association pour la Défense de la Famille et de l'Individu (ADFI) in France (1975), and Aktion für geistige und psychische Freiheit, Arbeitsgemeinschaft der Elterninitiativen e.V. (AGPF) in Germany (1977). By the time of the Jonestown tragedy other groups were beginning in other European countries as well as Israel,[10] New Zealand, and Australia. These groups quickly adopted the mind-control and brainwashing hypothesis as it developed in America.[11]

As in the United States, European concern over the new religions rose considerably, and by December 1980 had grown to the point that ADFI could host an international conference of anti-cult group representatives and other interested people in Paris. Representatives from fourteen countries were in attendance. Henrietta Crampton, one of the prominent leaders of CFF attended from the United States.[12] The international anti-cult network was put in place at that time. While Europe has not lacked in leadership on cult issues with the likes of Ian Haworth and Pastor Friedrich-Wilhelm Haack, it has continued to rely upon the theoretical perspective generated in the United States and has suffered as this perspective has proved inadequate.

Through the early 1980s a network was established across Europe which included such groups as SOS (the Netherlands), the Dialog Centre (Denmark), FRI (Association to Rescue the Individual, Sweden), Comitaro per la Liberazione dei Giovani dal Settarismo (Italy), and Association Pro-Juventud (Spain). Association Pro-Juventud hosted the next international conference in Barcelona in 1987 at which several of the prominent Cult Awareness Network theoreticians featured speakers. By this time the international network had spread to South America, and was especially strong in Argentina. In several countries, various anti-cult groups emerged as leaders disagreed over specific tactics and goals.

The strongest visible reaction to the Jonestown incident was in France where a government commission issued a report attacking sects as dangerous brainwashing groups, though no new laws or actions were taken against them.

## The rise and fall of brainwashing

In the mid-1970s, the primary understanding of destructive cults as centres engaged in 'brainwashing' their members through what was variously termed 'coercive persuasion', 'mind control', and/or 'thought control', was developed. Central to that development was the trial of newspaper heiress Patty Hearst in San Francisco in 1975. Hearst had been kidnapped by a radical political group, had undergone an intensive indoctrination programme that included being locked in a closet and other personal abuse. However, eventually Hearst converted to the group and participated in a bank robbery where she was photographed carrying a weapon. When finally captured, she was tried for armed robbery.

During the trial, the defence suggested that Hearst had been brainwashed and was hence not responsible for her actions. The jury rejected that argument and convicted her. However, Margaret Singer, one of the psychologists who had testified at that trial, even though for technical reasons not allowed to speak on the brainwashing issue, testified the following year as an expert in a case in which a conservatorship was sought over five members of the Unification Church. She testified that the members, all young adults, had been victimised by artful and designing people who had subjected them to a process of 'coercive persuasion'. As a result, the five should, she recommended, be sent for a period of reality therapy at the Freedom of Thought Foundation in Tucson.

Singer went on to found a counselling service for former members of the new religions, most of whom had been severed from the group through deprogramming. She presented the developing conclusions in several articles published in 1978, the most important being 'Coming Out of the Cults' in the popular news-stand magazine *Psychology Today* (January 1979).[13] The article was frequently reprinted in both Europe and North America. Through the early 1980s she developed her concept of brainwashing which was presented in the various legislative hearings, in testimony in trials, and in several talks given before meetings of the Cult Awareness Network. As developed by Singer, the concept of brainwashing became the keystone of the polemic against cults. Through the early 1980s, the testimony of Singer and several colleagues who accepted and reinforced her perspective became crucial in a series of multi-million dollar judgments against a string of new religions. She became a professional witness who devoted her full time to legal consultation. Her testimony was particularly effective as she had worked with E. H. Schein who had studied the Korean prisoners of war.

Singer's work, though difficult to assess as she wrote only a few papers laying out her thought, became the subject of intense debate in both psychological and sociological circles. The result of that debate was the overwhelming rejection of her approach to the new religions by her academic colleagues, though a handful of psychological professionals such as Louis J. West of UCLA's Psychoanalytic Institute were vocal supporters.[14] However, through the 1980s Singer's thought was accepted by the courts and strongly influenced the deliberations of juries.

The conflict between Singer and the great majority of her academic colleagues who had been studying the new religions finally led to a series of actions that has resulted in the collapse of her work on brainwashing. Those events began in 1983 when a proposal was made to the American Psychological Association (APA) that a task force be established to examine and report on the techniques of coercive persuasion being used by various psychological and religious groups. In 1984 the 'Task Force on Deceptive and Indirect Methods of Persuasion and Control' with Margaret Singer as chairperson was established. In the meantime Singer was called upon to testify in a case, *Molko v. The Holy Spirit Association for the Unification of World Christianity*, in which two former members of the Unification Church had charged it with psychological injury due to coercive persuasion. The lower court had dismissed the suit in part because it accepted arguments that Singer's testimony (and that of a colleague Samuel Benson) lacked scientific foundation.

The case was appealed. As the appeal process was working itself out, the APA board prepared and submitted an amicus brief critiquing Singer's stated position and supporting her and Dr Benson's exclusion. This brief was circulated among a number of scholars known for their work on new religions and many additional signatures (including that of this author) were added. As the submission of the brief became known, some supporters of Singer argued that it was improper for the APA board to submit such a document while it had a standing committee working on the very subject to which the brief proposed conclusions. Thus early in 1987 the APA board withdrew its support of the document, though those who had additionally signed on kept it before the court.

Meanwhile the Task Force report was submitted for review. Both outside reviewers and two members of the Board of Social and Ethical Responsibility for Psychology concurred in the inadequacies of the report and the Board rejected it. In a memorandum to Singer and the committee members dated 11 May 1987, it cited the report for its lack of both 'scientific rigor' and an 'even-handed critical approach'. It noted that, given the evaluation of the report, members of the committee could not use their work on the committee to credential themselves in the future.

The board could now resubmit the brief, but the Molko case had moved on and eventually collapsed when it was discovered that some of the stated facts in the case had been incorrect. However, almost immediately a new case appeared on the horizon, *US v. Fishman*. In his defence, which concerned the relationship between Mr Fishman and the Church of Scientology, Fishman called upon Singer and another colleague, sociologist

Richard Ofshe, to testify to the deleterious effects of the Church of Scientology's manipulation of him. The key document in the case became a lengthy restatement of the position of the previous APA brief and an analysis of the writings and statements of Singer written by psychologist Dick Anthony. Anthony argued persuasively that Singer postulated a 'robot' theory of brainwashing that lacked scientific support.[15] The court accepted his arguments and as a result, Singer and Ofshe were denied the stand. Fishman's defence collapsed. As a result of the Fishman ruling, both Singer and Ofshe were subsequently denied the stand in several additional cases. It became evident that the Fishman case had become the precedent through which the court accepted the position of the majority of scholars on the new religions and the idea of brainwashing.

The results of the Fishman ruling have been far-reaching. It has cost the Cult Awareness Network and those scholars who had accepted Singer's work a significant amount of credibility. This loss of position as a legitimate voice on cult issues was clearly demonstrated in the recent case of the Solar Temple. In spite of attempts to associate it with Jonestown, the media in America soon turned away from CAN spokespersons and allowed the incident to fade into oblivion. Most recently, in 1993 and 1994, Singer and Ofshe sued the APA, the American Sociological Association, and a number of individual scholars and declared that they had engaged in a conspiracy to deny them their means of livelihood. The courts dismissed both suits and in the second case ordered Singer and Ofshe to pay the rather significant legal costs of the defendants.

## The collapse of the Cult Awareness Network

Even as the courts were responding to the efforts of Singer and Ofshe to salvage their position, other events were occurring which would lead to the disbanding of the Cult Awareness Network. Through the 1990s, various individuals, but especially members of the Church of Scientology went on the offensive against the Cult Awareness Network. The Church of Scientology had attacked CAN as a hate-group and saw it as a source of many of their problems in the public sphere. Various Scientologists joined CAN and attempted to attend its annual meetings, but were turned away. Since attendance at the annual meeting was a clearly stated privilege for members, they sued CAN for what amounted to a breach of contract.

Although none of these suits ever came to trial, they became a time-consuming and expensive nuisance for CAN officials. More importantly, they occasioned a series of depositions by an array of CAN leaders and employees. Slowly, these depositions began to document CAN's continued involvement in de-programmings in the form of referrals from the national office to people in the field who made the direct referrals to the de-progammers; the use of the annual meeting as a place for de-programmers to meet potential clients (parents of members of new religions); and financial kickbacks from de-programmers to CAN. The information compiled from these various depositions found an unexpected use in the case of Jason Scott.

Jason Scott was the member of a congregation of the United Pentecostal Church International, a large older Pentecostal body with local centres across the United States and missions around the world. Scott's mother, a former member of the church, hired de-programmer Rick Ross who, with two assistants kidnapped Scott and attempted to convince him to leave the church. The de-programming did not work and Scott sued Ross. Rick Moxon, a lawyer who does most of his work for the Church of Scientology, agreed to take Scott's case *pro bono*. Using the material from the CAN depositions, he not only obtained a multi-million dollar judgment against Ross and his associates, but against CAN.

The million-dollar judgment against CAN forced the organisation into bankruptcy, and in 1996, a coalition of groups whom CAN had regularly attacked in its publications purchased the corporate name and the phone number (that had been widely publicised). Since that time, a new CAN office has been created by the coalition that continues to take calls from people seeking help with their 'cult' problems. In the meantime, the former leaders of the old CAN filed an appeal. The court's denial of that appeal in April 1998 has placed a significant obstacle blocking any reorganisation and revival of CAN in the foreseeable future. In the wake of the Scott decision, and the disruption of the CAN network, de-programmings have been brought almost to a complete halt in North America.

## The revival of anti-cultism in Europe

Even as anti-cult activity was being dealt a severe blow in North America, events conspired to give it new life in Europe. In December 1994, fifty-one members of a Swiss-based group called the Solar Temple were found dead following a group act of suicide/murder. Subsequently, bodies were found in Quebec, where in fact, most of the French-speaking group had settled. Then in March 1995, leaders of the Aum Shinrikyō, a Buddhist group in Japan, released nerve gas in a crowded subway station in Tokyo. Twelve people died, and in the wake of the arrests, a number of additional crimes (including homicides) committed by members of the group were uncovered. As had occurred fifteen years earlier following Jonestown, reaction to these events turned public attention towards other new religions. France was the first to act. Anti-cult sentiment that had continued in the Parliament since the days of Jonestown led to the formation of a commission, the holding of secret hearings with support from ADFI (the French anti-cult group), and the issuing of a report, 'Cults in France', in January 1996. The report listed 172 dangerous '*sectes*' which range across the spectrum of minority religions in the country from Buddhist groups to Evangelical Christians, from occult groups to the more controversial religious groups such as the Unification Church. As a result of the report, government funding of ADFI has increased substantially, new religions have been denied space to hold public meetings in hotels and similar facilities, and the Parliament has established an Observatory of Cults. Government actions were taken while ignoring the work of French scholars of new religions and the negative reaction of the scholarly community to the report.[16]

The reaction to the Solar Temple in France has been duplicated in Belgium which in 1997 issued a report that was even more extreme than the French one. It not only listed 189 minority religions but included several Roman Catholic orders, a variety of mainline Protestant Christian groups, and one Hasidic Jewish group. The statement against the Satmar Jews was particularly egregious as it recalled the old accusations about Jews kidnapping Christian babies. Again ignoring Belgian scholars, but reacting to Roman Catholic critics, the government moved in 1998 to establish an advice centre on harmful sectarian organisations which will operate under the Ministry of Justice. Quietly, the Austrian government also established a similar observatory.

In June 1998, the highly publicised report of the German inquiry commission on sects issued its final report which proved quite mild in light of its interim report. The German commission had worked within the context of raids on Pentecostal churches and an intense government campaign against the Church of Scientology which in 1997 placed the church under surveillance by the secret police (whose investigation has already embarrassed the government when an agent was arrested for extending surveillance activities to neighbouring Switzerland). During its two years of activity it had interviewed both scholars and anti-cult activists (several of whom have salaries from the Lutheran Church), and listened to reactions from American government officials. However, with the exception of Scientology, condemned as a 'political-extremist' endeavour, the report affirmed the constitutional guarantees of religious freedom, called for no new legislation (against 'brainwashing', for example), but did affirm the government's interest in intervening in cases of suspected crimes or acts detrimental to its own members by groups. The reports also called for the use of the term 'secte' to be discontinued because of its stigmatising effect.

As this article is being written, inquiry commissions are operating in Switzerland, and within the European Parliament. Although the European Parliament's interim report appears relatively mild, the Swiss commission was generated directly out of the Solar Temple affair and a report produced by the French-speaking canton of Switzerland calling for legislation against 'mind control' and the banning of cult members from government jobs, said report being sent to the national legislature for its consideration.

The reaction to new religion in French- and German-speaking Western Europe has given support to reactionary legislation in those countries to the east (from Russia to Bulgaria) in which the Orthodox Church has reasserted its position after a period of suppression through most of the twentieth century. The model for new suppressive legislation against minority religions (including the more well-known groups labelled 'cults' in the West as well as more traditional Protestant Christian groups) has been the Greek legislation adopted in the 1950s which established the Greek Orthodox Church and severely restricted other groups. In spite of World Court action against Greece, Russia moved to adopt similar legislation aimed at suppressing the many religious organisations that have emerged in the country since the fall of the Soviet Union. Meanwhile, the Russian example has served as a precedent for significant steps backward from its earlier legislation on religious freedom in Bulgaria (where a climate against minority religions has spread with the blessing of the Orthodox Church), and a set of repressive measures have been introduced into the legislatures of many of the countries of the former Soviet Union.[17]

The sum total of the actions taken through the mid-1990s suggests that continental Europe is passing through a period of adjustment to the new religious pluralism (a pluralism which can only be reversed by physical repression) quite similar to that through which the English-speaking world passed in the 1970s and 1980s. This adjustment is being made all the more stressful in Western Europe by the threats to national identities posed by the formation of the European Union, and in Eastern Europe by the long tradition of the governments exerting control over religious bodies and the reassertion of the Orthodox Church's role in shaping the identity of those countries in which it has been the dominant religious force. In reference to the cult controversy, it appears that the early decades of the twenty-first century will be a time of struggle, though in light of the German report, not as severe as some had imagined.

## The future

The string of court reverses has severely wounded the anti-cult movement in North America. The American Family Foundation continues to exist, though the primary support given anti-cultists by de-programmers has been taken away, and without any significant hope for government support, it appears an anaemic organisation. Media agencies are increasingly questioning the anti-cult movement's legitimacy in spite of the appeal their clear, if extreme, statements have as soundbites.

Slowly, the collapse of the brainwashing hypothesis in relation to the new religions is being brought to Europe, though as in America it will be some years before the strong prejudice against the new religions which has permeated Western culture will be dissolved. Indicative of the future, however, is the case of The Family (formerly the Children of God). Through the 1990s, The Family, which had kept a low key for many years, surfaced and let its presence be made known. Almost immediately it suffered a number of legal actions in several European countries. In spite of the disapproval of its sexually free lifestyle and its status as a cult (which gave substance to the charges against it), all of the cases have been resolved in its favour.

Meanwhile, since the opening of Eastern Europe, the new religions have emerged in strength and anti-cultism has reared its head. Cursory examinations of the situation as the century comes to an end, however, indicates that anti-cultists had been unable to attain the credibility needed to affect the overall activities of the new religions even though several governments have established observation agencies lest that situation change. Apart from the Scientology situation in Germany, new religious groups report France and Belgium as being the countries where anti-cultism exerts the strongest influence in the government and in legal proceedings, but there is every reason to believe that such influence will recede as public officials in both countries become better informed of the scholarly consensus on religious pluralism and the Solar Temple and Aum Shinrikyō incidents fade into the past.

## Notes

1  For a list of the large body of Jewish anti-cult literature, see Jack N. Porter, *Jews and the Cults: Bibliography*, Fresh Meadows, NY: Biblio Press, 1981. Porter's 49–page compilation, of course, covered only the first decade and the amount of Jewish literature has continued to grow.

2  Basic information about the first generation of the anti-cult movement can be found in Anson D. Shupe Jr and David G. Bromley, *A Documentary History of the Anti-cult Movement*, Arlington, TX: Center for Social Research, University of Texas, 1985; Anson D. Shupe Jr and David G. Bromley, *The New Vigilantes: Deprogrammers, Anti-Cultists and the New Religions*, Beverly Hills, CA: Sage Publications, 1980; Anson D. Shupe Jr, David G. Bromley, and Donna L. Oliver, *The Anti Cult Movement in America: A Bibliography and Historical Survey*, New York: Garland Publishing, 1984; J. Gordon Melton, *Encyclopedic Handbook of Cults in America*, New York: Garland Publishing, 1992; and Anson Shupe and David G. Bromley (eds), *Anti-Cult Movements in Cross-cultural Perspective*, New York: Garland Publications, 1994.

3  On the Children of God (now known as The Family) see: James R. Lewis and J. Gordon Melton (eds), *Sex, Slander and Salvation: Investigating the Family/Children of God*, Stanford, CA: Center for Academic Publication, 1994.

4  'What is Deprogramming?', *Citizens Freedom Foundation News*, 1(1), November 1974, p. 1.

5  Ted Patrick and Tom Dulack, *Let Our Children Go!*, New York: E. P. Dutton, 1976.

6  New York: W. W. Norton and Company, 1961.

7  Jean Merritt, 3 August 1975, quoted in Shupe and Bromley, *Documentary*, op. cit.

8  See for example: Christopher Edwards, *Crazy for God*, Englewood Cliffs, NJ: Prentice-Hall, 1979; Barbara Underwood and Betty Underwood, *Hostage to Heaven*, New York: Clarkson N. Potter, 1979; and Rachel Martin, *Escape*, Denver: Accent Books, 1979, for typical accounts by ex-group members.

9  It should be noted that the psychologists and other professionals who identified themselves with the anti-cult movement had a distinct problem. Almost none of them had ever studied the groups which they were now to evaluate as experts. Their entire knowledge of the new religions came almost totally from the stories of ex-members, accounts heavily distorted by the de-programming process. Their appraisals received constant negative critiques from the growing number of scholars who had actually studied the groups and were broadly familiar with the

literature, both pro and con, on the different groups. The work of these scholars (which by the mid-1980s numbered several hundred items) would be a major irritant for the anti-cult movement and in the end led to the destruction of the brainwashing hypothesis.

10 Cf. Benjamin Beit-Hallahmi, *Despair and Deliverance: Private Salvation in Contemporary Israel*, Albany, NY: State University of New York Press, 1992, pp. 35–48.
11 Cf. James A. Beckford, *Cult Controversies: The Social Response to New Religious Movements*, London: Tavistock Publications, 1985.
12 *Cult Awareness Network of the Citizens Freedom Foundation: Who We Are...and...What We Do*, Hannacroix, NY: Citizens Freedom Foundation, 1984.
13 M. Singer, 'Coming Out of the Cults', *Psychology Today*, 12, January 1979, pp. 72–3.
14 The details of the anti-cult position were best presented in the collection of papers in David A. Halperin (ed.), *Psychodynamic Perspectives in Religion, Sect, and Cult*, Boston: J. Wright, 1983. The critique can be seen in David G. Bromley and James T. Richardson (eds), *The Brainwashing/Deprogramming Controversy: Sociological, Psychological, Legal, and Historical Perspectives*, New York: Edwin Mellen Press, 1983. By 1984–5, the issue had largely been decided and while anti-cult scholars continued to publish and circulate papers reflecting the anti-cult perspective, these were published almost exclusively by anti-cult organisations such as AFF and found little audience in the larger scholarly community.
15 See Dick Anthony and Thomas Robbins, 'Law, Social Science and the "Brainwashing" Exception to the First Amendment', *Behavioral Sciences and the Law*, 10, 1992, pp. 5–29, for a discussion of this phase of the controversy.
16 Massimo Introvigne and J. Gordon Melton (eds), *Pour en finir avec les sectes: Le débat sur le rapport de la commission parliamentaire*, Turin: CESNUR/Milan: Giovanni, 1996 (2nd edition: Paris: Dervy, 1996; 3rd edition: Paris: Éditions Dervy, 1996).
17 Romania seems to be the exception to the rule, as efforts of the Romanian Orthodox Church to gain government support for its efforts to suppress competing new religions (including Protestant groups) have been rebuffed by the country's legislature. At present, the primary religious struggle in the country is between the Orthodox Church and the Eastern Rite Catholic Church in Transylvania over the assignment of some disputed church property.

# Summary of Chapter 12

Although responding to the same sort of challenge, and sometimes employing similar techniques, anti-cult movements have differed from one country to another in the type of support that they have been able to command, and in the sources from which it might come. Illustrating this diversity is the telling contrast with the situation in America of the anti-cult phenomenon in Germany, where the churches have played a much more open and aggressive role. They have appointed their own so-called 'cult experts' and sought quite systematically to promote a moral crusade against new religions. Dr Usarski documents the strategy and the tactics of the anti-cultists and reveals the more explicit involvement in Germany of both the churches and some agencies of the state in a campaign against the NRMs.

# 12 The response to New Religious Movements in East Germany after reunification

*Frank Usarski*

## The background

When in 1988 I offered a critique of the debate on so-called *Jugendsekten* ('destructive cults') approached on the basis of labelling theory, it could by no means have been foreseen that only a few years later my ideas would be relevant for Germany after reunification. In the former DDR (i.e. East Germany), there had been a few new religions operating in private circles,[1] but in general 'cults' were categorised as a problem belonging to Western capitalism.[2] From this perspective, the Wall, according to the official view, was still intact at that time. Because of this impenetrable barrier, the people of the DDR were protected from various developments which, from 1973 at the very latest, were classified even in the West as signs of decadence.

Since the Wall was dismantled, five new federal states have become members of the Federal Republic within the provisions of the 'Basic' (i.e. Constitutional) Law, and the citizens of the former DDR have been confronted with West German standards in every aspect of life. Almost everything that had determined social reality in the old federal states has now been extended to the whole of Germany. In this context, immediately after the Wall was torn down, the newspapers reported that the 'cults were also booming in the East'. This article referred to well-known organisations which, according to the author, 'acted as "newly discovered fodder" to fill the vacuum which prevailed in the political, social and religious life in the DDR'.[3] Even at that early stage, the presuppositions made when reporting on New Religious Movements in the re-unified Germany were the same as those that had hitherto prevailed in the Federal Republic.

At the end of the 1980s, I published a book on the debate about *Jugendsekten* in West Germany (BRD) from a basically different perspective. My concern was less with the New Religious Movements themselves than with the indignant reactions to these movements from the majority of BRD citizens. The scant regard that had already been shown towards empirical facts was the basis for the critical angle of my study. Anyone who closely examined the literature on New Religious Movements would have quickly gained the impression that there were good reasons for doubting both the supposed quantity and quality of the so-called *Jugendsekten* phenomenon.

With regard to the extent of the cult problem, whether deliberately or in all innocence, six-figure numbers for membership were sometimes mentioned. No one, however, could vouch for the reliability of these data. Global estimates have constantly been used, but all attempts to give a scientific definition to the term *Jugendsekten* have remained unsatisfactory. The term has usually been used to describe very different New Religious Movements. On the one hand, the term referred to groups such as ISKCON and the Children of God, each of which had relatively few members and were based on centralised organisational structures. On the other hand, the disciples of Bhagwan Shree Rajneesh or the Maharishi Mahesh Yogi were also simply included as members of dangerous *Jugendsekten*. In these cases, reference was made to a definite membership of an inner circle of active 'officials'. There were, however, many thousands of people who came on to the scene simply as occasional visitors to the Ashram in Poona or Oregon, or as participants in a weekend course on transcendental meditation.

Apart from these considerations, there has been until now a lack of any convincing scientific evidence which can be applied in a generalised form to show that involvement in a New Religious Movement has any destructive consequences for the psyche of the individual concerned. The same caveat applies to the criticism that these groups entice their members by using illegitimate means, completely taking them over, and making them financially dependent. The fact that, in all the ensuing years, no one has succeeded in verifying beyond reasonable doubt any of these claims, has, however, never been regarded as a reason to exonerate the groups in any way; instead, the causes of suspicion have continued. It has been alleged that the cults have never been convicted because they have managed to stay under cover through subtle subterfuge or have been able to pay large amounts to be represented in court by sophisticated lawyers. Thus, up to the time of writing, there has not been one single successful, legal conviction of the Scientology Church, even though this group has come to be regarded as the most dangerous of the new religious organisations. Recently, the Scientology Church has been used to exemplify the whole spectrum of problems which are supposed to be caused by *Jugendsekten*. The fact that even long-term investigations have as yet failed to produce the desired results continues to be ignored. An official report concerning possible legal proceedings to be taken with regard to the Scientology Church, published by the Senate of the City of Hamburg on 26 May 1992, declares:

> Up to the present time, no one has been prepared to testify in court against the SC [Scientology Church] as a witness who claims to have suffered personal damage, and no one has given evidence of a kind which would have enabled state prosecutors to take legal proceedings against the SC. Meanwhile, proceedings were initiated against the SC in

Stuttgart and Munich. Despite the fact that, in 1989, a very comprehensive juridical inquiry was set up, the court did not find any reason to sue any member of the SC. The case was abandoned. The Stuttgart state prosecutors have announced that, at the moment, they have not found any sufficient, concrete grounds to sue the SC.[4]

## Labelling theory and the *Jugendreligionen*

The extremely negative discussions about New Religious Movements in both the former BRD and in Germany after reunification cannot be adequately justified on the basis of empirical evidence. For this reason, in the following discussion I pursue the question: apart from the groups already under suspicion, what are the basic factors essentially responsible for the *Jugendsekten* thesis as it is now understood in the five new federal states?

From the perspective of labelling theory, collective processes by means of which, in their significance for the public consciousness, certain social phenomena undergo a gradual change, and become labelled by the whole society as deviant, are of particular interest. Within this framework, certain questions arise:

• What social interests were the driving forces of the so-called investigators in the context of this 'definition' process?
• What are the strategies used by the 'moral crusaders' or the protagonists of deviance labelling?
• What is the power base to which they appeal in their activities?
• What motivates these parties to take action against groups stigmatised as 'deviants'?

With regard to the *Jugendsekten*-debate in the former BRD, the attempt globally to categorise New Religious Movements as deviant orginated with members of the two main Christian Churches. Friedrich-Wilhelm Haack, the Bavarian Protestant expert mainly concerned with 'cults', emerged as the initiator of the anti-cult campaign and as the main Church protagonist in this area. In 1974, he coined the phrase *Jugendreligionen* by which he intended for the first time to define, under one heading, a supposedly global phenomenon. He attacked the *Jugendreligionen* in a totally undifferentiated manner. After Haack's death in 1991, Thomas Gandow, a clergymen from West Berlin established himself as an extremely committed activist in the campaign against the New Religious Movements.

An outsider might gain the distinct impression that the *Jugendsekten* phenomenon was brought onto the agenda as a permanent item by worried parents. It is, however, a fact that right from their outset, these initiatives, based on a shock response, came from Church officials concerned with cults and their long-term effects. Either Haack or Gandow or both were behind the founding of the most influential parent associations in Munich and

Berlin. Eventually, these and other shock response initiatives could hence-forth rely on regular support from, and representation by, so-called cult experts. This is also shown by the genuine involvement of Church represen-tatives in various other cases such as the activities of Pastor Rüdiger Hauth in Westphalia, of theologians like Joachim Biallas and Wilhelm Knackstedt in Lower Saxony, or Pastor Benrath in Schleswig-Holstein, Hamburg and Bremen.

Since their reports are not particularly convincing with regard to either quantity or quality, this involvement of committed cult experts, who have specialised in this field from a denominational point of view, is hardly a suit-able basis on which to establish an unbiased appraisal of parents or disillusioned former members. Rather, certain examples from the material would seem to support the suspicion that some individuals were used by the cult experts; but it must also be noted that this by no means implies that the personal feelings of the individuals who felt hurt by their experiences should in any way be called into question. Similarly, with hindsight, the undis-cerning way in which government circles, when acting in their official capacity, referred to the negative reports from parents and so-called drop-outs, can only appear to be very questionable.

## The moral crusade in the former East Germany

After the Wall came down, when interested parties became involved in generally raising the level of consciousness in East Germany in relation to the destructive danger of 'cults', the church officials responsible for dealing with *Jugendsekten* took measures which had already proved to be successful in the former Federal Republic. The media, especially the newspapers, became an essential element in the creation of a clear-cut image of the New Religious Movements. In addition, the fact that the journalists were also interested in sensational reports, and willingly adopted the negative rhetoric of their sources, worked to the advantage of the 'moral crusaders'. Together with Haack, Gandow came to prominence in this connection since he was now able to make more use of the central position of his office in Berlin for the whole of Germany.

Shortly after the demolition of the Wall, Haack began to issue public warnings against the 'cult boom' and its 'many victims' in eastern Germany.[5] Gandow did the same thing, informing reporters that, in what was still the DDR, cults were already mushrooming over the whole area with their enticing bait,[6] and that eastern Germany was virtually flooded by dangerous New Religious Movements.[7] In an article in a Berlin local paper in September 1990, Gandow declared, 'We have now almost reached the point where we can no longer talk about the advance brigade: the groups have now become completely established in the eastern block and DDR citizens seem to be easy prey for them.'[8] Gandow was also behind the unambiguous headlines which appeared at a later date in local papers in Leipzig[9] and

Schwerin,[10] and which had an influence on these activities beyond the area of Berlin.

In conjunction with their work with the press, the 'moral crusaders' concentrated their efforts on their colleagues in the East German churches. The goal here was to reach as generally binding a consensus as possible for a negative appraisal of the New Religious Movements. At the same time, they intended to recruit others from their own ranks to spread the *Jugendsekten* image that they wished to propagate. Already in February 1990, Stefan Weissflog, in his capacity as the Protestant 'cult expert' from Hamburg, made a plea to the DDR churches to involve themselves in the *Jugendsekten* problem.[11] That individual members of the Christian Churches were willing at such an early stage to become involved in this matter from their Western perspective is evident from an early newspaper interview with Haack when answering the question of whether the Protestant Church in the DDR felt helpless in the face of the cult phenomenon:

> On the whole, yes we do. But as officials from the West responsible for dealing with 'cults', we are trying to help the eastern churches. We have contacts with the Thuringian and Mecklenburg churches. I have been to the eastern part where I held some seminars to shed light on these matters.[12]

Gandow affirmed in a Berlin local paper in May 1990: 'It is necessary to spread information at every level and teaching materials must be made available.' 'Short intensive courses' were essential for all pastors involved with young people, local catechists and publicity officers for Church leaders.[13] In eastern Germany in 1991, Gandow circulated a pamphlet entitled 'Dialogue and Apologetics' which contained a list of possible seminar themes on the 'new religions phenomenon'. These extended further-education courses were to be available as a service for local parishes and were to be given by the church officials specialising in cults in Berlin. Apart from Gandow, the programme announced other competent speakers, among them members of the 'Evangelische Zentralstelle für Weltanschauungsfragen', a Protestant central office in Stuttgart dealing with both non-Christian philosophies and traditional Christian sects. The titles of courses included 'The invasion of cults into eastern Germany', 'Structures within religious fringe groups' and 'Within the vortex of the "psycho" scene'. Courses, seminars and conferences consisting of one-sided arguments from 'West German' speakers, were not only used for purposes within church communities, but, based on the models of former times, they also went hand in hand with political and state institutions to promote new initiatives and to cultivate connections. Thus, the conservative Konrad Adenauer Foundation (with CDU-links) made funds available to finance an 'information' conference in Leipzig in September, 1991, with well-known speakers from the West including Klaus Funke, the Catholic representative for cult matters from Berlin, and Klaus

Martin Bender from Karlsruhe. The high point in the proceedings was a lecture by Angela Merkell,[14] who was at that time a federal government minister, and whose presence gave a desired formal political gloss to the proceedings. Just two months later, a conference in Chemnitz on '"*Jugendsekten*", psycho-cults and the occult', funded by the Friedrich-Ebert Foundation (which has close SPD connections) had the active participation of Thomas Gandow, and the opening speech was given by the head of the municipal department for youth matters acting on behalf of the mayor. Thus the conference organisers had again succeeded in attracting the support of the authorities.

An occasion of much greater practical significance was a seminar for spreading the cult image. The Berlin-based 'Programme for Parents and Victims for Mental Liberation from Psychic Dependency', founded and supported by Gandow, was behind the conference which, once again, included well-known Western anti-cult officials amongst its speakers and which took place in Glienicke in March 1992. The organisers sought participants especially from the teaching profession, government workers, administration, communal advisory bodies and independent organisations, as well as politicians concerned with youth matters and workers from organisations for victims. To entice participants from the new federal states of eastern Germany, there was a concession for travel costs which only they could use.

Since, as early as the 1970s, the efforts of Church anti-cult experts had proved to be successful in voicing resistance to the new religions on behalf of their victims, it was only to be expected that similar initiatives would also be introduced to eastern Germany. In the meantime, initiatives such as 'further education seminars for teachers and local politicians', organised by the Berlin 'Parent and Victim Association', took place in East Berlin, in Leipzig, Dresden and Potsdam in 1990 and 1991.[15] Local organisations supported by Gandow sprang up in several eastern German towns such as Greifswald, Jena, Chemnitz and Leipzig, and encouraged him to say that 'Parents and Victim Associations' should be set up in the East based on the model for the conditions in the West: 'I think even there, every postal area must be fully covered.'[16]

The statements of Pastor Ingrid Dietrich, chairperson of the 'Parents and Victims Association against Psychic Dependence in Leipzig' are symptomatic. Reflecting on the origin of this parent initiative, she offered a revealing interpretation of the notion of 'being a victim', by saying:

> We formed an association after the first conference in Leipzig concerning information on cults with Mr Gandow and other experts; not just because we are parents who have lost children but because we ourselves were also affected. We were affected because there were a few rather serious cases in Leipzig of people who had come under the influence of the new religious groups and psycho-cults.[17]

It must also be added that Ingrid Dietrich was supported in her work as chairperson by the press spokesman, Markus Blume, who is a theology student, who thus introduced on his own behalf yet another church connection into the association.[18]

## Strategies in opinion formation

Among the strategies employed to form public opinion there was one well known in the former Federal Republic, which was characterised by posting negative leaflets to the addresses of the New Religious Movements containing explosive discussion topics, the conclusions of which, from the point of view of the majority of citizens, had already been decided. Given the prevalent public consensus with regard to the harmful effects of hallucinogenic or hard drugs which were widespread at that time, it was quite obvious from the outset of the *Jugendensekten* debate in the former Federal Republic that there was an attempt to label New Religious Movements in exactly the same way. Bearing this background in mind, the claim made in 1976 by Haack's Munich colleague, the Catholic theologian, Hans Löffelmann, seems to be an only too typical, paradigmatic example when he pleaded that it would have to:

> gradually sink into public consciousness that it was not only the drug dealers with their intoxicating poisons who were a life-threatening danger to young people and society in general, but also the 'bosses' of a *Jugendreligion* or *Jugendsekte* who, with their most sophisticated tricks, might not be able to ruin them physically – as the drug dealers could – but instead, could cause incalculable psychic damage.[19]

With such a background, it appears to be more than likely that the New Religious Movements will be lumbered with notions which have been very quickly crystallised into key words as part of the so-called 'coming to terms with the past'. Haack was highly sensitive to people's latent fears of traditional, centralised organisations, and alleged that after the collapse of socialism together with its organs of state, there would be an ominous danger of a swing-door 'effect'; just as the Eastern German FDJ (i.e. roughly the socialist equivalent of a boy scout/girl guide movement) 'goes out of the door, in comes the second best group with any set of beliefs'.[20] Gandow used a similar tone, when he re-emphasised the word *Kaderbildung* with its negative connotations alluding to socialistic elite education. Applying this expression to the *Jugendsekten* problem, he said:

> It must be added and emphasised that there [in East Germany after the breakdown of Communism], are some people who have lost their links with their view of the world as a whole and who are now searching for a new orientation.[21]

Earlier, he had said:

> The parallels are very worrying. Some of these totalitarian groups have
> even secured their grounds with barbed wire, thus achieving the collapse
> of the border between power and truth in their system. Critics are perse-
> cuted and expelled and there are even some cases of their being
> murdered. I have heard of some former members of the FDJ [i.e. the
> GDR socialistic youth movement] afterwards becoming enthusiastic
> disciples of the Reverend Moon. The Moon movement in particular
> now has some advantages. The structures are similar to those in the FDJ
> and 99 per cent of the ideology fits in with the FDJ.[22]

In using language of this kind, the 'cult' experts were right in expecting that
they would have a willing audience everywhere, which was especially the case
in the West. This is clear from the following extracts taken from the report of
a committee meeting in which the participants demonstrated a very rare
ideological uniformity of opinion. Kerstin Wetzel (CDU/CSU): 'In your
work, have you already had any experience in the new federal states of
Scientology infiltrating into the old structures in a clearly targeted
fashion?'[23] Elmer (SPD): 'The whole business reminds me of the Stasi.'[24]
Dobberthien (SPD): 'My dear Konrad Elmer, I should like to go one step
further: I regard them to be more a cross between the Stasi and the Mafia.'[25]

The article, 'Moon instead of Marx' in the *Konstanzer Südkurier* of 6 July
1991, may be regarded as representative of the widespread awareness of the
complex problem of *Jugendsekten* in eastern Germany', as in the following
extract:

> There are not only students from Halle and Jena who recently opposed
> the SED, sitting reverently at the feet of the new cult gurus, but also
> former convinced members of the SED and FDJ who seemed to have
> found their apparently suitable equivalents in the new religions. The
> main point is that they have people with leadership qualities and that is
> home territory for the young people from the former DDR. They are
> promoting the new man who is really 'in the know' – and likewise, that
> is nothing new for them. Those who do not know where to put their
> Honecker portraits can now find new idols.

While conjectures of this kind may well have broadly reflected the
mentality of most West Germans, they are by no means always in harmony
with the present self-awareness amongst the population in eastern Germany.
A different line of thought followed by cult opponents demonstrated its
effects even more in the new federal states than in the old. This alternative
kind of argumentation was directed at the deep-seated uncertainties which
surrounded the former DDR population in facing the challenges of what
was for them a new economic system. Capitalism required the citizens of the

DDR to act in circumstances which were strange to them, and then to find their place in an employment market based on the principle of individual competition. With this background, warnings about favouritism towards the New Religious Movements increasingly became an explosive issue, particularly as the former DDR citizens were demanding their justified incorporation into the labour market and were protesting against the western methods of stripping down their former assets. So, Gandow could rely on the fact that there would be a general widespread feeling of outrage when he stated that, by using public funds, the Erfurt employment exchange had promoted the BEP (i.e. Bewußtseins-Erweiterungs-Programm), which was regarded as a 'psycho-cult', and that the Berlin 'Treuhand' organisation had met the unreasonable demands of a subsidiary of the AAO (i.e. Aktionsanalytische Organisation) with regard to an item of real estate.[26]

## The case of Scientology

This kind of argumentation is, to a certain extent, very plausible and shows why, after unification, the *Jugendsekten* discussion for the whole of Germany had typically been limited, in a most conspicuous fashion, to the Scientology Church. This organisation – more than all the other controversial groups – was regarded as a 'pseudo-religion' which, therefore, only pretended to be a church to carry out dubious business dealings under the protection of the 'Basic' or 'Constitutional' Law in Germany. It is the case that the Scientologists do not deny their aim of gaining as great an influence as possible within the economic sphere. However, how far these activities are clandestine machinations of the whole organisation or are an application of the principles developed by Ron Hubbard by individual business people, generally remains a mystery to outsiders. Rather than making sweeping allegations, this very point could be something to be put under closer scrutiny. Meanwhile the extent to which the whole problematic subject of Scientology and the economy grew to become a controversial issue is revealed by a rumour constantly denied by the Warsteiner executives, but which, however, caused definite losses: it was maintained that the Warsteiner brewery had relations with Scientology.[27] Where it could be established that followers of this Church had become involved in business, the waves of discontent increased all the more. Individual cases in the new federal states such as the one where a Scientologist, Karl-Erich Heilig, got involved in some shady dealings, were soon blown up as typical examples of elaborate 'bounty hunts in the former worker and peasant state',[28] undertaken by the controversial Church. In the same breath, it was alleged that behind this kind of takeover, there was a programme developed by the Scientology organisation 'to train the apathetic "Ossis" (Easterners) to become hard-boiled managers and employees suitable for Western needs who could find their place and assert themselves in the jungle of the Western employment market'.[29] Once they had got such unscrupulous people to belong to the Scientology Church, then they would go on with what for a long time had been customary for the new religions in the West:[30] the running of disguised Scientology businesses and the acquisition of huge sums of money to the detriment of the German taxpayer.

When Ralf-Dietmar Mucha presented an actual invoice to a public authority in October 1991, this added fuel to the grounds for suspicion regarding the high fees for dianetics and auditing together with other allegations of this kind. According to this vehement Scientology critic from Düsseldorf, there are:

> about sixty businesses at present in action belonging to Scientology with new businesses starting up on a daily basis and they have greatly exceeded the profits they made at the end of the 80s, and the money now in circulation amounts to a sum between 300 and 500 millions.[31]

Ralf Abel, a Hamburg lawyer, regarded the profits from Scientology to be considerably higher when he referred to a turnover of the order of billions and demanded that this matter 'must be of interest to the Minister of Finance because the unpaid Value Added Tax for services alone must involve sums which, somewhere on the line, must have a depressing effect on the budget'.[32] With similar dramatic effect, the ex-Scientologist, Norbert Potthoff, made the following allegation:

> If we are estimating amounts of 300 millions, then that could be just about a third of the money leaving Germany and, of course without being paid to the taxman. Perhaps, Herr Waigel [the then German Minister of Finance] should look into this matter so that something will finally be done.[33]

With these kinds of figures, it is obvious that an attempt would then be made to extend the anti-cult lobby to include additional opposition groups with wider interests who could also exercise an extremely strong influence on society. In this regard, Gandow made the following demand: 'Trade unions and chambers of commerce should now face this problem, and not leave it to initiatives of parent groups and youth workers.'[34]

There was another similar rhetorical approach favoured by the Church cult experts which had been successful in the past. Its key character consisted in addressing from the outset the obvious weak spots in the anti-cult campaign with regard to their content and to introduce 'immunising' arguments into the debate. These initiatives sought to intimate that the whole extent of the 'cult danger' would be revealed in the future despite being based on failed predictions and, for this very reason, now was the time to take appropriate preventive steps. These were the kind of allegations the cult opponents had increasingly to assert in their reports, as it could no longer be denied that the invasion of New Religious Movements which had been predicted as an invasion into the new federal states had obviously failed to take place. Even in September 1990, Gandow had warned about a broad 'road of no return' because there were supposed to be several buses full of Scientologists and packed with 'dianetic' books coming from West Germany and heading eastwards to 'enable young DDR citizens to make their first contact with a Western sect'.[35]

It was not until thirteen months later that the Berlin 'cult' expert maintained in an official report that neither the Scientology Church, the TM Organisation nor the Unification Church were interested in 'putting a mass movement into action'.[36] The groups were more concerned with influencing elites according to the flexible motto: 'What are a hundred bank clerks compared with one bank manager?'[37] or: 'Why target thirty pupils if you can reach one teacher responsible for drug problems?'[38] The implication was that one should not be blinded by this subversive approach since the 'cults' had a long-term strategy. According to Ralf-Dietmar Mucha, one of the fiercest West German critics of Scientology, a 'time-bomb'[39] had been planted and now was the time to defuse it. There was a warning that a future increasing acceptance of the cults might be a delayed consequence caused by the current social circumstances, especially the rise in unemployment in the East and the increasing feeling of disorientation. Resorting to a study of a more general nature from the Leipzig research institute into youth matters, Gandow concluded that:

> There are a great number of important young people who are now either starting or finishing their higher education studies for whom either the loss of meaning in life or the search for meaning is a crucial factor in these kinds of organisations.[40]

Further, if there did 'happen to be a considerable number of new recruits to the cults in the East, then the pendulum could swing back again and initiate, as it were, a kind of "reverse mission"'. Thus, referring to what purported to be a new religious boom appearing in the East, he opined that 'people who are recruited over there (the East) but cannot make any money there will, of course, also be put into action in the western federal states'.[41]

The prospect of new religions dividing into smaller groups amongst themselves was envisaged, but this pluralism was unlikely to be less dangerous than the smaller numbers of the present 'classical' *Jugendsekten*. Harald Baer, a cult expert, took a similar view when, shortly after the Wall came down, he said that it was quite possible that what had already been the case in the former Federal Republic could be now repeated in the former DDR, i.e. that strictly hierarchically structured organisations such as Scientology, etc. functioning under a severe military discipline, would not be the real problem the people had to face, but instead an 'esoteric scene' would open the gate to a religious invasion.[42]

Norbert Potthoff expressed very irresponsible views which appeared deliberately at the end of this selection of arguments enlisted by the anti-cult brigade in order to divert attention from the lack of any substance in their accusations. Potthoff, specially recruited as the usual arch-witness against the Scientologists, was moved to make the following serious allegation in the context of a well-known inquiry in the presence of a parliamentary committee and various so-called 'cult experts':

> At the moment, I am 42, but when I am 80 I would not like to have to take on a similar task as in the White Rose Organisation with the Scholl brothers and sisters [a German resistance group in the Third Reich]. I can see things developing in this way. You may ridicule this idea, but Charlie Chaplin portrayed Adolf Hitler in his film *The Great Dictator* at a very early stage. At the same time, people laughed at him…and some-times, the film was even forbidden.[43]

## The role of the Churches

In so far as it is valid to base the significance of the German anti-cult campaign on the sociological insights of the labelling approach, the answer to the question concerning the power which enabled the relevant parties successfully to set up their moral crusade, is, in the main part, fairly obvious. The parties which became involved in the anti-cult campaign consisted mainly of officials of the Christian Churches who benefited from highly structured and wealthy organisations with various state-based centres of influence. This factor came more and more to the fore, the more vigorously the Western Church authorities became involved in the process of finding a sense of identity which the East German Churches were undergoing after unification. In this context, much of what had determined the Churches' campaign against the New Religious Movements in the former West Germany now went into the 're-building initiatives'. In case of need, material support was given from the West expressly for these purposes. The extent of the efforts made by West German Church officials to bring about a union of interests with their own traditional form of action against New Religious Movements, can be seen from the advertisement of 1 July 1992. What was advertised was an external position in the 'Evangelische Zentralstelle für Weltanschauungsfragen' responsible for East German churches within this Protestant Central Office for non-Christian philoso-phies and 'cults' with special emphasis on information concerning the attitudes of the groups flooding in from the West. An essential precondition for employment was 'willingness to work together with the main office in Stuttgart'.[44]

It proved to be generally satisfactory that, at the very beginning, a period distinctly characterised in the East by ideological uncertainty, there was an acceptable openness regarding the Western view of reality. These uncertain-ties corresponded to the subjective perception of former DDR citizens, who felt they had to rely on the knowledge and skills, and even in some cases on the 'doctrines', of a system which had finally proved to be 'victorious'. Gandow had noted 'increasing interest but combined with great ignorance' amongst the clergy and church youth workers.[45] Conscious that he, as a cult 'expert' coming from the West, had a great advantage as far as information was concerned, he had no scruples about making full use of his own monopoly of definitions. This was shown in an interview on the German channel 2 programme entitled 'The Religious Invasion into the DDR' broadcast on 1 August 1990. From his point of view, his East German colleagues were ignorant of these matters: 'Here they have experienced what it means for a Church to stand in opposition to an atheistic or, at any rate, secular state, but they have had no experience of what it is like to be one of many religious groups when some of them are playing with loaded dice; they must first be told about this.' The example of the 'Protestant work and research department for sectarian matters in the DDR' based in Potsdam attests to the fact that what was said by Western experts on *Jugendsekten* was eagerly accepted. Shortly after the Wall came down, this institute had arranged an infra-Church extended education course. Alongside various other convinced *Jugendsekten* opponents from the West, the panel of experts included Haack and Gandow as well as Gottfried Küenzlen, a member of the Evangelische Zentralstelle für Weltanschauungsfragen. The invitation read:

> We are very glad about the offer from a few of our expert brothers from the EKD [i.e. Protestant Church Services] to help us to fill in the most basic gaps in our knowledge of these matters in an intensive short course and we invite our colleagues most cordially to our intensive seminar on '*Jugendreligionen*', the guru phenomenon, the occult – a challenge to Church action.

The subsequent setting up of cult experts in East German parishes reveals in a most striking way how successful the attempts were to induce the Church representatives to fit into the traditional anti-*Jugendsekten* course from the West. The example of a working party on alternative religious communities from the Protestant Lutheran Church in the DDR[46] shows that unconventional forms of religion were, however, not completely new in the other half of Germany. The number of experts appointed after unification all over Germany including the East, bears no relation to what went before, and high staffing levels were attained in the meantime, both in the Protestant and Catholic Churches in East Germany.

Western colleagues were interested in giving official support to the theologians. Thus, Winfried Müller, for example, a theologian from Jena, already receptive to any information from the West in this field was selected by Gandow's 'Parents and Victims Association' in Berlin to be a counterpart responsible for similar activities.[47] In the same way, Chaplain Gerald Kluge, the Catholic expert from Pirna, appeared with his West Berlin colleague,

Klaus Funke, when giving lectures in schools, parishes, and other institutions in the Dresden-Meissen bishopric.[48] The influence of Western experts on the 'Parents and Victims Association against Psychic Dependence' in Leipzig was even more serious. In this association, all the thirty-five members regarded themselves as self-educated, but strove 'to acquire general knowledge about the cults from which specialised knowledge concerning the East German religious movements could be developed further'.[49]

With regard to the 'moral crusade' against 'cults', there is absolutely no doubt that religious and pastoral motives have played a not inconsiderable role. As both the ideology and spiritual practices of the so-called *Jugendsekten* are fundamentally opposed to Christian convictions, it is understandable that Christians turn against these alternatives and thus, reinforce their own beliefs. Alongside these factors which, as a rule, appear to outsiders to be the prime motives, a second level of motivation must be acknowledged, namely the need to combat secularisation. This second level of motivation might be said at least to overlap the first category, if not indeed, in its subjective significance essentially to overtake it.

## Clerical motivations

This weighting in favour of the second area of motivation arises from the fact that the relevant Church authorities have now been dealing with the so-called *Jugendsekten* for over twenty years. In this respect, they should be familiar with the discrepancy constantly pointed to by the critics of the *Jugendsekten* debate, between the state of empirical research and the unspecified allegations against the New Religious Movements. To illustrate this second level of motivation would have required more space than is available, including a more detailed discussion of the statistics confirming the trend of people leaving the Church which has continued as a dramatic tendency in Germany for years. On the other hand, these figures were to be addressed by the Churches' efforts to balance their losses in the form of large-scale and costly publicity drives.[50] Within the Churches there has been a growing awareness of a widespread decline in their influence on the surrounding society in contrast with what might have been for them an ideal, political field of influence.

With this background in mind, New Religious Movements which at the moment may be quantitatively insignificant might in the future possibly become serious rivals in the 'free market of Weltanschauungen'. At present, however, it is safer to assume that the *Jugendsekten* construct, with its negative connotations, is being used to set up an 'opposition' which can be seen by everybody as a challenge to the Western lifestyle in general. The intended outcome of such a strategy is to demonstrate that, more than other institutions, Christian agencies are competent defenders of Western social standards, traditional values and well-established philosophies which until now have been the basis of society. The *Jugendsekten* debate has been exploited for two purposes: in the background of a highly charged atmosphere amongst the public, there is concern for both the ideological aspects as well as for the Church as employer of staff.

In this context, the report[51] on the spiritual situation in the new federal states, produced by Helmut Obst, the Halle Professor of Ecumenical Studies, about eighteen months after the dismantling of the Wall, has acquired a very specific significance, because, although Obst stressed 'that a new spiritual and religious awakening was expected just like the peaceful revolution of the autumn of 1989', in fact, 'it did not take place for the majority of the people'. The report shows that Obst was taking into consideration that more than 70 per cent of people in East Germany had no religious affiliation.[52] As a consequence he had to ask himself what could be done on behalf of the Churches to raise their public acceptability.

This same issue appeared in the wider context of a questionnaire on environmental topics, formulated by the church shortly before the end of the DDR. The questionnaire in itself is of less interest than the conclusions later drawn from the results by the theologian, Hans-Peter Gensichen, who suggested that environmental themes and other current problems should be taken up to improve the image of the Christian Churches. He wrote:

> The adoption of environmental themes in the Church – together with other global problems – acts as kind of a counter-balance to the secularisation processes in society. A narrow-minded outlook within the Church and the faith will be broadened by accepting important social problems as genuine Church themes. In this way, both the Churches and Christians will acquire a new social relevance bringing about a new Christian momentum in society which could be important for the solution to global problems. This applies particularly to the East German Churches, but it is also relevant beyond their borders. In this area, the secularisation process has been accelerated.[53]

The labelling approach inspires the thought that the *Jugendsekten* debate, used in the way Gensichen suggests, was exploited by the Church. This approach seeks to show that the identification and persecution of deviance are a field of activity generally regarded by the public as fruitful, or even as extremely valuable, and provides an existence for great numbers of professional people. Seen from this perspective, it is important for the Churches, to have their *own* experts who are the sole specialists generally recognized in this field. This attribution of expertise reaches even to the highest government circles. At the same time it opens up a new field of professional activity since the Christian Churches do not seem to be consulted as urgently as they used to be as the 'final court of appeal'. As Susanne Rahardt-Vahldieck, in her capacity as a CDU member of parliament, commented during her attendance at a *Jugendsekten* conference in Leipzig, 'It must be noted that at the moment, mostly pastors and other clergymen will, of necessity, be the advisers on cults because people refer to them as they have no one else.'[54]

In conclusion, it has been established that the implications of the construct *Jugendsekten*, promoted mainly by the Church's so-called 'cult experts', have for a long time been a fixed component in the 'common sense' understanding of the majority of West German citizens. Despite the fact that various Church workers in East Germany have been acting as cult experts on a formally independent basis, they still remain bound to Western interpretations. In this capacity, the denominational colleagues in the East are on their own behalf and in a 'self-responsible' way still spreading a *Jugendsekten* image that has already been in existence for twenty years. They refer to political *Jugendsekten*-hearings,[55] supply information to representatives responsible for the local state parliament ministries,[56] or are commissioned by local state governments to participate in the creation of extended education seminars for teachers.[57]

This co-operation of political committees with church authorities dealing with the 'cult' problem shows that the *Jugendsekten* debate has developed in the new federal states according to the Western model. With regard to the public awareness of New Religious Movements, one can no longer speak, as has often been maintained, of the 'wall in the mind' a wall which is supposed to divide Germany, now as before, into 'West' and 'East' even several years after the opening of the border.

## Notes

1 In this matter, there is obviously a general consensus of opinion, see e.g. T. Gandow, 'Jugendreligionen und Sekten auf dem Vormarsch in die DDR I', in *Materialdienst der EZW*, 8, 1990, pp. 221–33, esp p. 224.
2 Note the typical subtitle by J. Lawrezki, *Seelenfänger ohne Gnade: Sekten, Kulte und Wundertäter in der kapitalistischen Welt*, Berlin (Ost) 1987 (Merciless Soulcatchers: Sects, Cults and Miracle Workers in the Capitalist World).
3 'Großer Zulauf zu Sekten in der DDR', *Hannoverische Allgemeine Zeitung*, 3. March 1990.
4 *Bürgerschaft der Freien und Hansestadt Hamburg*, 14 session, Report 14/2024 of 26 May 1992, p. 2.
5 'Pfarrer Haack: Boom für die Sekten. Viele Opfer', *Sonntag aktuell*, 22 July 1990.
6 'Sekten mit "Köderangeboten" flächendeckend in der DDR', *Berliner Sonntagsblatt*, 13 May 1990.
7 'Die Noch-DDR wird zur Zeit von Sekten, überschwemmt', *Berliner Morgenpost*, 11 September 1990.
8 'Sekten werden unterschätzt', *Volksblatt Berlin*, 9 September 1990.
9 'Weltherrschaft ist das Ziel', *Leipziger Volkszeitung*, 26 January 1991.
10 'Geschäftemacher in Sachen "Seelen" finden viele Abnehmer – Pfarrer Gandow warnt vor Sekten und Jugendreligionen', *Schweriner Volkszeitung*, 21 June 1991.
11 Cf. H. Spies, 'Sekten erobern die neuen Bundesländer', in *Weltblick: Beiträge zur Verständigung und Einheit*, 2 (3), 1991, 21–2, p. 21.
12 'Pfarrer Haack: Boom für die Sekten', op. cit.
13 'Schnellkurs' für die Kirchen gefordert', *Volksblatt Berlin*, 5 May 1990.

14 Pamphlet: *Invasion der Seelenfänger? Jugendsekten in den neuen Ländern.* Information conference in Leipzig (Brühlzentrum), September 1991 sponsored by Konrad Adenauer Stiftung.

15 See Bundestag. 12th term. Committee for Women and Youth. 14, Committee Report No. 13. Private hearing on *Jugendsekten*, p. 118.

16 Ibid. p. 119.

17 I. Dietrich, 'Was können Eltern tun? Orientierungshilfe für Betroffene', in *Sekten und Sondergemeinschaften in den neuen Bundesländern. Ergebnisse einer Tagung unter dem Thema: 'Jugendsekten, Psychokulte, Okkultismus' – Informationsvorträge und Seminare, Chemnitz, 15–16.November 1991*, Chemnitz 1992, pp. 126–31, p. l26.

18 See U. Dannert and T. Fugmann, 'Mythos Sekten', in *Kreuzer*, October 1993, pp. 16–18, p. 16.

19 H. Löffelmann, 'Das Geschäft mit der Religion. Neue Jugendreligionen schiessen wie Pilze aus dem Boden/Von allen Seiten wird gewarnt', in *Bundesvorstand des BDKJ (Hg.)*, Sonderdruck aus BDKJ-Informationsdienst, 15 March 1976, p. 2.

20 See 'Mun statt Marx', *Der Spiegel*, 36, 1990, pp. 97–9.

21 Bundestag, op. cit., p.93.

22 See the parallel interview in the periodical *Deine Gesundheit*, December 1990, p. 4.

23 Bundestag, op. cit., p. 80.

24 Ibid., p. 105.

25 Ibid., p. l06.

26 Ibid., p. 48.

27 See e.g., 'Scientology-Gerücht über Warsteiner: üble Nachrede', *Welt am Sonntag*, 15 May 1994.

28 See B. Schröder, 'Der Griff nach Osten. Scientologische Beutezüge im ehemaligen Arbeiter-und-Bauern-Staat', in J. Herrmann (ed.), *Mission mit allen Mitteln: Der Scientology-Konzern auf Seelenfang*, Reinbek bei Hamburg 1992, pp. 116–26.

29 Ibid., p. 118.

30 See e.g. Bundestag, op. cit., the corresponding statement of Hauser, the official for 'cults' in Baden-Württemberg, p. 86.

31 See ibid., p. 89.

32 Ibid., p. 84.

33 Ibid., p. 97.

34 As in Gandow's foreword to F.-W. Haack, *Jugendsekten. Vorbeugen – Hilfe – Auswege*, Weinheim, 1991, p. 8.

35 'Die Noch-DDR wird zur Zeit von Sekten überschwemmt', *Berliner Morgenpost*, 11 September 1990.

36 Bundestag, op. cit., p. 92.

37 Ibid.

38 Ibid., p. 116.

39 Ibid., p. 90.

40 Ibid., p. 93.

41 Ibid., p. 94f.

42 See ibid., p. 88.

43 Ibid. p. 135f.

44 In this context, I refer to the corresponding advertisement in *Deutsches Allgemeines Sonntagsblatt* of 6 December 1991.

45 'Sekten entdecken die DDR', *Rheinischer Merkur*, Christ und Welt section, 13 April 1990.

46 Oberkirchenrat Dr Münchow attached great significance to this fact in a letter of 11 September 1992 in which he responded to my questions concerning discussion of *Jugendsekten* in East Germany.

47 See 'Seelenfänger haben leider oft viel zu leichtes Spiel', *Thüringer Tageblatt*, 23 April 1991.

48 'Die Sekten sind da!', *Dresdner Nachrichten*, 25 October 1990.

49 Quoted from a letter written on 9 September 1992 on behalf of the initiative committee by Markus Blume, on the state of the East German *Jugendsekten* discussion.

50 See e.g. 'Himmlische Kampagne. Mit teuren Werbe-Kreuzzügen wollen Seelsorger Abtrünnige zur Umkehr bewegen', *Wirtschaftswoche*, 18 December 1992.

51 See H. Obst, 'Auf dem Weg in den weltanschaulichen Pluralismus. Zur geistig-religiösen Lage in den neuen Bundesländern', in *Materialdienst der EZW*, July 1991, pp. 193–205.

52 Eggers for example, cites these 1991 figures. Cf. Eggers, G.: 'Religion, Ethik und Lebensgestaltung als Inhalte schulischer Bildung: Entwicklungen und Probleme in den neuen Bundesländern und Berlin (Ost)', in H. Zinser, (ed.), *Herausforderung Ethikunterricht*, Marburg, 1991, pp. 39–52.

53 H.-P. Gensichen, 'Zur Religiosität umweltengagierter Bürger in der früheren DDR', in *Materialdienst der EZW*, May 1991, pp. 151–2, p. 152.

54 Bundestag, op. cit., p. 78.

55 I refer to a programme obtained at a meeting arranged by the CDU group of the Thuringian state parliament on 10 November 1993.

56 See 'Jeder zehnte Jugendliche hatte Kontakt zu Sekten', *Thüringer Allgemeine*, 12 February 1994.

57 State Parliament of Mecklenburg-Vorpommern, 1st term, circular 1/2048 (new), 30 June 1992, p. 9.

# Summary of Chapter 13

Many of the NRMs active in Britain are branches of organisations that have originated elsewhere, but the anti-cult bodies, even allowing for influences from abroad, and the imitation of American techniques such as de-programming and exit counselling, are none the less home-grown organisations. Dr Chryssides shows that some of these bodies were related to earlier Christian evangelical agencies whose self-appointed mission was to combat what they considered to be Christian deviations (such as Mormonism and Jehovah's Witnesses), but there were also other, more secular campaigners. It is perhaps not surprising that the anti-cult groups have also revealed fissiparous tendencies of a kind not altogether so different from those which anti-cultists have tended to identify as typical specifically of 'cults'.

# 13  Britain's anti-cult movement

*George D. Chryssides*

## Introduction

Britain's organised anti-cult movement did not come into existence until the 1970s. Previous decades had seen the spread of the older new religions – principally the Jehovah's Witnesses, the Mormons, the Christadelphians and Christian Scientists. Apart from Theosophy, all these major NRMs (New Religious Movements) which flourished in the 1950s and 1960s claimed a Christian identity, and hence became regarded by mainstream Christians as perversions of the gospel.

Opposition to such groups was spearheaded essentially by a few publications such as Horton Davies' *Christian Deviations* and short series of booklets published by the Society for the Propagation of Christian Knowledge and the Church Book Room Press.[1] Works such as Walter Martin's *The Maze of Mormonism*,[2] although originating in the United States, also circulated fairly widely in British Christian circles. Much of the written opposition to the 'cults' was aimed at enabling the mainstream Christian to know how best to proclaim the 'true' gospel to JWs and Latter-day Saints when they arrived at one's door. It was only the Jehovah's Witnesses who experienced systematic opposition in secular circles, by virtue of their refusal to fight in the Second World War – an act of defiance for which many British JWs had to pay fines or serve prison sentences.

It was the new generation of New Religious Movements that gave rise to a different form of opposition. Essentially, the older NRMs were much more staid in their lifestyle: only relatively minor adjustments were needed to one's way of life in order to become a Mormon, a Christian Scientist or a Jehovah's Witness. Giving up alcohol, or refusing certain forms of medical treatment were still thoroughly compatible with maintaining one's family life and pursuing one's occupation prior to conversion. Mormons and Witnesses tended to engage in dialogue with householders rather than with younger family members for obvious reasons, and parents rather than children were typically the first to convert within a household.

The new religions that entered Britain from the late 1960s onwards had a markedly different character. Only a proportion of them were 'New

Christian' in character.[3] Groups making their impact on Britain were now as diverse as the International Society for Krishna Consciousness (ISKCON), Nichiren Shoshu (now Soka Gakkai International), Transcendental Meditation and the Church of Scientology. The diverse character of the newer NRMs meant that the old style of Christian critique was no longer appropriate, since only a fraction could be construed as 'pseudo-Christian' impostors. Further, the early 1960s witnessed a dramatic decline in mainstream Christian allegiance, and hence fewer people found relevance in a distinctively Christian critique of 'the cults'. If 'the cults' were 'a problem' they were as much a problem for Christians and non-Christians alike.

There were other features of the new NRMs that the public found threatening. Several groups had taken to street evangelism rather than relying on responses at people's doors. All who ventured outside their homes were therefore potential conversion material, and young people as well as older ones were being 'recruited'. Eileen Barker reports that the average age of the full time UC member in 1989 was 23[4] – a radically different target population from the householders who were sought by Mormons and Witnesses.

The remarkable drop in the age of conversion was facilitated by a further feature of several groups: community living. The Unification Church (UC), the Children of God (now The Family) and ISKCON offered a radical change of lifestyle, which in general could only be taken up by younger members of society who had fewer ties. The 'loss' of one's children to NRMs, coupled with the radically different lifestyle that they appeared to demand, added fuel to public opposition.

Proselytising methods appeared to be more aggressive too. Not only did the public streets afford no door for the potential convert to shut; evangelisation tactics were believed to include deception regarding the group's identity, and techniques such as 'love-bombing' and 'flirty fishing' (enticement by sexual favours). In the case of the Church of Scientology, enquirers were drawn into progressive engagement in Dianetics courses, either by being persuaded to part with additional monies, or by working as a full-time staff member, offering labour in lieu of payment.

When the new NRMs were not attempting to gain converts, they were sometimes found selling wares such as candles, or soliciting donations from the public, who did not always realise their real identity. Some NRMs purported to collect 'for ecumenical work', for 'a children's home', or for some other seemingly good cause. Such activities were in marked contrast to the older NRMs, who seldom, if ever, sought public financial support. The Jehovah's Witnesses in particular had always made of a point of being the church that never even took up a collection during worship.

The fact that several of the new NRMs either came from the east or drew on eastern ideas provided an outlet for some of the prevalent British racism, expressed in the context of the mass immigration of the late 1950s and early 1960s. Some of the Unification Church's critics have remarked on 'all that eastern stuff' which *Divine Principle* contains. Recent objections to ISKCON's presence at Bhaktivedanta Manor in the Hertfordshire village of Letchmore Heath, which have Hertsmere Borough Council to seek its closure as a place of public worship, are much more plausibly explained by its threat to 'the British way of life' rather than any public nuisance that its visitors allegedly caused.[5]

The unfamiliarity of these immigrant religions' ideas often prompted comments that they were 'bizarre' and 'irrational'.[6] It therefore followed that there could be no good reasons for accepting them, and maybe not even bad ones. Since rational persuasion could not inculcate belief in the messiahship of Sun Myung Moon, or in Lord Krishna as the supreme personality of godhead, then – it was maintained – there must be some non-rational process at work that brought the seeker to faith. The 'brainwashing' theory was born.

## Types of opposition

Because of the apparently greater threat that was posed by the new wave of NRMs, many believed that there was a need for more active opposition than had been provided by the written critiques of Horton Davies and the like. Action, not just words, was needed. Accordingly, a number of individuals came together to form interest groups aimed at combating 'the cult problem'.

In all, it is possible to distinguish four categories of anti-cult group. First, there are secular groups who monitor NRMs, the best known of which are FAIR (Family Action Information and Rescue) and the Cult Information Centre (CIC). Second, there are Christian evangelical groups who continue the older-style Christian critique of 'cults', most notably the Deo Gloria Trust and the Reachout Trust. Third, several cult-specific groups have from time to time arisen, such as Counter Scientology Europe, EMFJ (Ex-Mormons for Jesus), CONCERN (a short-lived support group for parents and ex-members of the Children of God), and EMERGE, which was primarily an organisation dedicated to supporting ex-Unificationists. Finally, there are the de-programmers, who recommend and carry out the forcible abduction of members, usually for payment, from religious groups, and 'counsel' them back to the world of conventional reality. Few individuals and organisations will admit to de-programming, but one organisation that has unashamedly confessed to it is COMA (Council on Mind Abuse), run by ex-Unificationist Martin Faiers. (This organisation should not be confused with COMA in the United States, which is a totally separate body.) James Beckford refers to an organisation called POWER (People's Organised Workshop on Ersatz Religions), which existed briefly between 1976 and 1977, urging the need for 'hundreds, if not thousands of de-programmers', and the training of Jesuits for this purpose![7]

Although these four types of group claim to define their identity on the grounds I have indicated, they are not quite as distinct as may appear. Joint membership is often encouraged: FAIR, for example, at one stage picked up a sizeable proportion of its members through Deo Gloria. There is frequent collaboration amongst anti-cult groups: FAIR and Deo Gloria have held joint workshops, and FAIR itself has twice had clergymen as chairmen. It is not uncommon for one anti-cult group to refer enquirers to another: CIC sometimes refers its clients to Catalyst, an organisation run by a Christian chaplain by the name of Graham Baldwin, who provides 'exit counselling'. Baldwin in turn refers those who enquire about The Family to the CIC, where 'General Secretary', Ian Haworth, claims to have specialist knowledge. (Haworth's wife, apparently, was once a member of the Children of God.) The founder of the (Christian evangelical) Deo Gloria Trust, Kenneth Frampton, provided the financial resources for Ian Haworth to set up the CIC.[8]

Although the secular anti-cult groups claim to have 'no religious axe to grind' and to be opposed to cult practices rather than beliefs, *FAIR News*, its quarterly newsletter, from time to time lapses into theological critiques of NRMs. Its April 1985 edition, for example, launched into quite a detailed critique of the Unification Church's claim to have a Christian identity. Conversely, Christian evangelical groups are not exclusively concerned with the truth claims of new religions, but with their practices too.

Finally, cult-specific organisations can grow into broader ones. This has already happened in the case of FAIR, originally set up to oppose the Unification Church, but which now campaigns against all and sundry. Reachout began by targeting the Jehovah's Witnesses, but now has a much wider focus.

## The secular anti-cult groups

FAIR, the first and largest cult monitoring organisation, was formed in 1976 by Paul Rose, who was then Member of Parliament for Manchester Blackley. Rose's initiative was a response to mounting enquiries and complaints from parents whose sons and daughters had become involved in NRMs.[9]

As Beckford points out, FAIR offers no formal rehabilitation process, and does not employ any trained counsellors. It therefore offers no formal programme to those leaving NRMs to enable them to re-integrate to normal conventional life, and to cope with the predictable problems of losing a community of friends, finding accommodation, seeking employment or training, or explaining to others how they have spent a period of their lives 'inside a cult'. Enabling ex-members to deal with such problems provided the focus for another group called EMERGE (Ex-Members of Extreme Religious Groups), which was a self-help organisation providing mutual support for UC leavers. EMERGE was founded in 1980, but dissolved only five years later.

Although FAIR officials reject the term 'anti-cult',[10] FAIR's main strategy seems designed to hamper the progress of NRMs in a variety of ways. One important strategy is warning the potential 'recruit', and FAIR members are invited to use copies of a 'warning leaflet' adapted from the Citizens Freedom Foundation, America's largest anti-cult group. (The fact that various other anti-cult groups draw on CFF's leaflet explains similarities that have been noted between information from FAIR, COMA, Cultists Anonymous and CIC.)

FAIR is decidedly campaigning in character, and supporters are advised to write to Members of Parliament explaining the implications of cult membership, to contact church leaders, to demand information and explanations from NRM leaders, and to contact the media to gain publicity for those who are affected by the phenomenon. Such campaigning has no doubt been a major factor in FAIR's failure to gain a charitable status, for which it has twice applied and been rejected.

The secular anti-cultists' perception of NRMs is worthy of some comment. Their vocabulary is in itself sufficient indication of how NRMs are perceived. Cultism is a 'problem', making those who join 'victims' and those outside the cult 'vulnerable'. Members are 'recruited' (the word 'conversion' is never used) and the recruit becomes 'lost' to a cult, which is 'destructive' and 'damaging' to all those who come to 'depend' on it. This range of vocabulary would, of course, be considered quite inappropriate in other contexts where a young man or woman typically leaves home, for example, to go to university or to take up a post abroad in a multinational company, both of which have similar effects on family and social life.

NRMs are viewed stereotypically, frequently presented in the form of a list 'Marks of a Cult'. These 'marks' largely consist of the anti-cultist stereotype of one particular NRM, the Unification Church, which is extrapolated to all 'destructive cults' – a somewhat amorphous concept for which no anti-cult group has yet provided a clear definition. The list is normally tenfold, alluding to the secretive, deceptive way in which cults are deemed to operate, under the authoritarian leadership of a wealthy charismatic self-appointed guru or messiah, who subjects members to an intensive indoctrination programme and is thus able to demand total commitment to the cause.[11]

The typical stereotype of the 'vulnerable' is the impressionable young person, who is perhaps temporarily away from home, having a 'year out' from his or her studies, possibly travelling and feeling lonely, and maybe seeking for some meaning in life, having become disenchanted with mainstream religion's ability to meet his or her needs. Paradoxically, those same anti-cultists seem happy to embrace the contradictory thesis, that 'anyone is vulnerable' to the lures of a 'destructive cult'.

The perceived dangers of cult involvement are judged to be giving up one's studies, breaking up families, loss of one's material goods to the cult, abrupt personality changes for the worse, including a total dependence on the cult for all one's decision-making and a total inability to think for oneself. A recent television series – *Signs and Wonders* – depicted a member of a (fictitious) NRM as being unable even to chose a snack from a cafeteria menu after extradition from the group. At times it can be difficult to see the reason for the inclusion of certain alleged effects: Haworth, for example, suggests that one of the harmful effects of belonging to a cult is a 'reduced use of irony, abstractions and metaphors'![12] No evidence is presented, nor is it explained why this is undesirable.

Although the 'brainwashing' theory secures universal acceptance among anti-cultists, how brainwashing actually takes place is never convincingly explained. Haworth claims to have identified a total of twenty-six 'mind control techniques',[13] but it is not clear how these are supposed to induce acceptance or compliance on the enquirer's part. On the one hand, austere living conditions with food and sleep deprivation are somehow believed to induce trance-like states; yet, equally, the Unification Church has been accused of brainwashing clergy and academics at luxurious hotels in foreign resorts, where they were 'pampered'. At other times, it is suggested that NRM leaders are able to hypnotise members by making eye contact in a particular way, or by ensuring that members constantly accompany the new enquirer at all times. Faced with the difficulty of explaining how brain-washing occurs, anti-cultists have sometimes resorted to highly improbable, not to say bizarre hypotheses. Haworth's list of 'mind control techniques' includes 'inducing dependence on the group by introducing games with obscure rules',[14] and one ex-UC contributor to *FAIR News* accuses UC leaders alleging that 'we had been hypnotised while asleep'![15]

No attempt appears to be made to edit the 'marks' list to accommodate the changing features of the new religions. The presence of an authoritarian leader is posited as a distinctive 'mark', despite the fact that NRM leaders such as Prabhupada, L. Ron Hubbard, Osho and David Berg have all died in recent years, in each case without leaving any clear successor of similar putative charismatic quality.

Most, if not all, of these anti-cultist assumptions have been largely discredited by academic research, which on the whole is simply ignored. The suggestion that all (or even most) NRMs display a large number of common characteristics has been successfully challenged by Eileen Barker,[16] and by various other academic writers, such as Wallis, Melton and Turner, who have produced taxonomies which classify different groups into importantly different categories. As Wallis has shown, for example, some are world-renouncing, while others are world-affirming.[17]

The 'cults' are treated as unreasonable, despite the work of various researchers to demonstrate that at least some are capable of being systemati-cally treated as serious religions.[18] 'Anyone is vulnerable' still remains an anti-cultist dogma even though it has been demonstrated that there are defi-nite patterns of conversion, making those who come from specific backgrounds more likely to join certain NRMs rather than others.[19]

Occasionally anti-cultists take aboard academic findings to maintain credibility. Faced with Barker's undeniable conclusion that NRMs have important differences between them, FAIR now employs Haworth's distinction between two major types of cult: 'self improvement/counselling' and 'New Religious Movements'.[20] Faced with Barker's research findings that a typical UC member leaves the organisation after two years,[21] two speakers at a 1994 FAIR conference suggested that, although it may be possible for members to come out of a cult, it takes much longer for 'the cult to come out of the member'.

In 1994, FAIR members discussed an amendment to the organisation's name, since the word 'Rescue' at the end could be construed as an endorsement of kidnapping members. The fact that FAIR firmly rejected the substitution of 'Research' is no doubt a further indication of their disregard for academics, whom one former Chairman has dismissed as 'an inordinately complacent and self-satisfied lot of mystagogues'.[22] (In the end, it was decided that 'R' would henceforth stand for 'Resource'.) The anti-cult movement's contempt for academics is mirrored by the fact that few academics will endorse anti-cultism.

Faced with this almost unanimous lack of support from academics, the anti-cult movement relies on a small quartet of American psychiatrists who still support a 'mind control' thesis, notably Margaret Singer, Louis Jolyon West, Eli Shapiro and James Clarke. Haworth lists the following as his range of 'reliable cult aware contacts': 'mental health professionals, clergy, relatives of current cult members and ex-cult members'.[23] The omission of academic expertise is noteworthy, even though – or perhaps precisely because – many academic researchers have assumed a participant-observer role in studying NRMs. As Haworth writes: 'Accurate information on cults is not best obtained by trying to infiltrate a cult. This is far too dangerous.'[24]

Noteworthy also in Haworth's list of expert witnesses is the testimony of the ex-member, a testimony which is particularly valued within the anti-cult movement. Ex-members have been inside the cult, and hence know from first-hand experience what belonging to the group entails, and having been inside the movement they are also believed to have been party to any esoteric teachings that may be circulating. Again, it is a prevalent anti-cultist assumption that there is a significant difference between an NRM's publicly declared teachings and the real essential teachings that are divulged only to members in good standing. Unlike those who are currently NRM members, the ex-members have two further characteristics that make them of particular value to the anti-cult movement. Unlike current members, ex-members are no longer in a state of brainwashed indoctrination: they have seen the error of their ways, and are once more capable of viewing reality in a normal conventional way. Second – and most obviously – they are now on the side of the anti-cultist; unlike current members, who feel thoroughly defensive against the anti-cultist's jibes, ex-members are much more likely to have negative feelings towards the movement they have left.

## Christian anti-cult groups

While organisations such as FAIR and CIC have claimed neutrality on matters of doctrine, it remains a valid question whether the teachings of new religions are true or false. Since Christianity, particularly in its evangelical forms, appears to have insisted that one's eternal salvation might turn on the question of whether the seeker has accepted the right doctrines, it is a matter of vital concern that the errors of the new faiths should be exposed.

In 1981, Doug Harris lived in Twickenham, near London, where the Jehovah's Witnesses held their annual convention in the rugby stadium. Saddened by the thought that so many could apparently be in error, Harris vowed that he would take practical steps to ensure that they were won back for Christ. Together with a few like-minded people, Harris began by picketing the JWs' Convention, leafleting those attending. Within a short time, the work had expanded to nationwide proportions, and thus the Reachout Trust was formed to 'share the gospel' with such groups.[25] Reachout's activities are based on a statement of faith, which affirms the traditional Christian doctrines of the Trinity, humankind's state of sin and need for rebirth, Jesus Christ as the sole mediator between God and humanity, and the absolute authority of the Bible.[26]

Because salvation is important to the Christian, it is understandable that Reachout should wish to assess the potential of various new religions to enable the seeker to be 'saved'. Accordingly, Reachout's literature offers a taxonomy of NRMs which appears to address this question. 'Cults' are accorded a fourfold classification: (1) 'counterfeit Christian cults', (2) 'Christian cults', (3) 'commune cults' and (4) 'personality cults'.[27] This classification seems somewhat unsatisfactory in that it is hard to know, for example, where —say – the Unification Church ought to be placed, since it appears to have features of all four; ISKCON, equally, could be argued to be an example of either (3) or (4). Harris gives as examples of 'counterfeit Christian cults' the Jehovah's Witnesses, the Latter-day Saints, the Christadelphians and Christian Science; by contrast the Central Church of Christ, The Family, Seventh-day Adventists and the Word/Faith Movement are judged to be 'Christian', albeit 'with cultic tendencies'. The Unification Church and the Worldwide Church of God, however, appear to fall into neither category, but are nebulously labelled as 'Other Groups'.[28] No doubt the problems with this schema are partly due to the fact that Harris, its author, does not claim to be a scholar, and no doubt regards 'witnessing' to the cults as much more important than academic debate.

The need to differentiate between 'counterfeit Christian' and 'Christian' cults derives from a need for seekers and leavers to know for sure whether they have found true salvation in Jesus Christ, or whether some further act of commitment is needed. From the mainstream Christian evangelical standpoint, the 'counterfeit Christian group' is therefore particularly dangerous, since it purports to offer salvation but fails to do so. To qualify

as a 'Christian cult', then, it seems that an orthodox soteriology is not sufficient; an NRM's theology must be orthodox too.

Of course, it is not merely 'counterfeit Christianity' that fails to lead to
salvation, but any organisation or world-view that does not accept
Christianity's traditional doctrines. Accordingly, Reachout also targets
NRMs which stake no claims to a Christian identity, such as Transcendental
Meditation, ISKCON and Scientology, as well as the other major world reli-
gions, such as Hinduism, Buddhism and Islam.

Out of all the non-Christian world views, evangelical Christians have
expressed particular concern about the New Age phenomenon, which,
according to some, is the greatest current threat to Christianity.[29] This is no
doubt due to a number of factors. First, the New Age is eclectic and takes
aboard ideas from a variety of 'non-Christian' religions, for example Taoist
concepts of *yin* and *yang*, Hindu–Buddhist notions of rebirth, meditation,
chakras and so on. It also appears to encourage encounter with the occult,
expressing interest in channelling and spirit guides. Although the New Age
has a place for Jesus Christ and for apparently Christian concepts like
angels, it treats them in an unorthodox way, as is evidenced by its interest in
neo-gnostic ideas such as *The Aquarian Gospel of Jesus the Christ*, or suggestions by writers such as Holger Kersten that Jesus had a secret life in
India.[30]

The New Age's seemingly Christian components, together with its eclectic
nature, might encourage Christians to appropriate merely a few of its seemingly compatible ideas and to embrace them jointly with their Christian
faith. Herein lies the danger for evangelical Christians, for toying with New
Age ideas incurs the risk of unwittingly losing one's salvation. The boundaries of the New Age are also nebulous, and it is possible inadvertently to
use New Age concepts and artefacts unknowingly. Sounds of dolphins or
relaxing music may appear pleasant, but fail to signal their true New Age
origin. The New Age therefore offers a kind of Trojan horse to the unwary
Christian. Some evangelical Christians have gone so far as to outlaw forms
of healing which cannot be traced to conventional allopathic or Christian
roots.[31] One Christian attending a recent Reachout training day expressed
concern about a pair of earrings depicting a sun with a face and rays which
she had recently been given and which she feared might be 'New Age'.

## De-programming

My discussion of secular and Christian cult critiques serves to explain why
warnings, media publicity and political action are deemed necessary by
opponents of NRMs. However, according to certain cult critics, warning,
counselling and political action are insufficient to combat the 'cult problem':
more direct means are needed to get people out of the cults. In particular,
the supporters of de-programming reason, if members of NRMs are the
victims of mind control, they cannot be persuaded into seeing reason, for

one cannot reason with irrationality. If further justification is needed, those who favour de-programming will sometimes point out that those who have undergone it are sometimes grateful that they have been coerced into leaving.[32]

Because of the risks involved, it is understandable that de-programmers generally do not wish to be identified, and, although one hears rumours about certain anti-cult groups either recommending de-programming or having de-programmers in their midst, it is difficult to discover firm evidence about people who are willing to undertake de-programmings. Haworth is on record as having said, regarding de-programming, 'We aren't pushing that specific route, and we're not saying you shouldn't do it.'[33] FAIR has given publicity to and provided the addresses of US organisations such the Cult Awareness Network (CAN),[34] which was said to have been heavily involved in de-programming, until 1997 when it was taken over by Scientologists.

Parents of migrant British members have sometimes resorted to hiring American de-programmers who have undertaken the kidnapping abroad, as happened in the cases of Nicola Raine, Erica Heftmann and the Swatland sisters.[35] In its early days, FAIR appears to have debated the desirability of 'exit counselling', as it was then called, and concluded that it might indeed have a role to play. Cyril Vosper, at one time a FAIR official, himself turned de-programmer in 1987, and received a substantial prison sentence for work done in Germany.[36] FAIR has also on occasion given a platform at its meetings to supporters of CAN.

In 1985 there was within FAIR a body of opinion that FAIR had become too moderate and that firmer action was needed in response to the 'cults'. Accordingly, a breakaway organisation was formed which called itself Cultists Anonymous. CA leaders maintained that anonymity was needed for fear of reprisals by cult members, although it soon became fairly common knowledge that Lord Rodney was at its helm. Although CA went on record as being opposed to de-programming,[37] one correspondent, under the pseudonym of 'Mandy' (apparently all female CA correspondents and telephonists called themselves Mandy) admitted that CA referred enquirers to a variety of organisations, including COMA 'for information'.[38] Lord Rodney himself is said to have had his own daughter deprogrammed. Cultists Anonymous was short-lived, however, and returned to the fold of FAIR in 1991, but the fact that Lord Rodney became Chairman of FAIR in 1988 may well be an indication that there are those in FAIR who are not content with its warning leaflets and its media and political contacts.

Following the recent imprisonment of a number of de-programmers in Europe and the USA, de-programming has come under something of a cloud. At present Haworth and Baldwin in particular offer 'exit counselling', which they emphatically distinguish from de-programming, the main difference being that exit counselling does not entail forcible abduction. That apart, the same techniques of ensuring that the member is separated from the NRM, appealing to one's emotions, exposing his or her beliefs to forcibly stated objections and so on, are still employed.[39]

## Assessing anti-cult achievements

Anti-cultism has been greatly aided by negative media coverage of New Religious Movements. As Beckford points out, the media tend to use incidents involving NRMs as a means of achieving what Beckford calls 'negative summary events', reminding readers of a host of past atrocity tales.[40] There have been notable occasions where an NRM's activities have been severely damaged by negative publicity afforded by the media. The most notable case was an article published by the British *Daily Mail* in 1981, in which the Unification Church was described in a bold headline as 'the Church that splits up families' – a heading which gives due indication of the content. Faced with mounting criticism, the UC decided on this occasion that they had had enough bad publicity. They decided to sue, and lost.

This loss had two main consequences. One was a subsequent summons in which the UC had to fight for the right to maintain its charitable status – a task which occupied both the Attorney General and the UC between 1986 and 1988. UC members were jubilant when in the end the case was dropped through lack of evidence.[41]

The other consequence was potentially more serious for NRMs more widely, and consisted of attempts by several politicians to restrict NRMs' activities. The most successful was the Cottrell Report, presented to the European Parliament in March 1984. The Unification Church was singled out as the occasion for the report, but the recommendations applied to all NRMs. Although the report reaffirmed the European Convention on Human Rights and 'the full freedom of religion and opinion',[42] it went on to set out a code of practice, to which new religions should subscribe and which would serve as a means for assessing their integrity and eligibility for benefits afforded to bona fide religions.

The thirteen sections of the voluntary code included recommendations that NRMs should not call upon minors to make long-term commitments, that enquirers should have 'an adequate period of reflection' following contact, and that individuals should have the right of access to medical attention, and to family and friends at all times: letters and telephone messages should be immediately passed on. The identity of a movement and its principles 'should always be made immediately clear'.

The 'voluntary' nature of the code did not reassure NRM leaders, who claimed that they had not even been consulted on these matters, to which they were expected to agree. They also feared that a voluntary code was a stepping stone to compulsory legislation, a fear which was not without foundation, since one of Cottrell's clauses stated that 'such movements shall be required *by law* to inform the competent authorities on request of the address or whereabouts of individual members'.[43] Some of the Churches too had expressed some anxiety about the proposals, viewing them as unduly discriminatory: if it was wrong for NRMs to do such things, surely it ought to be wrong for any religious organisation, or indeed any secular one too? Further, if non-discriminatory codes or pieces of legislation were devised, then this could hamper mainstream religion, much of which could not comply with Cottrell's recommendations. After all, many mainstream churches accepted minors into long-term membership, and would not readily divulge confidential information about members to civil authorities. And could any mainstream Christian denomination make it immediately clear what was meant by the Incarnation, the Atonement or the Trinity?

On 22 March 1984, the European Parliament voted in favour of the Cottrell Report by a substantial majority, with 98 in favour, 28 against and 27 abstentions. This was an outcome which, predictably, was welcomed by FAIR.

In reality, the Cottrell proposals made little, if any, difference to NRM members. One obvious reason was that they lacked legal status, and awaited ratification by member states. The only subsequent attempt in Britain to introduce legislation specifically aimed at NRMs was by David Alton (MP for Liverpool, Mossley Hill) who attempted to introduce a Private Member's Bill in October 1984, to 'control the activities of religious sects and cults'.[44] The main provision of the proposed bill was to ensure that relatives had a legal right of access to those who had joined 'religious cults'. Like most Private Members' Bills, Alton's proposal was unsuccessful and did not progress beyond a second reading.

### Effects of the anti-cult movement

By way of conclusion, I shall attempt to evaluate the effects of the anti-cult movement. What has it achieved, and what differences have we seen in New Religious Movements as a result?

Faced with various setbacks, some new religions have decided to reappraise their activities, and in some cases move to parts of the globe where they may fare better. As a result of the *Daily Mail* libel case, for example, some 250 Unification Church members out of a 500 national full-time membership moved to the USA in 1982, where they believed they would achieve greater success. A further, obvious result of anti-cultist criticism is that it consumes time and energy on the part of NRMs. As one UC leader remarked to me, 'We could do far more good work if we did not have to spend so much of our time rebutting criticisms.'

Another response to negative publicity has been the creation of public relations officers or departments in certain movements. Ironically, some NRMs, somewhat naively, believed in their earlier years that they could use the media as a vehicle to spread their message to the rest of the nation, only to find that the media's construction of their message was a complete travesty. For example, Elan Vital (formerly known as the Divine Light Mission) publicised the advent of the child guru Maharaj-Ji in the early 1970s, only to find that he was portrayed as 'baptising crowds by water cannon'. (The multi-coloured water with which the crowds were sprayed on a few occasions was in fact no more than an exuberant act, and had no sacramental significance whatsoever.) Over two decades on, NRM leaders have considerably more experience, enabling them to decide when it is advantageous to talk to the media, and when it is best to seek no publicity.

It is sometimes difficult to determine whether changes are the result of anti-cultist criticism or whether they can be attributed to other factors, such as a religious movement's coming of age or becoming more affluent. The Unification Church's hectic street peddling and evangelism in the 1970s arose largely from to its need to acquire additional financial resources and its desire to let the world know that its new messiah was here. Now the UC's empire no longer has to rely on selling flowers and candles, and hence members' activities can be channelled elsewhere and living conditions have been much improved. Even attracting new members is no longer a priority, since non-members are now also invited to receive the Rev. Moon's 'Blessing' on their marriage.

In those groups that have liberal attitudes to sex, changes have perhaps been influenced more by the AIDS threat than by anti-cultism. The Family's 'flirty fishing' has now been totally abandoned, although the 'sharing' of marriage partners continues. Evidence of a negative AIDS test is now required at the late Osho's ashram at Poona before residence is permitted, and a six-month period must period must elapse before sexual activity is permitted between members.

One undoubted effect of the anti-cult movement has been to bring together a number of minority religious groups which would probably not normally have had cause to interact. Anti-cult activity has enabled NRMs to claim that they are persecuted minorities, victims of religious prejudice and discrimination. (There have been several instances of members losing jobs, being denied custody of their children, and even – in one case personally known to me – rejected for a place in higher education.) During the 1980s, the Church of Scientology was particularly instrumental in organising seminars on religious freedom, which were attended by NRMs, a few academics, and some members of the clergy who were more sympathetic than most to their plight.

The Scientologists in particular wanted legal protection to preserve religious freedom, and advocated the introduction of a Bill of Rights, based on the Universal Declaration of Human Rights (1948) and the European Convention on Human Rights (1968). They also expressed support for MP Ann Clwyd's Right of Reply Bill in 1988, which, if passed, would have entitled those who had been maligned by the media to publish their case in response. However, like Alton's Private Member's Bill, it was not allowed to proceed.

Anxious to correct its sinister public image, the Unification Church's strategy was to embark on a programme of 'Introductory Seminars', aimed at academics and clergy, in which The Principle was systematically explained over several days, and questions answered regarding the UC's activities. The Church of Scientology canvassed various academics to obtain endorsements for their definitive volume *What is Scientology?*[45]

The clergy have proved somewhat more difficult to win over than the academic community. However, the Churches' hierarchy tended to feel that the more hysterical response of the anti-cultists was unhealthy and counter-productive, and a number of denominations produced statements outlining their own recommended response. These included the United Reformed Church, the Methodist Church, the Church of England and the Roman Catholic Church.[46] The British Council of Churches (now the Council of Churches for Britain and Ireland) held a consultation on the subject in 1986, which was attended by representatives of most of the major denominations, the majority of whom championed a more moderate line. All these reports – especially the Roman Catholic contribution – advised caution, but all avoided the hysteria of the anti-cult groups.

The Church of England's report proposed a draft code of practice, which was a modification of Cottrell's, and which omitted some of the more problematic clauses mentioned previously. It also condemned de-programming, as well as misrepresentation of and unfair discrimination against NRM members, emphasising the right to freedom of belief.[47] Although the code of practice seemed more realistic than Cottrell's, NRM leaders with whom I spoke at that time still did not welcome it. The Board of Mission and Unity, which drafted the document, had deplored NRMs concealing their true identities, collecting money under false pretences, and using tactics such as 'heavenly deception', 'flirty fishing' and hypnosis. As one UC leader remarked, 'We can comply with the code, but it implies that we are guilty of these things.'

One further response to anti-cultism involved the setting up of INFORM (Information Network Focus on Religious Movements) in 1986 by Eileen Barker, with Home Office funding, and the support and patronage of the Archbishop of Canterbury, Cardinal Hume and the Moderator of the Free Church Federal Council. INFORM sought to provide more balanced and objective information than the other interest groups I have mentioned, a feature which some of the NRMs themselves welcomed. INFORM had a small number of full-time staff, some of whom are professionally qualified. Although they do not act as counsellors, they have access to a nationwide network of experienced workers in the field of NRMs who can offer advice and support.

INFORM's appearance on the scene has created some resentment by anti-cultists, some of whom had already applied for Home Office funding and been turned down. Yet the fact that INFORM had gained support in fairly prestigious circles spurred other groups on to improve their image. CIC managed to register itself as an educational charity in 1992, and gained quite an impressive list of patrons, including Dr Chad Varah, the founder of the Samaritans.

Nevertheless, the anti-cult movement's attempts to improve its image really fail to address the real problems. While one would hope for an increasing professionalisation of cult-monitoring organisations and more balanced media coverage of NRMs, there seems to be no obvious change of heart on the part of cult critics. Christian evangelicals are still as insistent as ever that Mormons, JWs and the like are in serious error. Media coverage is still quite negative, and television and radio stations still elicit the comment of the CIC and Catalyst, rather than the balanced views of INFORM staff and academic experts. Apart from the clergy, few of its members have any formal qualifications or training in counselling or in religious studies, for example – a situation that is becoming less acceptable at a time when increasing emphasis is being placed on specialist expertise, counselling skills and professional ethics. As Shaw rightly points out,[48] exit counselling is done at the instigation of others, without the consent of the NRM member, a practice which would certainly not be employed by any professional counsellor.

At the present time NRMs continue to cause a polarisation of views within society. On the one hand, increasing numbers of liberals continue to champion the cause of religious freedom, claiming that the NRMs have a right to fair representation in the media and more even-handed treatment from politicians and followers of mainstream religions.[49] On the other hand, there still remains the majority of citizens whose perception of NRMs is informed (or rather misinformed in many cases) by the popular press, which reinforces the anti-cultist stereotype. Whether the champions of religious freedom and media reform will triumph over the prejudices of the anti-cultism is debatable. Anti-cultist perceptions of reality are deeply embedded, and at best will only change gradually.

## Notes

1 Horton Davies, *Christian Deviations*, London: SCM, 1954. K.N. Ross, writing for SPCK between 1954 and 1958, discussed Jehovah's Witnesses, Christian Science, Spiritualism, Seventh-day Adventism, Mormonism and Astrology in a series of short booklets. M. C. Burrell's 'Modern Heresies' Church Book Room Press series addressed the Jehovah's Witnesses, Spiritualism, Mormonism, Christian Science and Christadelphianism, and was published in 1960.

2 Walter Martin, *The Maze of Mormonism*, Ventura, CA: Gospel Light Publications, 1978.

3 For an explanation of this term, see G. D. Chryssides, *The Advent of Sun Myung Moon*, London: Macmillan, 1991, p. 88.

4 Eileen Barker, *New Religious Movements: A Practical Introduction*, London: HMSO, 1989, p. 15.

5 G.D. Chryssides, 'Britain's Changing Faiths: Adaptation in a New Environment'; in G. Parsons (ed.), *The Growth of Religious Diversity: Britain from 1945, Volume II: Issues*, London: Routledge, 1994, pp. 55–84 (pp. 76–7).

6 *FAIR News*, October 1982, p. 2.

7 J. A. Beckford, *Cult Controversies: The Societal Response to the New Religious Movements*, London: Tavistock, 1985, pp. 228–9.

8 *Freedom Magazine*, 1995, p. 9.

9 Shirley Harrison, *Cults: The Battle for God*, London: Christopher Helm, 1990, p. 199.

10 *FAIR News*, October 1983, pp. 2–3; April 1984, p. 2.

11 Ursula MacKenzie and Barry Morrison, 'New Religious Movements in Britain Today', London: Church Youth Fellowships Association, 1982.

12 Ian Haworth, 'Cults on Campus', London: Cult Information Centre, 1993, p. 4.

13 Ibid., pp. 6–7.

14 Ibid., p. 7.

15 Brenda Henry, 'The Signs of the Times', *FAIR News*, Autumn/Winter, 1995–96, p. 4.

16 Barker, op. cit., pp. 9–11.

17 Roy Wallis, 'The Sociology of the New Religions', *Social Studies Review*, 1(1), September 1985, pp. 3–7. Harold W. Turner, 'New Religious Movements in Primal Societies', in John R. Hinnells (ed.), *A Handbook of Living Religions*, Harmondsworth: Penguin, 1985, pp. 439–54. J. Gordon Melton, 'Modern Alternative Religions in the West', in Hinnells, op. cit., pp. 455–74.

18 Chryssides, op. cit.; Kim Knott, *My Sweet Lord: The Hare Krishna Movement* Wellingborough: Aquarian, 1986; Robert Mullen, *The Mormons*, London: W. H. Allen, 1967.

19 J. Stillson Judah, *Hare Krishna and the Counter Culture*, New York: Wiley, 1974; Melton, op. cit.

20 Ian Haworth, 'Cult Concerns: An Overview of Cults and their Methods in the UK', *Assignation*, 11(4), July 1994, 31–4. *FAIR News*, October 1994, p. 5.

21 Eileen Barker, *The Making of a Moonie*, Oxford: Blackwell, 1984, p. 146.

22 *FAIR News*, October 1984, p. 16.

23 *Cult Information Centre* (information leaflet), 1993, p. 4.

24 Haworth, op. cit., 1994, p. 34.

25 *Reachout Quarterly Newsletter*, 1995, p. 1.

26 Reachout Trust, *Building Bridges to People in the Cults, Occult and New Age* (information pack), 1995, p. 2.

27 Doug Harris, *Cult Critiques*, Richmond, Surrey: Reachout Trust, 1995, p. 9.

28 Ibid., p. 4.

29 Harold J. Berry, *New Age Movement*, Lincoln, NE: Back to the Bible, 1988, p. 3.

30 Holger Kersten, *Jesus Lived in India: His Unknown Life Before and After the Crucifixion*, Shaftesbury: Element, 1994. Levi, *The Aquarian Gospel of Jesus the Christ: The Philosophic and Practical Basis of the Religion of the Aquarian Age of the World, transcribed from the Akashic Record*, Romford: Fowler, 1989.

31 Roy Livesey, *More Understanding Alternative Medicine: Holistic Health in the New Age*, Chichester: New Wine Press, 1985.

32 Erica Heftmann, *Dark Side of the Moonies*, Harmondsworth: Penguin, 1972, pp. 204–5.

33 *The Daily Mercury* (Guelph, Ontario), 1 February 1987.

34 *FAIR News*, April 1985, p. 3; 'Cult Awareness Network: The Serpent of Hatred, Intolerance, Violence and Death', *Freedom*, 1995, 27(2), pp. 1–35. Thomas G. Whittle (ed.), *The Cult Awareness Network: Anatomy of a Hate Group*, Los Angeles: Freedom Magazine.

35 Heftmann, op. cit. Nicola Raine, 'The Faith Breakers', *New Tomorrow*, 1983, no. 46, pp. 4–6, 17. S. Swatland and A. Swatland, *Escape from the Moonies*, London: New English Library, 1982.

36 'De-programming Decimated in America', *Freedom Magazine*, 1995, p. 9.

37 *The Sunday Times*, 28 July 1985.

38  Personal correspondence, 17 August 1985.
39  William Shaw, *Spying in Guru Land: Inside Britain's Cults*, London: Fourth Estate, 1994, p. 191.
40  Beckford, op. cit., 1985, p. 235.
41  Chryssides, op. cit., 1994, pp. 78–80.
42  Richard Cottrell (rapporteur), *Report on the Activity of Certain New Religious Movements within the European Community*, European Parliament, Committee on Youth, Culture, Education, Information and Sport. PE 82.322/fin, 22 March 1984, p. 5.
43  Ibid., para 2(l), p. 7 (my emphasis).
44  *Hansard*, 24 October 1984.
45  Church of Scientology International, *What is Scientology?*, Los Angeles: Bridge Publications, 1994.
46  G. D. Chryssides, C. Lamb, and M. Marsden, *Who Are They? New Religious Groups*, London: United Reformed Church, 1982; Maureen Edwards, 'New Religious Movements', in David Pendle (ed.), *MAYC Handbook*, Section G13, London: Methodist Association of Youth Clubs, 1985. 'Sects: The Pastoral Challenge', *Briefing 86*, 6 June 1986, 16(2), 142–52; republished as *New Religious Movements: A Challenge to the Church*, London: The Incorporated Catholic Truth Society, 1986; 'New Religious Movements: A Report by the Board for Mission and Unity', London: General Synod of the Church of England, GS Misc 317, 1989.
47  General Synod, op. cit., pp. 10–11.
48  William Shaw, 'Cults: Exit Counselling', *The Observer Magazine*, 28 May 1995, pp. 24–6.
49  See, e.g., R.A. Gilbert, *Casting the First Stone: The Hypocrisy of Religious Fundamentalism and its Threat to Society*, Shaftesbury: Element; G. D. Chryssides, 'The Right to be Religious', *The Modern Churchman*, New Series, 1987, 29(3), pp. 25–33.

# Index

Brahma Kumaris, Maharishi Mahesh
Yogi, Rajneeshism
Hinduism 146, 178, 199, 265
hippies 22, 214–15
holism 40, 47, 60, 66, 154
Holmes, Ernest 63, 70
Honen 203
Horton, Robin 70
Horus Centre 185
Hourmant, Louis 25
Hubbard, L. Ron 245, 262
Human Potential movement 22, 23, 35,
58–9
humanistic approaches to mental health
131
Hungary 23, 24
hypnosis 262, 270

ICD-9 126, 132
idealism 8, 39
idealist philosophy 39, 43
India 16, 61
individualism 23, 39, 42, 45
Information Network Focus on
Religious Movements (INFORM) 9,
16, 170, 177, 270, 271
Inner Peace Movement 57, 66
Institute for Research in Human
Happiness 61, 207–8
Institute of Oriental Philosophy, Taplow
Court xiii–xiv, 10, 11
instrumental activism, movement away
from 45–6
interfaith dialogue 177–8
international anti-cultism movement
225–6, 229–31, 232
International Foundation for Individual
Freedom 216, 222
international law 94
International Social Survey Programme
19
International Society for Krishna
Consciousness (ISKCON) 5, 6, 21,
23, 24, 176; American anti-cultism
214, 223, 224; British anti-cultism
258, 259, 264, 265; and
gender/women 144, 145, 146, 154,
157, 158, 159; German anti-cultism
238; and law 89; media 104; mental
health 128, 129, 137
Internet 31n19
Ishii, K. 109
ISKCON *see* International Society for
Krishna Consciousness

Islam 45, 169, 178, 265; influence on
NRMs 25; and law 83, 91–2; and
media 106, 107
Islamic countries 28
Israel 225
Italy 2; magical community of
Damanhur 183–94

Jacobs, Janet 148
Japanese NRMs 15, 22–3, 25, 123,
197–201, 229; in Brazil 197, 202–10;
media and 109, 112, 116, 199; and
New Age 61; religious freedom 3,
198; response to 29
Jehovah's Witnesses 4, 105, 257, 258,
260, 264, 271; and law 87, 88–9, 93,
94
Jenkins, Paul 60
Jesus Army/Fellowship 153, 167, 171,
172, 174–5, 176, 177, 178
Jesus People Movement 143, 214, 215
Jewish anti-cultism 215
Jewish faith 175, 178; opposition to
Hassidic Jews 230
Jews for Jesus 215
Jodo Shinshu Buddhism 202, 203, 204
John Paul II, Pope 39
Jonestown, Guyana 103, 104, 112, 123,
220–2, 228, 229; *see also* People's
Temple
*Journal of Managerial Psychology*59
Joy, Susy 60
Judaism *see* Jewish…
*Jugendsekten* 237–54
Jung, C.-G. 60, 61, 130, 146
Jungian archetypes 188

Kelly, Galen 224
Kersten, Holger 265
Key '73 215
King, U. 155
Kinsman, Francis 58, 66
Kiriyama, Seiyu 200
Kluckhohn, F.R. 46
Kluge, Gerald 249
Knackstedt, Wilhelm 240
Knott, K. 144
Kofuku-no Kagaku (Science of Human
Happiness) 61, 203, 207–8
Konkokyo (the Teaching of the Golden
Light) 197–8, 206
Korea 16
Koresh, David 110